Baseball
Memoirs of a Lifetime

To Adam, a great baseball fan. Please enjoy our book. Your mom is a great fan!

Baseball forever,

Ken Proctor

Nov. 15 2007

Sketch Ken Proctor batting, art credit to Pat Dooley.

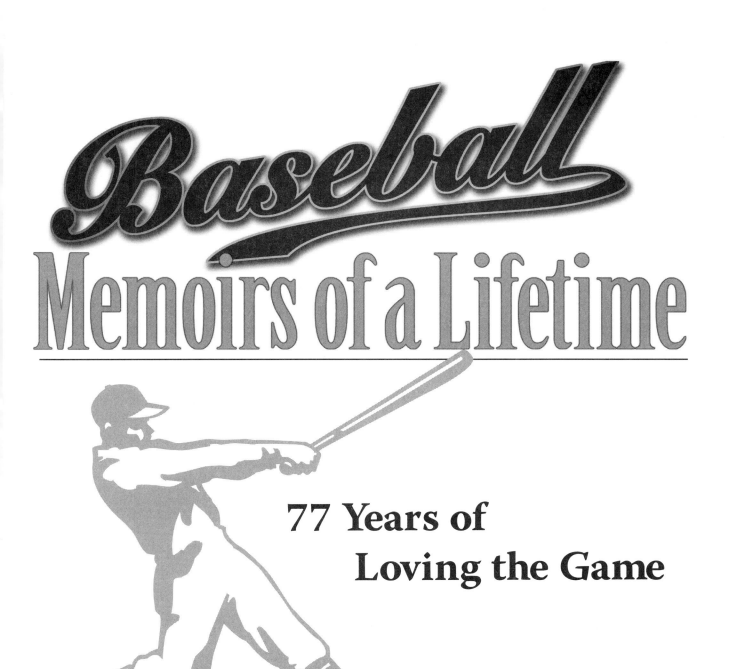

Baseball
Memoirs of a Lifetime

77 Years of
Loving the Game

by KEN PROCTOR

Baseball Memoirs of a Lifetime
Kenneth F. Proctor

Includes Index

Library of Congress Card Number: Available on Request

Softcover Edition $24.95:
ISBN-10: 0-9777281-0-2
ISBN-13: 978-0-9777281-0-7

Hardcover Edition $39.95:
ISBN-10: 0-9777281-1-0
ISBN-13: 978-0-9777281-1-4

PHOTO AND ART CREDITS
Pat and Dixie Dooley
Mike Proctor
Anne Jewell, Hillerich and Bradsby

Printed by Gorham Printing, Rochester, Washington USA
Cover and text design by Kathryn E. Campbell

DEDICATION

I wish to dedicate this book to my wife, Marilyn,

our three sons, Kenny, Mike, and Scott

and the players, friends, and fans

that have helped to make baseball such a vital part of my life.

◆ACKNOWLEDGMENTS

There are many people who encouraged, supported, and assisted me in putting this book together. I want to thank all of them.

Marilyn Proctor editing

First and foremost, I want to extend my gratitude to my wife, Marilyn, for her common sense, advice, suggestions, and logic in assembling the material found here. But, above those details, my deepest appreciation is for her many hours of editing. The picture of her in this section is emblazoned on my mind. When the book was supposedly finished she went over it again and again and found items that had to be corrected. She did an outstanding job. It turned out to be a good team effort.

Our son, Mike Proctor, was extremely helpful in his work on graphic arts, layout and design, cover art and copy, general photography, and editing. Thank you very much for your efforts, Mike. *(See Photo and Arts Credits)*.

We are indebted to Pat and Dixie Dooley for the creative sketches made for the book. Pat was excited to do those outstanding impressions and I appreciate the sharing of his exceptional talent. *(See Photo and Arts Credits)*.

For more than 75 years I have been collecting information and other memorabilia about baseball not knowing that someday they might be used to put in a book to share with others about our great game. To all those players, managers, administrators, and others who have been part of this grand scene, I say, thank you.

Mike Proctor today

I wrote a book published in 1960 titled *Successful Baseball*, that is being updated and rewritten in the near future. Please see more about that book in my Preface and Some Final Words at the end of the book. I wish to thank those readers of that book who have suggested I write about my personal experiences in *Baseball Memoirs of a Lifetime*.

Marsha Dashiell and Darlene Walker of Portland, Oregon, two devoted baseball fans, often asked me to tell baseball stories to them. Later they said, "why don't you put these stories in a book for others to read." That was one of the encouragements that prompted me to write this book.

A former high school student of the 1950s, Terry (Ben) Cain, suggested that I rewrite my earlier book and took me to an excellent printing company, Gorham Printing in Rochester, Washington, where the project was initially started. I owe a great deal of appreciation to Terry and his wife, Barbara, and to Kurt and Norma Gorham, Kathleen Shaputis, and Kathy Campbell of Gorham Printing for their valued advice and help.

I want to express my thanks to Dr. Bobby Brown and Coach Gary Adams for their Foreward statements. Our sincere thanks to Mrs. Adrienne Bratton, daughter of American League umpire, Emmett Ashford, for sending us pictures of her father. Ron and Susan Williams were very helpful in providing us expertise and suggestions on details of producing the book.

Our friends at the great Hillerich and Bradsby Company, maker of Louisville Slugger bats and other products, gave us excellent advice and assistance. They are Michael Hillerich, President; Rick Redman, Vice President of Communications; Anne Jewell, Executive Director, Louisville Slugger Museum; and Vickie Boisseau, Manager of Bionic Gloves, a relatively new division of the company.

Pat & Dixie Dooley

Ken Proctor is a long time friend and former teammate. While in the U. S. Navy V-12 Unit at UCLA during World War II we played on the UCLA baseball team. Ken was an excellent second baseman and made a major contribution to a very successful season. We played the keystone together.

He subsequently became an officer in the U. S. Navy, and postwar achieved an outstanding record as a high school baseball coach. He not only schooled his players in the art of playing baseball but imparted to them the highest of moral and spiritual ideals.

This book is about Ken's life and a perpetual love affair with baseball. While it is a baseball book, it's also about Ken's family, his friends, his teammates, his acquaintances, and his heroes. It's about his Christian faith, about his baseball playing and coaching careers, about his outlook in life. It's a baseball reference book with interviews, stories, and resumes of players, managers, owners, umpires, writers, and announcers. He describes a bat factory and how bats are made; he critiques ballparks and covers a multitude of facts concerning the origin and evolution of the game. The book lists "nicknames," famous sayings and quotes, and baseball terminology. There is a section in instruction, strategy, theory, and behavior.

This is not a book on just baseball. It is a publication on the exemplary life of an individual who has influenced generations of young high school students on the road to good citizenship.

This book represents the work and love of a lifetime and should be in the library of every baseball aficionado.

—**ROBERT W. BROWN, MD**
Bobby Brown, N. Y. Yankees, 1946-1954, President of the American League of Professional Baseball Clubs, 1983-1994, Physician, Private practice, Cardiology, 1958-1984

Bobby Brown and Ken Proctor at Yankee Stadium

When Ken Proctor was inducted into UCLA's Baseball Hall of Fame in 2002, it was not only because of his outstanding accomplishments on the baseball field but also because of the wonderful example he set for all those who knew him. He was truly a gentleman on and off the field.

Even his opponents, coaches and players, had the utmost respect and admiration for Ken. I was a player when Ken was coaching his great teams at Chaffey High School in Ontario, California. Whenever our Riverside Poly High School teams played Chaffey, all of us knew it was going to be a tough battle, not just because of the talented Chaffey players but because of their knowledgeable, dedicated skipper, Ken Proctor. Our entire team, including coach Ben Hammerschmidt, admitted, "Coach Proctor's teams will never beat themselves. We will have to play our best ball if we expect to win." In all of the games I played against our archrival, Chaffey, I do not remember them ever making a mistake, mental or physical.

In fact, I remember too well a play that Ken's team made against us that ended the game and beat us in our own ballpark. One of our best hitters and fastest runners hit a deep line drive to left center field that looked to all like a sure game-tying home run. The ball rolled to at least 420 feet from home plate before Chaffey's center fielder finally caught up with it. Against any other team our dug-out would have already celebrated the tie, but we all knew that this was not just another ordinary team. The center fielder never quit on the ball and he turned and threw a perfect strike to the shortstop who was nearly 300 feet from home plate. And he turned and threw another perfect strike to the first baseman in the cutoff position. He pivoted and threw a third perfect strike to the catcher who put the tag on the sliding runner. He was out by a whisker. It was a beautiful and perfectly executed play and the game was over.

Our team was stunned by the loss, but none of us were shocked by the execution of Chaffey's players, because they were a Ken Proctor team. No club was better prepared than Ken's. Every high school player and coach in Southern California knew that fact.

The quality of Ken's teams year in and year out was impressive and, yet, even more outstanding was the character of Chaffey teams, definitely a reflection of their outstanding coach. The teams played hard but they went about their jobs quietly, never ragging on their opponents. They won with humility and they lost with grace. Ken was their leader by example, always shaking hands with the opposing coaches after every game and giving credit to opponents in victory or defeat.

Gary Adams/Ken Proctor at UCLA Jackie Robinson Stadium

It was this kind of example that this man set for all of us to emulate. That is why he was a unanimous selection into the UCLA Baseball Hall of Fame and why everyone who knows him admires, respects, and loves him.

In all of my 41 years of coaching college baseball, I can think of no better person to write a book that speaks of life's lessons through experiences in this great game of baseball than Ken Proctor.

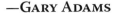

—**GARY ADAMS**
Head Baseball Coach, UCLA, 1975-2004, Head Baseball Coach, University of California, At Irvine, 1970-1975

One Of The Finest Men I Have Known

Knowing and learning from Coach Wooden is one the richest blessings of my life. Coach and my father were similar in personality. It seemed that everyone loved my father as I did. He was everybody's friend. We had many great experiences together. Coach is so much the same way.

When we visited Coach last year, at his request we took him to his favorite restaurant, VIP's, a few blocks from his home on Ventura Blvd. to have breakfast. As we walked into the place everybody greeted him. "Where have you been, Coach," or "It's good to see you, Coach," they said. He goes in there five or six times a week and eats with these special friends. It once again made us realize of the humility of this humble man. He does not see himself as anyone special but just another one of God's children.

After writing this chapter I sent a copy to Coach Wooden for his approval. A few days later Coach called me on the telephone and told me he would be pleased to have his story in the book. We spent nearly a half an hour just talking baseball among other things. He told me he gets down to the Los Angeles Angel baseball games from time to time. Manager Mike Scioscia is a close friend and welcomes Coach to visit anytime. He said he likes to go to New York Yankee games because he is a friend of Joe Torre, Derek Jeter, and Alex Rodriguez. He said some years ago he enjoyed going to see the Dodgers because former Dodger manager, Walt Alston and first baseman Gil Hodges were friends.

Coach told me he would have liked to play baseball at Purdue University but he was the star of the Boilermakers in basketball and kept his loyalties with renowned coach, Piggy Lambert. And with his shoulder injury, he passed on playing football or baseball. He said in their small high school in Martinsville they did not have a baseball program. That is why he gained his baseball experience in the summer leagues.

Coach told me one amusing story. He is very close friends with William "Dutch" Fehring. Both of them graduated from Purdue, both are Hall of Fame level players and coaches, and they have remained in touch through the years. John said that Dutch played some professional baseball. Dutch said above all his other honors and athletic experiences, the play he remembers most is when he tagged out Lou Gehrig at home plate while playing for the Chicago White Sox.

Recommendation

Department of Intercollegiate Athletics
University of California, Los Angeles
405 Hilgard Avenue • Los Angeles, California 90024

825-3236 or 825-3326

May 5, 1976

To Whom It May Concern
From - John R. Wooden, UCLA Basketball Coach (Retired)
Re --- Recommendation for Kenneth F. Proctor

It always is nice to be asked to write a letter of recommendation about a person for whom you have great respect and in
whom you have great confidence. Therefore, I am very happy
to write such a letter for Kenneth F. Proctor.

I have known Kenny for over twenty-five years - as an athlete,
as a teacher, as an administrator, and as a fine Christian
parent - and have no reservation in saying that he would be
a definite asset to any organization with which he might be
associated and to any community in which he might reside.

Kenny is a hard worker, intelligent, considerate of others,
loyal, cooperative, enthusiastic, friendly, and a person who
relates to all associates at every age or position.

I will not attempt to go into his background and experience
as that is available in his resume, but will say that it is
most impressive and shows his versatility.

Therefore, it is my honest and sincere opinion that you should
give him strong consideration for the position for which he
has applied.

Respectfully yours,

John Wooden

John R. Wooden

JRW:tw

In the spring of 1976 I was updating my files and asked Coach if he would provide me with a recommendation for my resumé. He responded on May 5th of that year with the letter shown here. It is one of my most prized possessions.

◇ PREFACE

Ken in 1948 at UCLA

Ken at Chaffey
High School

ART CREDIT TO PAT DOOLEY

I was born in 1924 and baseball has been a part of my life since I was a small boy. I enjoyed it as a child, a teenager, an adult, in pre-retirement years, and as a retiree. It continues to give me interest, enthusiasm, pleasure, and challenge.

I have had the privilege of sharing America's great game with my wife, sons, grandchildren, family, players and friends. Many of these experiences hold fond memories for me.

It is my sincere desire to pass along some of these moments in the hope that others may derive from baseball some of the times of satisfaction that have occurred for me. I owe significantly to this wonderful sport that has provided me with much more than I could ever return.

Following a hitch in the U. S. Navy and five years of college training I embarked on my baseball-coaching career. I decided to keep notes and records and pass along information about what I had learned through the years. I wrote and published a book in 1960 titled *Successful Baseball*. Basically, it was a book emphasizing baseball fundamentals, coaching techniques, and how to organize a baseball program. I have found that the principles covered in the book are still true today. It is my intention to edit, update, and reprint the book in the near future.

When I chose to write a second book my concentration was more about personal moments I had experienced in over seventy-five years in the grand old game. It contains more than 220 stories. Many of these stories involve baseball people with whom I have crossed paths over the years. Also, I have tried to include some history and interesting facts about baseball. I have personalized many of the stories that I hope the reader will find interesting.

Since I first discovered the game at age four, now, in my golden years, I am enjoying it more than ever and I am aware there are others out there who love it and benefit from it as they grow in knowledge and respect for this fascinating and intriguing pastime. In addition, the book is designed for the novice baseball fan to enjoy and understand more about the fundamentals and inner workings of this game that has been played in America for the past century and a half.

Yes, baseball is more than a game. It has a life of its own just waiting for participants to delight in it and learn from it. I was impressed with a comment made by our UCLA basketball coach, John Wooden. Here is a man who is one of the outstanding coaches and gentleman in the sports world. His teams won ten national championships in basketball. He is known the world over for his accomplishments. He said to me, "Ken, throwing out the first pitch at the 2002 World Series was the biggest thrill of my life in sports." I write more about him in Chapter 10 of this book because of his love for baseball. Along with Coach Wooden, I am just one of millions of baseball fans and I hope some of my observations will provide enjoyment for others.

I grew up in Southern California and some of this book will refer to baseball in that locale. However, I realize that all Americans had personal experiences in their own particular locations. It is my hope that readers will relate to their own geography whether it is Texas, Florida, New York, Chicago or some small town in Kansas, Colorado, the Pacific Northwest, or anywhere within our land and possessions. Frankly, I get excited when I think of our great sport of baseball being played through the years in every nook and cranny of this great nation. Baseball has a way of bringing us all together. It is a wonderful camaraderie that we have been privileged to experience.

My major purpose in making this book available to others is to try and give something back to the game. It is my sincere hope that you enjoy *"Baseball Memoirs of a Lifetime."*

—KEN PROCTOR

Ken Proctor today

Ken, age 70, on top of Mt. St. Helens

 **TABLE OF CONTENTS**

CHAPTER 1 Treasured Personal Baseball Stories

Story 1:   Dad Gave Me a Baseball When I Was Four 22

Story 2:   The Panthers 23

Story 3:   A Day At the Ball Park 26

Story 4:   Dizzy Dean's Promise 28

Story 5:   Phil Cavaretta's Bat 30

Story 6:   An Incredible Event—The Big Baseball Drop 31

Story 7:   World War II Duty on Guam with Mace Brown 32

Story 8:   Playing Against the Yankee Clipper, Joe DiMaggio 34

Story 9:   Hey Kid, You Got My Number 35

Story 10:   A Major League Pop Up by Larry Doby 37

Story 11:   Mike Gazella, A Former Yankee 38

Story 12:   Marilyn Proctor, My Best Baseball Buddy 39

Story 13:   Developing a Youth Baseball Program in Ontario, California 40

Story 14:   The Ontario-Upland Pirates 41

Story 15:   Who Is Hiram Bithorn? 42

Story 16:   We All Watched Willie in Amazement 43

Story 17:   Wrigley Field, Los Angeles 44

Story 18:   Gilmore Field, Los Angeles (Hollywood) 45

Story 19:   Umpires Do a Great Job 49

Story 20:   The Dodgers and Giants Come West 53

Story 21:   Our First (and Only) Live World Series Game 58

Story 22:   Sandy Koufax Strikes Out the Side 59

Story 23:   Don Zimmer (Popeye) Throws Out Musial 60

Story 24:   A Shot Heard 'Round the World 61

Story 25:   Scouting for the Baltimore Orioles 63

Story 26:   Denny McLain Goes for 32nd Win 64

Story 27:   Mickey Mantle's Last Game at Yankee Stadium 66

Story 28:   The Dodger All Switch-Hitting Infield 68

Story 29:   A Great Memory of a 1964 Detroit Conference 69

Story 30:   The Fellowship of Christian Athletes 70

Story 31:   Will You Pitch Batting Practice To Me, Mr. Feller? 72

Story 32:   Make It Go Through 75

Story 33:   Hal Reniff, A Special Guy 76

Story 34:   Visiting Hillerich & Bradsby (Louisville Slugger Bats) 79

Story 35:   Happening on Ty Cobb's Home Town 83

Story 36:   Yankee Stadium With Dr. and Mrs. Bobby Brown 85

Story 37:   Twenty-eight Ballparks and Counting 88

Story 38:   The Baseball Hall of Fame 106

Story 39:   Dick Butler, A Gentleman of Class 108

Story 40:   Baseball At the Tokyo Dome With Yashitoka 109

Story 41:   Spring Training Fun 110

Story 42:   Throwing Out the First Pitch at Major League Baseball Games 112

Story 43:   Ken Griffey Jr.'s Signature Disappearing Act 114

Story 44:   Celebrating Our Anniversaries at Safeco Field 115

Story 45:   Catching Foul Balls at Baseball Games 116

Story 46:   Music and Poetry of Baseball 117

Story 47:   Introducing Joe Garagiola 125

CHAPTER 2 Stories About My Favorite Baseball Announcers

Story 48:   Mel Allen—How About That? 128

Story 49:   Red Barber—The Ol' Redhead 128

Story 50:   Hal Berger—An Old Time Baseball Announcer 129

Story 51:   Jack Buck—He Is One to Remember 130

Story 52:   Harry Caray—A One-Of-A-Kind Great Broadcaster 131

Story 53:   Ken Coleman—An Unending Love For the Game 132

Story 54:   Dizzy Dean—Twenty Years Behind the Mike 133

Story 55:   Ron Fairly—High Quality Player and Announcer 134

Story 56:   Ernie Harwell—An Accomplished Gentleman 135

Story 57:   Russ Hodges—A Top Leader And Announcer in Broadcasting 137

Story 58:   Gordon McClendon—The Old Scotchman 138

Story 59:   Jon Miller—One of the Gems of Baseball Announcing 139

Story 60:   Lindsey Nelson—A Classic Voice to Remember 140

Story 61:   Ronald Reagan—A Great Leader And Auspicious Broadcaster 141

Story 62:   Vin Scully—The King of the Hill, The Best of the Best 142

CHAPTER 3 My Baseball Memories At The University Of California At Los Angeles (UCLA)

Story 63:   1944 Team—Champions Of Two Baseball Conferences 146

Story 64:   1947 Team—Back From the War 148

Story 65:   1948 Team—Playing More Against the Pros 149

Story 66:   1949 Team—My Last Year in College Baseball 150

Story 67:   UCLA Baseball Hall of Fame—Eighty-One Members to Date 151

CHAPTER 4 Leading The Chaffey High School Baseball Tigers In Ontario, California In The 1950s

Story 68:   1950 JV Team—My Very First Squad 160

Story 69:   1951 JV Team—We Have Some Experience Now 161

Story 70:   1952 JV Team—Another Great Bunch of Kids 162

Story 71:   1953 Team —A Good Varsity Start 162

Story 72:   1954 Team —Breakthrough, a Great Team 163

Story 73:   1955 Team —Close Pays Off Only in Horseshoes 165

Story 74:   1956 Team —We Catch the Golden Ring 165

Story 75:   1957 Team —Two In a Row 168

Story 76:   1958 Team —Back to Back to Back 170

Story 77:   1959 Team —Almost Perfect (39-1) 172

Story 78:   Commentary—Putting It All Together 174

A. Chaffey School District & Administration Support 174

B. No Cuts in Baseball—Everyone Plays 174

C. Chaffey Baseball Coaches, 1949-1959 175

D. Ontario Kiwanis Club 176

E. Pomona 20/30 Club Baseball Tournament Participation 177

F. Citrus Belt & Montview Leagues Titles 178

G. Overall Record from 1950 through 1959 178

H. C.I.F. (California Interscholastic Federation) Playoff Record 179

I. Everyone Had a Job 179

J. Dimes and Quarters 180

K. Banquet Speakers 180

L. Riverside's Competitive Horsehiders 180

M. Attitude of My Players and Managers 181

N. Sportswriters 182

O. Jim Bryant, Sportswriter Deluxe 182

Story 79:   TBF—Torques, Buzzards, and Friends 184

CHAPTER 5 Stories About Some Of My Favorite Major League Baseball Players

Story 80:   Rich Amaral—Utility Man Deluxe 188

Story 81:   Wally Berger—My Buddy's Uncle 188

Story 82:   Yogi Berra—Funny and Great 188

Story 83:   Hiram Bithorn—First Puerto Rican in the Majors 189

Story 84:   Jim Bouton—A Tough Knuckleballer 190

Story 85:   Bobby Brown—Destined to Succeed 191

Story 86:   Mace Brown—A Great Relief Specialist 192

Story 87:   Dick Butler—A Class Act 192

Story 88:   Phil Cavaretta—One of My First Heroes 192

Story 89:   Roberto Clemente—A Legend of Puerto Rico 192

Story 90:   Ty Cobb—He Did It All 192

Story 91:   Del Crandall—A Winner On and Off the Field 193

Story 92:   Dominic Dallesandro—More Power Per Pound 194

Story 93:   Dizzy Dean—It Ain't Braggin' When You Can Do It 194

Story 94:   Joe DiMaggio—Player of the Century, 1869-1969 195

Story 95:   Larry Doby—Check Out His Great Numbers 195

Story 96:   Bobby Doerr—Babe Said He Was the MVP of the Red Sox 196

Story 97:   Ryne Duren—You Better Duck! 196

Story 98:   Carl Erskine—In a Rundown Between First and Home 197

Story 99:   Bob Feller—They Don't Come Any Better 198

Story 100:   Rollie Fingers—More Saves Than Anyone 198

Story 101:   Whitey Ford—The Leader of the Pack 198

Story 102:   Augie Galan—Joe "D" Was His Replacement in the PCL 199

Story 103:   Mike Gazella—He Faced Walter Johnson 200

Story 104:   Troy Glaus—MVP of the 2002 World Series 200

Story 105:   Ken Griffey Sr.—A Member of the Big Red Machine 201

Story 106:   Ken Griffey Jr.—A Future Hall of Famer? 201

Story 107:   Marvin Gudat—Broke Up a No Hitter 201

Story 108:   Fred Haney—First Angel General Manager (Amer. League) 202

Story 109:   Gabby Hartnett—Why Gabby?...Because He Was So Quiet 202

Story 110:   Babe Herman—One of the Three Men on Third Base 203

Story 111:   Jackie Jensen—Ted Williams Said Jensen was Best Outfielder Ever 203

Story 112:   Walter Johnson—Modest, Decent, Quiet, Awesome 204

Story 113:   Marty Keough—A Most Gifted Performer 205

Story 114:   Sandy Koufax—A Great and Humble Young Man 206

Story 115:   Chris Krug—I Will Build a Baseball Field (Like the Field of Dreams) 207

Story 116:   Rusty Kuntz—One of Sparky Anderson's Guys 208

Story 117:   Denny Lemaster—A Fireballer From Oxnard 208

Story 118:   Gene Lillard—An Old and Great Angel 209

Story 119:   Johnny Lindell—Another Great Yankee 209

Story 120:   Walter Mails—"Duster" Was a Character 210

Story 121:   Eddie Malone—One Tough Cookie 210

Story 122:   Billy Martin—"Wanna Fight? I'm Your Man!" 211

Story 123:   Cal McLish—Just Call Me Tuskahoma 211

Story 124:   Denny McLain—What Might Have Been 212

Story 125:   Mickey Mantle—One of the Greats of All Time 212

Story 126:   Willie Mays—An Incredible Performer and Gentleman 212

Story 127:   Steve Mesner—A Pacific Coast League Phenom 213

Story 128:   Bill Moisan—He Threw a Pitch That "Sailed" 213

Story 129:   Wally Moon—An Excellent Model to Follow 213

Story 130:   Stan Musial—They Say He Was the Most Consistent Ever 214

Story 131:   Mike Radford—A Cup of Coffee With Kansas City 215

Story 132:   Jimmy Reese—Seventy-eight Years in the Game 215

Story 133:   Hal Reniff—A Very Competitive Yankee 216

Story 134:   Phil Rizzuto—Holy Cow, What a Ballplayer 216

Story 135:   Jackie Robinson—The Man Played All the Sports 216

Story 136:   Gary Roenicke—Two Brothers and a Great Dad 217

Story 137:   Ron Roenicke—Los Angeles Angels' Bench Coach 217

Story 138:   Babe Ruth—The Babe Was and Is "BASEBALL" 218

Story 139:   Art Schallock—His Curve Had Lots of Bite On It 218

Story 140:   Arnold "Jigger" Statz—The Greatest Angel of Them All 218

Story 141:   Lou Stringer—Louie Was Quick, Quick, Quick 219

Story 142:   Bobby Thomson—In the Giants' All-Time Outfield 219

Story 143:   Nick Tremark—"I Played Some Baseball in New York" 220

Story 144:   Omar Visquel—This Guy is a Tiger Out There 221

Story 145:   Bump Wills—A Quality Young Ballplayer 221

Story 146:   Don Zimmer—A Genuine Credit to the Game 222

CHAPTER 6 Personal Stories About Friends, Fans, And Former Players

Story 147:   Harry Amend—He Wanted To Be At the Plate 223

Story 148:   Gary Adams—A Standing Ovation at Bovard Field 224

Story 149:   Gene Adams—Dr. Adams, An Accomplished Professor 225

Story 150:   Chuck Bennett—"Should I Go For It, Coach?" 225

Story 151:   Terry "Ben" Cain—A Quality Pair of Friends 226

Story 152:   Rob Campbell—A Veritable Baseball Encyclopedia 227

Story 153:   Moose Clauson—He Brightens Up a Room 227

Story 154:   Howard Collins—A Good Man to Have On Your Side 227

Story 155:   Ross Cutter—Baseball Is His Middle Name 227

Story 156:   Marsha Dashiell—An All American in Sports and Life 228

Story 157:   Joe DeMaggio—A Colleague Who Has Earned Respect 229

Story 158:   Pat Dooley—Pat and Dixie, Two Talented & Valued Friends 229

Story 159:   Elvin C. "Ducky" Drake—My Coach, Trainer, and Brother 230

Story 160:   John Fabian—Mr. Baseball Fan 231

Story 161:   Chuck Giordano—Best Second Baseman in the CIF, 1957 231

Story 162: Hal Handley—This Great Catcher Could Nail Them 231

Story 163: Jerry Hendon—A Loyal Baseball Fan Saw the Finals 231

Story 164: Ben Hines—If You Want to Learn About Batting, See Ben 232

Story 165: The Knudsons—A Baseball-Loving Family 232

Story 166: Jim Lisec—Steady Jim Always Did the Job 232

Story 167: Jody Marker—A Fine Player With a Big Heart 233

Story 168: Larry Maxie—CIF Player of the Year—Twice 233

Story 169: Daryl Moss—130 Pounds of Dynamite 233

Story 170: Andy Prevedello—Kept Centerfield Under Control 234

Story 171: Hannah Proctor—A Quality Young Lady With a Good Eye 234

Story 172: Jesse Proctor—A Fine Athlete and Gentleman 235

Story 173: John Proctor—My Dad Was Everybody's Friend 235

Story 174: Ken Proctor Jr.—A Smooth-Hitting Lefty 236

Story 175: Marie Proctor—She Could Lick a Polar Bear 237

Story 176: Marilyn Proctor—This Lady Makes Things Happen 237

Story 177: Mike Proctor—His Talents Know No End 237

Story 178: Penny Proctor—What a Gal—She Does It All! 238

Story 179: Rebekah Proctor—Music, Basketball, Graceful Character 239

Story 180: Scott Proctor—A Great Son and Athlete 239

Story 181: Dave Reinhart—Super Dad, Therapist, and Baseball Fan 240

Story 182: Harry Reinhart—Fine Dad & Musician Who Loves the "Sox" 240

Story 183: Jerry Snider—A Clutch Performer 240

Story 184: Phil Sultz—A Genuine Friend, Artist, and Baseball Fan 241

Story 185: Hal Thomas—Los Angeles Angels Forever Plus Good Buddy 242

Story 186: Darlene & Terry Walker—Great Grandma & Grandpa Fans 242

Story 187: The Tim Walkers—Total Baseball Family 243

Story 188: Don and Shirley Warner—TBF Leaders and Baseball Fans 243

Story 189: Gary Wright—Top of the Line PR Man 243

CHAPTER 7 Extra Innings

Story 190: Baseball Is a Perfect Game 246

Story 191: Tips on Watching Baseball Games 247

Story 192: Baseball's Language of Its Own (Baseball Lingo) 255

Story 193: Lefties and Righties Today 261

Story 194: Grandmas Like Baseball, Too 261

Story 195: Baseball As Told To a Foreigner 262

Story 196: Batting Practice Around America 263

Story 197: Baseball Fun Games As Kids 263

Story 198: Softball vs Hardball 264

Story 199:   Family Fly Ball Fun at City Park 264

Story 200:   Scott Proctor's Kitty League 265

Story 201:   A Telephone Call From Out of the Past (57 Years Ago) 267

Story 202:   Watching World Series—A Tradition 268

Story 203:   Baseball Nicknames Are Fun 268

Story 204:   Jinx and Superstitions 270

Story 205:   Billy Kilmer, An Incredible Athlete 271

Story 206:   Wally Moon Baseball Camp 271

Story 207:   The Old Pacific Coast League 272

Story 208:   Four Pitches and You're Out 272

Story 209:   One of Baseball's Famous Brawls 273

Story 210:   Brothers in Baseball 274

Story 211:   Rip Sewell's Eephus Pitch 274

Story 212:   Mordecai "Three Finger" Brown 275

Story 213:   Casey Stengel, God Love His Soul 275

CHAPTER 8 Baseball Quotes, History, Trivia, & Humor

Story 214:   Memorable Quotes in Baseball 280

Story 215:   History of the Grand Old Game 282

Story 216:   Trivia for Horsehide Fans 283

Story 217:   Humor on the Diamond 287

CHAPTER 9 Major League Clubs' Names And Location Changes

Story 218:   Club Names and Location Changes 289

CHAPTER 10 Coach John Wooden's Favorite Sport

Story 219:   The First Time I Saw John Wooden 294

Story 220:   My Annual Notes to Coach Wooden 294

Story 221:   Coach's Early Days of Baseball 295

Story 222:   Marriage and Coaching 295

Story 223:   Enjoying the Game Through the Years 295

Some Final Words 297

Bibliography 299

Index 301

CHAPTER 1

Treasured Personal Baseball Stories

Dad Gave Me A Baseball When I Was Four

When I was four years of age my dad, John Fred Proctor, gave me a baseball. He was my hero and model and I cherished the ball. Little did I realize what the influence of receiving that ball was to mean to me in later years. I discovered that I was becoming interested in the game and I followed it closely in my early years. And as my dad and I went to watch various contests my love for the grand old game increased and I became more and more absorbed with baseball.

Ken Proctor, four years old

I heard names like Babe Ruth, Lou Gehrig, Carl Hubbell, Casey Stengel, Connie Mack and many others. As I grew up I was aware of almost every major league player on every team complete with batting and fielding averages and what was happening in the game at that time. I have met many others who had the same experience. I was obsessed with it. In those early days of the 1930s and 1940s we listened to the games on radio every spare moment for there was no television at that time.

We had all kinds of dreams of being baseball stars. I recall having a game I played with a tennis racquet and balls. I would make line-ups on a score sheet. I hit the balls against the back of a huge auditorium wall that had no windows. I had certain spots on the wall that went for singles, doubles, triples, and home runs. Other spots were for different kinds of "outs." My mind ran wild with my made-up games.

Also, we had a big field with lots of rocks in it. We would get a sizeable stick as a bat and hit those rocks until we were dead tired. In that game it was mostly to see how far we could hit the rocks. We imagined ourselves as Babe Ruth, Lou Gehrig, and other sluggers of that era.

When I reached twelve years of age I asked several of my baseball friends to join me as I organized a team. We did not have Little League or any type of youth baseball so we were on our own. My friends were pals Harley Cross, Bill Horn, and Don Miller. Please enjoy a short story about our cherished youth team of the 1930s.

STORY 2

The Panthers

Harley Cross, Bill Horn,
Ken Proctor , Don Miller

I decided to name our team THE PANTHERS. Somehow, that visual of a sleek, black panther was powerful. And nobody else had that name. We chose deep blue and white for our colors, bought sweatshirts, and purchased six-inch white felt block "P's," (for Panthers) and our mothers sewed them on the shirts. Now more than 70 years later, I still have that sweatshirt. The only uniforms that we had were the shirts, baseball caps of various types, and baseball shoes. Some of the players wore sneakers or tennis shoes. The day that we could save up enough money for real spiked shoes was a red-letter day for each of us.

More and more players were added to our team and we joined the Harvard Playground Senior League (ages 12 to 15) of Los Angeles, California. It was the closest thing to youth baseball at that time and in a nice park in our community. Some of the other teams were the Angels, Cubs, Dodgers, Giants, Our Nine, Pirates, and Stars. None of the teams had sponsors and each squad had to pay for all necessary baseball items.

I still have score sheets from some of those games. We were very competitive and played and practiced at every opportunity. We had a pitcher named Bill Flaugher who was good enough to get a tryout with the local triple-A team of the

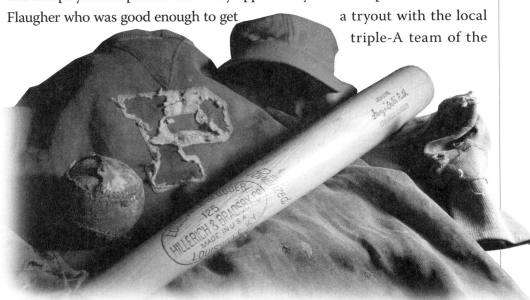

Old baseball, bat, and my old Panther sweatshirt.

Panthers Clowning, Harley Cross, Ken Proctor, Bill Horn, Don Miller

Pacific Coast League, the Los Angeles Angels, a minor league franchise of the Chicago Cubs. He had a very good fast-ball. I recall Bill playing with the Angels for a period of time. I have an old Wrigley Field sheet called "The Bulletin." It has a story that reads, "17 year-old Bill Flaugher, Dorsey High School graduate, will be getting a starting assignment soon, according to manager Arnold "Jigger" Statz. Incidentally, Dorsey is where the renowned Sparky Anderson went to high school.

The Angels played at Wrigley Field (Los Angeles version), an almost exact duplicate of the Chicago major league park. The team and ball park was owned by the Wrigley Gum Company. It so happens my favorite gum was Wrigley's "juicy fruit". Please see Story 17 (Wrigley Field, Los Angeles).

My grandfather, John T. Gear, gave me an old alligator leather satchel. It was filled with used baseballs. We had to sew some of them with heavy thread as they wore out. That was usually a nightly chore after practice. We may have had one or two bats that were not broken, but the rest were repaired with screws and tape. Some of the bats stung our hands when we made contact with the ball. Any batter will understand this experience and know what I am saying.

As I think about it, we were the luckiest kids on the planet with not a care in the world and out there playing baseball together. Our entire universe was Harvard Playground and we were there everyday. When the Lord takes us home I hope we can do it again. It was our "field of dreams."

We used old Peterson Scoremaster sheets (and others) for scoring games. Everyone took turns completing the score sheets. After an official game was played we turned in the results to a local paper, the Southwest Wave, a free weekly that was delivered to all homes in the greater southwest area of Los Angeles. So, we even had our games in the paper. As old Yankee announcer, Mel Allen, used to say, "how about that?"

If we had the money, after practice or games we would head for the small grocery store near the playground and buy frozen Pepsi Colas for five cents each.

Young Hurlers Help Los Angeles Club In Winning Ball Games

Followers of the Los Angeles Baseball club were overjoyed when Bob Weiland, veteran left hander, and Frank Totaro, young southpaw, made such an excellent showing against San Francisco.

Manager Arnold Statz opened the series by using Ray Prim, also a left hander, and the three southpaws won their games.

Another young player on the Los Angeles ball club will receive his first starting assignment soon. He is Bill Flaugher, 17-year-old Dorsey high school graduate.

Manager Statz is planning to start him soon.

Bill Flaugher story from Wrigley Field Bulletin

The owner had a method of freezing the glass bottles to a certain point and the soda pop would flow out with little pieces of ice in it. I can still taste it in my mind. After a hot day of baseball that was a very refreshing drink.

The Panthers of Harvard became known around the area. And The Southwest Wave carried the news. This is where we learned how to play baseball. I threw my first curve ball there. It delighted me to see the ball curl in toward the batter and make him duck out of the way. We learned a lot about "change of speeds," too. It was found that we could keep the batter off balance by mixing speeds with our pitches and throwing a curve ball now and then. The fine arts of hitting and fielding were studied. We discovered how to use strategy to win games. It became an art form. We could have performed better by working on the location of our pitches. I think young pitchers today have more knowledge of "hitting the right spots." That aspect of pitching has improved through the years.

Umpiring our own games was necessary. When two teams met each would provide an umpire. Balls and strikes were called from behind the pitchers' box (there was no mound). Occasionally we would have a disagreement on a call but, in general, I think honor prevailed and calls were made accordingly. It was similar to a pick-up tennis match whereby calls are made by the players, themselves.

Some great friendships were made there. Teammates such as Bob Clark, Harley Cross, Don Dufek, Leo Helfrich, Bill Horn, Sol Israel, Frank Latronica, Jack Lombard, Lloyd McClanahan, Don Miller, Carl Moore, Ed Moreno, and Jim Nickoloff, and Dick Runcie became lifelong pals. In fact, Harley, Bill, and Don Miller served in our wedding some years later when Marilyn Knudson and I were married. The Panther pictures still have a place of honor in my den.

Panthers Beat Manchester

A ninth inning rally enabled Harvard playground's Panthers to come out on the long end of a 6-5 count in the last baseball game with Manchester.

The Panthers drew first blood, scoring in the first, but Manchester tied it up in the third. In the seventh Manchester rallied three runs across the plate on a double by Hayes with the bases full.

Two errors brought in two runs for the Panthers in the eighth after two walks were issued. Going into the last half of the ninth with the score 5-4 against them, the Panthers staged an uprising. Proctor drove a double over the left fielder's head. Nickoloff then sent a double down the left field line, scoring Proctor with the tying run. McClanahan singled Nickoloff home with the winning run.

Panthers Capture Harvard Contest

Continuing their winning ways, the Panthers, scourge of the senior baseball league at Harvard playground, took a firmer grip on first place recently by defeating the Pirates, 4 to 0.

The Panthers got off to an early lead in the first frame on two walks and an error. They put the game on ice in the last stanza with a triple by Virgil, a double by Nickoloff, and Proctor's triple.

Dufer, Panther hurler, pitched one-hit ball and fanned four men. Garcia, losing chucker, also fanned four batters but was hit freely.

In another game, the Angels conquered the Stars, 5 to 3.

Harvard Champs Receive Medals

The Panthers of Harvard playground were winners of the Harvard senior league baseball championship this season. The boys on the team received medals.

Members of the team were Kennie Proctor, Jim Nickoloff, Lloyd McClanahan, Leo Helfrich, Sol Israel, Ed Moreno, Bob Dufek, Don Miller, Harley Cross, Bob Clark. These boys went through the season undefeated.

Glenn Landis organized and supervised the league. He also directed the Harvard junior baseball league.

A Day At The Ball Park

In looking at some of my memoirs I found the following story tucked in among some clippings. It is written in my own handwriting and I estimate the date was in the summer of 1934. I was ten years old. It is titled, "Just Another Win." My name is printed on top of the page (see illustration).

It goes as follows, word for word as written: "On a bright sunny day two boys and myself decided we wanted to go see the Los Angeles Angels beat the Seattle Indians (Pacific Coast League teams). First, we all went home and got some lunch and some money. Next we sat down and tried to think of some way to get to Wrigley Field (about three miles away and mentioned previously in this section). After a few minutes I saw a big boy down the street with his automobile. We all knew him and so we went down to where he was. I asked him if he would take us and he said he would if we would give him 7 cents. So I gave him three and the other two boys gave him two apiece. We finally got started. This was Bobby's (who is one of the boys) first baseball game. When we got there we thanked the big boy and started in. Finally after two or three hours the game started. In the first inning the Indians made one run but Marvin Gudat, the Angel right fielder in the Angels half of the first inning knocked one clean over the right field screen (being a left handed batter) into the bleachers. The game stayed tied at 1-1 until the ninth inning when Gene Lillard hit a homer with one out to win the game, 2-1." I don't remember how we made it back home. We probably had to walk. It was a great day for three young boys.

STORY 4

Dizzy Dean's Promise

When I was twelve years old I was a regular attendee at our triple-A baseball park, Wrigley Field, of the Los Angeles Angels. They were a farm team of the famous Chicago Cubs.

One day we heard that an exhibition game was to occur between the St. Louis Cardinals and the Angels. I listened to our baseball radio station announcer, Hal Berger, who interviewed Jay Hanna "Dizzy" Dean, Cardinal pitcher. Dizzy said he would meet in the parking lot after the game to sign autographs for all baseball fans.

When the game ended I went to the parking lot with my scorecard to get it signed. But, Dizzy never showed up. I am sure that important obligations and commitments kept him from keeping his promise that day. It was beyond his control, I concluded. But, I made up my mind to try and not make promises I cannot keep. This twelve-year old was very disappointed.

Dizzy Dean was a true character of the game and a great performer. One of Dizzy's famous quotes was as follows: "It ain't braggin' when you can do it" (1934). Along with his brother, Paul "Daffy" Dean, they made a sensational pair of hurlers for the St. Louis Cardinals of the 1930s.

Dizzy signed with the Cards at age 21. He pitched the last game of the season for them defeating Pittsburg 3-1 on September 28, 1930. For the next five seasons he averaged 24 victories per year. He was one of the most successful players in the majors with outstanding fielding, good hitting and excellent speed on the bases. In addition to his great pitching in his regular starts, he also came in out of the bullpen in relief roles. He led the league in complete games and pitched over 300 innings a year.

In 1934 Dean predicted he and his brother, Paul, would win forty-five games even though Daffy had never pitched a game in the major leagues at the time. The prediction was low because Dizzy won 30 games and Daffy won 19, four more than his estimate. He led the league in wins, strike-outs, shut outs and won the MVP award. The Cardinals played the Detroit Tigers in the World Series and Dizzy won two games and had a shut out in the seventh game. Please see Story 93 (Dizzy Dean).

He continued to achieve with the same success until 1937 when, at the All Star game, suffered a broken toe. This altered his pitching motion to favor his bad foot and he developed bursitis in his right arm. Dean was traded to the Chicago Cubs.

He never regained his sensational achievements although he was successful by replacing his great fastball with an outstanding curve ball and change up. He was able to record a 1.81 ERA and a 7-1 record to help the Cubbies to the National League pennant.

After his retirement at age 30 he became a broadcaster for the old St. Louis Browns. He actually went back on the mound from the broadcast booth three times. In the last game of the year he shut out the Chicago White Sox for four innings and rapped out a base hit in his one at-bat.

I will always remember him announcing games on television and singing the strains of "The Wabash Cannonball," a tune of the old days about a train written by country singer, Roy Acuff. Dizzy had a great southern drawl and a language of his own. One time he said that arguing with Umpire Beans Reardon was like "argyin' with a stump." He and Pee Wee Reese, an old Brooklyn Dodger, made a great announcing team. He announced with other fine broadcasters as well. He spent twenty years in that business. Please see Story 54 (Dizzy Dean) about Dean's announcing career.

It was always fun to hear Dizzy sing as described above. These are the words to his favorite tune:

THE WABASH CANNONBALL by Roy Acuff

Listen to the jingle the rumble and the roar,
As she glides along the woodland, ore the hills and by the shore,
Hear the rush of the mighty engine hear the lonesome hobos call,
He's riding through the jungle on the Wabash Cannonball.
Now the Western states are dandies so the southern people say,
From Chicago and St. Louis and Peoria by the way,
To the lake of Minnesota where the rippling waters flow,
No chances to be taken on the Wabash Cannonball.
She pulled into the station one cold December day,
As she rolled up to the platform you could hear the people say,
Now there's a gal from Birmingham, she's long and she is tall,
She came down from Georgia on the Wabash Cannonball.
Now here's to daddy Claxton, may his name forever stand,
And always to be remembered in the courts of all the land,
His earthly race is over and as the curtain falls,
We'll carry him back to Dixie on the Wabash Cannonball.

It is players like Dizzy Dean that makes baseball the interesting game that it is and our hats are off to this great Hall of Famer.

Phil Cavaretta's Bat

Another day at Wrigley Field I had an experience that is forever etched in my mind. I went with some of my baseball pals to see a game between the famous Chicago Cubs and the Los Angeles Angels. It occurred in March of 1936, and the Cubs were in the area because they had a spring training site on Catalina Island just a few miles off the Southern California coast. It was at that location where some of the old Joe E. Brown baseball movies were made such as "Elmer the Great," and "Alibi Ike." Ring Lardner, a famous author of the 1920s, wrote a number of these books. Incidentally, those who enjoy good baseball stories, you will be rewarded if you find some Lardner books to read.

On this particular day we were excited to realize we had the chance to see the Chicago Cubs play baseball. Phil Cavaretta was a young left-handed first baseman and a very powerful hitter. Phil played with the Chicago Cubs from 1934 to 1953. He was with the Chicago White Sox in 1954 and 1955. He played in 2,030 games with a lifetime batting average of .293, 95 home runs and 920 RBIs. He was an All Star in 1944, 1946 and 1947. He had 17 at bats in World Series games with a .317 average. In his first professional game in 1934 at 18 years of age, Phil hit for the cycle (single, double, triple and home run). In 1945 Cavaretta was the batting champion of the National League with a .355 average.

Back at Wrigley Field, in the fifth inning Phil came to bat and took a ferocious swing at the first pitch and the bat came apart. It split in four pieces but all quite even and parallel to the grain of the bat. The batboy picked them up and laid them down at the bat rack. I kept my eye on those pieces the rest of the game.

When the game ended I found my way down to the field where I asked the batboy if I could have those bat pieces. He said I could have them because they would throw them away. I took them home and carefully pieced them together, put glue on the bat to hold it together, and I added screws and countersunk them. It was a beautiful bat, a Hillerich and Bradsby Louisville Slugger, Model 125. Of course, Phil Cavaretta's name was burned into the heavy part of the bat at the end. I treasured that bat. I had it for years.

Somewhere in moving from one place to another I lost track of the bat. I wish I had it today. It was my real connection to the major leagues, one that had been used by a famous and genuine player. It still excites me when I think of the thrill I received to take it home, fix it and keep it in my room. When Marilyn and I later visited the Louisville Slugger plant my recollection of the Cavaretta bat became fresh in my mind, a young boy's dream.

STORY 6:

An Incredible Event—
The Big Baseball Drop

The following story occurred in 1939. A very unusual baseball-related event happened.

I was a sophomore attending Washington High School in southwest Los Angeles. Four hundred miles north of Los Angeles, the city by the bay, San Francisco, was holding a gigantic World's Fair. It was called The Golden Gate International Exposition." Various activities were taking place all over the city and environs, but the major action was occurring in a remote area called Treasure Island located in the middle of this great bay.

High school students all over the West and beyond were offered a very unique opportunity. For a mere $40 per person, we were provided an 800-mile round trip train ride on the Union Pacific Railroad, two nights in a hotel and a pass to the Exposition. We were on our own for purchasing food. We traveled as a group from our school and it was well organized and properly supervised. That was a much easier task in those days.

The San Francisco-Oakland Bay Bridge opened in 1936 and the Golden Gate Bridge opened in 1937. The Exposition celebrated the completion of these two incredibly impressive bridges.

At the approximate mid-point of the new Bay Bridge was Yerba Buena Island. To the north of this island, man-made Treasure Island was built which became the site of the Exposition. To reach the grounds one had to use the Bay Bridge or ride a ferry. Treasure Island was built of bay dredged dirt. It was planned that the area would be used as an international airport when the Expositon ended. However, when World War II came, plans were changed and an exchange of lands occurred and the airport was built where it still stands on the west side of the bay south of San Francisco.

On the exposition grounds was a 450-foot structure called "The Tower of the Sun." One area baseball team was the famous San Francisco Seals. A publicity promoter, former major league pitcher Walter "The Great" Mails, came up with the idea that a ball dropped from the tower and caught would be a notable public relations stunt. A well-known star, Seals manager Frank "Lefty" O'Doul, who was formerly one of the great major league baseball players in America, was selected to make the "drops."

Joe Sprinz and Larry Woodall, San Francisco catchers, were selected to try and catch the dropped balls. It was Joe's 37th birthday on August 3. I was fortunate enough to be there on that very day. Joe caught five and Larry caught three and the event was a huge success. However, Mails was not satisfied and negotiated the "Great Balloon Drop," whereby the catchers would attempt to catch balls dropped from a blimp that was flying 1000 feet above a baseball diamond on Treasure Island. When they dropped the first ball all backed away except Joe Sprinz. The first ball hit in the empty bleachers. A second ball embedded itself in the ground. Even so, Joe tried to catch the next ball and it glanced off his mitt and violently hit him in the side of the face. He woke up in the hospital with twelve broken bones, a badly injured face and five teeth knocked out. Joe spent three months in the hospital and had five more years of headaches. They estimated the speed of the ball at 150 miles per hour.

Joe went on to play with the Seals through 1946. When he was 43 years old he caught 106 games and batted .303. He went into another type of work but did come back to be the catcher at the "Old Timers" game in the Oakland Coliseum at age 67.

STORY 7:

World War II Duty on Guam with Mace Brown

In early November 1945 our ship, the USS LST 839, pulled into Apra Harbor, Agana, Guam. We had just completed thousands of miles in the war zones in the South Pacific. The war had ended in the previous summer as the Japanese had surrendered on August 14 with the dropping of some atomic bombs in southern Japan. Demobilization began, and older and married service personnel were sent back to the USA, and some of us were assigned in different locations to wind down the war. I was in the latter category and was assigned to duty on Guam under the command of the United States Marine Corps.

My station was at Island Command, the headquarters of all military operations in the various South Pacific islands. My Marine commander was Col. Donald Sult. My job was to direct athletic programs on these islands and to provide recreational activities for the many service people still performing jobs in the area.

I worked with an outstanding gentleman by the name of Lt. Mace Brown. Mace, like myself, was a naval officer. We organized tournaments of all kinds including softball, basketball, volleyball, and other sports. We even brought a major league all-star baseball group to split into two teams and compete with one another for several games. The service people loved it.

Mace was a great friend and co-worker. He had played for the Pittsburg Pirates, Brooklyn Dodgers, and the Boston Red Sox having first signed professionally in 1935. When he returned home after his Guam duty, he played another year, 1946, for the Red Sox. He was a gentle and gracious man and became one of my mentors. Mace was sixteen years my senior at 36 years of age.

He played ten years in the major leagues and posted a 76-57 pitching record with a lifetime earned run average of 3.46. He played in two World Series, in 1941 for the Dodgers and in 1946 for the Red Sox and was an All Star in the 1938 season.

Brown was one of the first relief specialists having made 50 appearances in a season (1937) without recording a complete game. He repeated this feat in 1938 by appearing in 51 games.

In total, Mace pitched 1,075 innings and had a career fielding average of .967.

When Babe Ruth hit home run number 714 (his last homer) he was playing for the Boston Braves. He hit three dingers that day. The last one was hit out of Forbes Field where Boston was playing Pittsburg and was measured at 600 feet. Mace told me the Babe sat down next to him after that home run and said, "that

The LST839., Ken's home in 1944 and 1945.

July 31, 1967. Republic of Vietnam, Mechanized Landing Craft LCM 912 and the Tank Landing Ship, LST839, veteran of World War II, recommissioned as USS Iredell County, docked at Cua Viet LST-ramp, where supplied from Da Nang are loaded on small craft for transport to Nang Ha combat base. Official US Navy photograph released for publication.

felt good!" I looked it up and, indeed, the Babe did sit down next to Mace on the Pirate bench. That sounds like something the Babe would do.

My good friend, Mace Stanley Brown, passed away March 24, 2002 at age 92. This outstanding baseball player from North English, Iowa was a wonderful colleague. God bless you, Mace!

STORY 8:

Playing Against The Yankee Clipper, Joe Di Maggio

In the baseball season of 1941 the game was very popular and some of the biggest games were making the news. I can remember players like Ted Williams, Phil Rizzuto, Bill Dickey, PeeWee Reese, Cookie Lavagetto, Stan Musial, Hank Greenberg and many others. They were the heroes of baseball fans all over the country.

But, one name seemed to stand out above all others. That was the incomparable Joe Di Maggio. He had helped the New York Yankees win four consecutive World Series titles from 1936 through 1939. By 1941 Joe was at his peak. On May 15 he hit a single in a game against the Chicago White Sox. He continued to get hits in 56 consecutive games finally ending his streak on July 17 against the Cleveland Indians. He was named the Most Valuable Player that year beating out Ted Williams, Boston Red Sox star, who batted .406.

This is an interesting note. Following July 17 Joe hit in 16 consecutive contests bringing his total to 72 out of 73 games. To say he was hot is an understatement. To further show his consistency, eight years previously in 1933, Joe hit in 61 consecutive games for the San Francisco Seals in the old Pacific Coast League. I was just nine years old that year and went several times to watch Joe and the Seals play at Wrigley Field in Los Angeles.

Joe was my personal hero in a way. Even though I was a Los Angeles Angel fan as a local boy, I admired DiMaggio and his skills. He was everything a young hopeful wanted to imitate.

The following is an amusing story I think readers might enjoy.

I recall one day after a game I walked by a corner bar in the Wrigley building and I saw Joe drinking a beer. I was crushed! We were always taught to never drink or smoke and to take care of our bodies in every way. I know some would laugh at this today but after some of the sad stories of today's professional athletes and their personal problems, perhaps we need to establish some training standards for young players. The steroid problem is a case in point in addition to drugs and alcohol. I know plenty of coaches who stress clean living.

Born Giuseppe Paolo DiMaggio, Joe was solely a Yankee having never played for another major league club. He played in ten World Series and was an All Star thirteen times. His records in so many areas of baseball achievement were phenomenal. He compiled a .325 lifetime batting average. He was considered among the best in hitting, hitting for power, fielding, throwing and running.

Joe's records are in a class by themselves. He led the Yankees to World Championships in nine different years (1936 through 1939 as mentioned plus 1941, 1947, 1949, 1950 and 1951). He played through some difficult injuries after the war years and continued to be the Yankee's quiet leader.

In 1969, the centennial year of professional baseball was celebrated and a poll was conducted among sports writers as to who was the greatest living baseball player. DiMaggio won that poll hands down.

I was playing second base for the UCLA Bruins in 1944 in the old California Intercollegiate Baseball Association (CIBA). During that year we often played local service teams. One such team was that of the U.S. Air Force stationed nearby. We learned that the famous Joe DiMaggio was on that team. He was just as competitive and aggressive there as he had been with the New York Yankees for the past eight years from 1936. It was a privilege to be on the same field with the Yankee Clipper. Please see Story 94 (Joe DiMaggio) about more DiMaggio accomplishments.

STORY 9:

"Hey Kid, You Got My Number!"

On Tuesday, May 4, 1948 our UCLA baseball team was playing the Santa Barbara Gauchos in a doubleheader. The day before at practice our coach, Art Reichle, told us we were going to have the privilege of meeting the great Babe Ruth just prior to the start of the first game. The Sultan of Swat was in Los Angeles to supervise the filming of his life story.

The moment arrived when "the Babe's" big black limousine pulled up and parked right over home plate at Joe E. Brown Field, the UCLA baseball diamond. On that very spot Pauley Pavilion now stands, the home of the famous UCLA basketball team led by John Wooden for so many years. Our catcher at that time, Hal Handley, told me recently that his job during the week was to care for the ball field and he clearly recalls that the big car parked right over the top of his "neatly-trimmed" batter's box.

Coach Reichle told us to line up side-by-side and to wear our warm-up jackets to meet the great home run king. We were told not to speak to Babe because he had cancer of the throat and it would have been a strain on him to reply.

As twenty of us lined up in front of our dugout the Babe stepped out of his big automobile. He was dressed in a long black overcoat and wore a small cap with a little bill in front. I recall I was seventeenth in line. Mr. Ruth passed along the line one-by-one and met each player. No words were exchanged, just smiles and handshakes. When he arrived to me, once again he extended his hand and grinned. As he did so he glanced at my UCLA warm up jacket. His face widened to a deeper smile and, in a raspy, throaty voice, he looked me in the eye and said, "Hey, kid, you got my number!"

Yes, I was number "3," The Babe's number all those years with the famous New York Yankees. I squeezed his hand a little more and thanked him as he moved to the next player. Needless to say, I was overwhelmed that he spoke to me.

FULL OF SMILES—The Sultan of Swat arrived in Los Angeles this week to supervise the filming of his life story. The Bambino stated that major league baseball isn't up to the par it was when he bowed out of the game.

UCLA DAILY BRUIN   9
Wednesday, May 5, 1948

BASEBALL RESULTS
AMERICAN LEAGUE

Detroit   001 002 000   3   9   2
Boston   001 014 00x   6   10   3

    Houtteman, Gentry (7) White (8) and Wagner; Ferris, Galehouse (7) and Tebbetts.

    Chicago at Washington, Night Game.
St. Louis   000 100 000   1   4   3
New York   110 000 31x   6   9   0

    Potter, Stephens (6) Widmar (7) and Partee, Moss (7); Shea and Berra.
Cleveland   012 003 000 0   6   12   1
Philadelphia   103 200 000 2   8   12   0

    Muncrief, Gromek (3) Klieman (7) Christopher (7) Wensloff (9) and Gegan; Marchildon, Harris (3), Savage (6) Brissie (8 and Guerra.

NATIONAL LEAGUE

    Philadelphia at Chicago, postponed, rain.
    Boston at Pittsburgh, night game.
    Brooklyn at St. Louis, night game.

Ken's number on the arm
of his UCLA jacket.

A few minutes later, my teammate, outfielder Marty Weinberger, said, "Hey Proc, the Babe talked to you." I acknowledged that momentous occasion and told Marty it was very exciting to meet him but to have him make a personal comment was unbelievable.

The Babe sat on our bench for several innings before he had to leave. Doug Sale told me he stayed a little longer than expected because he wanted to see Jack "Moose" Myers bat one more time. (Jack was one of our sluggers who later played with the Philadelphia Eagles NFL football club). What an honor it was for all of us to have this legend of baseball be with us that day! Please see Story 138 (Babe Ruth) for more information on "The Bambino."

I still have my chenille number "3" displayed in my den as a memoir of that special moment in my life. Mr. Ruth passed away just three months later on August 16, 1948.

Many years later my wife, Marilyn, was called to jury duty in a local county office. It so happened that the judge in attendance and his wife had gone to a Seattle Mariner baseball game with us previously. In the course of our conversation at the game the judge learned that I had played at UCLA and had met Babe Ruth in 1948.

In the courtroom that day, the judge recognized my wife and while the jury was out mentioned to those in the court room that this particular lady's husband had met Babe Ruth years ago. When Marilyn and the jury returned, she noticed that the baliff and some officers of the court were smiling at her. Later when I picked Marilyn up, some of these people wanted to shake my hand. This occurred because her husband had met Babe Ruth. We all had a good laugh out of that experience.

To this day it still amazes people to meet someone who actually met and shook the hand of the great Babe. It was such a privilege for me, one I shall never forget.

STORY 10:

A Major League Pop Up
By Larry Doby

It was a beautiful spring day in March when I first saw Larry Doby. He was playing for the Cleveland Indians at Sawtelle Field in Los Angeles where our team, UCLA, sometimes played home games. In fact today, interestingly enough, that field is called Jackie Robinson Stadium and is, indeed, the home field of the UCLA Bruin baseball team.

Midway through the ball game Larry hit one of the highest pop ups I have ever seen. The wind blowing in from Santa Monica blew the ball around and it was so high that the right fielder and I lost it and allowed it to fall in for a double.

Larry was the first African-American to play in the American League. He did not get the publicity as did Jackie Robinson but he certainly proved his worth as the next thirteen years passed. In fact, Larry actually had better numbers than Jackie. He compiled an enviable record during his career. Larry played in 1,533 games with a .283 batting average. He hit 253 home runs and had 970 RBIs. He was in ten World Series games in 1948 and 1954, all with Cleveland. He played in six All Star games. In 1962 Larry and Don Newcombe became the first former major leaguers to play for a professional Japanese team, the Chunichi Dragons.

On June 30, 1978 Larry became the second African-American manager as he took over the reins of the Chicago White Sox. He was elected into the Hall of Fame on March 3, 1998, certainly a well-deserved honor. Larry passed away on June 18, 2003.

STORY 11:

Mike Gazella, A Former Yankee

One of my teammates at UCLA in 1949 was Mike Gazella Jr. His father, Mike Gazella Sr. played with the New York Yankees in 1923 and 1926-1928. He played alongside Babe Ruth, Lou Gehrig and other greats of those Yankee teams. Also, he played on a champion 1934 Pacific Coast League team, the Los Angeles Angels, as well as other minor league teams.

Mike Sr. came to our games and practices often. He was scouting for the Boston Braves at the time. He had been a regular on the club and did a creditable job in both the field and at the plate. We asked Mike what his greatest thrill in baseball had been. He came up with a humorous reply that had all of us in stitches. To understand Mike's answer, one has to know that the great Walter "The Big Train" Johnson threw very hard when he was pitching in the big leagues. Mike said, "Well, one time I recall that I popped up foul off Walter Johnson." Great comment!

Incidentally, the Boston Braves eventually became the Milwaukee Braves and currently are the Atlanta Braves. Please see Chapter 9, (Major League Clubs' Names and Location Changes.)

STORY 12:

Marilyn Proctor, My Best Baseball Buddy

I want to move ahead in time somewhat to introduce my best baseball buddy, my wife, Marilyn Knudson Proctor. We were married in 1949 and almost immediately baseball became a very important part of our lives. I considered signing a professional baseball contract at that time but I had been in the U.S. Navy for seven years, four of them in active service in World War II, and was 25 years old. So, I decided to teach and coach baseball as a profession and make it my life's work while Marilyn and I raised our family. This proved to be a wise decision in my opinion. My chances at making it to the major leagues were undoubtedly slim anyway. I signed a contract with the Chaffey Union High School District in Ontario, California and started coaching and teaching in January 1950.

Marilyn was familiar with baseball having gone to games with her father and brothers at Gilmore Field in the old Pacific Coast League. Also, we went to Wrigley Field before we were married. Soon, we were sharing baseball experiences together as I coached high school teams every year. In addition, I was active in developing a youth baseball program in our new town. Please see Story 13 (Developing A Youth Baseball Program in Ontario, California).

I choose to put this story here because our baseball relationship will be referenced to in several other parts of the book. I will discuss our sharing of the grand old game in various ensuing segments.

Marilyn has become a student of the game through the years. One of the lines I hear from her most often is, "Now we need a double play ball." She tells me "The pitcher is coming in too high and needs to keep the ball down." She will say, "See how he hit his cut-off man perfectly on that play." Or occasionally she will comment, "Our team needs work on running the bases." She is very knowledgeable, no question about it. We have been enjoying this camaraderie for more than fifty years.

There is only one person on this earth who understands all the stories and experiences in this book. And that person is my best baseball buddy, Marilyn Proctor.

Marilyn Proctor clapping at game

39

Developing A Youth Baseball Program In Ontario, California

When I started my teaching at Chaffey High School it was not long before some local people asked if I would be interested in working to develop a youth baseball program. I was excited and honored they would ask me to be involved. I met with them and accepted the task of being "player agent" for the Little League and provided leadership in holding clinics and try-outs for the players. The first year of the league I umpired every contest of a 30-game season. I might say I should have sought out some sort of shoulder protection and shin guards. I did not realize how hard those youngsters could throw and there I was behind the catcher taking foul balls all over my body. My new colors were " black and blue."

Youth baseball in our town, just like any other city, required the combined work of many people. We had to secure sponsors who provided money for equipment and uniforms. The cooperation of the city government was important in order to have properly cared-for fields on which to play. The local newspaper, *The Daily Report* (now called the *Inland Valley Daily Bulletin*), was very cooperative and covered all youth league news and game results.

There were so many individuals involved that I would be remiss if I tried to name people. Suffice it to say that the total community was behind the effort and it was a huge success.

Later, as the Little Leaguers grew up it was necessary to provide programs for older players. I became involved with the Pony League that was developed for 13 and 14 year-olds, with the Colt League for 15 and 16 year-olds, and American Legion baseball was the next step for older players.

I have one regret and that would be that we did not have such a program for girls. Today that problem has been remedied and girls' programs flourish all over America.

Ken Proctor w/young ball players

STORY 14:

The Ontario-Upland Pirates

A semi-professional team existed in our area that was composed of players of all ages but, generally, for players from twenty to forty years of age. The Ontario-Upland Pirates were very popular and played in a group called the Sunshine League. It was composed of our Pirates, San Bernardino Hornets, San Bernardino Dancers, March Field Air Force Base, and teams from Pomona, Riverside, Colton and Corona. We played on Sundays and occasionally during the week at night. Our local ball field, called John Galvin Park, seated about 2,000, had great lighting and was an outstanding diamond. It was the former site of spring training for the Los Angeles Angels and Hollywood Stars of the old Pacific Coast League..

Much credit is due a gentleman named Ken Smith who coached and organized the Pirates. Ken worked hard to make this league a success. Actually, there were other semi-pro teams all over Southern California, and, for that matter, all over the nation. I do recall that we played a team from Santa Barbara that was coached by Gene Lillard, a former star third baseman with the Los Angeles Angels of the Pacific Coast League. Many of the old ball players went to the semi-pro leagues in their later years.

I was in my upper 20s in those years and played second base for the Pirates. As my high school players graduated, some chose to play on the semi-pro club. I enjoyed playing along side of them. Also, in the months of November through February a number of major league players were added to rosters. They were playing for enjoyment and to keep in shape over the winter. Some were working on improving injuries in order to report to their clubs at spring training in good condition.

One such player on the Pirates was Marty Keough who played eleven seasons in the big leagues. He was a great teammate and an excellent player. I had occasion to observe Marty on other occasions that are described in Story 113 (Marty Keough). Also, I discussed his family there because they all were outstanding athletes.

I really enjoyed playing with Pirates. We had an outstanding team and did our share of winning against tough competition. In all of my playing days, the times competing with the Pirates was among

Proctor Tops Hitting

Two Kens—Ken Proctor and Ken Smith—are showing the way to the rest of the Ontario-Upland Pirates in connecting with Sunshine league pitching for basehits.

Ken Proctor, veteran second sacker, paces the club with a lusty .412 mark. The Pirates manager is second with .385.

The Pirates will probably need all this power at the plate and some more when they bump into the league-leading Pomona Chevs Sunday afternoon at the Ontario Baseball park.

A double Pirate win would put the locals even with the front runners.

Ken Smith has called for a practice tomorrow afternoon at 2:30 at Upland Memorial park for the Pirates.

BATTING AVERAGES

	AB	H	Avg.
Bob Wolfe, ss	2	2	1.000
Ken Proctor, 2b	17	7	.412
Ken Smith, 3b	13	5	.385
Buster Gladson, 2b	8	3	.375
Bill Morris, p	8	3	.375
Bob Sachs, of	25	9	.360
Wayne Specht, c	34	12	.353
Lou Vasquez, ss	15	5	.333
Don Seely, ss	6	2	.333
Van Huppert, 1b	27	8	.296
Don Black, 3b	15	4	.267
Bob Staudenmayer, 3b	23	6	.261
Buzz Gardner, of	23	5	.217
Arlen Downs, 1b	5	1	.200
Dick Zuccato, 3b	5	1	.200
Hal Biggers, p	5	1	.200
Ken Roberts, of	16	3	.188
Fred Fernandez, of	11	2	.182
Jerry Wulf, p	12	1	.083
Fred Kennedy, of	12	0	.000
Odis Baker, c	3	0	.000
Ray Baker, c	3	0	.000
Pat Williams, p	0	0	

my favorites. I was a little older than college days and had picked up more experience. I batted .414 with the team, a career high for me, and thoroughly enjoyed having the opportunity to play against major leaguers after foregoing possible chances to play professional baseball.

STORY 15:

Who Is Hiram Bithorn?

I had mentioned that I was aware of almost every baseball player in the game when I was a youngster. Along with friends it was competitive and entertaining to know the batting and fielding averages of players, but especially those players in our local Pacific Coast League.

As I am writing this book I find names popping up I have not heard in sixty or more years. One such player was that of a pitcher in the Pacific Coast League named Hiram (Hi) Bithorn. My pronunciation of his name was "Hi-ram Bithorn." However, in the 80s Marilyn and I took a trip to Puerto Rico and went to the baseball stadium in San Juan, the capital city, which was called "Bithorn Stadium," or in Spanish, "Estadia Bithorn." Hiram's name in Spanish sounds like "Ee Ram Bee Thorn." It was a surprise to realize one of the players of my boyhood was famous in Puerto Rico. We saw a very professional ball game and the fans were very knowledgeable. Of course, everything had a Hispanic flavor from the food to the announcing. It was really fun to experience baseball there. Some of the players were major leaguers from the United States who were keeping in shape during "winter baseball." The attendance was approximately 3,000.

Earlier, Hiram played for the Chicago Cubs in 1942-43 and for the Chicago White Sox in 1946-47. He had a lifetime ERA of 3.16 and had 34 wins and 31 losses. In 1942 Bithorn was 18-12, fourth in the National League in wins and led the league in shut outs with seven. His ERA that year was 2.60 which was among the leaders. Hiram was a burly fellow and after two seasons in the military service increased his weight to 225. He was sold to the Pittsburg Pirates in 1946 and went on to the White Sox the same year. But his effectiveness was gone. He played in the Pacific Coast League later.

The major baseball stadium in San Juan, Puerto Rico was named after him following his death. The stadium is still in use in San Juan. In nearby Caroline, Puerto Rico, the new Roberto Clemente Municipal Stadium is now in use.

STORY 16:

We All Watched Willie In Amazement

In March of 1951 I was coaching my second year at Chaffey High School. I had a good junior varsity team and wanted to do something nice for them. So I organized a trip to Wrigley Field in Los Angeles so we could watch an exhibition game between the New York Giants and the Los Angeles Angels. It was a beautiful sunny Saturday afternoon and with the help of parents, we car-pooled into Los Angeles, roughly a 90-mile roundtrip.

We had good seats and really enjoyed the game. As the various plays occurred I had the opportunity to point out certain fundamentals to my players. It was a great opportunity to do some coaching at a real major league baseball game.

Sometime in the middle of the game with the Angels at bat and a man on third base and one out, a long fly ball was hit to centerfield. Nineteen-year old Willie Mays caught the ball at the 380 foot mark, and threw the ball to home plate on one hop. I believe it was one of the most incredible throws I had ever seen. Many of us recall the great catch Willie made in the 1954 World Series of a 460-foot drive off the bat of Vic Wertz of Cleveland. It has been dubbed,"The Catch." It has been shown over and over again on television. Well, I believe that throw we saw ranks right up there with that catch. Willie Mays was a phenomenal player. Later in Story 20 (The Dodgers and Giants Come West) please read about the first time Marilyn and I saw the great Willie Mays "live" in a regular league game. What happened still gives me chills.

On that day with my players, however, we all watched Willie in amazement. He was truly one of the greatest of all baseball players and had an great attitude to match.

STORY 17:

Wrigley Field, Los Angeles

I was ten years old when I first visited Wrigley Field. (Please see Story 3 (A Day at the Ball Park) Etched in my memory forever is the experience of walking into the park and seeing that elegant green field with its white lines, perfectly trimmed, with the outfield walls enclosing the entire scene. It was a sight all of us who love this game have experienced. And as we go into ballparks again and again, the same thrill and stimulating feeling goes through our bodies.

I attended games at Wrigley Field many, many times. My dad and mother took me and a friend or two to both night and weekend games. It was our favorite activity as a family. As with many youngsters, I knew the names, batting and pitching statistics and records of all the players. They were our heroes.

This park is a nearly exact model of Wrigley Field in Chicago. The Southern California ballpark was the home of the Los Angeles Angels Baseball Club. In 1921 the club was purchased by chewing gum company owner, William K. Wrigley, for $150,000. This was just one year after Wrigley purchased the Chicago Cubs.

The Pacific Coast League team had played it's games at Washington Park in downtown Los Angeles from 1903 to 1924 and when the city refused to build proper parking facilities, Wrigley decided to build a new park similar to his ballpark in Chicago. In addition to the parking problems, Washington Park held just 15,000 "kranks," the name given to fans at the turn of the century. The new park's capacity was 20,500. While small for major league standards it would permit more income than the old park. Construction began in 1924, my birth year, by the way. The new million-dollar park opened on September 29, 1925 when I was just over one-year old.

Lights were installed on July 22, 1931. This was a major change from the park in Chicago. No lights were there until August 8, 1988, fifty-seven years later (there is some trivia for you). It was a beautiful facility and fans came in droves to watch baseball. As it turned out the new Cub farm team dominated the PCL. They won twelve championships in their 55-year history. The 1934 club had a record of 137-50 winning nearly three of every four games. They finished 30 games ahead of the San Francisco Seals, led by Joe DiMaggio. They were so good that the All Star game that year featured the Angels against a team of stars from the other seven franchises...and the Angels still won the game!

At that time players refused to go to the American and National League teams in many cases because they would have to take a pay cut. But, when the Dodgers moved to Los Angeles in 1958, the PCL's plans to become a third major league in America were doomed.

STORY 18:

Gilmore Field, Los Angeles (Hollywood)

In 1949 I played at Gilmore Field, Los Angeles, when our UCLA Bruins faced the USC Trojans in a Pacific Coast Conference baseball game. This park was the home of the minor league Hollywood Stars baseball club owned by movie people Bing Crosby, Barbara Stanwyck, Cecil B. DeMille, and others.

Gilmore Field was built in 1938 to accommodate the Hollywood Stars club. The stadium was probably the most intimate park ever developed as a professional site for the grand old game. Home plate, ordinarily 60 feet from the backstop, was just 34 feet from the nearest seats. The corners at first and third bases were just 24 feet away.

Arthur F. Gilmore came west in 1870 from Illinois looking for a good home for his family. He purchased 256 acres in Los Angeles and developed a dairy farm. He drilled for water for his cattle and struck oil. It was not long before the farm was gone and the Gilmore Oil Company was a successful business.

By that time, the elder Gilmore's son, Earl Bell Gilmore, was directing the family business. The area became known as The Farmers' Market in 1934 and it still exists today. It has been magnificently developed and is known all over the world. But, Mr. Gilmore saw much more potential there. He built Gilmore Stadium and it served as a racecar track for midget racers. Along with his Farmers' Market, the area became an international landmark. The stadium became the venue for the Bulldogs, Los Angeles's first professional football team. Other events took place there including boxing, wrestling and rodeos.

In 1925 the Vernon Tigers of the Los Angeles area, moved to the Bay area of San Francisco. The original Hollywood Stars, having been playing their games at Wrigley Field on the eastside side of Los Angeles, moved to San Diego to become the Padres. Later, the San Francisco club under the name of Mission Reds decided to move to Los Angeles and take over the name of the Hollywood Stars. They played in Wrigley Field for one year, 1938. They had need of their own ballpark and Earl B. Gilmore built Gilmore Field to provide them that park and

Baseball Centennial
1839 — 1939

A CENTURY OF BASEBALL 1839 - - 1939

HOLLYWOOD STARS

OFFICIAL PROGRAM

GILMORE FIELD

43

Louisville Slugger Baseball Bats

HILLERICH & BRADSBY CO. LOUISVILLE KY. LOUISVILLE SLUGGER

Standard Wherever Baseball Is Played

10¢

they moved from Wrigley Field to play their first season in their new ball park.

The Hollywood Star president, Victor Ford Collins, and Robert Cobb, vice-president, organized a company to purchase the Stars. They acquired support from such prominent movie stars and Hollywood elite as Robert Taylor, Gary Cooper, DeMille, Stanwyck, Crosby, Gail Patrick, Leon Schlesinger, Lloyd Bacon, Harry Warner, Herbert Fleishacker, Wade Killefer, and many others.

Gilmore Field was an immediate success. It was a new and exciting place for the Hollywood fans. Menu prices were interesting. All of the following items were sold at 10 cents: Red hots (hot dogs), ice cream, peanuts, popcorn, lemon lime, orange, Coca Cola, and Canada Dry. William Penn cigars were 5 cents each. Other cigars were 10 cents and better cigars were two for a quarter. Cigarettes were 15 cents a pack. Scorecards and cushions were 10 cents each. Coffee was 10 cents and Pabst Beer was 20 cents. Eastside and ABC beer was 15 cents. All candy was 5 cents each.

Marilyn's father, Luther, took his family to games at Gilmore Field in the 1940s. He took wife, Dolly, daughter Marilyn, and sons Lyle, Howard and David. Lyle lives in Los Osos, California at present and I called him to hear his version of attending games at Gilmore Field. He said most of the time he, dad, and brother Howard went together. They sat in the grandstand (80 cents) or the bleachers 40 cents). He vividly recalls players like Bobby Bragan, Babe Herman, Carlos Bernier, Cliff Dapper, Len Gabrielson, Joe Hoover, Jack Salveson, Hiram Bithorn and Frenchy Uhalt among others. Lyle said it was usually a full house. They especially enjoyed the Sunday doubleheaders. He recalls a big Lion as a symbol. It reminded me that the Gilmore's motto was "Roar With Gilmore," referring to their oil business.

I attended some games at Gilmore Field in the late 1940s but most of the time I went to Wrigley Field because it was closer to my home and I was a devout Los Angeles Angel fan.

Generally, the stands were full of movie stars. George Burns and Gracie Allen, Jack Benny, Cyd Charisse and Tony Martin, Crosby, Stanwyck and George Raft attended regularly. It was reported that Raft brought a different girl to each game. Guess who served as the Bat Girl? It was none other than teenager Elizabeth Taylor. CBS Television City was built next door and many TV stars came to games right after work.

Spencer Harris

MENU

Red Hots	10c
Beverly Ice Cream	10c
Mellos Jumbo Peanuts (big bag)	10c
Popcorn, Big Bag	10c
LaVida Lime 'N Lemon	10c
Green Spot Orange	10c
New Yorker Beverages	10c
Coca Cola	10c
Canada Dry	10c
Charms	5c
Christopher's Candy Bars	5c
Wm. Penn Cigars	5c
Santa Fe Patties	10c
Santa Fe Panatelas	2 for 25c
Santa Fe Biltmores	2 for 25c
Santa Fe Imperiales	15c
Camel Cigarettes	15c
Raleigh Cigarettes	15c
Kool Cigarettes	15c
Philip Morris	15c
Cushions (Rented)	10c
Score Cards	10c
Pabst Beer	20c
Eastside Beer	15c
ABC Beer	15c
Huggins-Young Coffee	10c

The weather in Southern California made it ideal for baseball. A rained-out game was extremely rare and the temperatures were good for both fans and players. With the huge crowds at both Wrigley and Gilmore Fields, owners were pushing to make the Pacific Coast League the third league with major status. Bob Cobb, as vice-president of the Stars (also, he was owner of the famous restaurant, The Brown Derby), pushed hard to make this happen but MLB owners did not want PCL franchises cutting in on their profits. Also, having to pay to transport teams over the Rocky Mountains did not help as well.

The Hollywood Stars, drawing more than 600,000 every season, won pennants in 1949, 1952 and 1953. Many of their games were wild and woolly. In a game with Oakland one night, Bllly Martin, covered in blood, was carried off the field with spike wounds in both legs. The doctor, who was called in from the stands, gave Billy a shot of whiskey and the wounds were stitched up without the aid of any anesthetic as his teammates held him down.

A memorable moment in the Stars history was on April 1, 1950 (April Fools' Day). The players showed up in shorts, with stockings knee-high, and flashy baseball shirts. They used that uniform until 1953. I recall those shorts and wondered how the players would make out with injuries when they slid. But, while they did have their share of "strawberries," the shorts did not seem to add more wounds than normal.

"Miss Hollywood Stars" of 1955 was buxom Jayne Mansfield. At one point her picture was put on the cover of the official program and it made quite an impression on everyone. Believe it or not, I still have an official program of the Hollywood Stars on display in my den at home. It is not the Mansfield program but one from 1939, their first year of existence. It's emphasis was "A Century of Baseball," 1839-1939, referring, of course, to the beginnings of modern baseball and referring to Abner Doubleday, the inventor of the game in 1839.

The Stars was the first baseball team to broadcast home games on television. Stars tickets were hard to come by in the 1950s. The team enjoyed tremendous popularity. However, it was a time of change for baseball and when the Dodgers came to Los Angeles in 1958 the old PCL became history. But the Hollywood franchise was certainly significant in the changes that were occurring.

In 1953 a Stars/Angel game produced the greatest professional baseball fight in history. The two teams fought for a full half hour. The fans and television audience were delighted. Chief of Police William Parker, watching the game on TV, called fifty policemen who came on the field to restore order. Afterwards, police were placed at each dugout and just nine players were allowed out at a time. Order was necessary as it was a doubleheader and a second game still had to be played. Please see Story 209 (One of Baseball's Famous Brawls) and Story 121 (Eddie Malone) for more on the fight.

After playing ten years for the Stars, the popular Frankie Kelleher, left baseball in 1954. Jayne Mansfield cried. He was probably the most famous of all the Star players. He was a power hitter and I recall his lifting his front (left) leg in the air as he swung giving him additional momentum. The fans gave him a long, standing ovation as they retired his number 7. Frank was kind enough to come to our Chaffey High School baseball banquet after our 1956 season and provide us with an excellent address as speaker. Please see Story 74 (1956 Varsity Team).

On September 5, 1957 the last game was played at Gilmore Field. Sadly, it was an end of an era. They presented Bob Cobb with a new car and honored him for a job well done. There were several offers to purchase the team but a Utah businessman, Nicholas Morgan, bought the franchise for $175,000 and moved it to Salt Lake City. The ballpark was taken down in 1958. There were more than 1,700 baseball games played there. The lights were sold to the Dodgers' Spokane franchise and are still being used.

Interestingly enough, after several changes in league status, the old franchise has become the Tacoma Rainers and play baseball games today in old Cheney Stadium under the auspices of the Seattle Mariners. Those years of the Hollywood Stars were special times for baseball. Once again, we baseball fans have a reason to think back and shed a tear or two and recall a wonderful chapter in baseball history.

STORY 19:

Umpires Do A Great Job

Obviously, every baseball coach has had contact with umpires in many different ways. In fact, I officiated basketball for fifteen years and football for 21 years. Many coaches officiate in their "off seasons." Going through all the training and preparation for officiating makes one respect the task of performing that job in any sport. Also, I did some umpiring in my various baseball experiences.

I have always felt that umpires do a great job. An umpire is like a judge. He or she wants to be fair. They work hard at their task and do many hours of preparation to do a good job. Most fans do not realize the time taken by officials to make sure they perform well. The old line, "they call 'em as they see 'em" is certainly true. And all that hard work makes most of their calls correct.

I had a rule on our teams that when a batter is at the plate and questions a

Emmett Ashford in uniform—You're Out! First Afro-American major league umpire. Alan J. delay, *The Oregonian*

Emmett Ashford reading paper

call, he stays in the batter's box, looks out at the centerfield fence, and says to the umpire, "where was it, sir?" Most umpires will merely tell the batter the truth. Some answer could be "on the outside corner," "inside corner at the knees," or "right down the middle." In any case, our players were never to turn and look at the umpire or to give the impression they thought it was a bad call. When a player asks where was the location of the pitch, the umpire gets the message. There is a rule that players, coaches, and managers may not question balls and strikes. That rule should be followed. Inciting fans to yell at the umpire is not good for the game. That umpire is there to make the situation fair for both teams.

When one of my teams played for the California Interscholastic Federation championship in the 50s, I had a very nice card from a gentleman named Eric "Dutch" Bergmann. Dutch, the lead umpire that day, wanted to compliment our ball team in their demeanor and behavior on the field. I cherish that communication. The respect went both ways.

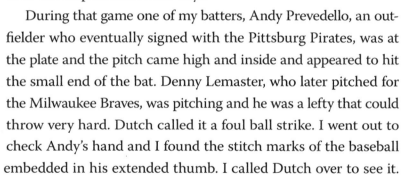

During that game one of my batters, Andy Prevedello, an outfielder who eventually signed with the Pittsburg Pirates, was at the plate and the pitch came high and inside and appeared to hit the small end of the bat. Denny Lemaster, who later pitched for the Milwaukee Braves, was pitching and he was a lefty that could throw very hard. Dutch called it a foul ball strike. I went out to check Andy's hand and I found the stitch marks of the baseball embedded in his extended thumb. I called Dutch over to see it. Upon observing it, Dutch called and pointed, "first base." In officiating, we call that "getting it right." There have been times in officiating whereby an umpire will never change his call. This was a case of Dutch making the correct call, even though he had first judged it as a foul ball.

Incidentally, an old-time baseball left-handed pitcher worked the bases in that game. His name was Tillie Schafer. Tillie was very effective as a pitcher with a good fastball and an understanding of changing speeds. I had batted against him when our UCLA team played his Pacific Coast League Portland team in the spring of 1948. I don't recall what happened but I expect he put me back on the bench. He was a fine umpire and well-respected for his sharp eyes and fairness.

When playing at UCLA we often had a gentleman working behind the plate named Emmett Ashford. "Ash," as he was known to close associates, was considered to be one of the best in the business calling balls and strikes. He became a professional umpire in 1951 and eventually worked many years in the Pacific Coast League. At age 61, he became the first African-American umpire to be assigned in the American League. He worked the 1967 All Star game and the 1970 World Series. Emmett was always dressed immaculately and had a tendency toward humor and good showmanship. His first major league game was on April 11, 1966 in Washington D.C. where the Senators faced the Cleveland Indians.

At UCLA, I was seldom a long ball hitter but occasionally I made good contact and hit one deep. There was no outfield fence at the Bruin's Joe E. Brown Field when I played there. One day when Emmett was working the plate, I hit one to right centerfield and it rolled on between the two outfielders. I circled the bases and coming around third the signal was given to me to go for the plate. As I came toward home I realized that I was going to make it. Players sense that fact when they are running the bases. I slid under the tag and touched the plate. Safe, I thought! There was one problem. Emmett exclaimed in a very loud voice, "YOU'RE OUT!" As I laid there for a second or two I looked up at the umpire's face and said in a kind of sad tone, "Emmett, you missed it!" Later, Emmett and I laughed about that scene many times.

A few years later when I was coaching at Chaffey High School I took on the job of officiating basketball games around Southern California. One night in Fullerton I was working a Fullerton JC vs Riverside JC game and my partner was none other than Emmett Ashford. In the middle of the first half he blew his whistle loudly somewhat quieting the crowd as they listened to see what call was being made. And Emmett pointed at a defensive player, raised his fist in the air and yelled, "YOU CAN'T DO THAT TO THAT MAN." It brought down the house. Uncontrollable laughter prevailed. That was Emmett. He always brought joy to the game.

We lost Ash in 1980 at the young age of 65. He was a great credit to the game. I felt fortunate to be a friend of this excellent umpire and fine man. As I was gathering information for this book I had the privilege of contacting Adrienne Ashford Bratton, Emmett's daughter. She kindly provided me with the pictures of her great dad seen here. We are grateful to Mrs. Bratton for sharing these photographs and other information about our good buddy, Emmett.

Adrienne held a book-signing gathering at her Sisters of Bubic Boutique Café in Old Town Pasadena, California in October 2005. She featured Emmett's book, "My First Biography." Also, Adrienne has written a book titled, "STRRR-IKE!!" It tells the story of her father as an umpire. Adrienne is an excellent dance teacher as well.

Adrienne gave me this quote: "In 1941, while Jackie Robinson was breaking UCLA's athletic records, my dad was at Chapman College, a small private Christian school breaking different kinds of records. He not only played baseball for the

Chapman team, but was the first black sports editor of the campus newspaper. It may not be recorded anywhere in history but he may have been the only sports editor—even to this day—to write about himself as a player. For his achievements on the field, behind the typewriter, and as one of the greatest umpires baseball has ever seen, he is honored in the Chapman Athletics Hall of Fame and is admired by all who knew him and those who know of him."

There are literally thousands of umpires throughout America. Many of these are close friends of mine. After my playing and coaching days I worked in Seattle at a company called PEMCO Financial Services. I met and still have many fine friends there. One of these associates is a man who happens to be an umpire. His name is Rick Froman. Rick does an excellent job in whatever he attempts. This includes umpiring. He is highly respected at PEMCO as well as in his umpire work. Rick is typical of so many fine people that give help to the youth of our country by umpiring games. He is a former military man and his devotion to country carries over to his love for baseball and plays out in his second career, umpiring.

I did a survey on major league umpires and currently there have been approximately 350 umpires in the major leagues. The general count was 185 in the National League and 165 in the American League. The active number now is about 65.

It was nostalgic going through the names of umpires. I know that many readers of this book will have memories of some of the umpires mentioned here. Here are several: Lee Ballanfant, Al Barlick, Larry Barnett, Joe Brinkman, Nestor Chylak, Al Clark, Drew Coble, Nick Colosi, Jocko Conlan, Terry Cooney, Derryl Cousins, Gerry Crawford, Henry Crawford, Don Denkinger, Augie Donatelli, Bob Engel, Jim Evans, John Flaherty, Dale Ford, Bruce Froemming, Rich Garcia, Larry Goetz, Tom Gorman, Doug Harvey, George Honochik, Cal Hubbard, Ed Hurley, John Kibler, Bill Klem, Greg Kosc, Bill Kunkel, Stan Landes, George Magerkurth, Randy Marsh, Larry McCoy, Bill McGowan, Jim McKean, John McSherry, Durwood Merrill, Ed Montague, George Moriarty, Larry Napp, Jerry Neudecker, Hank O'Day, Steve Palermo, Joe Paparella, Chris Pelekoudas, Babe Pinelli, Paul Pryor, Jim Quick, Beans Reardon, Mike Reilly, Dutch Rennert, Rocky Roe, Ed Rommel, Ed Runge, Paul Runge, Marty Springstead, Bill Stewart, Ed Sudol, Bill Summers, Terry Tata, Ed Vargo, Vic Voltaggio, Harry Wendelstedt, Joe West, and Lee Weyer. This, by no means, includes all the umpires we might remember but most of these men called games for twenty years or more.

An umpire named Steve Palermo had his career cut short when he and another gentleman came to the aid of two women in a Dallas restaurant as a robbery

KIRKLAND   008

MEMBER #300694240000

198315 BK-BASEBALL   15.99 A

   SUBTOTAL   15.99
A 8.90% TAX   1.42

   TOTAL
VF EFT/DEBIT   17.41

XXXXXXXXXXXXX3819   SWIPED
Seq#: 000200 Ref#: 121030
EFT/DEBIT   Resp: AA

   APPROVED
   AMOUNT: $17.41

0008 011 0000000054 0005

CHANGE   .00

TOTAL NUMBER OF ITEMS SOLD - 1
CASHIER: SCOTT M   REG# 11
11/15/2007 10:10 0008 11 0005 54

SHOP WWW.COSTCO.COM
   ** THANK YOU - COME AGAIN **

COSTCO
WHOLESALE

KIRKLAND   008

MEMBER   R30G9242A0000

19835 BK-BASKETBALL   15.99 A

SUBTOTAL   15.99
A 8.90% TAX   1.42

TOTAL   17.41

VF   EFT/DEBIT   SWIPED
XXXXXXXXXXXXX3813
Seq#: 000200 Ref#: 121030   Resp: AA
EFT/DEBIT

APPROVED
AMOUNT: $17.41

0008 011 000000054 0005

CHANGE   .00

TOTAL NUMBER OF ITEMS SOLD =   1
CASHIER: SCOTT M   REG# 11
11/03/2011 10:10 0008 11 0005 54

SHOP WWW.COSTCO.COM
** THANK YOU   COME AGAIN **

was taking place. One report said he was shot in the stomach while another said he was shot in the back. In any case, he was forced to retire from umpiring. His ability to walk was in jeopardy at first but he eventually improved. When active in umpiring, Steve was considered one of the top ball-and-strike umpires in the business. He signed on as an Umpire Supervisor in 2000 and at age 56 continues to serve in that post.

I feel compelled to say here that an umpire's job is often a thankless one. But, like the police or anyone in authority, we are fortunate to have individuals who are willing to take on such responsibilities. We should teach all players at any age to show respect for the umpire and display good sportsmanship. That may sound old-fashioned to some but I believe we need that kind of behavior from fans, players, coaches and managers to help restore order in our society. We have seen some signs of behavioral weakness in various sports events recently and for the good of all we could use some common sense by everyone.

STORY 20:

The Dodgers and Giants Come West

In 1958 Walter O'Malley negotiated to bring his Brooklyn Dodgers to Los Angeles. The same was true for Horace Stoneham and the New York Giants. For years there were people who wanted to make the Pacific Coast League the "third" major league just like the National League, the senior circuit, and the American League, the junior circuit. However, when Mssrs. O'Malley and Stoneham brought their teams west that dream was finished.

Of course, the newspapers were full of news of these moves. So, in this pivotal year two National League teams made their debuts on the west coast. The Dodgers and Giants had been rivals for years when they played in New York. A new intense and special rivalry now developed as the two teams played each other home and home several times during each season. As Dodger announcer Vin Scully used to say, "The Dodgers and the Giants are rolling in the dirt again."

O'Malley had tried to buy land in Brooklyn earlier in order to build a more modern and up-to-date stadium than Ebbetts Field. Though that field was almost a shrine for Dodger fans it was getting old and had only 32,000 seats. Income was decreasing for O'Malley as attendance dwindled in the 50s. So in 1956 O'Malley, seeing that buying new land in New York was becoming less and less of a possibil-

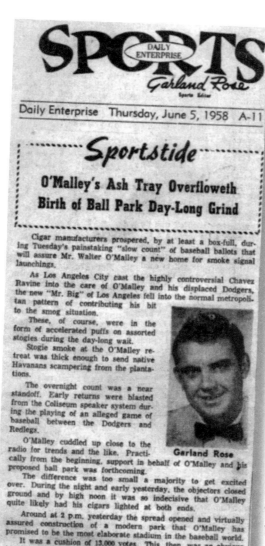

SPORTS
DAILY ENTERPRISE

Garland Rose
Sports Editor

Daily Enterprise   Thursday, June 5, 1958   A-11

········ *Sportstide* ········
O'Malley's Ash Tray Overfloweth
Birth of Ball Park Day-Long Grind

Cigar manufacturers prospered, by at least a box-full, during Tuesday's painstaking "slow count" of baseball ballots that will assure Mr. Walter O'Malley a new home for smoke signal launchings.

As Los Angeles City cast the highly controversial Chavez Ravine into the care of O'Malley and his displaced Dodgers, the new "Mr. Big" of Los Angeles fell into the normal metropolitan pattern of contributing his bit to the smog situation.

These, of course, were in the form of accelerated puffs on assorted stogies during the day-long wait.

Stogie smoke at the O'Malley retreat was thick enough to send native Havanans scampering from the plantations.

The overnight count was a near standoff. Early returns were blasted from the Coliseum speaker system during the playing of an alleged game of baseball between the Dodgers and Redlegs.

O'Malley cuddled up close to the radio for trends and the like. Practically from the beginning, support in behalf of O'Malley and his proposed ball park was forthcoming.

The difference was too small a majority to get excited over. During the night and early yesterday, the objectors closed ground and by high noon it was so indecisive that O'Malley quite likely had his cigars lighted at both ends.

Around at 2 p.m. yesterday the spread opened and virtually assured construction of a modern park that O'Malley has promised to be the most elaborate stadium in the baseball world.

It was a cushion of 13,000 votes. This, then, was an obvious trend.

Walter O'Malley &
Dodger Stadium plans

---

ity, realized he needed an alternative plan. In a sense New York administrators pushed the Dodgers out the door by refusing to allow O'Malley buy land to build a privately owned stadium in New York.

In the meantime administrators in Los Angeles had been seeking to bring major league baseball to their city. Besides the effort to make the Pacific Coast League a major circuit, some had their eyes on securing a team such as the Washington Senators. O'Malley made contact with officials in Los Angeles for discussions in the matter. He found that people in Los Angeles offered what New York city fathers would not offer. And that was an opportunity to purchase land on which to build a new baseball park. The whole matter left Brooklyn fans in disbelief. As the 1957 season was played out, the biggest story was not current baseball games, but rather the publicity that the Dodgers might actually move to California.

Then came the one of the biggest sports stories of the decade. Mr. O'Malley made an announcement at the end of the 1957 season that the Dodgers would move to Los Angeles the following season after having played sixty-eight seasons in Brooklyn. Additionally, he urged Mr. Stoneham to move the Giants to San Francisco at the same time. This became a reality and on April 15, 1958, the two teams met in San Francisco for three games followed by another three game set in Los Angeles. These two series started what was to become one of the biggest rivalries ever in major league baseball. The first game in Los Angeles was played in the Coliseum with 78,672 fans in attendance. The Dodgers won that game over the Giants, 6-5.

I had to teach on April 18 and could not attend. But, on Saturday morning, one day later, my best buddy, Marilyn, and I attended the second big league game ever played in Los Angeles. The Dodgers, with an aggressive marketing department, gave to every high school and college baseball coach in Southern California free passes for two to every home game for the entire season. Armed with our pass, binoculars and a small portable radio, we headed for the Coliseum from our home in Ontario, forty-five miles east of Los Angeles.

I should comment at this point that the Coliseum was basically a football stadium. The 1932 Olympic games had been held there. And other significant events took place from time to time. An annual football game by a dozen city schools occurred there each year in the early days and was called The Milk Bowl. It was a fund-raiser to provide milk for underprivileged children. Each of the participating high schools brought their cheerleaders and other groups to march. Marilyn was in the Washington High School Drum and Bugle Corps and marched with the group as she played her bugle.

On April 18 a most unusual baseball experiment occurred in the Coliseum. Home plate was placed in the southwest corner of the stadium and it was 60 feet from the batters' box back to the stands. There was not enough room for a deep left field fence so the third base line ended at a distance of 240 feet. A giant 40-foot screen was built so that a ball clearing the fence would have had to travel some 330 feet or more depending on its trajectory. Center field was well over 400 feet to the fence. There was plenty of room toward right field and a small low fence was built which ran from 330 feet at the end of the first base line and much deeper as the fence was built diagonally toward center field.

Top: Coliseum, deep right field.

Bottom: Coliseum, right field line

An interesting situation developed due to this huge left field screen. The Dodgers had a player named Wally Moon who had been secured from the St. Louis Cardinals. He was a very capable left-handed batter and a good outfielder. Wally had the ability to hit to all fields and he developed an opposite-field long ball swing. He became able to "go the other way" and hit the ball over the big screen. These hits became very popular with the fans and were coined "Moon Shots." The sports writers wrote about these "blasts" at every opportunity and the fans would call for them when Wally was at bat. It electrified the crowds every time.

The Coliseum was not ideal as a baseball park but it served well until Dodger Stadium was opened April 10, 1962 with its seating capacity of 56,000. That location, not far from downtown Los Angeles, had been known as Chavez Ravine for many years.

I recall the following experience like it was yesterday. It was on Saturday, April 19, 1958. All around the Coliseum, cars were parked long distances away because of the huge crowd that attended that day. We searched and searched for a space to park. Finally finding one, we set out walking for the park. I turned on the little radio and listened to pre-game ceremonies. We still had not reached the stadium when the first Giant batter stepped in to bat. It was Jose Pagan. As we crossed Figueroa Street, Jose grounded out to Junior Gilliam at third base. We ran across the Coliseum grounds to reach the long stairs that led to an opening at the top. As we arrived at the base of those stairs, Jim Davenport flied to Duke Snider in center field. Two out!

The Dodgers lost the game that day 11-4. But the score paled compared to what we were about to see. It was the highlight of the day for us. We reached the top of the stairs just as Giant centerfielder Willie Mays stepped to the plate. I suggested to Marilyn that before going to our seats, we sit down and watch this historic moment and not block others' views. It was our very first experience of seeing an official major league baseball game. What we saw in the next two minutes has been etched in our minds for almost fifty years.

We watched a young player, 26 year-old Willie Mays, step into the batters' box. He had already been on All Star teams, was the Most Valuable Player one year, he led the league in batting and homeruns and had won Gold Gloves. Willie took the first pitch for a ball. On the next pitch he lined a drive over first baseman Gil Hodges. It caught the fence in right field just as right fielder Carl Furillo tried to stop the ball. It went by Carl and center fielder Duke Snider had to come over to stop it.

In the meantime Willie was on his way to third base running like the wind. We can still picture that pigeon-toed runner flying around the bases. A second later we realized that Willie was trying for an inside-the-park home run. We could hardly believe what we were seeing. Duke picked up the ball and threw it to Charlie Neal, the second baseman, who turned and threw a bullet to home on one hop. The ball and Willie arrived simultaneously as catcher John Roseboro put the tag on the runner. It was a very close play and umpire Jocko Conlon yelled, "YOU'RE OUT." Willie was up in the umpire's face momentarily but not with any real emotion. It was just his competitiveness. He quickly accepted the decision and headed to his defensive position. It was a VERY exciting play.

I turned to Marilyn and with tears in my eyes and exclaimed, "Honey, major league baseball has come to Los Angeles." We had never seen anything like it. It was truly a dramatic and impressive play. Willie Mays and many others were to give us many more thrills through the years. We realized that this was just the beginning of much rich enjoyment of the grand old game in the future.

The Dodgers captured the attention of sports fans, not only in Los Angeles, but in the entire west. Vin Scully, Dodger baseball announcer, was probably the most influential person with this ball club. I venture to say that literally thousands of baseball fans, and particularly women, went to baseball school with Vinny. He taught all of us how to enjoy this great game. It became all the more exciting when just one year later the Dodgers played the Chicago White Sox in the 1959 World Series. The record attendance for a single World Series game still holds up from that series in the Coliseum—92,706 fans.

Coliseum scoreboard, World Series, October 3, 1959, Game 4

Filled Coliseum

STORY 21:

Our First (And Only) World Series Game

Having received a free pass to all Dodger home games that first year gave Marilyn and me the opportunity to see many games and know the Dodgers from top to bottom. Our interest continued in 1959 and we attended as often as possible. Of course, we were paying customers this time since the passes were for 1958 only.

This was a time of change in the baseball world. Besides the move west by the Dodgers and Giants, the Boston Braves moved to Milwaukee, the St. Louis Browns made Baltimore their new home, and Connie Mack's old Philadelphia A's became the Kansas City A's (Athletics). This was the post-war decade and competition at the major league level was at a peak. Former players such as Bob Feller, Joe DiMaggio and Jackie Robinson retired and new men were taking their places. These included such stars as Duke Snider, Hank Aaron, Ernie Banks, Mickey Mantle, Willie Mays, Whitey Ford, Roberto Clemente, Frank Robinson, Warren Spahn, Yogi Berra, Eddie Mathews, and many more.

As the season progressed we knew the Dodgers had a good ball club and were "in the hunt" for the National League pennant. They had been dominating the league much of the decade and the Milwaukee Braves had won in 1957 and 1958. But, it appeared the Dodgers were back in control. However, the season ended in a flat tie between the Dodgers and Braves who had 86 wins and 68 losses each (.558). The Dodgers won the first two games of a three-game playoff and were in the World Series.

Their opponent from the American League was the Chicago White Sox who was in the Fall Classic for the first time since the infamous "Chicago Black Sox" and Shoeless Joe Jackson lost in 1919. The series opened in Chicago's Comiskey Park where the "Sox," as my Chicago friend, Harry Reinhart, calls them, blew out the Dodgers 11-0. But, from here on out it was the Dodger's series as they won four of the next five games to become world champions.

Marilyn and I were fortunate to obtain two tickets for game four in the Coliseum. We sat far down the right field line in that huge bowl which

Two World Series tickets, Los Angeles Dodgers *vs* Chicago White Sox World Series

usually housed football games. Frankly, we needed field glasses to see very well.

We were among 92,650 fans that day, the second largest crowd to ever attend a World Series game. Actually, it was the largest-ever crowd for twenty-four hours. The next day an additional 56 people attended bringing the new record number to 92,706. That mark is the record still standing today. And, in fact, that total series attendance of 420,784 fans, while only six games, is the all-time record as the largest ever for any series.

STORY 22:

Sandy Koufax
Strikes Out The Side

As the 1958 season progressed Marilyn and I attended as many baseball games as our schedule would allow. Here we were seeing all the exciting National League teams including the St. Louis Cardinals, Pittsburg Pirates, Milwaukee Braves, Philadelphia Phillies, Cincinnati Reds, Chicago Cubs and, of course, the San Francisco Giants. For us it was a dream-come-true. And announcer Vin Scully made it all come to life.

We learned that the young phenomenon, Sandy Koufax, was pitching one evening and we headed for the Coliseum. Parking this time was easier and we were there in plenty of time. To our dismay, Sandy walked the first three batters to load the bases. He was throwing high and could not find his rhythm. The Dodger pitching coach went to the mound and chatted with Sandy. Then, just like magic, the young lefty proceeded to strike out the side.

Little did we know of the sensational career this young man was to have during the next several seasons. Four no-hitters including a perfect game were in the offing. His pitches were awesome. He made hitters look bad. And I don't think I ever saw a player more humble than Sandy Koufax. He was truly a champion.

STORY 23:

Don Zimmer (Popeye) Throws Out Musial

Another time in 1958 Marilyn and I went to the Coliseum to see a Dodger game. They were playing the famed St. Louis Cardinals whose earlier teams were coined the "Gashouse Gang." Stan "The Man" Musial was in his sixteenth year of playing for the Cards, the only major league team for which he ever played. This was the year that he reached his 3000th hit.

But, this story is not about the great Musial. We saw a play that will be imprinted on our minds forever. Playing shortstop for the Los Angeles Dodgers was Don Zimmer. Yes, this is the man currently nicknamed "Popeye." In this Cardinal game he was a trim 170 pounds and made a play to remember. Early in the game, Musial was in his familiar coiled batting stance and hit a hard drive up the middle. Zimmer dashed to his left and sprawled flat out to glove the ball. He quickly hopped to his feet and threw out Musial by a half step. It was as good a play by a shortstop anyone would ever see. Today, Zim, as he is also called, is certainly not the agile shortstop we saw that day. But, he is a total baseball man.

Two years later Zimmer had been traded to the Chicago Cubs.

On April 14, 1960 he returned to the Coliseum as he was playing third base for the Cubbies alongside the unforgettable Ernie Banks. The capable Richie Ashburn was in center field for Chicago. Zim led off the third inning with a homerun off Don Drysdale, the famous Dodger pitcher on this Opening Day. Drysdale went eleven innings to win 3-2 and contributed a triple at the plate. Don walked four and struck out fourteen. Add to those stats the fact that Bob Anderson and Don Elston, the Cub pitchers for the day walked six and struck out twelve between them. Twenty-six strikeouts in eleven innings displayed pretty good pitching. By checking you will find that Zim was back with the Dodgers in 1963 after they moved in the new Dodger Stadium.

Zimmer was born in Cincinnati in 1931. He has been a manager, coach and assistant for more than fifty years. Don likes to brag that he never received a paycheck outside of baseball. He played with several minor league teams before joining the Brooklyn Dodgers in 1954. He had been hit in the head by a pitch in 1953 and nearly died. He was "beaned" again in 1956 but survived to stay in the game for many years. Many will recall his getting hit in the head once again in the New York Yankee dugout. As a gag, they put an old Army helmet on Zim's head. That was a classic shot on TV and in the newspapers.

His playing days included such teams as the Brooklyn and Los Angeles Dodgers, Chicago Cubs, the first New York Mets team in 1962, the Cincinnati Reds and finally the old Washington Senators. Don played for twelve seasons, in two World Series and was selected to the All Star team in 1961.

He coached in the minor leagues and was manager of the San Diego Padres, Boston Red Sox, Texas Rangers and Chicago Cubs. He was most recently known for his coaching with the successful New York Yankees when they won four World Series titles. Currently, he is a senior advisor for the Tampa Bay Devil Rays.

Zim was named Manager of the Year with the Cubs in 1989.

STORY 24:

The Shot Heard 'Round The World

If you go to the Internet you will find that there are two references to "the shot heard 'round the world." One, of course, discusses the Midnight Ride of Paul Revere. When we were school children we can recall the poem lyrics, "Listen my children and you shall hear, of the midnight ride of Paul Revere….!" Yes, on the night of April 18, 1775 a shot rang out as the American colonists (Minutemen) and the British faced each other in Lexington and then Concord (Massachusetts). The beginning of the Revolutionary War had begun. Marilyn and I visited the spot where that first shot rang out. It was excitingly historic to be there and hear the story.

The second "shot" occurred on October 3, 1951 when New York Giant third baseman, Bobby Thomson, won the National League pennant on the last pitch of the season with a home run into the left field bleachers at the Polo Grounds. It was later to become known as "The Little Miracle of Coogan's Bluff." The New York Polo Grounds was sometimes known as Coogan's Bluff, the location of the site.

There are so many unusual facts in this incredible story. The Giants won thirty-seven of their last forty-five games to close from 13½ games to draw even with the Dodgers. On the final day of the regular season they were tied for the league lead. A two-out-three playoff ensued and they split the first two games. In the rubber match the Dodgers were leading 4-1 after scoring three runs in the eighth inning. In essence, it was over. But, the Giants were not finished.

Alvin Dark led off with a single off Gil Hodge's glove at first base. Don Mueller followed with a line drive single to right field. With runners at the corners,

Monte Irvin popped out to first base. Monte shattered his bat on the ground going back to the dugout. Whitey Lockman, batting left handed, doubled to the left field corner scoring Dark. Score now was 4-2, Dodgers. Manager Charlie Dressen replaced pitcher Don Newcombe with Ralph Branca. He warmed up with his eight-allowed pitches and they were ready to play. First pitch, strike one on the inside corner. The next pitch was a fastball and Thomson hammered it, a line drive into the left field stands for a three-run homer to win the game, 5-4, and the National League pennant.

Then came the celebrated words of Giants announcer, Russ Hodges, "The Giants win the pennant, the Giants win the pennant, the Giants win the pennant, the Giants win the pennant." He could hardly contain himself. Russ was so excited he never did mark in the Thomson home run on his scorecard. That scorecard can be seen in Cooperstown, New York, at the National Baseball Hall of Fame.

The players carried Thomson around the park on their shoulders. There were 34,329 paid that day. Some unfortunately had left the park, thinking the Dodgers had won the game. But, the many Giant fans who remained were "going crazy," as Hodges had put it. It was truly one of the greatest, if not the greatest, moment in sports history.

Some may not remember that the on-deck hitter after Thomson was young Willie Mays. And Blanche McGraw, the widow of legendary Giants manager, John McGraw, was watching from her box seat that day. Asked what her late husband would have thought about the game, Mrs. McGraw responded, "It would have made him happy just like the old Orioles."

Giant second sacker, Eddie Stanky, was on the top step of the dugout as Branca came into the game and ferocious Eddie was giving him the choke sign. When Thomson hit the winning homer films show Eddie leaping onto Giant manager, Leo Durocher, with a lovable embrace.

The best part of this story for me was that I saw it live on television. We had just purchased our first TV set, a round-screen Zenith a few weeks earlier. The home run was hit at 3:58 p.m., Eastern time, and it was 12:58 p.m. on the west coast. I had a lunch break from my teaching job in the middle of the day and was due back at 1:30 p.m. This gave me the rare opportunity to see much of the last part of the ball game in addition to the famous home run and post-game activities. Somehow, even then, I realized what a memorable major sports event happened that day.

Scouting for the Baltimore Orioles

When I was coaching Chaffey High School I received a telephone call from a gentleman named Jim Wilson, the chief baseball scout on the west coast for the Baltimore Orioles. He asked if I would be interested in checking various prospects as I went about my coaching duties. I eagerly accepted and was pleased to have the opportunity to work for a major league club

I was assigned to check on a catcher with La Puente High School, Andy Etchebarren. La Puente was in the Montview League where Chaffey had been placed in 1958. Andy was a fine catcher and was a strong hitter. Eventually we signed him to a $100,000 contract and that was big money in those days.

Andy succeeded at Baltimore and was their catcher through some of their great years when they were winning both the American League and the World Series. Andy played in 948 major league games and had 309 RBIs. His strength was his handling of pitchers. He was the catcher when manager Earl Weaver was running the team.

Another player I followed was Phil Ortega of North Phoenix High School. He had a great fastball. We decided to pass on offering him a contract and he eventually signed with the Los Angeles Dodgers where he struggled for several years and retired a few years later with the Washington Senators.

Jim Wilson was a great guy and a capable major leaguer in his playing days. He played for the Boston Red Sox, St. Louis Browns, Boston Braves, Milwaukee Braves, Baltimore Orioles, and the Chicago White Sox. On June 12, 1954 he pitched a no-hitter for the Milwaukee Braves against the Philadelphia Phillies. Jim had 1,539 innings in 13 years with an ERA of 4.01.

Our boss at Baltimore was Harry Dalton, an experienced baseball executive. He was instrumental in the success of the Orioles in their glory years.

Denny McLain Goes for 32nd Win

I was in Baltimore, Maryland on business on Monday, September 23, 1968. Having finished my work at the end of the day I went out to Memorial Stadium to see the Baltimore Orioles play the Detroit Tigers. This is where Johnny Unitas and the Baltimore Colts had made football history and were still making it. And besides having the rare opportunity to see a major league baseball game, it was somewhat of an historic evening in baseball. Tiger pitcher, Denny McLain, was trying to win his 32nd game of the season. Obviously, he had been very successful and there was every reason to believe he would record a victory that night.

It was my very first visit to Memorial Stadium. I had scouted for the Baltimore Orioles in the early 1960s and I was getting my first live taste of this storied ballpark. McLain was the first 30-game winner since Dizzy Dean accomplished that feat in 1934. Denny had won well over 50 games in his first few years with the Tigers. Earlier in September he had even pulled off a triple play against Baltimore when Boog Powell lined out to him.

Here I was nearly 3,000 miles from home watching some of my heroes like the Oriole's Brooks Robinson, Mark Belanger, Don Buford, Paul Blair, Dave Johnson (who later became their manager), and, of course, Powell. Tiger stars were Jim Northrup, Al Kaline, Norm Cash, Bill Freehan and McLain. I was in seventh heaven. Baltimore won the World Series Championship just two years earlier in 1966 and I had to pinch myself to realize I was sitting where it happened. They had shut out Los Angeles, 4-0, when the Dodgers had their heralded all-switch hitting infield plus Don Drysdale and Sandy Koufax. The final two victories of that playoff were 1-0 ball games. Great series!

The night I attended, Baltimore scored in the first and seventh innings while Detroit could manage only one run in their half of the eighth. Denny's competitiveness was evident. He allowed just one earned run but five walks and two errors proved his downfall and he was denied win number 32 by the score of 2-1 in Baltimore's favor.

McLain tried for that 32nd win two times before the season ended but it was not to be because the Tigers suffered two consecutive 2-1 losses with McLain on the mound. However, he helped Detroit to the American League championship, was the league MVP and a unanimous Cy Young Award winner with a record of

31-6, 28 complete games, an incredible ERA of 1.96 and led the league in strike-outs with 280.

The Tigers defeated the St. Louis Cardinals and their great pitcher, Bob Gibson, in the World Series. McLain lost his first two starts against Gibson but came back to win the sixth game on two days' rest to set up the classic seventh game in which popular Mickey Lolich won his third game of the series besting Gibson, 4-1. It was Detroit's first World Championship since 1945.

I would like to make a few more comments about Denny McLain. In his career he pitched with Detroit, Washington, Oakland and Atlanta. Denny was an extrovert. He even did an act in Las Vegas at one time. He was on the Ed Sullivan show and performed in other TV programs. He was the son-in-law of Hall of Fame shortstop Lou Boudreau.

In 1969 the Tigers gave him a $100,000 contract (high in those days) and McLain won a second Cy Young Award with a 24-9 win/loss record and a team-record nine shutouts. But things turned sour for Denny about that time.

Toward the end of his baseball playing days he was in trouble with the Commissioner, Bowie Kuhn and the law, and spent some time in jail. What might have been a sensational career was over at the tender age of 28.

However, McLain was one of the finest pitchers in the game. In his career he pitched in 1,886 innings with a record of 131-91 and an ERA of 3.39. He was an All Star in 1966, 1968 and 1969. They never found out what Denny might have done in the future. In Mickey Mantle's last game at Tiger Stadium he threw one right down the middle on purpose to give The Mick his next-to-last career round tripper to pass Jimmy Foxx on the all-time home run list. The Mick tipped his cap to Denny as he rounded third base.

Again, we find Denny McLain to be one of "characters of the game." One often wonders what might have happened with a different direction. He was a true individualist. That September evening in Baltimore was a great experience for me and certainly one I will always remember.

Mickey Mantle's Last Game at Yankee Stadium

I had a conference to attend in New York following my 1968 Baltimore visit and I had the opportunity to go to Yankee Stadium on Wednesday, September 25. I saw the incomparable Mickey Mantle play his last home game. Once again, here I found myself in a ballpark filled with history. That vast stadium was the scene of many exciting baseball moments. It was sometimes called "The House That Ruth Built." To say I was in awe is an understatement. I was overwhelmed to say the least.

At the time I was not aware that this was Mickey Mantle's last game at Yankee Stadium. His last game ever was played three days later in Fenway Park against the Red Sox. I walked around the stadium and took pictures. I was excited the entire game although the game itself was commonplace and very routine. It was simply spine-tingling just to be there. Between innings I went down to the field level next to the Yankee dugout and took several pictures. In one shot Mickey looked directly at me as if to ask "who is this guy taking pictures of me?" And no one in the stadium, to my knowledge, knew this was Mickey's last game in the shrine of baseball, Yankee Stadium.

Cleveland was the Yankee opponent that day and the great Luis Tiant was pitching for the Indians. The day ended with Luis shutting out New York, 3-0. And, guess what? The Mick had the only hit off Tiant, a single. As it turned out it was the last hit in Mantle's career. I always thought how remarkable it was that I would see one game in Yankee Stadium and it was Mickey's last game there. And to top it off I saw his last major league hit ever.

Mickey Mantle looking at camera, Sept. 25, 1968, Mickey Mantle's last game at Yankee Stadium

I was 27 years old when Mantle played his first game for New York. He was 20 years old having been born in 1931. I can recall he played alongside Joe DiMaggio his first year and in 1952 he took over for the Yankee Clipper in centerfield. He was truly outstanding in everything. He could run down fly balls, throw with strength and accuracy, hit from both sides of the plate and to this day was the greatest switch-hitter in the history of the game. He hit with tremendous power and, yet, could drag bunt with the best of them and run to first base in 3.1 seconds. Many say he was a better hitter right-handed but it is a fact that of his 536 home runs, 373 were hit from the left side.

He developed some injuries as he played non-stop in every game so, occasionally, he was placed in left and right fields to reduce his running. In 1967 and 1968 he was brought in to play first base to further limit his running. He was in great pain in his last few years but he kept trying. There was no quit in the kid from Commerce, Oklahoma. He nickname was the "Commerce Comet."

Mickey was born to be a ballplayer. He was named after the famed Detroit catcher, Mickey Cochrane. In his early years Mantle teamed with Yogi Berra. Each of them averaged 25 home runs per season and, as a duo, they produced 150 to 225 RBIs. In 1956 Mantle hit .353 and had 52 home runs along with 130 RBIs

Mickey Mantle swinging, Sept. 25, 1968, Mickey Mantle's last game at Yankee Stadium

to win the Triple Crown. His accomplishments began to pile up as he received award after award. Many remember Don Larsen's perfect game in the 1956 World Series but few may recall that Mantle made a saving defensive play in that 2-0 ball game. Also, Mickey hit three home runs and scored six runs in that outstanding series in which New York defeated Brooklyn four games to three.

My old friend and assistant coach at Chaffey High School, Clyde Francisco, is still a Yankee fan through and through. Mantle was his favorite player. The two of us often compared Mickey and Willie Mays, two of the greatest players ever to play at the same time. When those two played they really put on a show. Incidentally, Clyde is now a member of the Board of Trustees in the Chaffey School District, Ontario, California.

We would be remiss if we did not mention the M&M Boys, Mickey and Roger Maris. They put on a home run duel in 1961 and as the baseball world knows, Roger hit 61 that year to break Babe Ruth's long-standing record of 60. Mantle hit 54 dingers that year.

Mickey played the last eight years as one of the most popular ever. He was on

12 American League champions and seven World champions. He holds a number of World Series records, that of 40 RBIs, 18 home runs, 42 runs, 26 extra base hits, 123 total bases, and 43 bases on balls. Also, he was known to have hit several home runs well over 500 feet with the longest estimated at 565 feet.

Please see my comments in Story 29 (A Great Memory of a 1964 Detroit Conference) about Mantle's final World Series.

STORY 28:

The Dodger All Switch-Hitting Infield

In the mid-sixties I was an administrator at Whitworth College in Spokane, Washington. Our local team was the Spokane Indians of the Pacific Coast League. It was the breeding ground of the Los Angeles Dodgers. Marilyn and I enjoyed going out to the Indian's ballpark and we saw some of the up and coming stars of MLB.

One of these players, Maury Wills, had played shortstop there previously. Tommy LaSorda was the manager of the club before taking over the reins of the Los Angeles Dodgers. Maury's eldest son, Bumpy, played football and baseball for Central Valley High School and our sons, Kenny, Mike and Scott played in the Mead School District.

Bumpy and Kenny, being just about the same age, battled back and forth in their league games with each other. I recall a game when Bumpy scored a touchdown on the opening kickoff of a CV/Mead contest. CV kicked off to Mead and Kenny returned it for a touchdown. Score: 7-7. They were less than one minute into the game and two TDs were already on the scoreboard. They had the same kind of competition in baseball. Bumpy was a right-handed batting second baseman while Kenny hit from the left side of the plate and played third base.

We followed the Dodgers and Indians about equally. In 1965 the Dodgers had a very unique group of infielders that were all switch-hitters. I do not recall ever seeing a set of infielders that all hit from both sides of the plate. I refer to shortstop Maury Wills, third baseman Junior Gilliam, second baseman Jim LeFebvre, and first baseman Wes Parker. That was very unusual.

In Story 193 (Lefties and Righties Today) I mention the number of switch-hitters in baseball today. At the time of my research there were 76 "switchies" playing in MLB. Of course, that can move up or down at any given time. When I was a young boy in 1934, I followed a player named Augie Galan who played for the Chicago Cubs. To my knowledge he was the only switch-hitter in the game at that time. Please see Story 102 (Augie Galan) for more information about this fine player.

So, to have all four infielders on one team bat from both sides of the plate was extremely unique. In fact, it was a great advantage for the Dodgers. Later both Wills and LeFebvre became MLB managers. This is an additional note about the 1965 Dodgers. They had a utility infielder named Dick Schofield. Interestingly enough, he, too, was a switch-hitter.

Several years later Marilyn and I had moved to Seattle. When the Texas Rangers were in town we visited the Seattle Kingdome and went onto the field to see Bump (as he was now called in MLB) Wills who was the second baseman on that team. It was fun talking over old times of Spokane high school baseball and football with Bump. He developed into a very competitive major leaguer. Please see Story 145 (Bump Wills) for more information about him. It is my understanding that Bump eventually followed his dad's ability to become a switch-hitter.

STORY 29:

A Great Memory of a 1964 Detroit Conference

In my job as Director of Admissions of Whitworth College (Spokane, Washington) I attended a number of conferences through the years. In 1964 I went to Detroit where the Association of College Admissions Counselors held their annual meeting.

We were housed in the Hotel Cadillac in the heart of the downtown area. From my hotel window I could see the celebrated old Tiger Stadium where so many famous Detroit baseball teams had played. The lights were dark there because the baseball season was over and the World Series was being played in New York and St. Louis. This turned out to be Mickey Mantle's last World Series.

When I was free I watched some of this series on television in my room. It was a series in which many great baseball memories occurred. Mickey Mantle scored eight runs to tie a seven-game Series mark. He won the third game with a home run in the ninth inning. He hit a three-run homer in Game 7. He had three home runs and six RBIs.

But, this Series went to the Cardinals, 4-3, based on the excellent pitching of

Bob Gibson, the timely hitting of Tim McCarver (.478) plus home runs by Mike Shannon, Ken Boyer, and McCarver. Also significant was the pitching of Jim Bouton author of the book, Ball Four)(Please see Story 84 (Jim Bouton), home runs by Tom Tresh and Joe Pepitone, and the record of 13 hits by Bobby Richardson, all of New York.

It was a great Series and one I shall always remember as Mickey Mantle's final one.

STORY 30:

The Fellowship of Christian Athletes

This organization had a profound influence in our lives. I belonged to the Ontario Kiwanis Club when I was coaching at Chaffey High School and our group of approximately 100 men accomplished many projects to help our community. If the project was worthwhile and we could fund it, we did so.

One such project was support of the Fellowship of Christian Athletes. The club provided half the funds to send an athlete to a special camp in Ashland, Oregon. The athlete was responsible to provide the other half. During the years I was the leader of this program we sent more than 30 young men to these five-day camps. There were some twenty-five camps around the nation with about 400 to 500 young men participating at each location.

Many of these men were led to lives of service and character through the program. Many young athletes became ministers as a result. Our son, Mike, a minister and missionary, is one of those young men. The "FCA" still exists today.

Marilyn and I were asked to serve on the staff at Ashland and we did so for several years. In the late 1960s we were asked to serve on two staffs, one at Ashland and the other at Estes Park, Colorado (near Rocky Mountain National Park). It was at the latter camp where we became good friends with Dallas Cowboy football coach, Tom Landry, and his

Ken & his FCA huddle, August 16, 1963 at FCA camp, Ashland, Oregon

family. We lost Tom a few years ago. He was a very positive influence on his players and associates through the years.

Many famous athletes attended these camps. At one Ashland camp, former Brooklyn Dodger pitcher, Carl Erskine attended and was a main speaker.

Erskine was well known in those days as a pitcher who had thrown two no-hitters, one in 1952 and another in 1956. Also, he struck out 14 batters in Game Three of the 1953 World Series, a record that stood up for fourteen seasons. In that game he struck out Mickey Mantle four times, a feat in itself. He told a story which I would like to relate.

It seems that Erskine was not a very good hitter as is often the case with pitchers who do not practice batting often. But, on this particular day an opposing pitcher walked Carl on four pitches. There were no outs and Erskine went to second on a passed ball. The next batter grounded to second and Carl moved over to third base. Old-timer Babe Herman was coaching third base that day and walked up to Erskine to give him some instructions. Before Babe could speak, Erskine said, "You know, Babe, I feel real good today. I think I could steal home." To which the no-nonsense Herman replied." "Listen, Erskine, it took you eleven years to get over here. Don't louse it up now!" Needless to say, the room full of young athletes howled with laughter. Please see Story 98 (Carl Erskine) for more information on this fine player.

Some of the other athletes involved with the FCA in those days were Bob Pettit, great basketball star of the St. Louis Hawks, Cleveland Baseball Hall of Fame pitcher, Bob Feller, Dallas Cowboy coach and Hall of Fame pro football player, Tom Landry, Yankee second baseman Bobby Richardson, and Green Bay

Top: Ken & Marilyn & Kenny, Mike and Scott at FCA, August 15, 1963, Ashland, Oregon

Bottom: Ken & Spokane FCA boys

quarterback Bart Starr.

Marilyn and I attended church our entire married life. But, our involvement with the Fellowship of Christian Athletes provided us with a much deeper experience and in those years Jesus Christ came alive to us.

It all started in Ontario, California when the local aforementioned Kiwanis club asked me to attend a meeting in Pasadena to evaluate the program of the FCA. I heard a young 18-year old athlete give his Christian testimony in a way I had never heard previously. I was excited. I was talking about it with some outstanding personalities including Rafer Johnson, Olympic track star, Elvin "Ducky" Drake, Johnson's coach and UCLA head trainer, Billy Wade, quarterback of the Chicago Bears, Raymond Berry, receiver of the Baltimore Colts, and John Wooden, famous UCLA basketball coach. During the meeting, Rev. Towler said, "Hey, you seem to be on fire!"

Indeed, I was on fire and soon thereafter, Marilyn and I gave our lives to Jesus Christ. All of this story is described in a book written by Gary Warner titled, The Home Team Wears White in Chapter 13 (see Bibliography).

STORY 31:

Will You Pitch Batting Practice To Me, Mr. Feller?

In the late 1950s and early 1960s I served as President of the Fellowship of Christian Athletes Chapters (FCA) in three separate locations, Southern California, Spokane and Seattle.. This is an outstanding program that has positively influenced thousands upon thousands of young people.

At Chaffey High School in Ontario, California, through membership in the Ontario Kiwanis Club I had the opportunity to send more than 30 students to a summer camp of the FCA at Southern Oregon College in Ashland, Oregon. Marilyn and I served on the staff of the group at both Ashland and in Estes Park, Colorado. Please see Story 30 (The Fellowship of Christian Athletes).

During the summer of 1963 we were at Ashland with our family. All of us participated in the five-day camp. Professional, college and high school athletes were involved at every gathering. On this particular occasion, featured was Cleveland Indian Hall of Fame pitcher, Bob Feller, aptly named "Rapid Robert." This nickname was given to Bob because of his ability to throw a baseball nearly 100 miles an hour. When he broke into the major leagues at age 17 he was already striking out some of the game's greatest batters. He gave notice of his potential when he struck out eight St. Louis Cardinals in a three-inning exhibition game.

Our nine-year old son, Mike, knew of Mr. Feller and walked up to him and asked the question, "Will you pitch batting practice to me, Mr. Feller?" Bob generously replied in the positive and began throwing Mike's old baseball. Mike took his cuts and after several minutes took the worn ball to Bob and asked him to autograph it. That ball sits among many of our family baseball memorabilia items today. Mike, now in his 50s and a minister and a firefighter, still recalls the day that he batted off the great Bob Feller.

As we talk about great baseball players, Feller was certainly among the greatest. He has the most wins of any pitcher in Cleveland Indian history. He was the first hurler since the great Walter Johnson to be elected to the Hall of Fame in his first eligible year. He was a strong farm boy from Van Meter, Iowa, who signed his first contract in 1936. His capabili-

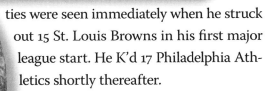

Top: Mike, age two, swinging a bat, Mike and neighbor Mickey Stewart, summer 1956

Middle: Mike, age nine, walking to batting practice, Southern Oregon College, Ashland, Oregon, August 16, 1963

ties were seen immediately when he struck out 15 St. Louis Browns in his first major league start. He K'd 17 Philadelphia Athletics shortly thereafter.

Bob had control problems in the beginning. In 1938 he was a regular starter for Cleveland and won 17 games his first year. He led the league in strikeouts with 240 but also led in walks with 208. He continued to be wild but as he matured he progressively improved his control. In his second,

Bottom: Bob Feller signed baseball, August 16, 1963 at Ashland, Oregon

73

third and fourth years he led the American League in wins and strikeouts. In 1940 he won 27 games. On opening day against the Chicago White Sox he threw a no-hitter.

As World War II began Bob joined the U. S. Navy and earned eight battle stars. Four years later he returned to Cleveland and was better than when he left. In 1946 he won 26 games and established a new strikeout record with 348. In addition he tossed a no-hitter against the famous New York Yankees. In his career Feller threw three no-hitters and twelve one-hitters.

In 1948 he again led the American League in strikeouts (seventh time) but it was evident his blazing fastball had lost something. However, he won six straight games to end the season and was instrumental in giving Cleveland their first pennant in twenty-eight years.

He continued to pitch well even though he was using more control pitches with curves and change ups. He posted a 22 and 8 mark in 1951 to lead the American League in victories and winning percentage. Cleveland retired Bob's uniform number 19 in 1957. Twelve years later in 1969 he was declared baseball's greatest living right handed pitcher at the meetings of professional baseball's centennial.

And it was just six years later that Mike Proctor said, "Will you pitch batting practice to me, Mr. Feller?" Perhaps Bob's batting practice helped Mike because he went on to star in high school in the Interscholastic League of Honolulu as a leading hitter. Mike was all-league in both baseball and basketball. Please see Stories Nos. 175, 178, and 180 (Ken Proctor Jr., Mike Proctor, Scott Proctor).

Feller ended his career with 3,827 innings pitched, a record of 266-162 (.609), an ERA of 3.60, on the All Star team eight times, and led the league in wins six seasons. He was elected into the Hall of Fame in 1962. He was a gentleman in every respect and a genuine credit to baseball.

Make It Go Through!

When I was coaching I put reminder signs in the dugout to refresh the players' minds about certain fundamentals. Some of these were "Be Tough With Two Strikes," "Watch the Ball Into Your Glove," and "No Three Ball Counts." Please see Story No. 191 (Tips On Watching Baseball Games).

In those same years Marilyn and I put reminder signs about our home to remind our own boys about certain fundamentals and philosophies. I recall one sign we liked that said, "Be Selective." We were referring to both baseball and life with this one. In baseball we were asking the boys to be selective in the pitches they chose to hit. We were telling them to swing at good pitches, those with which they might make good contact. In life, we were encouraging the boys to be selective in the friends they made, those with good character and behavior.

Another sign simply said, "Make It Go Through." My baseball philosophy was, when on second base as a runner and the ball is hit to the left side, one does not run unless the ball goes through the infield (past the third baseman and shortstop). If the runner goes to third base on this type of ball he can easily be thrown out at third base. There can be an exception here with an extremely slowly hit ball, but, in general, you "make it go through." It is a fundamental that nearly every baseball player knows.

When Mike was attending Mead Junior High School in Spokane, Washington he was playing a game at Greenacres Junior High School. The score was tied 3-3 in the last inning and Mike was on second base with two outs. And guess what! The ball was hit to the left side and Mike took off for third base. The shortstop threw the ball to third as Mike slid. The ball went through the third baseman and Mike went home and scored the go-ahead run. They put Greenacres down in the last of the inning and won the game, 4-3.

After the game Mike came over to see us in the grandstand. We said to him, "Good game, son, on scoring the winning run." I continued saying, "But do you recall the sign with four words on the wall at home?" Mike pondered for a second and replied, "Trust in the Lord?" That was another sign we had at home and Mike had me on that one.

This reminds me of a time when Scott nailed me. He came in the kitchen one day and said, "What is that foul smell in here." I reminded him that he was never to criticize his mother or anything she did. Scott looked at me and said wryly, "Dad, we are having chicken tonight!" Boy, was I caught on that one!

Back to the reminder signs; I really like them. They are no different than reminding ourselves we have a doctor's appointment, to wash the car, mow the lawn, or pay a certain bill. Reminders are such great teachers for athletics. It is the old game of repetition. Repeat it over and over until it sinks in! And other signs are applicable, too, like "Love One Another," or "Do Unto Others As They Do Unto You," or "The Base on Balls Will Beat You."

STORY 33:

Hal Reniff, A Special Guy!

Hal Reniff pitching

In 1953, my first year as head baseball coach at Chaffey High School, my program whereby no player was cut from the tryouts was active and working well. As I was looking over the prospects, one young freshman (a ninth grader) was obviously talented. He was 5'11" and around 170 pounds. His blond hair made him stand out. His name was Hal Reniff.

Though a freshman, Hal played some games on the varsity. No other freshman made the varsity then or later. He was a pitcher and could throw hard. In March 1954 we played in the Pomona Tournament, a quality competition, composed of 32 of the best high school teams in Southern California, a hotbed for major league baseball prospects. To win the tourney a team had to win five consecutive games. We played and defeated Lynwood High School in the finals, 3-2. Hal, now a sophomore, won two of those games and was the Most Valuable Player of the Tournament.

Hal went on to compile a pitching record of 22-2 in his final two years. He was the winning pitcher in the California Interscholastic Federation (C.I.F.) finals against Oxnard High School, 3-0 in 1956, the same year, incidentally, that Don Larsen of New York, Hal's future teammate, pitched a memorable and dramatic perfect game against the Brooklyn Dodgers and won 2-0.

After graduation, Yankee scout Gordon Jones signed Hal to a New York contract. His first few years he played in the minor leagues including Modesto (California) and Richmond (Virginia). When he reported to Richmond in 1960, Joe DiMaggio saw Hal and reported to Yankee manager, Major Ralph Houk, that Reniff should get a shot at the big club. Joe's analysis proved correct and Harold was a Yankee from 1961 to 1966. He was their leading right-handed relief pitcher. Hal ended his major league career by playing in 1967 with the New York Mets. In his big league career, Hal pitched 471 innings and had an ERA of 3.27.

Hal was on the Yankees in 1961 when Mickey Mantle and Roger Maris were having their heralded home run duel. And, of course, the year ended with Roger beating Babe Ruth's record by one, 61-60. Also, Hal was on World Series Yankee teams in 1962, 1963 and 1964.

When Hal returned home after the championship 1961 season, I asked if he would go with me to a father-son church banquet in the nearby town of LaVerne, California. Hal told me that Yankees in those days were paid several thousand dollars for any appearance but he would be glad to go just for the dinner served that evening. We had a great time and all enjoyed hearing Hal speak.

Hal Reniff & Ken Proctor at Laughlin, Nevada, March 27, 2004

He brought signed New York Yankee baseballs for our three boys, Kenny, Mike and Scott. One of those balls sits with our family baseball memorabilia today with the signatures of Hal, Mickey Mantle, Yogi Berra, Hank Bauer, Whitey Ford, Jim Bouton, Ralph Terry, Bill Stafford, Roger Maris, Joe Pepitone, Hector Lopez, Tom Tresh, John Blanchard, Tony Kubek, Harry Bright, Clete Boyer, Marsahll Bridges, Elston Howard, Phil Linz, Jake Gibbs, Al Downing, Jack Reed, Steve Hamilton, and Ralph Houk and the other stars of that great 1961 Yankee club. Hal was good friends with Jim Bouton whom I met a few years ago. Please see Story 84 (Jim Bouton).

Hal was a fierce competitor. One of my catchers, Daryl Moss, told me a story that demonstrates Reniff's enormous desire to succeed. Chaffey was playing a game at San Bernardino High School that was to determine the championship for the season. Late in the game we were leading by three runs and Hal was looking very strong. San Bernardino had two men on base and Hal unexpectedly walked a batter to load the bases. This brought their leading hitter, Jim Turner, to the plate. His average was near .500 and he had home run potential. Hal struck him out on three pitches. What I did not know and learned later from Daryl was that Hal wanted to face Turner in that situation to prove his ability to put him down. Daryl said he walked the previous batter on purpose to get that opportunity. It was not a move I would have wanted, of course, but Hal was so confident he took it upon himself to face Turner. It is no surprise that Reniff became one of the New York Yankee's outstanding relief pitchers. Many years later I was taking Bouton to the airport in Seattle, and he told me he always felt comfortable when Hal came in to save a game for him.

I have many other memorable stories about Hal but I just want to say that seeing and chatting with him in March of 2004, was so very special. We were having a reunion of the Chaffey players in Laughlin, Nevada and Marilyn and I had the opportunity to sit and talk with Hal for a long time. We reminisced about the old days and he shared some of his stories about the Yankees. For example, he told of the many nights he, Mickey Mantle, Whitey Ford and Billy Martin would run around together between games on the road. He said they were a great group to enjoy. When Hal first saw Marilyn, he said "Hi Blondie." He remembered her as a young bride of the coach in those early days.

This is very emotional for me to write because last fall we were stunned when we were told that Hal had passed away of cancer. What a shock it was to all of us. He didn't tell anyone. He kept it all inside. He knew death was coming and he requested of his family that he did not want a funeral or a memorial service. I talked to his sister, Carol, and she said he did not want any commotion. He simply wanted to pass on quietly and not be a bother to anyone. That was Hal. We wish our condolences to Hal's mother, Grace, and Carol and other members of the family.

Incidentally, I was a good friend of Hal's dad, Harold Sr., who passed away recently. We would often get together and just talk. One time he told me that if you looked inside Hal's head you would find a baseball in there. I believe he was correct.

Down deep Hal was a loner. He was an individualist. He did his own thing. As with all my players, I loved Hal. I am happy for the times we had together but I wish they had been more and longer. In a way, Hal represents the quality and richness of character of my Chaffey students, both players and non-players. Please see Story 79 (TBF) about a Chaffey group called "TBF."

One thing is for sure, all of us connected with Chaffey do love each other and, somehow, Hal's passing has brought that fact to the fore. Chaffey High School has a hallway where Hal's memory is preserved. Some of his equipment and Yankee memorabilia is on display there. It has been collected and prepared by Pat Dooley, a 1956 Chaffey graduate. Pat, a fine professional artist, has done the sketches found in this book. Please see Story 158 (Pat Dooley).

Yes, to be sure, Hal Reniff was a special guy!

Visiting Hillerich and Bradsby (Louisville Slugger Bats)

When I was a kid, owning a Louisville Slugger bat was a dream. We called them "Looey-ville" Sluggers. Some of the gang called them "Lose-e-ville" Sluggers (not a put-down—that is just the way they thought it was pronounced). Later when I was Director of Athletics at Chaffey High School we had a coach named Charlie Rupert who was from Louisvile, Kentucky. He told us the correct way to pronounce that great city's name was "Lou-a-vul." In the 1980s Marilyn and I took a boat trip on Lake Okefenokee in Georgia. The boat tender asked us if the capital of Kentucky was pronounced "Louis-ville" or "Louie-ville?" Each one gave his own version of the pronunciation. And, of course, both answers were wrong as the tender said, "I always thought it was pronounced "Frankfort." He got us on that one! In the Louisville brochure prepared by the Greater Louisville Convention & Visitors Bureau, they print five different ways to spell or say the city's name—Looavul, Luhvul, Loueville, Looaville, and Looeyville.

Big bat in front of Hillerich & Bradsby, © H&B.

For this application I will stick with "Looey-ville" Sluggers because that is what we called them years ago. Bats were usually Model 125 and had the signature of a big league player on the heavy end. The theory was that player models were shaped and sized according to the desires of that particular ball player. The big leaguer would give the specifications to the factory and the bat was designed to fit his needs. For example, a 35-inch Joe DiMaggio model had a thin handle and was somewhat heavy on the end. That is what Joe liked. The bats were made in various lengths including 32, 33, 34, 35, and perhaps longer. They had been stained and finished with a smooth and shiny surface. They are still making bats the same way today.

All of us knew the various bat characteristics and each of us had a favorite model. When we could save up enough money we purchased our own bat. I recall many different models including Charlie Gehringer, Nelson Fox, Babe Ruth, Mickey Mantle, Stan Musial,

Ernie Banks, Ralph Kiner, Harmon Killebrew, Pee Wee Reese, Gil Hodges, Brooks Robinson, Enos Slaughter, Ted Williams, Bobby Thomson, Jackie Robinson, Bobby Doerr, and many others.

In 1993 Marilyn and I took an extended automobile trip between Florida and Missouri and many points in between. One of our stops was Jeffersonville, Indiana to see the famous Louisville Slugger plant. The firm was known by several names in the early years and in 1897 the company name was changed to J. F. Hillerich & Son. By the time we visited there nearly 100 years later, they were then known as Hillerich and Bradsby Company. That was the name I knew in the 30s. Mr. Frank Bradsby joined the company in 1911 and became part owner in 1916. The same name exists today.

The tour of the factory was fabulous. They showed us how bats were designed, treated, produced and finished. They showed us every aspect of the company's production. We saw the bat of each and every player of the previous World Series. Other famous bats were on display from the early days.

First opened on July 17, 1996, the new facility in Louisville is better than ever. When I decided to write something about this great company I contacted Mr. Rick Redman, a vice-president of the company. He said they would be very happy to have us include them in the book. His cordial reply included much information about Hillerich and Bradsby and its history and we are greatly indebted to Mr. Redman for his cooperation and assistance. He indicated they get over 200,000 visitors a year.

Some friends, Don and Shirley Warner of Lewiston, Idaho, visited there recently and said it was most impressive. Please see Story 79 (TBF) about the Warners. Many interesting facts and experiences await the visitor. Exhibits feature information about the trees that are destined to become baseball bats, data about the great hitters of the game, what it is like to face a 90-mph fastball, a working batting cage, and, of course, the production of bats and other items. A well-equipped gift shop is available that gives the visitor an opportunity to take home some nice memoirs. As with the Warners, we, too, were greatly impressed.

In 1916 they had begun to produce golf clubs. This became a large part of the company's business. They continue to produce wooden bats and golf clubs, and are producing aluminum bats and hockey sticks. Also, they own some tree farms to assure production of wood for bats. They now have nine separate locations for their various departments and employ nearly 500 people. It is a highly successful

Top: Anne Jewell, Executive Director of Louisville Slugger Museum, Rick Redman, Vice-President of Communications, Hillerich and Bradsby

Middle: Louisville Slugger executives with Ken and Marilyn

Bottom: Vickie Boisseau, Director of Sales & Marketing, Hillerich and Bradsby.

business and continues to expand.

A huge bat stands in front of the Louisville Slugger Museum, 11.5 degrees off center. It was raised on this site on October 21, 1995. It is 120 feet long making it the world's tallest bat. It has a 9' diameter at the base and is 3'6" at the handle with a 6'6" diameter knob. The interior is hollow and yet the total weight is 68,000 pounds. It took over six months and 1,500 man-hours to complete. It has five layers of paint including a hand-painted wood-grain coat. It is an exact-scale replica of the model R43, 34" wood bat, designed to specifications requested by Babe Ruth in the early 1920s. The "Bud Hillerich" signature that appears with the famous oval logo is a tribute to John A. "Bud" Hillerich, who turned the company's first bat in 1884.

There is a sculpture in the museum commissioned by the Kentucky Crushed Stone Association. It is known as the Big Glove. It is 12' long, 9' wide and 4' high. It is made of 450-million-year-old Kentucky limestone. It weighs 34,000 pounds, about half the weight of the Big Bat. A relative of the original owners, artist Kim Hillerich, was involved in the creation of it. It was installed July 21, 1998.

The following is information about securing Personalized Signature Bats. They can be purchased in regular or smaller sizes. There are a large number of options. They come in a variety of colors including natural, black, brown or wine. The adult size is 34 inches long. Youth sizes are 28 through 31 inches long. Check with the company for prices and shipping costs. I have one of my own and we gave one to each of our three sons. They are terrific!!!

A recent news story tells about the 100th anniversary of Hall of Famer Honus Wagner's bat contract. It is believed to be the first equipment endorsement ever signed by a professional athlete. On September 1, 1905 the Pittsburg shortstop signed a contract with the Hillerich and Bradsby Co. whereby no money was involved. They simply made an agreement that the company would provide Wagner Louisville Slugger bats at no cost and custom-made to his specifications in exchange for using his name. As we look back we realize this was the beginning of endorsement transactions by professional athletes. Wagner was the first to have his name engraved into a barrel of a bat. Since that time more than 8,500 players have signed similar deals.

On our Louisville visit Mr. Redman hosted us and

Top: Dan Luckett, lead bat maker with his bat machine

Middle: Dan Luckett making bats

Bottom: Dan Luckett holding bat

introduced us to various key personnel of the company. Anne Jewell, Executive Director of the museum, is a delightful lady with quality experience in heading up all museum activities. She has met and dealt with hundreds of major league stars. I was informed that her ideas and follow-through continue to improve an already successful venture. In addition to executive capabilities Anne is an athlete in her own right having played volleyball and basketball in her college days. She was kind enough to allow us to interview her, and she introduced us to her immediate staff.

We met Vickie Boisseau, Director of Sales and Marketing for the Bionic Glove division of the company. This phase of business is relatively new. We understand they are growing at a 400% rate currently. Their types of gloves are marvelous. They continue to add more choices and are top-of-the-line quality items. They produce many kinds of gloves including baseball, gardening, driving, dress, equestrian, golf, and heavy duty pro types. Marilyn has two pair for gardening, one with long arms for rose care, and another with extra-strong fingertips for working in the dirt. We purchased a heavy-duty pair

Top: Ted Williams, Bobby Doerr, Rudy York selecting bats at H&G, photo provided by Louisville Slugger Museum.

Middle: Don Greene operating batting cage at Louisville Slugger

Bottom: Old Slugger building, photo provided by Louisville Slugger Museum.

for our son, Mike, who is a firefighter and has obvious protective needs.

A thirty-six year veteran of Hillerich and Bradsby Company is Dan Luckett. When he joined the company in 1969 he was turning bats by hand on a lathe. Today he operates a machine that can turn out a bat in twenty seconds. It is computerized and Dan can make a bat with specifications requested by any player under contract with the company. He feeds into the machine a piece of ash or maple called a billet. It is 40 inches long and round in shape. The computer tells the machine the shape of the bat required. The player's signature and logo of the company is added later. At this point the bat is given a professional finish and shipped to the player in question. While we watched Dan work (see pictures) he completed an order for six bats in just minutes.

The machine was made in Germany at a cost of $250,000. The price to ship it to Louisville was $10,000. Dan was very proud of it and rightly so. One can imagine the work required to turn all the bats by hand as he did years ago.

There are a number of tour leaders including Don Greene. He covers other responsibilities at the factory and is very good at his job. He is very clever with his words and has a good knowledge of baseball that enhances his presentation. At the conclusion of the tour each person in the group receives a miniature Louisville Slugger bat, a nice souvenir to take home. Part of Don's job is operating the batting cage where a hitter can put on a helmet and batting glove, select a bat, and hit several balls pitched by an automatic pitching machine. I gave it a try and had fun doing it (I think I hit 0 for Monday).

Ken Proctor in batting case at Louisville Slugger Museum.

Angie Grammer was one of the first persons we met when we entered the corporate office. She is a great receptionist and made us feel completely welcome. Her pleasant voice greets all callers and she gives a good impression both at the desk and on the telephone.

We highly recommend your visiting Louisville Slugger when you visit that fine city. Louisville is the 16th largest city in America and you would find it most interesting and enjoyable. From our standpoint visiting Louisville Slugger was the highlight of our trip.

The new facility is just a few blocks from the original 1875 location. The company may be contacted by telephone at (502)-588-7228 or by mail at 800 West Main Street, Louisville, Kentucky 40202.

STORY 35:

Happening On Ty Cobb's Home Town

Marilyn and I have traveled a great deal in these United States. We visited Georgia several times in the 1980s and tried to see as many special locations as possible such as Augusta National, site of the Masters Golf Tournament, the famous Bobby Jones Golf Course north of Atlanta, the campus of the Georgia Institute of Technology (Georgia Tech), etc. As we were motoring from Atlanta one day where we saw the Braves play at Fulton County Stadium, we headed on to Athens to tour the University of Georgia campus. We drove on a few miles and came upon Royston, a small town of about 2,500 people. A sign on the edge of town said "Home of Ty Cobb."

To say I was excited when I saw that sign is an understatement. We knew

Cobb's home was in Georgia. Here we found ourselves in the hometown of Tyrus Raymond Cobb with plenty of time on our hands. We asked a few questions in town and learned that there was a Ty Cobb Museum there. In addition we learned that he and most of his family were buried there.

First, we went to the museum. It was fascinating. It contained every kind of memorabilia imaginable. Cobb's entire career was represented with bats, balls, uniforms, shoes, scorecards, jackets, baseball programs, Hall of Fame documents, trophies and other awards, pictures, newspapers, and on and on. I have seen museums of other players but none better than this Royston monument to Ty Cobb.

Following, we drove out to the small cemetery on the edge of town. It was quiet there with nary a soul in sight. We found Mr. Cobb's grave as well as several members of his family. My mind was running wild with thoughts of Cobb's baseball achievements. He was very competitive, spirited, fierce in his desire to win, controversial, unrelenting and asked no favor nor gave one. He had a lifetime batting average of .367, the highest of any major league player in baseball history. He led the American League in batting for nine consecutive years. Many experts feel these two records may never be broken.

Actually, even though Royston is considered as Cobb's hometown, he was born in a small community by the name of Narrows, Georgia which is located about 25 miles from Royston near the South Carolina border. His father moved the family to Royston in order to be on a major rail line. Narrows was too small to accomplish their goals. I looked on a map of Georgia and went to the Internet and Narrows does not appear to exist today.

Most fans are not aware that Cobb batted just .240 in 1905 as he made his first appearance in the major leagues on August 30. Those nine consecutive years of leading the American League in batting were from 1907 to 1915. He repeated from 1916 to 1919. He managed Detroit from 1921 to 1926. Interestingly enough, after playing 22 years with Detroit, Cobb played his final season, 1927, with Connie Mack and the Philadelphia Athletics. That fact is a story in itself.

When the Baseball Hall of Fame was initiated in 1936 Cobb was elected to that celebrated group and led in the number of votes submitted. He received 222 of a possible 226 votes. He had more votes than Walter Johnson, Babe Ruth, Christy Mathewson, Honus Wagner or any other inductee. In 1950, the Sporting News selected him as the most important player in the first fifty years of Major League Baseball.

During his playing days he invested his money wisely in real estate, automobiles, and cotton, and purchased a large number of Coca Cola shares. At retirement, Cobb was one of the wealthiest men in the game.

His records and achievements are countless but these are a few more of note. He had 11,434 at bats, 4,191 hits, 892 stolen bases and 2.245 runs. He hit over .400 three times including his high average of .420 in 1911. That year he beat out the infamous "Shoeless Joe" Jackson who batted .408. He played in 17 World Series games with a .354 batting average.

The following story supposedly took place in the 1950s. Cobb was asked how he would hit under modern (current) conditions. He answered, "Oh, I'd hit .310 or .315. To which the interviewer replied, "But, Mr. Cobb, you averaged .367 over a career! Why would you hit only .300 now?" Cobb replied, "Well, you have to remember. I am 72 years old now." True story? I guess we will never know for sure but it is good for a laugh, isn't it?

In his later years Cobb contributed $100,000 for a new hospital in Royston, a sizable sum in those days. He endowed a number of hospitals in northeast Georgia known as the Ty Cobb Healthcare System. The Ty Cobb Museum is housed in one of these buildings today.

That is just a small amount of information about one of the most colorful players in major league history. Yes, "The Georgia Peach" was one of a kind! Please see Story 90 (Ty Cobb) about more fascinating details of Cobb's life.

STORY 36:

Yankee Stadium With Dr. And Mrs. Bobby Brown

On December 7, 1942 I signed up to join the Navy. I had just graduated from Washington High School in Los Angeles and attended the University of California at Berkeley for the first half of my freshman year. Before joining the Navy I transferred to the University of California at Los Angeles (UCLA). The Navy assigned me to UCLA in the Naval Reserve Officers Training Corps (NROTC). Along with recruits of the Navy V-12 and Marine Corps programs, all several hundred of our men lived on the UCLA campus.

We were required to enroll in at least 18 units per semester, with many of those being naval courses. Our purpose was to complete our work as soon as possible and join the fighting forces of World War II against Germany and Japan. Along with the studies we were encouraged to get involved in college sports. Staying in good physical condition was one of our requirements.

In addition to our daily physical conditioning programs I chose to play base-

Dr. & Mrs. Bobby Brown host Ken and Marilyn Proctor in the Stadium Club, Yankee Stadium

Dr. & Mrs. Bobby Brown host Ken and Marilyn Proctor in box seats at Yankee Stadium

ball, basketball and football. In baseball I played second base alongside a great teammate, Bobby Brown who enlisted in the U. S. Navy and was assigned to the Navy V-12 Unit at UCLA when he was called to active duty. We formed a double play combination on the UCLA Bruin varsity baseball team. After our baseball experience together I was sent to Virginia to Amphibious Training School and Bobby continued at UCLA.

After spending three semesters at UCLA, Bobby was sent to the Tulane University School of Medicine. He spent five semesters there before being assigned to medical school. He graduated in June 1950 with a Doctor of Medicine degree.

This became one of the highlights of my baseball experience as our 1944 team participated in two separate conferences, namely, the Pacific Coast Conference, and the Southern California Intercollegiate Baseball Conference. The former included the University of Southern California (USC), the University of California at Berkeley plus UCLA, while the latter was composed of Occidental College, California Institute of Technology (Cal Tech), Redlands University, USC and UCLA. Our Bruins were champions of both conferences. The Northwest universities from Washington and Oregon were not included at that time because of limitations of wartime travel. Bobby was our captain and our leading hitter.

Bobby and I liked to throw batting practice to each other. We would get a bag of baseballs and stay out until nearly dark pitching and batting baseballs. Bobby was bound and determined to make it to the major leagues. Shortly after graduation from UCLA he went to medical school in Louisiana and kept playing baseball when possible. The Yankees had their eye on Bobby and signed him when the opportunity arose.

Bobby Brown, later more well-known as Dr. Robert W. Brown, became an excellent cardiologist. He practiced professionally from 1958 to 1984. Also, in the 1950s, "Bobby" played for Casey Stengel and the New York Yankees. Please see Story 85 (Bobby Brown—Destined to Succeed) for more details.

In the 1980s, he was named President of the American League in baseball. Marilyn and I visited New York City in 1985 and had the opportunity to meet with the Browns. On Friday, June 14 we had dinner together in The Stadium Club and took in a baseball game. On our way to the stadium from the Yankee private parking lot we unknowingly walked in with Phil Rizzuto, former great New York shortstop who was now announcing the games for the Yankees.

As we sat in the restaurant having dinner we had to pinch ourselves. All around us were large paintings of former Yankee stars and managers such as Babe Ruth, Joe DiMaggio, Casey Stengel, Joe McCarthy and Bill Dickey. Here we were in the "House That Ruth Built." Bobby and Sara Brown were treated like the king and queen. Of course, he is part of that rich Yankee his-

1944 UCLA team picture

tory and everyone knows him. This was as close to a being in a dream than anything we have ever experienced.

We sat in the "League President's Box" in the first row next to the Yankee dugout. They were playing Detroit that evening and we met Sparky Anderson, manager of the Tigers. Also, the current manager of the Yankees, Gene Michael, came up to say hello. In about the third inning, Bobby excused himself to say he had to go up to the executive area to meet a friend. He said to me, "You remember Eddie Lopat, don't you? Did I ever! He was one of my favorite Yankees during their hey-day of World Series victories in the 50s.

I sat there with two great ladies, Sara Brown and Marilyn Proctor, awaiting Bobby's return. These two had a very close relationship because of their commonality in Jesus Christ. Both had attended the Womens' Bible Study Fellowship in their past.

Bobby returned and we enjoyed a very good ball game. It was an evening these two old baseball fans will remember forever. Marilyn and I still reminisce about that great evening.

Because Bobby was living in New York, he seldom had the chance to visit his aunt, Florence Fuerbach, who was living at Crista Ministries Nursing Home in north Seattle near where Marilyn and I live. We would go to the nursing home and look in on Florence from time to time. It was enjoyable to see "Auntie Florence" and fill in for Bobby occasionally.

Now and then, Bobby came to the Northwest to visit our local major league club, the Seattle Mariners. He always called and invited us to the ballpark to have dinner with him.

One evening in 1995 he and Sara came to Seattle to represent the American League when the Mariners were playing the New York Yankees for the Western Division championship. The Mariners were down. 2-0, having lost the first two games of the five-game set in New York. The last three games (if necessary) were played in Seattle. We attended all three games and it was the year that the M's came through to defeat the Yankees for the American League West Division title. In the final game, Marilyn sat with Sara and I sat with Bobby the first few innings. Then, I sat with former Mariner owner, George Argyros. Finally, I had the opportunity to sit with Baseball Commissioner, Fay Vincent for a few innings. I was certainly out of place but enjoying every minute of it. Marilyn and I shall always remember that exciting evening. To complete the evening the Mariners won the championship on the last play of the game when Edgar Martinez doubled home Ken Griffey Jr. with the winning run. As one might expect the place was a madhouse.

We recently talked to the Browns on the telephone. They are now retired and living in Fort Worth, Texas. Bobby still plays tennis and he and Sara are near some of their family there. We contact each other occasionally although we have not had the chance to visit together for a number of years. I will always remember Bobby as one of my most cherished teammates. He was an inspiration to all. The Browns are a wonderful pair of friends.

STORY 37:

Twenty-Eight Ball Parks and Counting

Watching baseball has been a pleasure for Marilyn and me. We watch it for the enjoyment of the game and all that is around it. It is so much fun to see dads, moms and grandparents at the games with their youngsters. How many times have you heard someone say, "I will never forget going to the ballpark with my dad, my mom, my grandparents, or my folks when I was a kid?" It is a part of the fabric of America.

I did a survey of the many times we have attended games in some of the ballparks of our nation. At last count we had gone to twenty-eight parks including the following teams alphabetically by league.

AMERICAN LEAGUE (13)

Baltimore Orioles, Camden Yards:

We visited Camden Yards twice. It is an excellent stadium with good views of the field from every seat. Of course, there is a rich history of baseball in this great city. The waterfront has been outstandingly upgraded and the ballpark is situated very close to the center of town. We were impressed with the layout of the entire complex. They had markers embedded in the cement to display where various memorable home runs had been hit. It was enjoyable checking out each one. Great place to see a ball game!

Our first time seeing a game here was on Thursday, September 15, 2000 at 7:05 p.m. The Seattle Mariners faced the Orioles and won 10-2. We were thrilled to see Cal Ripken, Jr. and Brady Anderson play for this storied franchise. It was doubly exciting for us as we brought with us several shipmates of our former ship, the LST 839. We were having a reunion in that great city full of American history.

Marilyn and I returned to Baltimore after taking a trip around the east and saw the Toronto Blue Jays play the Orioles on Thursday, September 28 at 7:05 p.m. It was an unusual game as Baltimore pummeled the Jays 23-1. Pat Rapp tossed a two-hit masterpiece. Eight Oriole batters each had two hits or more and they had a 10-run fourth inning.

Baltimore Orioles, Memorial Stadium:

This storied field does not exist anymore. Sports fans everywhere know of the baseball and football accomplishments achieved here. This was where Johnny Unitas and the Baltimore Colts dominated NFL football at one time. Please see Story 26 (Denny McLain Goes for 32nd Win). On that September evening I watched McLain try for his 32nd victory that year against one of the Oriole's great teams. When I returned there with Marilyn in the 80s, a tear came to my eye as I thought about the many years of enjoyment fans experienced there. Like old Ebbetts Field (Brooklyn), Comiskey Park (Chicago), Tiger Stadium (Detroit), Polo Grounds (New York), Crosley Field (Cincinnati), Forbes Field (Pittsburg), Sportsman's Park (St. Louis), and others, many memories linger here. In a way it is a shame that these old fields could not have been saved. It has been a matter of money, I guess and "time marches on."

Boston Red Sox, Fenway Park:

Two times we visited this oldest existing park in major league baseball and each time it was a unique experience. We sat in different locations and enjoyed both of them. Our first visit on June 16, 1985 found us in the right field bleachers. The fans there were loud and demonstrative. Brooms were everywhere throughout the stadium because Boston was trying to win a third consecutive game against Toronto and sweep the series. The fans certainly enjoy themselves. We were impressed with security people. They were strong young men dressed in blue blazers and gray pants. They put up with no nonsense. I saw several occasions where fans creating problems were challenged and, in some cases, arrested. I might say, however, that watching recent difficulties with fan interference at Fenway, the security people are dressed differently. Maybe there is more than one group of them.

The second visit was on September 30, 1987 and we sat in the box seats not more than thirty feet from the visitor Baltimore's bat rack. We sat close enough to see the blue in Cal Ripken's eyes. I asked a young fan sitting in the next box if he always sat in this location. He told us his family had owned this box since 1912 when the park opened. We were astounded. Apparently, many people have owned their seats there for years. Both visits we came early and enjoyed the festivities and pre-game salesmanship calls of the vendors, like "pretzels, pop corn, peanuts, hot dogs...." yelled in a sing-song fashion and very unique. There were shops with all kinds of baseball gifts and memorabilia everywhere. It is an exciting ballpark.

Just to give one some appreciation for the age of this famous old stadium, the park opened the same week as the Titanic disaster (famous ship sinking). That kind of puts everything in perspective, doesn't it?

Chicago White Sox, Comiskey Park:

When I was a young boy I can recall hearing radio broadcasts from old Comiskey Park on Chicago's south side. Charles Comiskey opened that park on July 1, 1910. Before it was torn down in 1991 it produced eighty years of wonderful baseball memories. On September 30, 1990 the two parks sat side-by-side. The old park was torn down in the next two months to make room for a huge parking lot.

The New Comiskey Park opened April 17, 1991. Marilyn and I attended our first game there on June 8, 1998, to see the Cardinals meet the White Sox. Chicago pitcher, Jason Bere, bested Mark Petkovek in an 8-6 game. It was a rainy evening but not enough to delay the game. We were impressed with the park in general but certainly wished we could have attended at the old original ballpark. We saw Mark McGuire hit his 29th home run of the season with one of his prodigious blasts, a "400-foot plus shot" into the leftfield bleachers.

On September 6, 2001 we took the Red Line (elevated) from near our North Chicago hotel, the Majestic, which was just six blocks from Wrigley Field. We went into town and transferred to the Orange Line taking us directly to Comiskey Park. We saw the White Sox play the Detroit Tigers. The game started at 1:05 p.m on a beautiful sunny afternoon. Detroit pounded out 12 hits as Jeff Weaver defeated Chicago 6-2. White Sox first baseman Paul Konerko hit his 30th home run. Along with 13,601 fellow baseball fans, we just sat back and enjoyed major league baseball at its best. It is certainly a beautiful baseball park!

Detroit Tigers, Tiger Stadium:

As previously stated, I had seen Tiger Stadium from my hotel room while attending a conference in Detroit in 1964. However, in 1985 my work took me to various stops across the country. One was Detroit where Marilyn and I had the opportunity to visit old Tiger Stadium.

The Detroit Tiger's first field was called Bennett Park in 1901. Twelve years later a beautiful ballpark was constructed on the same site and renamed Navin field after owner, Frank Navin.

Old Tiger Stadium. It has been replaced by Coamerica Park in Detroit.

In 1938 the park was renamed Briggs Stadium after owner, Walter O. Briggs. Finally, in 1961 the historical old park was named Tiger Stadium and held that name until 1999. That was a sad year for Detroit fans for the old ballpark was torn down and Coamerica Park was built where the Tigers play today. Only three of the old original parks remain today including Yankee Stadium, Fenway Park and Wrigley Field.

The day Marilyn and I visited the Tigers they were on the road. However, we walked into the stadium on a beautiful sunny day and the head groundskeeper gave us a short tour. It was an awesome feeling to wander around those grounds where so many baseball memories existed. The franchise today is well over 100 years old and names such as Mickey Cochrane, Harry Heilmann, Ty Cobb, Al Kaline, Hank Greenberg, Freddie Hutchinson, Sparky Anderson and many others give the Tigers a rich history. Frankly, I was astonished doing my research when I realized how many baseball people were greatly affected by Detroit's incredible background. And there we stood soaking it all in and trying to feel the reality of being in one of the pinnacles of baseball achievement.

This story is worth telling. On April 24, 1901 the Tigers were to play their very first baseball game against Milwaukee. Inclement weather postponed the game to the following day. It was played before 10,000 fans at old Bennett Park. The Tigers were having a dismal day. They went into the ninth inning behind 13-4. But, as they say, good comes to them who will wait and have patience. As the home team they batted last and scored ten runs to win, 14-13. What a start!

Kansas City Athletics, Municipal Stadium:

When the Kansas City Athletics moved to Oakland in 1968 the Royals took over that wonderful city. I was attending a conference in 1967 when I had the opportunity to see a game at Municipal Stadium. The team I saw was the old Philadelphia Athletics who had moved to Kansas City in 1955. The Philadelphia club had been managed by the famous Connie Mack until 1950. The Kansas City Royals became an expansion franchise when owner Charles Finley moved his Athletics to Oakland in 1968. Today the new field is called Kauffman Stadium.

Los Angeles Angels, Angels Stadium:

Though I lived in Southern California for many years I went to old Anaheim Stadium just once. I took my dad and mother there for a special evening. My dad was an avid Angel fan. Gene Autry, owner of the Angels and famous cowboy movie star, is known far and wide for his love of baseball and his team. Also, he was Marilyn's hero when she was a child. I doubt if she ever missed a Gene Autry cowboy movie. It was a great day for the franchise when they won the 2002 World Series against the San Francisco Giants. My basketball coach at UCLA, John Wooden, threw out the first pitch in one of the games. Coach said it was one of the thrills of his life. Please see Chapter 10 (John Wooden's Favorite Sport.)

Yankee Stadium from East River. (It will be replaced in the next few years by a stadium immediately next to Yankee Stadium.)

Minnesota Twins, Metrodome:

On a business trip east in 1985 Marilyn and I had the opportunity to visit Minneapolis. The Twins were out of town and we did not see a game. But, we saw the Metrodome that is located right in the middle of downtown. Currently, I understand there is a move to build a new stadium in the city.

New York Yankees, Yankee Stadium:

My first visit to Yankee Stadium on September 25, 1968 is described in Story 27 (Mickey Mantle's Last Game at Yankee Stadium). Here I was, a 44-year old man feeling like a kid again with that special visit.

But, seventeen years later on June 14, 1985, Marilyn

and I were there with American League president, Dr. Bobby Brown, and his wife, Sara, watching a game between the Yankees and Tigers. Please find details of that experience in Story 36 (Yankee Stadium with Dr. and Mrs. Bobby Brown). The Yankees have announced that a new stadium will be built soon in the same area of the famous old structure. As has happened with other new stadiums there will be many unhappy fans expressing regret over the tearing down of Yankee Stadium. If this happens there will be only two old original parks remaining, those being Fenway Park in Boston and Wrigley Field in Chicago.

Seattle Mariners, Kingdome:

Marilyn and I went to countless games at this park after it was built in 1976. The Mariners first game there was played April 6, 1977. While the Mariners never had a "rained-out" game at the Kingdome, they never had a game in the sunlight either. This situation brought about the new Safeco Field in 1999.

Seattle Mariners, Safeco Field:

On July 15, 1999 Safeco Field opened with its first baseball game. Of course, now Seattle can plays games in the bright sunlight because they have a roof that can be opened or closed. It is a great ballpark. People can purchase all kinds of food and drinks on the promenade in view of the field. I know many people who wander around the park and watch the game from different locations. Fans can look at the two

Ken and Marilyn at Safeco Field

bullpens from ground level or one floor above. The "Hit It Here Café" allows fans to eat and watch baseball simultaneously.

Marilyn and I go often to Safeco Field and see games in the afternoon or evenings. We feel it is the best ballpark in the major leagues. It is certainly fan friendly and there is not a bad seat in the entire stadium. Since the opening, Seattle fans have averaged between 30,000 and 40,000 per game.

Toronto Blue Jays, Exhibition Stadium:

As president of the Kiwanis Club of Seattle I attended an international convention in the summer of 1985. Marilyn and I drove to this event stopping at various business locations on the way. The convention was held in Toronto and we had the opportunity to attend a Toronto Blue Jay game against the New York Yankees at Exhibition Stadium. Our visit was on Wednesday, July 3 and it was a 12:35 pm game.

We saw a good pitchers' battle between two outstanding hurlers, Phil Niekro, the super knuckleballer, and Dave Stieb, a veteran who was very effective. They

Safeco Field, Seattle, Washington

finally gave way to several relief pitchers and Toronto survived, 3-2, in the 10th inning. Yankees of note were Ken Griffey (Sr.), Dave Winfield and Don Mattingly. For the Blue Jays were Jesse Barfield, George Bell, Willie Upshaw and Jeff Burroughs.

The park was adequate but certainly not up to major league standards. We heard that new stadium planning was "in the works."

Toronto Blue Jays, Skydome:

Indeed, the new planning was, "in the works." Marilyn and I attended a baseball game between the Toronto Blue Jays and the New York Yankees on Tuesday, September 19, 2000 at the marvelous Skydome. This stadium, with a retractable roof, is big enough to put a 31-story building in centerfield. The Video Board is 110 feet by 33 feet in size. The structure sits immediately next to the huge CN Tower that is 1,815 feet high. The stadium is an impressive structure and was the first of its kind in the world.

The Blue Jays had on their "hitting shoes" that night. They banged out 19 hits beating lefthander Andy Pettitte 19-4 though Andy sported a record of 18-8 at the time. Steve Trachsel tossed a four-hitter for Toronto and led the rout. Home runs of note were by Yankee outfielder, David Justice who hit his 38th. On the Blue Jay side of the ledger, Tony Batista swatted his 39th.

We found that getting to the Skydome via public transportation was inexpensive and relatively easy. Good views are available from any seat. Attending a baseball game there is certainly a unique experience. We recommend it.

NATIONAL LEAGUE (14)

Arizona Diamondbacks, Bank One Ballpark:

Marilyn and I have been going to spring training games in Arizona for many years. We always attend with two good friends, Ross and Shirley Cutter from Spokane, Washington. Ross (Dr. Cutter) is an Emeritus professor from Whitworth College. Both of them are great baseball fans. Please see Story 155 (Ross Cutter).

On Friday, March 29 we attended a game between the Diamondbacks and the Cubs at the field locally known as "BOB," Bank One Ballpark. It is a beautiful stadium with all the amenities. Our seats were down the leftfield line at the

300- level. We had great views of all the action. Parking was somewhat difficult mainly because a professional basketball game was being played that same night in an edifice very close to the baseball park.

"BOB" has a retractable roof, inside air conditioning and natural turf. It has multiple screens for good viewing and can accommodate more than 50,000 fans for a baseball game. It is certainly a ballpark worth attending.

Atlanta Braves, Fulton County Stadium:

I get the feeling that a new sports complex is being built in Atlanta every few years. At least it seems that way. But, we saw a game in this older stadium in May 1988. The Braves were playing the Montreal Expos. The old stadium was built in 1965 and was the home of the Braves until 1996. It met the wrecking ball in 1997 and Turner Field now serves as the Brave's home yard. Its capacity is 52,000 and it has a natural grass field.

The All Star game was played at Fulton County Stadium in 1972, several World Series were played there in the 90s, it was the site of Hank Aaron's 715th home run and where Pete Rose's 44-game hitting streak was stopped in 1978. Some tried to save the old stadium before it was demolished but failed. We certainly enjoyed watching baseball there.

Our day there on May 11 was rather unique. The Braves won the game 3-2 in a well-played game. Interestingly, Paul Runge Jr. played third base for Atlanta while his father, Paul Runge Sr. was an outstanding umpire in the major leagues. Bruce Sutter earned the save that day for Atlanta. He had more than 300 saves in his career and had 45 for the St. Louis Cardinals in 1984. One of my favorites, Dale Murphy, played center field for Atlanta.

Chicago Cubs, Wrigley Field:

This is our favorite baseball park. First, it feels like home to Marilyn and me because our park in Los Angeles, also named Wrigley Field, was almost an exact replica of the old Chicago stadium. Also, when we go to see a game there the place is "electric." The fans are really into the game and understand what is happening. They are extremely knowledgeable about the various facets of baseball. It has that feel of a park of the early days. Fenway Park and Yankee Stadium are similar in that both are thick with the history of the grand old game.

Our first visit to Wrigley Field was on June 8, 1985, three years prior to the installation of lights for night games. The Cubs were playing Pittsburg in an afternoon game. The place was packed. Jody Davis was the catcher for the Cubbies and he was a fan favorite. When he batted they all yelled in unison, "Jo-dee,

Jo-dee, Jo-dee." Chicago sent the fans home happy as they defeated the Pirates 7-3. Some of the players in addition to Davis were Ron Cey and Larry Bowa for Chicago and Lee Mazilli and Bill Madlock for Pittsburg. Steve Trout was the winning pitcher with a 6-1 record.

The upcoming visits described here were the first of several to Wrigley Field for Marilyn and me. In 1998 we found a small hotel, The Park Brompton, located about six blocks from the ballpark. It was moderately priced and comfortable and an easy walk to the baseball games. On June 7 we saw the White Sox play the Cubs in their renowned cross-town rivalry. It was a hitters' game with the Cubs winning 13-7 and with 25 hits recorded between the two teams. We saw Sammy Sosa, Mark Grace, Leon Durham and Frank Thomas, all bonafide big leaguers. The exciting part of this day was a stadium full of brooms because this was the third consecutive victory by the Cubbies over the Sox. The traditional chant of "sweep, sweep, sweep," echoed throughout the old ballpark at game's end. It was a magic sound for a couple of west coasters.

We went to a reunion of my Navy shipmates in Milwaukee and returned ten days later to see Milwaukee edge the Cubs 6-5. Sosa hit a home run and Fernando Vina, Mark Loretta and Jeromy Burnitz played. This was the Brewer's first year in the National League.

In 1999 we returned to the same little hotel now with a new name, the Majestic. Incidentally, the inn was very old and formerly housed movie stars and other dignitaries in the old days. It is unique and, if still in existence when visited, it should be one that would be a great place to stay. They serve a continental breakfast including their famous "sticky buns," a sweet type of pull-apart. It has good food and pleasant surroundings. We saw a trio of games this time all against the Los Angeles Dodgers. Unfortunately for the Cubs, the Dodgers swept the series.

The first game, played on Friday, September 3, was a night game won by Los Angeles 8-6 although the Cubs out-hit the Dodgers 12-9. Prominent players were Gary Sheffield, Eric Karros, Adrian Beltre, and Mark Grace. Sosa hit his 57th homerun. On Saturday, Kevin Brown threw a two-hitter shutting out the Cubs 6-0. Karros hit his 30th home run. The following day Dodger pitcher, Darren Dreifort won 4-1 as he threw a seven-hitter and had two RBIs to boot. Even in losing causes, excitement fills the air at Wrigley Field. The 2:20 p.m. games are special. What a ballpark!

Two years later (2001) we returned to the Majestic Hotel and went to see the Atlanta Braves play the Cubs. On Friday, September 7 we saw Greg Maddux return to his former team, the Cubs, to pitch a four-hitter and win 3-2 in an afternoon game. On Saturday, September 8, again in the afternoon, Tom Glavine defeated Chicago 11-7 as Chipper Jones hit his 35th round tripper. Both games were sell-outs at the "The Friendly Confines," as Wrigley Field is often called.

Marilyn and I still think of seeing the elevated Red Line gliding past the ballpark right field stands. Neighbors beyond both left and right field fences have constructed seats and "watching" areas on their rooftops and we are told they have made good businesses out of their developments. However, there has been some litigation about this situation.

Following the games, we often linger for a while just taking in the whole aura of the ballpark and its surroundings. The classic old scoreboard still operated by hand was built in 1937 and gets the job done. This is the second oldest park in major league baseball and was built in 1914 (Fenway Park was constructed in 1912). First called Weeghman Park, the name was changed to Cubs Park in 1920 when the Wrigley family purchased the club. Finally it was called Wrigley Field in 1926 in honor of William Wrigley, Jr., owner of the club and the chewing gum magnate. This park at Clark and Addison in Chicago just drips with baseball history.

In 1932 Mr. Wrigley passed away and his son, Philip K. Wrigley, took over the operation. Since that time control was handed down from father to son until the franchise was sold to the Chicago Tribune Company in 1981 ending 65 years of Wrigley family direction.

Cincinnati Reds, Riverfront Stadium:

On May 26, 1993, we were taking a vacation in the Midwest and had the opportunity to visit a great city, Cincinnati. Our baseball goal was to see a game at Riverfront Stadium, the home of the Big Red Machine of the Cincinnati Reds of the 70s. We had dinner at the Spaghetti Factory just a baseball-throw away from the ballpark. We watched Red's pitcher Tim Belcher one-hit the Braves in a 4-0 victory. The losing pitcher was Greg Maddux. Third sacker Chris Sabo hit a circuit clout for the Reds and the only hit for the Braves was a double by Deion Sanders.

They had a walkway from the stadium into town with large signs describing some of Cincinnati's great moments in baseball such as Johnny Vander Meer's back-to-back no-hitters in June of 1938 that I remember well, Sparky Anderson's great teams of the 70's, or the first night game ever played in the major leagues on May 24, 1935. Additionally, Cincinnati was the first team to use an airplane to transport its team to another city, Chicago in this case, in 1934. Baseball history abounds in Cincinnati.

Riverfront Stadium was demolished December 31, 2002 and the Great American Ballpark now stands in a similar location on the Ohio River. Old Crosley Field in Cincinnati was a favorite of mine when I was a youngster although I never saw it. Marilyn and I are happy we went to Riverfront Stadium before it met the implosion that took 37 seconds that day as more than 25,000 local citizens attended. There is much baseball history in that old Ohio city. Incidentally, in 1944 I was in the Navy and my ship, the LST 839, sailed down the Ohio River and right by the location of Riverfront Stadium. Little did I know what was to happen there in ensuing in the future.

Cincinnati Reds, Great American Ball Park:

Knowing we were going to be in Cincinnati in September, 2005, we purchased some tickets for the game to be played by the St.Louis Cardinals and Cincinnati Reds on September 20, my birthday. As we drove up from Knoxville and through Lexington we became excited to know we were going to see another of America's great parks. We had heard what a super job they did with this fine stadium and after touring the Louisville Slugger factory in Kentucky, we headed for this storied baseball city to see the game. The park had opened March 31, 2003. We saw a good ball game with the Reds coming out on top, much to the delight of the Cincinnati fans.

The first professional baseball game ever played was reportedly by the Cincinnati Red Stockings in 1869. The manager of the team was Harry Wright. The Cincinnati Hall of Fame, now housed in the Great American Ball Park, has some exhibitions of that memorable team. Also in this outstanding Hall of Fame are complete records of all Cincinnati teams through the years. They have a model of one of the famous Cincinnati ballparks. It was built in Roman and Grecian style and was called "The Palace of the Fans," and dedicated in 1902. A fire two years earlier had demolished the previous park called the " Union Grounds." In 1912 the park was re-named Redland Field that eventually became Crosley Field in 1934. Riverfront Stadium was opened June 20, 1967 and served the Reds until the Great American Ball Park was dedicated.

Top: Ken and Marilyn Proctor visiting the Great American Ball Park.

Bottom: Great American Ball Park baseball field, Cincinnati, Ohio.

Los Angeles Dodgers, Coliseum:

In 1958 the old Brooklyn Dodgers came to Los Ange-les. What a boon for this "triple-A baseball city!" The first question was, "Where will they play their games?" There were two sizable baseball parks in the area, Wrig-ley Field and Gilmore Field. Both were inadequate for one main reason. They were limited in seating capac-ity. Ebbetts Field in Brooklyn could seat only 32,000 but the anticipation of large crowds in Los Angeles was certainly justified for this baseball-hungry community. In fact, the first year the Dodgers averaged 34,000 per game. Please see Story 20 (The Dodgers and Giants Come West).

The Los Angeles Memorial Coliseum was known far and wide. The 1932 Olympic games were held there. It had a capacity of nearly 100,000 people. The Dodger organization put their heads together with city officials and came up with a plan. They figured they could build an almost-adequate field at the west end of the struc-ture. There was an infinitesimal distance available toward

Los Angeles Coliseum, Los Angeles, looking east.

right field but, on the other hand, left field would provide a foul line distance of just 240 feet. No major league park had a distance that short.

They solved the problem to some degree by building a 40-foot high fence from the left field foul pole to deep left-center field. While many singles were hit off that fence they saw that it would take a blow of 325 feet or more for a ball to clear the giant left field screen. The arrangement proved adequate though not highly desired. Also, we relate some of our experiences during those first four years of Dodger baseball in Los Angeles. We saw many games in the Coliseum and had some of our most memorable experiences there along with our children and good friends.

The attendance consideration was certainly revealed on Opening Day at the Coliseum when 78,762 fans came through the turnstiles. The Bums (Dodgers) defeated the Giants 6-5.

On September 15, 1961 we headed for the Coliseum to see what turned out to be a unforgettable ball game. It was a beautiful Friday evening and a shirt-sleeved crowd of 23,911 watched the Dodgers meet the Milwaukee Braves. The great Sandy Koufax (15-11) was facing the equally famous Warren Spahn (19-12). The two lefties were scheduled to hook-up in a classic pitchers' battle. But, it did not turn out that way. In the second inning the Dodgers got to Spahn for six runs and the Brave hurler never did get an out before being relieved.

The game ended up an 11-2 victory for Los Angeles as Koufax threw a nifty five-hitter. In addition to Sandy, Dodger stars were Maury Wills, Wally Moon, Frank Howard, and Gil Hodges.

And besides Spahn, Brave notables were Eddie Mathews, Hank Aaron and Joe Torre, the catcher and current Yankee manager.

There was something about the Coliseum that was very special. Of course, it was the first place the Dodgers played official MLB games in Los Angeles, and it had that unusual giant screen in left field. But, in those four years of being home to the Dodgers, fans became used to it and Los Angeles quickly became a major league city as announcer Vic Scully gave many westerners baseball knowledge never known previously there. Marilyn and I have commented how unique it was to be in those stands during those historical years. Again, please see Story 20 (The Dodgers and Giants Come West) about more details of the Los Angeles Coliseum.

Los Angeles Dodgers, Dodger Stadium:

The Dodgers played their first game at their new Dodger Stadium on April 10, 1962. It had taken four years for them to purchase land and build their new stadium.

It is one of the most scenic ballparks in MLB. There is a great view of the city of Los Angeles, the San Gabriel Mountains and the Elysian Hills. It has parking for 16,000 automobiles and has easy access to and from the park. It is known as the cleanest stadium in the big leagues because at the end of every season the entire structure gets a new coat of paint. With a capacity of 56,000 people and a high annual attendance record the Dodgers have accommodated millions of fans as it approaches its 50th year in Los Angeles.

We had attended our first Dodger game on April 19, 1958. We attended many more games those first four years at the Los Angeles Memorial Coliseum including a World Series game in 1959. When Dodger Stadium opened we continued to see games there. One game In particular was very interesting to us. It was May 16, 1963 and the Dodgers faced the Pittsburg Pirates. This was the famous team that had beaten the New York Yankees in the seventh game of the 1960 World Series when second baseman Bill Mazeroski hit a walk-off home run in the bottom of the ninth inning to win 10-9. What a finish and what excitement that day! We had seen it on television and here we were watching that great club playing our home team. There was Bill Mazeroski at second base, the great Roberto Clemente was in his regular right field spot and Bill Virdon in center field.

The Dodgers also had their share of outstanding world champions from the 1959 World Series when they defeated the Chicago White Sox four games to two. We saw rightfielder Wally Moon, second baseman Jim "Junior" Gilliam, third baseman Maury Wills (who played shortstop for many years following), and the outstanding catcher, Johnny Roseboro, who had replaced the injured Roy Campanella sometime earlier.

The game, itself, was fun to watch as pitcher Johnny Podres out-dueled Don Schwall in a super pitcher's battle, 1-0. Johnny had that outstanding curveball that "dropped off a table." It was a thing of beauty to watch. Roseboro singled in Jim Gilliam to win it in the bottom of the ninth inning. It was another example of the great baseball games we were destined to see in the future.

Marilyn and I have attended many games at Dodger Stadium. It is an excellent place to watch baseball. It is a "must" for baseball fans visiting Southern California.

Milwaukee Brewers, County Stadium:

On June 7, 1985 we drove to County Stadium, Milwaukee to see the Brewers play the New York Yankees. It was a beautiful summer day and ended up in a slugfest with the Brewers winning 10-9. The two clubs pounded out 27 hits between them. We had commitments in the city and decided to skip the game, get our business done and drive on to Chicago the next morning. We were impressed with the old ballpark that served the fans of Milwaukee from 1970 through 2000.

Milwaukee Brewers, Miller Field:

On September 7, 1999 we were visiting Milwaukee at a reunion of my old navy ship, the LST 839. It gave us an opportunity to visit the new Miller Park under construction. A tragic crane accident in which three workers lost their lives had occurred in July. Their goal of having the opening game in the new park in April 2000 was moved up to April 2001. It took months to get the project back on schedule. There were as many as 500 workers on the project at any one time.

We viewed the damage of the accident and tried to imagine how the new park would look. As it has turned out Miller Park is one of the best in major league baseball. They did, indeed, open their season at Miller Park on April 6, 2001. President George W. Bush threw out the first pitch and a sellout crowd of 42,024 were in attendance. The Brewers defeated the Cincinnati Reds 5-4 as Brewer Richie Sexson hit a home run to win it.

Montreal Expos, Olympic Stadium:

As we headed toward Toronto for our 1985 Kiwanis International Convention we stopped in Montreal to see that great city. On June 28 we went to Olympic Stadium (Stade Olympique) to watch the Montreal Expos meet the Philadelphia Phillies. This was a unique experience with the combination of English and French languages interpreting the game to the fans. We were told that 21 radio stations beamed out their broadcasts in French.

It was well played early in the game. Suddenly, the skies opened up and a cloudburst caused a deluge on the field through the oblong opening of the roof. There was so much water that they had to bring in a vehicle-like vacuum that sucked up the water off the astroturf and emptied it through a huge tube to the side. We were amazed to see how quickly they removed all that water from the field. In twenty minutes the game resumed.

The Expos won the game 5-3. Players of note that night were Mike Schmidt, Hall of Famer, and Garry Maddox of Philly. For Montreal it was Tim Raines and Terry Francona. The latter went on to manage the Boston Red Sox in their historical victory in the World Series over the New York Yankees in 2004.

In 2003 the Expos played 22 games in Puerto Rico's Hiram Bithorn Stadium. In 2005 the franchise was moved to Washington D.C. where they became the Washington Nationals.

They played their first season in Robert F. Kennedy Stadium but a new park is being planned for the future.

Montreal Expos, Hiram Bithorn Stadium:

On November 10, 1993 we started a tour of Puerto Rico to see baseball stadiums on the island. Our first experience was at Hiram Bithorn Stadium (Estadio Hiram Bithorn) where the Montreal Expos were to play 22 games in 2003. We saw the Santurce Crabbers play the Mayaguez Indians. It was excellent baseball. That really was not surprising when one realizes that many Puerto Rican players are in the American and National Leagues.

The name of the stadium was chosen because Hiram Bithorn was the first Puerto Rican player going to the major leagues after signing with the Chicago Cubs in April 1942. Please see Story 83 (Hiram Bithorn) for more information.

The stadium, itself, is small by big league standards holding just 19,000 fans. It is 315' down the left field line and 313' to the right field corner. The distance to center field is 396'. It had a grass field when we attended but Astroturf has been installed recently.

We saw some of the other ballparks on the island. These make for a good winter league. Many American players come to play there in the off-season. In addition to Hiram Bithorn Stadium, the following teams and stadiums are currently active: Caguas Criolles (Creoles), Caroline Gigantes (Giants), Manati Athenians, Mayaguez Indios (Indians), and the Ponce Leones (Lions). All the parks are well kept and adequate for their communities.

As a side note, I would like to recommend that visitors going to Puerto Rico try and see El Yunque, the only tropical rainforest in the national park system. It is located about 35 miles east of the capital city of San Juan. It has some excellent hiking trails, unique colorful parrots and other animals, various plants and trees and interesting sights. I recommend this in a book about baseball because it was such an excellent experience for us as we visited ballparks.

New York Mets, Shea Stadium:

Ken & Marilyn Proctor at empty Shea Stadium.

When the Dodgers and Giants departed New York in 1957 the city was left with just one baseball team, the Yankees. By 1962 the city was awarded an expansion franchise, the New York Mets (Metropolitans). Ground was broken in 1961 for a new stadium at Flushing Meadows and in the meantime the Mets played for two years at the old Polo Grounds. While it was admittedly antiquated, the name of that old park always had a romantic ring to it.

But on April 17, 1964 Shea Stadium was opened. It was named after a lawyer, William A. Shea, who was instrumental in ultimately securing the expansion franchise for New York. It was a grand stadium with five tiers. It had a remarkable elevator system and seated 55,601 fans. It had a natural grass field and supported both baseball and football games. It is still pretty much the same stadium now with the exception of having seats added or replaced. I am told that the only negative at Shea Stadium is the constant drone of airplanes landing or taking off at nearby LaGuardia Field.

An interesting note is that the New York Yankees played there in 1974-1975 while Yankee Stadium was being renovated. There has been talk of building a new stadium nearby to replace Shea Stadium but such a plan has come to a halt. There have been discussions, however, about renovating Shea.

We arrived at the ballpark in 1985 on a day when the Mets were out of town. But, as with Tiger Stadium in Detroit, a friendly field manager allowed us to come, look around, and take pictures. It was another awesome experience for us as we recalled "The Miracle Mets" of 1969. Little did we know that one year later it would be the sight of an unbelievable world championship victory over the Boston Red Sox.

Philadelphia Phillies, Veterans' Stadium:

Our annual reunion of my World War II ship, the LST 839, ended Sunday morning, September 17, 2000 in Baltimore, Maryland. We drove up the east coast in time to go to Vet's Stadium in Philly, a 1:35 p.m. game. It was a beautiful sunny day and 15,486 showed up to see it. Randy Wolf effectively scattered five hits for the Phils to defeat Florida, 6-5. Another Philly, Bobby Abreu hit his 24th home run while Marlin Preston Wilson hit his 28th of the season.

We had always wanted to go to "The Vet," (Veteran's Stadium) and, in this case, even more so because a new stadium was in the works and the old Vet was going down like so many in the past. This, of course, was the scene of many of Philadelphia's great successes over the years. Names came to mind like Robin Roberts, Mike Schmidt, Steve Carlton, Richie Ashburn and the Whiz Kids, Tug McGraw and even the Cincinnati pair, Pete Rose and Joe Morgan, all Philly stars. And when one mentions Philadelphia, almost automatically pops up the name of Connie Mack, the sage old manager.

As we headed out of town we stopped at "Pat's" for the traditional Philly cheese steak sandwich. Ummm, good!!! If you go there don't miss it. They say that at "Gino's," that is directly across the street from Pat's, sandwiches are equally tasty.

"The Vet" was demolished in 2004 and the Phillies moved into their new field, Citizen's Bank Park. It holds 43,500 and is located immediately next to the old Veteran's Stadium site. It has natural grass and is beautiful. They have done an outstanding job of providing the Philadelphia citizenry with a great ballpark.

Candlestick Park, San Francisco.

San Francisco Giants, Candlestick Park:

This wind-blown park received its name because of its location overlooking Candlestick Cove on San Francisco Bay. The name was derived because of the now-extinct "Candlestick bird" that lived there at one time.

The first game was played at "The Stick," its nickname, on April 12, 1960. The big stadium was completed two years before Dodger Stadium opened four hundred miles south. The two franchises were in competition with everything from baseball itself to the type of facilities it provided fans.

Candlestick Park was known for its winds which blew in from left centerfield and out towards right centerfield. When constructed it held 43,765 fans and was enlarged later to 58,000 capacity. Originally, there was an opening in the outfield toward the bay. It was enclosed and seats were added to, presumably, keep out the howling winds. But, when completed the winds swirled about the stadium and were just as strong as before.

Often, fog would roll in on summer evenings and make the park a dismal place to watch baseball. It would become cold and was often accompanied by those swirling winds. Some estimate that if Willie Mays had been playing anywhere else he might have hit 800 home runs. The heavy wind from the left field line held up many of Willie's long balls.

The last Giant game was played there on September 30, 1999 although the San Francisco 49er football team still plays there. Four years previously the 3Com Corporation bought the naming-rights and it was known as 3Com Park for several years. In 2004, the naming rights of the ball park were purchased by Monster Cable Products and some call it Monster Park. But, in many minds it will always be Candlestick Park.

It is interesting to note that the park originally had bluegrass in 1960 and it was changed to artificial turf in 1970. But, in 1979 bluegrass was replanted and is there today. Six World Series games and two All Star games were played there.

Marilyn and I went to see ball games there several times. On one occasion we took Marilyn's ninety-year old mother. We caught a beautiful sunny day and "Dolly," a real baseball fan, thoroughly enjoyed it. On July 10, 1977 we saw the Giants meet the Atlanta Braves. Two big innings for the Giants wrapped it up, 12-5. That was the last time we saw the incredible Willie McCovey play a game. Willie hit 28 home runs that year and ended his career three years later with a total of 521 round trippers and 1,555 RBIs.

We have not attended a game at San Francisco's Pacific Bell Park or SBC Park, as it is now called. It is a beautiful stadium, well placed and convenient for fans. With the bad reputation of Candlestick Park and its strong winds, they now advertise that this park is located where it is warmer and the winds are not a problem. It would be fun to go there and see a home run hit into the water of McCovey Cove over the right field fence.

St. Louis Cardinals, Busch Stadium:

St. Louis was always of great interest to me because when I was a youngster my mother told me of going into town from her little community of Troy, Missouri, 50 miles north of the big city. Her father (my grandpa), Johnny Gear, took the family to Sportsman Park many times to see the Cardinals play baseball. She said it was one of her favorite activities. Rogers Hornsby was one of her favorites.

On May 20, 1993, Marilyn and I were in St. Louis where we saw the Cards defeat the Cubs 6-3. Bob Tewksbury scattered six hits and walked none to get the victory. Ozzie Smith, Ray Lankford and Todd Zeile starred for the Cardinals while Mark Grace and Sammy Sosa played well for Chicago. Zeile is a fellow UCLA Hall of Famer who has 16 years of major league baseball behind him. Todd has 253 home runs and has driven in 1,110 runs. He played for 11 different clubs over his career, his first seven with St. Louis.

We enjoyed going to Busch Stadium. It is located right downtown very near the Mississippi River and the huge St. Louis Gateway Arch. The stadium and the arch both opened in April 1966. The old Busch Stadium is being demolished and the New Busch Stadium will open in April 2006.

Final Comments: According to my count Marilyn and I have ten more parks to visit to complete all major league cities. These would be Cleveland, Colorado, Florida, Houston, Oakland, Pittsburg, San Diego, Tampa Bay, Texas and Washington. Of course, in the meantime more parks may be built and others perhaps torn down. It is even possible that new cities will be added. But, whatever the future holds for major league baseball parks, Marilyn and I would not change a thing with our hobby. It has given us many great memories and we have enjoyed it. In addition to these major league parks visited, we have gone to various minor league and community parks. They all have the one common characteristic —baseball games are played there and many Americans love it!

STORY 38:

The National Baseball Hall Of Fame

As long as I can remember I had heard of the celebrated "Baseball Hall of Fame." I never dreamed I would ever have the opportunity to see it. However, my dreams came true. On June 11, 1985 Marilyn and I had our first opportunity to visit this shrine of baseball. And on September 21, 1987 we once again visited there. One visit was just not enough to soak up all that baseball history.

The route to Cooperstown, the location of the celebrated hall and museum, is in beautiful upstate New York. There are small towns, farms and low hills. Lakes and streams are scattered all over the area. What a setting! It lies between the Adirondack and Catskill Mountains and seventy miles from the state capital, Albany.

When we arrived we did not know where to go first. The decision was made to go inside the hall and museum. It was an incredible experience. We looked at the many historical items from baseball's past. As we entered there was a large statue of Babe Ruth along with other distinguished relics of the past. It was almost too much to take in at one time. One source said there are more than 2.6 million items on display.

Many changes have been made since. While our visits seem like yesterday to us, twenty years have passed and improvements have made it even more outstanding. We understand many more additions are planned for the future.

They now have a Grandstand Theater on the second floor in which visitors can enjoy a 13-minute movie titled, "The Baseball Experience." They

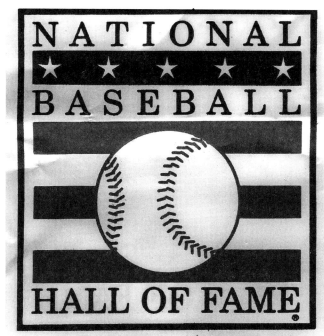

www.baseballhalloffame.org ★ 888-Hall-of-Fame

recommend seeing this movie before you start your tour. The next step is to move into the "19th Century Exhibit" depicting the game from its earliest roots right up to current baseball. Still on the second floor, "Today's Game Exhibit" gives one access to a major league clubhouse and a manager's office.

Moving up to the third floor, one may see the popular "Records Room." It features all kinds of statistical records of past and current players. The "Baseball Awards" exhibit shows actual awards including Most Valuable Player trophies, Gold Glove awards, Silver Bats, Cy Young awards and more. The "Autumn Glory Post-Season" exhibit is next where one may see every World Series program dating back to 1903. The exhibit has "touch-screen" capabilities describing every World Series ever played.

"The Plaque Gallery" features bronze plaques of all members of the Hall of Fame. They are very impressive and are displayed beautifully. Then comes the "Beyond the Plaque Gallery" which has memorabilia about baseball's announcers and sportswriters. It includes various movies about baseball.

The hall and museum are open from 9:00 a.m. to 9:00 p.m. from May 27 to Labor Day. In the "off-season" it is open from 9:00 a.m. to 5:00 p.m. Admission fees are $14.50 for adults, $9.50 for seniors, $5.00 for children 7-12 and children under 7 are free.

We walked over to the nearby legendary Abner Doubleday Field and sat in the grandstands trying to take in where we were and all of the long history behind it.

We wandered around the stadium with a feeling of awe. It is a beautiful little field. An annual Baseball Hall of Fame game is played there every year in the spring.

There are wonderful gifts and souvenirs to be purchased in the Museum Store. It has 4000 square feet of many interesting items. The address is Museum Store, 25 Main Street, Cooperstown, NY 13326. The telephone number is 1-888-Hall of Fame. I have purchased a number of items by mail. They accept credit cards.

Another location of interest is the Sandlot Kids' Clubhouse located in the Library Atrium. It is a hands-on area designed especially for children. Additionally, they have a Bullpen Theater for kids with daily programming in the spring and summer.

It was on June 12, 1939 when the National Baseball Hall of Fame and Museum was dedicated. At this monumental event a quote was made by the commissioner, Kenesaw Mountain Landis. He said, "To the pioneers who were the moving spirits of the game in its infancy and to the players who have been elected to the Hall of Fame, we pay just tribute. But I should like to dedicate this museum to all America."

On that day they enshrined the first five players who had been previously elected in 1936. They were Ty Cobb, Babe Ruth, Honus Wagner, Walter Johnson, and Christy Mathewson.

STORY 39:

Dick Butler, A Gentleman Of Class

I met Dick Butler in 1989. He was assisting my good friend and former teammate at UCLA, Dr. Bobby Brown, president of the American League. Dick was working for Bobby as special assistant to the AL President. His job, as it had been since 1969, was Supervisor of Umpires for the American League.

When Dick was visiting Seattle for his umpire observations he would call me from his office in Fort Worth, Texas, and set up a time for us to get together. In my conversations with him it seemed as if he knew everyone in baseball. I recall one time in the early 1990s when we were having breakfast that I asked Dick if he ever had occasion to be with Mel Ott. Mel was a favorite of mine who played outfield for the New York Giants. And Dick replied, "Oh, yes, Mel and I ran a baseball clinic together in Japan one time." I never mentioned a baseball person he did not know.

Dick started his baseball career in 1946 as an assistant to Commissioner

A. B. "Happy" Chandler. Incidentally, Mr. Chandler was the governor of the state of Kentucky at one time. Marilyn and I toured the governor' mansion in Frankfort, Kentucky, just recently and heard some good stories about "Happy" who was a very popular governor and commissioner. After his work with Commissioner Chandler, Dick became a minor league executive in 1953 as President of the South Atlantic League serving in that post for two years. He held the same position in the Texas League for the next eight years. From 1964 to 1969 he was the vice-president and general manager of the Dallas-Fort Worth Spurs. He became the Supervisor of Umpires working for American League Presidents Joe Cronin, Lee MacPhail, and Dr. Bobby Brown.

Dick retired in 1994 and spent his remaining days in Fort Worth, Texas. He passed away at age 92 on December 20, 2003. His burial took place in his hometown of Paris, Kentucky three days later. A special memorial service was held on January 16, 2004 at the ballpark in Arlington, Texas.

In the short time I knew Dick I found him to be a genuine, honest, and likeable friend. In his 49 years in baseball I understand his colleagues all felt the same way. He was truly a gentleman of class.

STORY 40:

Baseball At The Tokyo Dome With Yashitoka

In the winter of 2000 I was asked to represent the Kiwanis Club of Seattle at the International Convention in Taipei, Taiwan to be held in June 2001. Going that far from home, I accepted and decided to make a vacation of it and take Marilyn to Taipei, Tokyo, Beijing and Hong Kong.

Later in the spring of 2001 we were attending a Mariner game at Safeco Field in Seattle and happened to meet a young Japanese man by the name of Yashitoka. He was an exchange student from Japan. He sat at the game quietly not making sound and took in everything about him. It was obvious he enjoyed baseball and seemed to understand what was taking place on the field even though he was limited with his ability to speak English. We struck up a friendship and kept in touch by email afterwards.

Since we were going to Tokyo the following June we decided to meet there and see a game together at the Tokyo Dome. We kept him informed of our plans and location of our hotel in the city and he met us there at an appointed time.

Yashitoka "showed us the ropes," what trains to take, where to get food for the game, how to buy tickets, etc. We took him as our guest and watched a Pacific League game between the home team, Nippon Ham Fighters, and the visitors, Fukuoka Daiei Hawks. He made us aware of the many leagues and the development of baseball throughout Japan as a result of American exhibition games there years before.

Attendance was very good. In leftfield the bleachers were occupied by fans of the home team. They had horns and banners and all kinds of noisemakers. When their team was at bat they were constantly shouting and cheering for their team. On the other hand, the visitors occupied the right field bleachers and they demonstrated loudly when their team was at bat. Occasionally, both groups would be cheering and shouting at the same time making for a lively scene.

Yashitoka-san watched us and enjoyed our "taking everything in." The food was unique, of course, and we enjoyed some oriental goodies. Food prices as well as ticket costs were similar to those in America. And they played a good brand of baseball. We were amused when, in the middle of the game, the dirt part of the infield was smoothed out, as in the United States, but one thing was different. A group of girls came out on the grass part of the infield and danced and sang to the tune of "Y----M----C----A," American style.

The entire evening was fascinating. As we left our hotel the next day heading for Beijing, there was Yoshitaka with arms full of gifts for us. He was proudly wearing the tee shirt we had brought him which said, "Seattle Mariners." We hope our paths cross again to enjoy our common interest that speaks all languages, baseball.

STORY 41:

Spring Training Fun

With all of our interest in baseball through the years, attending spring training games and all that goes with it may be our most favored activity.

When I was working at my "day job," I could never get away for spring training baseball. Various friends encouraged us to do so but it did not happen until we fully retired. We know many people who plan their vacations around this unique and special experience. We sometimes think we might have used vacation time to start it sooner. There are two choices for spring training in the United States. That would be Arizona, dubbed "the Cactus League, and Florida, "the Grapefruit League."

The people who really convinced us it would be the intelligent thing to do were Ross and Shirley Cutter of Spokane, Washington. Ross, as an emeritus professor from Whitworth College and a former colleague of mine when I was on staff there, has an annual schedule compatible with the joys of spring training. He and Shirley, and sometimes their family members, have been going for more than ten years.

We have now joined them and have been going for five years ourselves. We meet in Phoenix, Arizona in March where we have the opportunity to see six teams in each league. In the American League we watch the Angels, A's, Mariners, Rangers, Royals and White Sox. In the National League we see the Cubs, Brewers, Diamondbacks, Giants, Padres and Rockies.

The parks are great. They each hold about 10,000 fans and most are usually full or nearly so. We stay in a location where we can be reasonably near the Angels, A's, Cubs and Giants. It is a bit of a drive to the others. In fact, the Diamondbacks, Rockies and White Sox play in Tucson located about a two-hour drive south. To date, we have not driven that far. We sometimes buy our tickets ahead of time in order to be sure to secure seats. Many games sell out. It is amazing to see how many people travel to these locations to watch spring training baseball.

It is our usual procedure to try and see as many different teams as possible. Of the twelve clubs in Arizona it is not uncommon for us to see eight or nine of them during our standard two-week stay.

Ross and Shirley know many of the good eating establishments in the area. They lived there previously when Ross was doing some academic work at Arizona State University. They know how to get around the city. Our eating experiences always prove to be a very enjoyable part of the trip.

We rent a car when we arrive. One really needs a car to get around. There is a good bus system in the greater Phoenix area, but having a car is a must. Insofar as housing is concerned, one needs to search around for a hotel or motel that fits his needs. Some people come for more than a month and lease a home, condominium or apartment.

All of us are acquainted with various

Top: The Ross Cutters and Ken Proctors at Phoenix Diablo Stadium

Middle: The 7th inning stretch and Ross Cutter loves to sing, one, two, three strikes, YOU'RE OUT!"

Bottom: Ken and Marilyn Proctor at Peoria, Arizona

friends living in the general area. We try to take them out for a meal or go to games together when the opportunity arises. One good friend is Marcia Dashiell, a former All American basketball player from Whitworth College. She meets us for dinner and/or baseball games from time to time. She is a true baseball fan. However, her favorite team is the Atlanta Braves and they train in Florida, much to the dismay of Marcia. She would like to have them in Arizona. Please see Story 156 (Marcia Dashiell).

Another great Phoenix friend of our's is Howard Collins. He played for me at Chaffey High School in the 1950s and was on two of our California Interscholastic Federation (CIF) championship clubs. Howard played in the infield and generally at third base and went on to star at Chaffey College and UCLA. He worked with the FBI for many years and now works in Phoenix in another business.

Marilyn and I have traveled in Florida and visited most of the spring-training baseball parks there. However, we have never visited in March when they train. We had a great time in the mid-80s visiting Vero Beach where the Dodgers train. It was our favorite venue down there.

We certainly recommend going to see spring training games. It is an opportunity for serious baseball fans to study the various teams and attain a reasonably good knowledge of how each team might fare for the upcoming season. Try it! We think you will like it!

STORY 42:

Throwing Out The First Pitch At Major League Baseball Games

When I went to work at the PEMCO Financial Center in Seattle, Washington, I discovered that the firm was active in all kinds of children's and young people's activities. This was due basically to the philosophy of the PEMCO CEO, Stanley O. McNaughton. His company had been very successful from a business standpoint and it was his intention to give something back to the community. In fact, he gave much back to the community by his support of, not just children, but all kinds of people. He was truly a generous citizen and typical of many of his generation who supported a plethora of good causes.

Because major league baseball provided a venue of fun for many Seattle families, Mr. McNaughton backed the sport by purchasing season tickets annually and advertising PEMCO on the "big screen" in the outfield. Consequently, the

Seattle Mariners asked to have one of our people "throw out the first pitch" at various American League games. Fortunately for me I was asked to throw out the first pitch on a number of occasions.

The person in charge of this activity for the Mariners was Al "Moose" Clauson, one of the great guys in the baseball world. Please see more information in Story 153 (Moose Clauson).

The first time I did so was in 1991 at a Seattle/Toronto game. My catcher was Rusty Kuntz, a former major leaguer with the Sox, Twins and Tigers. Rusty was the M's first base coach.

I had the privilege again in 1992 at a Seattle/ Oakland game when my receiver was Omar Visquel, the Mariner shortstop. We had previously met Omar's fiance at a Tacoma Rainier Triple-A game when he was in the minors and that made our experience that evening somewhat special. Omar has gone on to be one of the great shortstops in major league history. Not only is his defense remarkable but his hitting has been vital to all his teams including Seattle, Cleveland and San Francisco.

When one throws out the first pitch the Mariners do a great job for the partici-

Top: Ken throwing first pitch at Kingdome.

Bottom: Omar Visquel, Moose Clauson, and Ken (after Ken threw out first pitch).

pant. They put the individual's picture on the big screen in the outfield, provide a personalized photograph with the catcher, and give him or her the baseball as a personal gift. I bring up the last point because in 1991 I asked "Moose" if he would get Ken Griffey, Jr., to sign the ball for me. Please see the following amusing account, Story 43 (Ken Griffey Jr.'s Signature Disappearing Act), regarding my gift baseball.

I would like to thank my best baseball buddy, Marilyn, for helping me with my "first pitch" responsibilities.

Whenever I was scheduled to pitch, she became my catcher during the days prior to the event and caught a few dozen pitches. She did a great job and the activity helped her to improve her throwing arm as well.

STORY 43:

Ken Griffey Jr.'s Signature Disappearing Act

Throwing out the first pitch at the Mariner/Blue Jay game in 1991 was exciting for me. I wanted a good memory of it and, as described in Story 42, I asked "Moose" to get a signature on it by Ken Griffey, Jr. "Moose" kept the ball for several weeks because it was difficult to get signatures from players during the season. Ultimately, he gave the ball to Junior who took it home.

Griffey went home for the winter and was unavailable. When spring rolled around "Moose" said that Melissa, Ken's wife, urged him to sign the ball and get it back to "Moose" since so much time had passed. As the 1992 season started, "Moose" gave me a call to tell me he had my signed ball. Success!! I placed it in my den along with all of my ball collection.

Time passed and about a year later I noticed the signature was fading. I did not think much about it but eventually the signature disappeared completely. I took the ball back to "Moose" and showed him. Both of us were baffled. He took the ball to Junior and he signed it again with a special pen. Success once again!!

The ball again sits in my den between "Hank Aaron" and "Bob Feller." It is a special ball in my collection especially because it lived once, faded, and came back to life.

Ken Griffey Jrs. signed baseball

STORY 44:

Celebrating Our Anniversaries At Safeco Field

Marilyn and I try to make our anniversaries special. After our fiftieth commemoration, instead of celebrating just once during the year, we start remembrances in the spring and continued right through until fall. Of course, the day itself, July 24, is the highlight of the year for us.

When we celebrated our Golden Anniversary, our minister son, Mike, gave us our original vows. It was a small ceremony just with the family. We dressed up for the occasion. Hannah and Rebekah, our granddaughters, wore long dresses and Mike and wife, Penny, wore special clothes. Grandson Jesse looked great, too. Son Scott took movies of the ceremony. Since that day we have spread it out from spring to fall.

On our 54th anniversary we came up with idea of putting the announcement on the huge Mitsubishi screen at Safeco Field during a baseball game. Along with birthdays and anniversaries of other fans involved, the screen read, "Ken and Marilyn Proctor, 54th anniversary." Since then we have had two more anniversaries placed on the big screen again and hope to continue this commemoration each year.

Some people have used such a venue to get married. It is fun for everyone and nice to have thousands of people cheer when two "tie the knot."

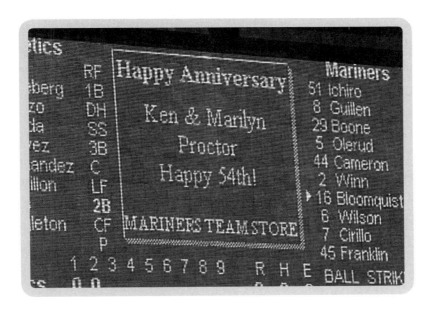

Ken & Marilyn's 54th Anniversary on Safeco Field Big Screen (they celebrate at Safeco Field every year).

Catching Foul Balls At Baseball Games

One would think that catching or securing foul balls at baseball games is largely a matter of "being in the right place at the right time." That is probably true. I have noticed that some people make a game of this achievement, wear a glove and position themselves to try to be in what they consider the right place.

I have never attempted to put myself in a position to get a foul ball. But, I certainly can say I have been fortunate to capture eight baseballs over the past twenty years. I do not use a glove. I think my favorite instance was in 1984 when I was seated in the right field bleachers at the Seattle Kingdome about twenty-five feet from the foul line. During batting practice rookie Alvin Davis hit a long drive and it came directly to me. I caught the ball and had a prize. I secured two more in that same area at other times.

On May 30, 1990 Marilyn and I took two friends, Erik and Mary Poulsen, to a baseball game between Seattle and Milwaukee. Erik was a colleague at work and had just recently moved to Seattle from Wisconsin. He and Mary wanted to see Milwaukee play. Also, Ken Griffey, Jr. was his favorite player.

In the fourth inning Griffey fouled off a ball and it came right to me. I caught it and handed it to Erik all in one motion. He was flabbergasted to think he was holding a ball off the bat of Junior. He put the ball in his jacket pocket to take home.

The next day at work Erik approached me and said, "I have some bad news. Last night I threw my jacket in the washing machine and forgot the baseball was in the pocket." One can imagine what happened to the ball. Erik was depressed to say the least. His Griffey ball was "mush." Incidentally, Erik left the job when he was elected as a state representative in the State of Washington Legislature. He still holds that position today.

Interestingly enough, a few nights later we were sitting down the left field line in the 12th row. A ball came to me once again off the bat of none other than Ken Griffey, Sr. Oddly enough, no one around me went for the ball and it was an easy catch.

In 1993 I went to a game with two other colleagues from work and a foul ball came to me in the upper deck (300 level). I was able to catch that ball although my boss, Ray Lundeen, swears I mauled a lady sitting in front of us as I tried to catch it. That simply was not true. (Well, it is possible we came in slight contact).

I think that was my seventh ball.

I read about a gentleman named Zack Hample who has collected more than 2,750 baseballs from forty different baseball parks. He must hold the national record. I don't think he has to worry about me overtaking him.

In March 2005, at spring training, Marilyn and I attended a game with Ross and Shirley Cutter at the Milwaukee Brewer Stadium in Maryvale, Arizona (Phoenix area). I secured a foul ball off the bat of Mariner catcher, Dan Wilson, who incidentally, retired from the team in 2005. It was my eighth ball to date and I hope to have Dan sign it for me.

Getting foul balls at baseball games has developed into an important tradition. It is fun and brings joy to the fans. Fans never know when a ball is going to hit and bounce right in their hands. I do not plan to fight to get a foul ball. Diving over seats, etc., is not for me. I wait until they come directly to me.

However, it is fun to see youngsters go after them with all the energy and strength they possess. More recently, ball girls or boys have made it a point to give foul balls to smaller children when possible. It is a joy to see their faces light up when that ball is placed in their little hands.

It is a fun tradition and one I hope they will never change. It has become a part of the game. I enjoy it when the fans clap for a good catch as the recipient holds it overhead for all to see. Thus far, I have never had a tossed bat come my way. Perhaps I should be happy with that fact.

STORY 46:

Music And Poetry Of Baseball

I think one of the most enjoyable experiences for baseball fans is singing "Take Me Out to the Ball Game," during the seventh inning stretch at ball games. It seems to bring us all together. When we enter the ballparks all over America we all become equal. We have no other identity except that we are baseball fans enjoying our great game together. And as we sing that wonderful old song, it seems to put on the finishing touches. The following version was written by Jack Norworth in 1908, composed by Albert Von Titzer and published by the York Music Company.

TAKE ME OUT TO THE BALL GAME
by Jack Norworth and Albert Von Titzer

Katie Casey was baseball mad.

Had the fever and had it bad,

Just to root for the home team crew,

Ev'ry soul Katie blew.

On a Saturday, her young beau,

Called to see if she'd like to go,

To see a show but Miss Kate said,

"No, I'll tell you what you can do.

"Take me out to the the ball game,

Take me out with the crowd,

Buy me some peanuts and crackerjack,

I don't care if I ever get back,

Let me root, root, root for the home team,

If they don't win it's a shame,

For it's one, two, three strikes, you're out,

At the old ball game."

Katie Casey saw all the games,

Knew the players by their first names,

Told the umpire he was wrong,

All along good and strong.

When the score was just two to two,

Katie Casey knew what to do,

Just to cheer up the boys she knew,

She made the gang sing this song.

Take me out to the ball game,

Take me out with the crowd,

Buy me some peanuts and crackerjack,

I don't care if I ever get back,

Let me root, root, root for the home team,

If they don't win it's a shame,

For it's one, two, three strikes, you're out,

At the old ball game."

Another version of the song was written by Mr. Norworth in 1927 which featured "Nelly Kelly" rather than "Katie Casey." Norworth was a successful vaudeville entertainer/songwriter.

When I was a youngster I heard a marvelous song on the radio one day. The sound of it and the words still haunt me. It was a big band with a young girl singing about "Joltin' Joe DiMaggio."

I still have the disc. It was recorded on Okeh Records at a speed of 78 RPM. The ballad was written by Ben Homer and Alan Courtney. Published in 1941, it was first performed by Les Brown and His Band of Renown. The vocalist was Betty Bonney.

It paid tribute to Joe DiMaggio and his celebrated 56-game hitting streak. Very popular with baseball fans, it went like this:

JOLTIN' JOE DIMAGGIO
by Ben Homer and Alan Courtney

Hello, Joe, whatta you know?
We need a hit so here I go,
Ball one (Yea!),
Ball two (Yea!),
Strike one (Boo!),
Strike two (Boo!),
(sound of the ball hitting a bat)
A case of Wheaties.
He started baseball's famous streak,
That's got us all aglow,
He's just a man and not a freak,
Joltin' Joe DiMaggio.
(CHORUS)
Joe, Joe DiMaggio,
We want you on our side.
He tied the mark at forty-four,
July the 1st you know,
Since then he's hit a good twelve more,
Joltin' Joe DiMaggio.
(CHORUS)
From coast to coast that's all you'll hear,
Of Joe the one-man show,
He's glorified the horsehide sphere,
Joltin' Joe DiMaggio.
(CHORUS)
He'll live in baseball's Hall of Fame,

He got there blow by blow,
Our kids will tell their kids his name,
Joltin' Joe DiMaggio.
We dream of Joey with the light brown plaque,
Joe, Joe DiMaggio,
We want you on our side.
And now they speak in whispers low,
Of how they stopped our Joe,
One night in Cleveland, Oh, Oh, Oh,
Goodbye streak, DiMaggio.

The copyright of this song is currently held by the Alan Courtney Music Company.

Baseball Titles

There are more than four hundred musical works and songs related to baseball. They range from comedy and frivolity to seriousness and reality. As baseball developed in the early part of the twentieth century writers, songwriters and others coined baseball as "The National Pastime." By the mid-20s it was generally designated America's National Game.

Songs poured out of the music establishments describing this game that had captured America's interest. It had become a diversion to help the population get through difficult times. Many of the songs told about that story.

The oldest published song I could find was titled "The Base Ball Polka" (1858). Please note that around 1910 they started putting the two words, "base" and "ball," as one word, "baseball." These are a few more interesting titles in chronological order:

Base Ball Waltz (1867)

Tyro Base Ball March (1870)

Our Noble Giant Nine (1889)

Play Ball (1890)

(There were eleven songs titled "Play Ball" between 1890 and 1955)

American League March (1901)

Take Me Out to the Ball Game (1906)

Watching the Ball Game March (1908)

Take Your Girl to the Ball Game (1908)

Those Grand Old Words, Play Ball (1909)

Baseball On the Brain (1910)

My Old Man is Baseball Mad (1910)

A Two Bagger (1910)

You've Made a Home Run With Me (1911)

When the Baseball Season's Going, I'll Be There (1916)

Casey At the Bat (1920)

I'm Baseball Crazy (1924)(the year I was born)

Ripp, Ripp, Ripp, Zipp-Zipp-Zipp (the Cardinals Won the Championship (1927)

Babe Ruth, Babe Ruth, We Know What He Can Do (1928)

Turn Me Loose at the Ball Game (1930)

It's a Grand Old Game (1931)

Our Team is Leading the Hit Parade (1936)

Joltin'Joe DiMaggio (1941)

Baseball (Fourteen songs written with this title 1919 to 1947)

Bronx Bill Is A Dyin' (cause the Dodgers Lost Their Last home game (1948)

Brooklyn Dodger Jump (1949)

It Happens Every Spring (1949) *(see comments at end of list)*

Say Hey, Willie Mays (1954)

Mickey Mantle Mambo (1956)

Shoeless Joe From Hannibal, Mo (1957)

Gimme the Good Ol' American League Pastime Baseball (1959)

Southpaw Waltz (1971)

There Used To Be a Ball Park Here (1973)

Willie, Mickey and the Duke (1981)

The ever-popular "Casey At the Bat" is well known as a poem and was also written as a song in 1920. Read through it and see how Ernest L. Thayer made it come alive as a never-to-be-forgotten baseball experience for the 5,000 fans attending.

Casey At the Bat
by Ernest L. Thayer

The outlook wasn't brilliant for the Mudville nine that day,
The score stood four to two, with but one inning more to play.
And then when Cooney died at first, and Barrows did the same,
A pall-like silence fell upon the patrons of the game.
A straggling few got up to go in deep despair,
The rest clung to the hope which springs eternal in the human breast.
They thought, "if only Casey could but get a whack at that,
We'd put up even money now, with Casey at the bat."
But Flynn preceded Casey, as did also Jimmy Blake,

And the former was a hoodoo, while the latter was a cake.

So upon that stricken multitude, grim melancholy sat,

For there seemed but little chance of Casey getting to the bat.

But Flynn let drive a single, to the wonderment of all,

And Blake, the much despised, tore the cover off the ball.

And when the dust had lifted, and men saw what occurred,

there was Jimmy safe at second and Flynn a-hugging third.

Then from five thousand throats and more there rose a lusty yell,

it rumbled through the valley, it rattled in the dell.

It pounded through on the mountain and recoiled upon the flat,

for Casey, mighty Casey, was advancing to the bat.

There was ease in Casey's manner as he stepped into his place,

There was pride in Casey's bearing and a smile lit Casey's face.

And when, responding to the cheers, he lightly doffed his hat,

no stranger in the crowd could doubt t'was Casey at the bat.

Ten thousand eyes were on him as he rubbed his hands with dirt,

Five thousand tongues applauded when he wiped them on his shirt.

Then, while the writhing pitcher ground the ball into his hip,

defiance flashed in Casey's eye, a sneer curried Casey's lip.

And now the leather-covered sphere came hurtling through the air,

and Casey stood a-watching it in haughty grandeur there.

Close by the sturdy batsman the ball unheeded sped-

"That ain't my style" said Casey. "Strike one!" the umpire said.

From the benches, black with people, there went up a muffled roar,

like the beating of the storm waves on a stern and distant shore.

"Kill him! Kill the umpire!" shouted someone in the stand,

and it's likely they'd have killed him had not Casey raised his hand.

With a smile of Christian charity, great Casey's visage shone,

he stilled the rising tumult, he bade the game go on.

He signaled to the pitcher, and once more the dun sphere flew,

but Casey still ignored it, and the umpire said, "Strike two!"

"Fraud!" cried the maddened thousands, and echo answered "Fraud!"

But one scornful look from Casey wouldn't let that ball go by again.

The sneer had fled from Casey's lip, the teeth are clenched in hate,

He pounds, with cruel violence, his bat upon the plate.

And now the pitcher holds the ball, and now he lets it go,

And now the air is shattered by the force of Casey's blow.

Oh, somewhere in this favored land the sun is shining bright.

The band is playing somewhere, and somewhere hearts are light.
And somewhere men are laughing, and little children shout,
but, there is no joy in Mudville—mighty Casey has struck out.

This poem has been known and appreciated since 1920, taught in schools, and heard in groups and lectures in all the world. It is one of the treasured poems of scholars everywhere. America owes a debt of gratitude to Mr. Thayer for making it part of our nation's history.

Willie, Mickey and The Duke by Terry Cashman

Later in the 80s another great song hit the charts. When the great baseball decades of the 50s, 60s, and 70s went by, many memories had been established in the minds of fans everywhere. An avid baseball fan, Terry Cashman, seemed to capture the feelings of all baseball aficionados in 1981 when he wrote a long titled, "Willie, Mickey and The Duke." His theme was "I'm talking baseball." These are the words to his popular song:

The Whiz Kids had won it,
Bobby Thomson had done it.
And Yogi read the comics all the while,
Rock 'N Roll was being born,
Marijuana we would scorn,
So down on the corner
The national past-time went on trial.
(Refrain)
We're talkin' baseball
Kluszewski Campanella
Talkin' baseball
The Man and Bobby Fella
The Scooter, the Barber, and the Newc
They knew them all from Boston to Dubuque
Especially Willie, Mickey, and The Duke
Well Casey was winning,
Hank Aaron was beginning
One Robbie going out, one coming in,
Kiner and Midget Cadell,
The Thumper and Mel Parnell,
And Ike was the only one winning down in Washington.

(REFRAIN)

Now my old friend

The Bachelor

Wee he swore he was the Oklahoma Kid.

And Cookie played hooky

To go and see the Duke,

And me I always loved Wil Willie,

Those were the days.

Well now it's the 80's,

And Brett is the greatest,

And Bobby Bonds could play for everyone.

Rose is at the Vet,

Rusty again is a Met,

And the great Alexander is pitching again in Washington.

I'm talkin' baseball,

Like Reggie, Quis and Berry

Talkin' baseball,

Carew and Gaylord Perry,

Seaver, Bobby Schmidt and Vida Blue,

If Cooperstown is calling, it's no fluke,

They'll be with Willie, Mickey, and the Duke.

Willie, Mickey, and the Duke (Say hey, say hey, say hey)

It was Willie, Mickey and the Duke (Say hey, say hey, say hey)

I'm talkin' Willie, Mickey and the Duke (Say hey, say hey, say hey)

Baseball is woven into the fabric of American life and music has been an important part of it.

STORY 47:

Introducing Joe Garagiola

On Friday, May 21, 1999, ARC, a philanthropic organization of King County in Seattle, had invited
Joe Garagiola to be the featured speaker at a special
luncheon. They asked if I would do the honors in
introducing him. A group of us met mid-morning
at Tully's, a gourmet coffee shop downtown, to get
the aforementioned noon program organized. Tom
O'Keefe, owner of Tully's and a friend of Joe, hosted
the meeting.

Ken & Joe Garagiola
(Joe Garagiola had just
finished speaking at
the Cavanaugh Inn in
downtown Seattle).

I had not met the famed NBC host and announcer previously. We had the opportunity to sit and chat
for better than an hour about the day's program and other things. I found that Joe
and his wife, Audrie, were married within months and in the same year as Marilyn and I. Also, Joe and I were almost exactly the same age within a few weeks.

It was enjoyable talking baseball with the former major leaguer-turned TV
star. We had much in common. I queried him about various historical points
of his past and I included the information in my introduction. Joe had grown
up in St. Louis and lived directly across the street from Yogi Berra. They played
baseball together as youngsters. Both are in the St. Louis Walk of Fame with
more than 250 of other St. Louis dignitaries. These individuals come from many
areas of life including baseball, politics, theater, military, art and more. To name
a few, they are Branch Rickey, Stan Musial, Dizzy Dean, Rogers Hornsby, T. S.
Eliot, Charles Lindbergh, Virginia Mayo, Ulysses S. Grant, Tennessee Williams,
Joseph Pulitzer, William T. Sherman and Charlie Russell. This is an impressive
list to say the least.

The most unusual happening occurred. In our conversation, Joe mentioned he
was looking for a Charles S. "Chub" Feeney baseball to give to the National Base-
ball Hall of Fame in Cooperstown, New York. He wanted to get Henry "Hank"
Aaron's signature on the ball because Feeney was the president of the National
League at the time Hank hit his home run number 715 to move ahead of Babe
Ruth's old record of 714.

Here is the interesting part of this story. I cannot tell you why but in the trunk
of my car I had a number of "Chub Feeney" baseballs. When I told Joe the balls
were just a couple of blocks away in my automobile his mouth dropped. He said,

"You're kidding me, aren't you?" I said, "Give me a few moments and I will be right back." I went to the car and brought back five balls. I gave him three balls, one for the Hall of Fame, one for himself, and one to get Hank Aaron's signature and send it back to me. Joe signed the other two balls, one for our 50th anniversary just two months away, and one for my baseball collection in my den to go with many others. I assume the original ball is in the Hall of Fame and I do not know what happened to the ball for me. However, Joe gave me another ball (not a Chub Feeney ball) with Hank's signature on it and one I cherish very much.

I saw Joe later in Arizona at a Diamondbacks game at Bank One Ballpark during spring training. Marilyn and I were there with Dr. and Mrs. Ross Cutter. Please see Story 41 (Spring Training Fun). Joe tried to meet us after the game. He was not able to make it and I am sure his schedule was tight and something came up. I have written back and forth with him and am in brief touch today.

Joe signed a baseball contract with the St. Louis Cardinals in 1946 and stayed with them until 1951 when he went to Pittsburg. Having stayed with the Pirates only two years, he went with the Chicago Cubs in 1953-1954. He made a quick move to the New York Giants and the same year retired from baseball to announce St. Louis Cardinal games. Joe finished with 676 games player, a .257 lifetime batting average, 42 home runs, and 255 RBIs. His World Series marks were five games, with a .316 batting average and four RBIs.

Later he signed with NBC where he spent thirty years doing baseball announcing and other shows.

Garagiola is considered by many as one of the true characters of the game of baseball. I certainly enjoyed meeting and chatting with him. His speech that day in Seattle was well received. I found Joe to be an interesting gentleman and considered it a privilege that our path's crossed.

CHAPTER 2

Stories About My Favorite Baseball Announcers

The baseball announcers named here are by no means an all-inclusive list of the great broadcasters of all time. No, they are simply a group of outstanding announcers who were influential somehow in my baseball life. Certainly these people have been an important part of the game as it has developed through the years. Let's start alphabetically with Mel Allen and work our way to Vin Scully.

STORY 48:

Mel Allen—How About That?

To some baseball fans including this baseball fan, Mel Allen brings back childhood memories that will last forever. His voice was known by millions of fans as he announced New York Yankee games from 1939 to 1964. He grew up in Alabama and attended law school at the University of Alabama in Tuscaloosa. Perhaps this is why his melodic voice had a tinge of that beautifully sounding southern drawl. His love for baseball among other sports led him to a place among the best in his profession, sports announcing.

Fans knew him for his famous line, "How about that?" He was among those to describe a home run as "going, going, gone!" Please see Chapter 8, Story 216, Baseball Trivia, Item 6 about Harry Harman. Interestingly enough, Mel's first broadcast was an Alabama/Tulane football game. He was associated with the CBS radio network and did all sorts of announcing. He even did "Truth or Consequences," a game show.

Mel did 24 All Star baseball games and 20 World Series. Also, he announced 14 Rose Bowls, 2 Orange Bowls, and 2 Sugar Bowls. He did voiceover narration for Fox Movietone newsreels.

He returned to the Yankees in 1976 on SportsChannel and did Yankee games once again until the late 80s.

Three years earlier, 1977, he hosted "This Week in Baseball" (TWIB), a highly popular syndicated show that captured the imagination of baseball fans across the nation. He did that show until his death in 1996.

Allen is a member of the Baseball Hall of Fame as well as the Radio Hall of Fame. In my mind, he was certainly one of the best announcers and broadcasters in baseball history. The tone of that great voice will always be in my memory.

STORY 49:

Red Barber—The Ol' Redhead

As a young teenager I enjoyed hearing "the ol' redhead" about as much as any baseball announcer. His southern accent was classic. Even though he was known as the "Voice of the Brooklyn Dodgers," many fans are not aware that he spent thirteen years with the New York Yankees and five years with the Cincinnati Reds.

He blazed the announcing trail in a number of ways. On August 26, 1939, Red broadcasted the first professional baseball game ever televised. It was a double-header at Ebbetts Field in Brooklyn between the Dodgers and the Reds.

Officially he was Walter Lanier Barber. His manner was renowned for flare, liveliness, fairness and accuracy. He was a professional in every sense of the word. Red was known for more than his baseball announcing although the grand old game was his real forte. He covered five Army/Navy football games and four NFL championship contests. He announced 13 World Series and four All-Star baseball games.

In my baseball world, Red's greatest contribution to the game was to help make fans aware of the prowess and skills of Vin Scully. Red discovered Vinny in a happenstance manner as he, as Sports Director of CBS, asked Vin to do a Boston/Maryland football game on a Saturday. One thing led to another and Barber asked Scully to be the number three man in the Dodger's booth. Vin was just 22 years of age. Please read Story 62 (Vin Scully) for more of this drama about these two "redheads."

Red passed on in 1992 after entertaining listeners on the "Morning Edition" of National Public Radio with Bob Edwards for many years. Red Barber was one-of-a-kind and certainly among the most prolific in his field. He was inducted into baseball's Hall of Fame in 1984.

STORY 50:

Hal Berger— An Old Time Baseball Announcer

When I was a " baseball-nut" ten-year old in Los Angeles in the 1930s, my favorite local announcer was Hal Berger. He made the Triple A Los Angeles Angel games exciting. When the team was out of town playing in Seattle, Portland, San Francisco, and Sacramento among others, Hal re-created these games in a small booth at the radio studio.

I was "living those games." I made up a scoresheet, entered the line-ups, and kept score of every part of the game. Hal Berger made it live for me whether the Angels were home or away (re-created games). Many who read this book will think back of the announcer in their hometowns who did exactly the same thing for them. In fact, Ronald Reagan was known for re-creating games on the radio in the 1930s. Please see Story 61 (Ronald Reagan).

Hal was not inducted into any type of hall of fame in his work. But, he made baseball live for me. Hal was a great part of my life. I am deeply indebted to him for many pleasurable days of enjoying his broadcasts.

STORY 51:

Jack Buck—
He Is One To Remember

The gravel-voice of Jack Buck is deeply embedded in my sub-conscious. He is among a number of announcers who could be labeled "Mr. Baseball." The famous Harry Carey was the lead St. Louis Cardinal announcer in 1954 when Jack Buck joined him. Jack continued to broadcast the Cardinals as well as many other important events for nearly 50 years.

Buck called World Series, Super Bowls, and professional bowling on a national scale over those years. He was a walking encyclopedia of baseball. Here is an interesting bit of trivia. When Jack obtained his job with the Cardinals he won the position over Chick Hearn, celebrated Los Angeles Laker Basketball announcer. It was a good decision for both of them.

Jack and I had similar birthdays. He was born just one month before me in August of 1924. We have other similarities. Jack went overseas with the Army to Germany in the mid-1940s while I was heading to the Pacific in the Navy. Jack returned to attend Ohio State University and began his career in broadcasting at the school's radio station. At the same time I returned to UCLA to start my profession of teaching and coaching.

Some of Buck's quotes are classic. In game one of the 1988 World Series the Dodger's Kirk Gibson hit a game-winning two-run homer off Oakland's Dennis Eckersley in the bottom of the ninth inning. Joe exclaimed, "I don't believe what I just saw." And when the Cardinals would finish a game with a victory, Joe traditionally said, "That's a winner!" The comment each time made him dear to St. Louis fans. When a key homerun was hit, Jack would say, "Go crazy, folks, go crazy." In 1998 when Mark McGuire tied Roger Maris' home run record, Jack commented, "Pardon me for a moment while I stand up and applaud," as the crowd noise told the story.

Jack was inducted into the Baseball Hall of Fame broadcaster's wing in 1987. He is a member of radio's hall of fame as well. Many other honors were bestowed upon John Francis Buck and all well deserved. He is a member of the storied St.

Louis Walk of Fame. Jack's son, Joe, is now the lead play-by-play broadcaster for baseball and football at Fox. So, the Buck announcing tradition continues. Jack Buck gave us many exciting baseball moments from behind the microphone.

STORY 52:

Harry Caray— A One-of-a-Kind Great Broadcaster

When the name of Harry Caray is mentioned most fans think of two things. First, the great line of Harry's, "Cubs win, Cubs win!" And, secondly, they visualize Harry leading the singing at Wrigley Field of "Take Me Out to the Ball Game." Harry sensationalized this tradition in 1971. Harry was singing the famous old tune and a microphone was placed in the broadcast booth in order that the fans could hear him. From that time on the tradition was in place.

Harry began his radio career at age 19 and spent a few years in Illinois and Michigan "learning the ropes." Soon thereafter, he became the announcer for the St. Louis Hawks NBA basketball team and broadcast for the University of Missouri. In the meantime he covered three Cotton Bowl games.

Caray's baseball career began in 1945 when he announced for the St. Louis Cardinals. He continued that job until 1969. As described in Story 51 (Jack Buck), he brought Jack on the scene in 1954 to eventually broadcast Cardinal games for almost fifty years. Harry moved to Oakland in 1970 to cover the A's at the microphone. This was quickly followed by a move to Chicago where he broadcast White Sox games for ten years.

Then came the move where Harry was best known. He became the Cubs lead announcer in 1982 and remained there until his death in 1998.

Two other sayings that Harry created were, "It might be, it could be, it is," and the memorable "Holy Cow!" Harry is a legend in Chicago and will always be known for his "down home" attitude and manner. He was a lovable guy who loved people. He leaves a son and grandson, Skip and Chip Caray, who carry on the name in broadcasting. Skip is the lead announcer at Atlanta for Brave's baseball and Chip now is the play-by-play broadcaster with the Cubs.

Harry was inducted into baseball's Hall of Fame, broadcasters' wing, in Cooperstown, New York in 1987. There are three "Harry Caray's" restaurants in the Chicago area where people still remember one of the great characters of the game. He is one broadcaster I will always remember as a genuine baseball fan. I listened to him whenever the opportunity arose. I miss him!

STORY 53:

Ken Coleman— An Unending Love for the Game

Marilyn and I were in Boston visiting the Henry Longfellow House on October 4, 1987. We had attended a Boston/Milwaukee game at Fenway Park the day before and decided to do some history searching this last day of the season.

We listened on our hand-held radio as Boston announcer Ken Coleman wrapped up this final game of the year. Roger Clemens had just bested Paul Mirabella 4-0. So, it was a Red Sox victory although they were mired in division standings some 15 games out of first place.

But we will never forget that special broadcast by Ken Coleman. He was so sincere as he talked sadly about the fact that the season was over. It was reality-check time. He reminisced about various happenings during the year and who would or would not return next year. It was like a funeral when remembering a great and wonderful friend. Baseball was over, at least for a time. His story went on as if he did not want to stop because when he did there would be no more baseball for six months. Finally, he relished the fact that the months would pass and April would soon be upon us. Baseball would return and the world will be good again.

Ken's voice was rich and deep. To us he sounded like the premier of announcers. He certainly knew his baseball inside and out. But it was his love for the game that shown above all else. It was beautiful. We will never forget it as we prepared to enter Longfellow House near Harvard University on that fall day in October.

Coleman spent many years in broadcasting. He covered the Cleveland Browns from 1952 to 1964. In 1966 he took over the Red Sox lead announcing job from Curt Gowdy, another prominent and distinguished announcer, who was moving on to NBC. Ken stayed with Boston until 1974 when he had a brief four-year stint with the Cincinnati Reds. Coleman returned to the Red Sox and was the play-by-play broadcaster until 1989. He has said that one of his favorite moments was announcing Carl Yazstremski's 3,000th hit and there were many more great moments for him.

Ken did the 1967 World Series for NBC and had previously covered Ohio State football as well as Cleveland Indian baseball. He authored many sports books. Also he often served as Master of Ceremonies of the famed annual New Hampshire Baseball Banquets where hundreds of baseball greats were honored through the years. We lost a fine announcer when Ken passed on in 2003.

He was among the best in the business for us. We are appreciative of his profound love for our great game.

STORY 54:

Dizzy Dean— Twenty Years Behind the Mike

Without question, Dizzy Dean was among the most interesting characters in baseball history. He had an amazing career until age 30. He was a rookie with the St. Louis Cardinals at age 21 in 1932. For the next eight years he built an incredible record. It was an injury received in an All Star game that essentially ended his playing career. Please see Story 4 (Dizzy Dean's Promise) regarding my first experience in trying to meet Ol' Diz.

In 1941, Dean joined the St. Louis Browns as their regular announcer until 1946. He actually left the booth and briefly pitched successfully for the Browns in 1947. He stayed with the Browns as broadcaster for the next two years when he left to do television broadcasting in New York City. He was very popular there with his unusual style. Dizzy returned to the Browns from 1952 to 1954 and was there until St. Louis moved to Baltimore to become the Orioles.

He joined the CBS broadcast of "The Game of the Week" and was an instant success. With his candid opinions, Dizzy "pulled no punches." He told as he saw it. Fans loved his high-spirited descriptions and homespun humor of events on the field. And his incorrect English complete with double negatives made it all the more interesting to fans. He once described the word, "slide", in the past tense. Dizzy's word was "slud." In addition to all these traits, Dizzy had trouble with names. It all added to the "Dean mystique." In the early 1960s Dizzy and Pee Wee Reese are given credit for bringing more and more fans to the game. They made a great team on the weekly CBS show.

Baseball lost one of its true individualists when Diz passed away in 1974. He played only six full seasons in the majors. There is no telling what he might have accomplished had he been able to play a normal number of years. Even with just six years he was inducted in the Baseball Hall of Fame in 1953. His announcing helped fill in the gaps for fans that wanted to see him play more active years. I know he was one of my favorites.

STORY 55:

Ron Fairly—
High Quality Player and Announcer

My first awareness of Ron Fairly was in 1956 when I was coaching at Chaffey High School in Ontario, California. Ron was a senior at Long Beach Jordan High School in Southern California.

My shortstop at Chaffey High School, Jerry Snider, who later signed with the Boston Red Sox, and Ron, were both batting in the mid-.500s and it appeared one or the other would be the top batter in the California Interscholastic Federation (CIF) that year. As it turned out Jerry ultimately had the highest average on the basis of his last turn at bat that year. Please see Story 183 (Jerry Snider). And Ron, along with Mike McCormick of Alhambra High School, was co-CIF Player of the Year. Ron went on to become one of baseball's top players and broadcasters for nearly 50 years.

I had lettered at UCLA in 1944, 1947, 1948, and 1949. I had many friends playing at USC across town (Los Angeles) and kept up with their ensuing teams. Ron was on some of those teams in the late 1950s and was an outstanding player for the Trojans.

Of course, Fairly's accomplishments as a major league baseball player are familiar to most fans. He played in the major leagues from 1958 to 1979. He has a .266 lifetime batting average with 215 homeruns, 1,044 RBIs in 2,442 games. He played for Los Angeles, Montreal, St. Louis, Oakland, Toronto and California. In four separate World Series, Ron played in 20 games batting .300 with two home runs and six RBIs. He won two World Series rings with the Dodgers.

After retiring in 1979 from baseball he became Sports Director of station KTLA in Los Angeles. In 1982 Ron turned to broadcasting. He was with the Dodgers until 1986, joined the San Francisco Giants in 1987 and spent six years there until 1992. He came to Seattle in 1993 and is still with the Mariners.

When Fairly came to Seattle I had occasion to meet him in a business arrangement with PEMCO, our company which was active in supporting the Mariners at that time. Ron was kind enough to visit us and help with a baseball promotion we were doing.

Fairly is noted for some of his radio and/or TV quotes. He commented one time, "Last night I neglected to mention something that bears repeating." A second one was, "It could permanently hurt a batter for a long time," as he spoke of an injury. Another was, "he fakes a bluff." The fact is that Ron is a teacher on the airwaves. I wrote a letter-to-the-editor of the Seattle Times Sports Section saying essentially that Ron takes the fans to baseball school everyday. It is true that he is one of the most prolific broadcasters in the business. He knows the game thoroughly and expresses his thoughts clearly and precisely.

This is a man whom I have enjoyed and appreciated both as a player and announcer. He is a credit to our great game.

STORY 56:

Ernie Harwell— An Accomplished Gentleman

In the summer of 1984 I received a call from George Toles, a Seattle friend of mine. He asked if I would like to join a few pals to have lunch with Ernie Harwell, the long-time Detroit Tiger announcer. I gave my reply in about three-tenths of a second. What an opportunity! This man is one of the "greats" in baseball broadcasting.

Ernie called major league baseball games for more than six decades. He was another of those with the rhythmic and mellow southern sound. The words just flowed from his mouth. They were so pleasant to the ear.

Oddly enough, Harwell had speech difficulty as a youngster. But with the help of his parents and several speech therapists Ernie overcame his problem by the time he reached twenty years of age. Because of his father's influence Ernie knew at an early age that he wanted to be a baseball announcer. Talk about fulfilling one's dream, Ernie knew where he was going and he went there.

Ernie was born in 1918 in Washington, Georgia, a small town in the northeastern part of the state. His father lost his furniture business and the family moved to Atlanta. Soon thereafter, the senior Harwell became ill and passed away. The family struggled to make ends meet. Ernie had a newspaper route earning two or three dollars a week. An interesting note—one of his customers was Margaret Mitchell, author of Gone With the Wind. He continued to listen to baseball games as he grew up.

After gaining some experience in sports by working for a newspaper, Ernie joined the Marines and wrote for their publication, Leatherneck. Ernie had a break by working some football games at Georgia Tech and doing two Masters Golf Tournaments in 1940 and 1941. It was not long before he was doing play-by-play for the Atlanta Crackers, the professional baseball team there at that time.

Harwell was the only broadcaster ever traded for a player when the Crackers sent him to Brooklyn in exchange for farmhand, Cliff Dapper in 1948. There is an interesting story regarding Cliff. It so happened that he and I went to the same high school, Washington, in Los Angeles. Later, in 1944, I was playing for UCLA against the U. S. Naval Training Station in San Diego. Please see Story 63 (1944 Team) when Cliff was a catcher on that San Diego team. Some of his teammates we faced were Bob Lemon, who later managed the Cleveland Indians, Ike Boone of the famous baseball Boone family (Bob, Bret, Aaron), Ed Bockman of the New York Yankees, Bob Sturgeon, Cubs and Braves, and George Vico of the Detroit Tigers.

Ernie joined the Dodger broadcast team in 1948. By 1950 he was lured to the New York Giants and broadcast the debut of Willie Mays. Then, from 1954 to 1959 he was the voice of the Baltimore Orioles. In Baltimore, Ernie and Hall of Famer George Kell became a team and in 1960 they formed a tandem known as Detroit's famous "twosome at the mike." In 1965, Kell took over the television duties and Harwell stayed with radio where he was most comfortable.

Many fans are not aware that Ernie was a writer and lyricist having authored several books and scores of songs. He even worked with the famed Johnny Mercer on some of his music. He has served as speaker at chapel services in team clubhouses. Ernie gave his testimony at an internationally televised Billy Graham Crusade. There is no end to the man's accomplishments. He even shot a hole in one on the golf course!!

Ernie was the first active announcer inducted into baseball's Hall of Fame at Cooperstown. That occurred in August 1981 and since then he has entered eight more Halls of Fame. His honors are too numerous to list here. Suffice it to say that this gentleman is an outstanding person in many ways. He has succeeded in whatever he has attempted and done it in a most humble manner. Ernie retired on September 15, 2002.

But, let's go back to that luncheon in Seattle in 1984. The Tigers were in town to play the Mariners and Ernie was free between games to have lunch with us. As I listened to him I realized the man is a veritable encyclopedia of baseball information. He was so kind and generous to field every question thrown his way and he did it with enthusiasm. Ernie displayed his Christian attitude in his responses. What a privilege we had to meet and chat with this American treasure.

In 1940 Ernie met Lulu Tankersley at Emory University. They were married a year later and will be celebrating their 65th anniversary in 2006. Ernie has said that God has been good to him. That is a certainty, friends. What a pillar of strength!

Russ Hodges— A Top Leader and Announcer in Broadcasting

When the New York Giants and Los Angeles Dodgers moved west in 1957 it opened up a whole new world for me. I had been a baseball fan as long as I could remember and now two famous major league teams called California their home. My mind wandered back to that exciting day in 1951 when I took my lunch hour at home.

"The Giants win the pennant! The Giants win the pennant! The Giants win the pennant!" Those words were shouted one more time before announcer Russ Hodges permitted the crowd to tell the story and he then said, "They're going crazy, they're going crazy." Yes, it was the historic Bobby Thomson home run that disappeared into the left field bleachers at the Polo Grounds in New York that placed the Giants as National League champions. Please see Story 24 (The Shot Heard 'Round the World).

Just minutes before almost everyone had acknowledged that Brooklyn had proven their superiority over the Giants in that fateful ninth inning. Hodges was so excited that he did not complete his scorecard. That document can be seen in the Baseball Hall of Fame with Thomson's home run unrecorded. And, in fact, a Dodger fan put a small recorder in front of Russ to capture the moment that Hodges would have to tell the world the Giants had been beaten. Instead of defeat, Russ was revealing to baseball fans around the globe that the impossible had happened. And, surprisingly, that little recorder was the only taped version of Russ's voice. It is certainly one of the most famous moments in baseball history.

Russ was born on June 18, 1910. He went to the University of Kentucky in his home state and obtained a law degree. His interest in baseball was evident, however. He announced for the Cincinnati Reds, Chicago Cubs, and Washington Senators before joining Mel Allen on New York Yankee broadcasts in the 1940s.

In 1949 Russ made a major move signing with the New York Giants as their lead announcer. He spent 22 years with them and moved west with the team when they made their new home in San Francisco in 1957.

Willie Mays hit 633 home runs with the Giants and Russ called all but two of them. He became known for his description of a Giant home run and that was,

"Bye-bye baby," his personal trademark.

Hodges first broadcasted in 1929 and soon moved to the major leagues to eventually become one of baseball's premier announcers. Russ was known for many other achievements. He was founder and president of 3 Roads Communications, the most successful communication production company for television, video and web production operations at that time.

With this company Hodges produced award-winning programs including the "Gift of Life," a documentary about seriously ill third world children. He did a public television series titled "Legends of Airpower," about great aviators. Also, Russ headed up the John McLaughlin "One on One" program and the "McLaughlin Group." He received many awards for his work including an Emmy.

Hodges died on April 19, 1971 at the age of 60. He was elected into the Baseball Hall of Fame posthumously in 1980. Hodges died much too young but accomplished many important goals in those sixty years. Russ was certainly one of my favorites in the baseball world.

STORY 58:

Gordon McClendon— The Old Scotchman

In my opinion, Gordon McClendon was never given the credit he deserves regarding baseball announcing. He filled in gaps that major networks had not yet covered. Gordon owned many radio stations all over America in the 1940s. Since the major networks had legal control of all broadcasts of any type, McClendon came up with the idea of re-creating games on a national level. Re-creating games was not new. They were being done on a local level in many parts of the United States in the 1930s. Please see *Story 50* (Hal Berger) and *Story 61* (Ronald Reagan).

On March 1, 1951 McClendon, a Texan, launched the Liberty Broadcasting Network. His purpose was to send these re-created games over the airwaves to every corner of America.

I remember them well. I was hungry to hear baseball games over the radio. They were talking about my heroes of the various franchises in the East and Midwest.

It is not generally known that McClendon was in a broadcast booth at the 1951 playoff game in the Polo Grounds between the Giants and the Dodgers. His description of the "shot heard around the world," Bobby Thomson's dramatic pennant-winning home run, is thought to be the only complete recording known to exist. It was beamed out over the Liberty network.

As stated in Story 57 (Russ Hodges, One of the Greats in the Broadcasting Business), Hodge's famous recording was made by a Dodger fan who wanted to hear Russ cry when the Giants lost. Fate turned it the other way around. The fan sent Hodges the tape after the fact and it was the source for all the many times we have heard Hodges give his renowned exclamations of that great victory for the Giants.

On August 1, 1952, the Liberty network folded due to legal difficulties. A $200,000 settlement was made between baseball and McClendon and he went off the air. Shortly thereafter, however, he made an agreement with the Mutual Broadcasting Co. and the "Mutual Game of the Day" was born. As writer Bill McCurdy wrote in 2004, "All we had available to help us follow the big leagues were our local sports pages, The Sporting News, and the daily radio broadcasts of the Mutual Game of the Day and the fabled Gordon McClendon."

He was not elected to the Baseball Hall of Fame, but was certainly valuable to baseball fans in those days. "The Old Scotchman," as McClendon was called, was positive and was an outstanding baseball announcer. I was one of his most ardent fans.

STORY 59:

Jon Miller—One of the Gems of Baseball Announcing

Like so many baseball fans, I discovered Jon Miller by listening to Sunday Night Baseball on ESPN. He and Joe Morgan do a great job in my opinion.

However, I first met Jon at the San Francisco Giant spring training site in Scottsdale, Arizona. He was covering the Giants there for radio station KNBR 680, San Francisco. I had the opportunity to chat with him and express my admiration and appreciation of his work. I have enjoyed Jon's great ability to describe baseball games with his golden voice, knowledge of the game, and sense of humor.

Jon has been announcing baseball for more than twenty-seven years. He was with the Texas Rangers in 1978-79, with the Boston Red Sox from 1980 to 1982, and with NBC-TV from 1986 to 1989. He occasionally worked with Tony Kubek and Joe Garagiola in those years. In 1983 he began broadcasting for the Baltimore Orioles and was with them for 14 years. At that time, he went with ESPN and has been with them ever since. His work on the Sunday night games is classic.

Concurrently, Jon has been the "voice of the San Francisco Giants on KNBR radio and KTVU-Fox 2 television and continues that job today.

For seven years Jon has covered the World Series for ESPN radio. He has broadcast hockey, basketball, and soccer as well. He was nominated six times for ACE Awards (excellence in cable television) and won that award in 1991 and 1996 for his play-by-play work. And he was nominated twice for a national Emmy Award in 1995 and 1996.

Jon is a Bay Area native and currently resides with his family in Moss Beach, California. He and his wife, Janine, have three daughters and a son.

It is my opinion that in Jon Miller we have one of the brightest and eloquent broadcasters in the business. His positive manner attracted me to him and I predict history will credit him as a true leader in his profession.

STORY 60:

Lindsey Nelson— A Classic Voice to Remember

This icon of sports announcing was born in Campbellsville, Tennessee on May 25, 1919. He was one of the most versatile broadcasters in his field. Lindsey is best known for his work at the New York Mets lead announcer plus his coverage of college football. His southern voice left one with a feeling of warmth.

A graduate of the University of Tennessee, his first job in sports was as a reporter for the Columbia (Tennessee) Daily Herald newspaper. He was the first announcer for the "Vol Network," set up to broadcast games of his university. He did an outstanding job there and soon signed to cover announcing for the Cotton Bowl that he did for 25 years. For 13 years he was the voice of Notre Dame football. Lindsey called NFL games from 1974 to 1977 on the Mutual Broadcasting System's Monday night radio.

Nelson's baseball broadcasting career began with the NBC television network in 1957. Five years later he was hired by the New York Mets and for 17 years did both radio and television with sidekicks Ralph Kiner and Bob Murphy. In 1979 the San Francisco Giants lured him west to do Giant games for three years. In 1985 he worked for CBS doing radio broadcasts of Major League Baseball. Lindsey was the first announcer to feature the use of "instant replay."

He was inducted into several halls of fame including the Writers' Wing of Baseball's Hall of Fame in Cooperstown, the New York Mets Hall of Fame, the

National Sportscasters and Sportwriters Hall of Fame, and the American Sports-casters Association Hall of Fame. In 1988 Lindsey received the Ford C. Frick Award for contributions to baseball and an Emmy in 1991 for Life Achievement.

Lindsey Nelson's voice was a fond memory for me. I heard him whenever the opportunity arose. His broadcasts were synonymous with pleasurable listening. He was the ultimate professional. He passed away on June 10, 1995 leaving a legacy difficult to equal.

STORY 61:

Ronald Reagan—A Great Leader And Auspicious Broadcaster

Have you been to the Ronald Reagan Library in Simi Valley, California? If not, I certainly recommend you put it on your schedule. Obviously, among many other accomplishments, it provides a very interesting story of President Reagan's radio experiences in the early days.

He graduated from Eureka College in Illinois in 1932 and his foremost desire was to be a radio sports announcer. He tried to catch on with a several stations in the Chicago area but failed. Not to give up, he walked into the studios of WOC, Davenport, Iowa a short time later, did an audition, and received the following message from the station manager. "You get five dollars and bus fare to Iowa City. You're doing the Iowa-Minnesota game."

President Reagan, known as "Dutch" in the early days, became the general announcer for WOC, Davenport. It was sister station with WHO, Des Moines. These two 1000 Khz stations were given authority in 1932 to increase power to 50,000 watts. From 1933 to 1937 Mr. Reagan broadcast a wide variety of sports events including Iowa football, swimming and the Drake Relays. It was at this time that Mr. Reagan re-created baseball games for the Chicago Cubs and Chicago White Sox.

This is an interesting note. As a youth Mr. Reagan had always wanted to ride horses. While at WHO Des Moines he obtained a commission in the Citizens' Military Training at Fort Des Moines to train as a horseman. In this way he fulfilled a lifelong dream.

In 1935 Mr. Reagan began spending vacations at the Chicago Cubs spring training site on Catalina Island in California. As he interviewed a number of movie stars he arranged to get a screen test in 1937. This led to his leaving station

WHO and he began making movies in Hollywood. His aforementioned presidential library is a wonderful place to visit. One can enjoy every phase of President Reagan's life. Also, it documents all of his radio broadcasting experience and verifies his great love for baseball. It confirms his great leadership abilities and it certainly confirms his excellence in announcing and broadcasting.

STORY 62:

Vin Scully—The King of the Hill, The Best of the Best

"The Dodgers and Giants are rolling in the dirt again today." When those two teams moved to the west coast we knew we would be hearing those words from Vin Scully several times each season. Honestly, friends, the most pleasant and melodious sound I have ever heard anywhere, radio or otherwise, is that of Vince Scully. He is popularly known as the "voice of the Los Angeles Dodgers." When he came to Los Angeles he virtually taught thousands, particularly women, how to enjoy and understand baseball. As one would sit in the Coliseum, and later Dodger Stadium, Vinny's voice could be heard everywhere like music off in the distance. Vin was the Dodgers!

Having grown up in Southern California, our family radio was tuned to KFI, a 50,000-watt station whenever the Dodgers were playing. The mellow tones of this Irish tenor are magical. They capture you! In my mind the man is the epitome of those announcers who translate information to listeners. He is brilliant! His command of the English language is nothing short of phenomenal. I feel as though there really are no words to properly describe Scully's capabilities. Just off the cuff, he comes up with words and phrases as though reading from a carefully prepared script. And this talent, combined with his vast knowledge of the game of baseball and its history, makes his broadcasts absolutely incomparable.

One of the best descriptions of Vin's incredible ability to report a baseball game is in an article by Gary Kaufman on a website called Salon Brilliant Careers. Try it on your computer. It is an outstanding description of Vin. Read it. I think you will enjoy it.

I will mention one thing Kaufman said that I personally verify. He said "If you have not heard Vin Scully on radio, you haven't heard him." That is so true. He paints a picture for you. He includes all that needs to be included but nothing more. I read where one famous announcer said he, personally, keeps a set of cards with anecdotes on them. During the game he would pick one up and read it. That is fine and probably the way I would do it. But, with Vinny, those anecdotes just flow out of his reservoir of stories in his mind.

Scully was born on November 29, 1927 in the Bronx. When he was eight years old he knew what he wanted to do. Recently he said, "I would crawl under the old radio so the loudspeaker and roar of the crowd would wash all over me, and I would get goose bumps like you can't believe." Doesn't that sound like Vinny? Further, he said, "I wanted to be that fella saying, whatever, home run or touchdown. It really got to me."

Actually, Vin played baseball at Fordham Prep and went to Fordham University on a partial baseball scholarship in 1945 where he played two years in the outfield. He served a year in the Navy and returned to finish his education in 1949. Vin was a New Yorker, through and through. He was a stringer for the New York Times, and sang in a barbershop quartet. With those vocal cords he is bound to have a great singing voice.

Scully's first big job was at WTOP, the CBS affiliate in Washington. Upon a recommendation of a network executive, Red Barber called Vinny's home to assign him a duty. Scully later said, "My mother took the message but she said it was from Red Skelton." Please see Story 49 (Red Barber), about Vinny's first big opportunity in broadcasting.

In the mid 1950s Barber went to the Yankees and Scully became the lead announcer for the Dodgers. In 1958 when the Dodgers moved to Los Angeles it was quite traumatic for Vin. Everything he knew and loved about the game was in the Big Apple. But it wasn't long before Vinny was the toast of the town in Los Angeles and the Dodgers were winners. They were world champions in 1959, 1963, 1965, 1981 and 1988. In addition they were National League champions in 1966, 1974, 1977 and 1978. Vinny's voice literally meant victory to Dodger fans not just in Los Angeles but all over the country.

Scully has worked for the various networks now and then doing baseball, football and golf. I have some classic tapes of Vinny teaming up with Sparky Anderson, Joe Garagiola, Johnny Bench, Jeff Torberg, and many others. This may sound crazy but it really is not. I turn on these tapes from time to time just to hear Vinny's voice. It doesn't matter if it is game that was played years ago. His voice is like hearing a quality piece of music. It is soothing and pleasant. His rhythm and pace is simply stimulating to hear.

In researching for this study on Scully I found literally dozens of awards and honors given to him. There are so many it is overwhelming. To cap if off, thirty-two years after joining the Dodger broadcast team Vin was inducted into the Broadcasters' wing of the National Baseball Hall of Fame as the Ford C. Frick recipient. He is by far the most capable broadcaster in the minds of most experts and fans.

Please allow me to express my appreciation to a man who has been instrumental in my life in bringing my beloved baseball more alive. But, even more than that, he has given all of us a model of a gentleman, a scholar and a friend. We salute you, Vincent Edward Scully!

He had been a football and baseball star at the University of Nebraska. Later he graduated from Harvard Law School and used his degree in many ways. "Sturzy," as he was affectionately called, was a great coach and very well liked by everyone. He coached both baseball and football at UCLA.

Our team members were Burt Avedon, Bobby Brown (Captain), John Derdivanis, Dave Fainer, John Finch, Frank Frericks, Baker Garrison, Sid Gilmore, Sam Gravely, Warren Haynes, Hal Holman, Mike Knauff, Bert Leisk, Don Malmberg, Doc Mason, Bill Matcha, Don Miller, Jack Myers, Lyle Palmer, Jack Porter, Ken Proctor, Don Reaume, Bob Ritzman, Nick Russin and Dave Stauffer.

Don Miller, an outfielder, and I were friends since boyhood. We graduated from Washington High School together in 1942. We still see Don and his wife, Ali, ever so often. They live at Huntington Harbour in California. Also, we keep in touch with Bobby and Sara Brown who make their home in Fort Worth, Texas. Also, our manager was a high school friend by the name of Dave Tomlinson who now lives in Seattle.

Sam Gravely passed away several years ago. He played outfield for us and was honored earlier as the Navy's first African-American admiral. Jack "Moose" Myers, our first baseman, eventually played for the Philadelphia Eagles in the National Football League. Lyle Palmer was a fine outfielder and we later played against each other when he transferred to the University of California at Berkeley after the war ended. Don Malmberg was an exceptional football player and was a fullback for the UCLA varsity.

Our success in winning two conferences came on strong in the last few weeks of the season when we won most of our games. We defeated USC in a two-game series to bring home both conference titles. We defeated the Trojans three out of four games during the season and had the highest team fielding and batting averages on the West Coast. "Sturzy" was quoted as follows: "This is the finest Bruin baseball team in my coaching career." At season's end, he received the award as "Coach of the Year" by the University.

Ken in UCLA uniform in 1944 kneeling.

1947 team picture, (Ken Proctor's 1947 UCLA team)

STORY 64:

1947 Bruins—Back from the War

When World War II ended I returned to UCLA and joined the Bruin baseball squad coached by Art Reichle. We had a formidable schedule including the St. Louis Browns, Hollywood Stars, San Diego Marines, Los Angeles Police and, of course, the tough Pacific Coast Conference squads. The team held its own with a better than .500 record.

Players included Lou Briganti (Captain), Jack Brooks, Bob Call, Jim Daniels, Dick Dowlin, Frank Frericks, Bob Hana, Hal Handley, Joe Hicks, Mark Mauer, Evan Murphy (Manager), Ed McKenzie, Jack Myers, Ken Proctor, Cal Rossi, Gene Rowland, Doug Sale, Bill Schneider, Bob Selzer, John Stanich, Phil Steinberg, and Jack Stuart.

We had a number of two-sport men on the squad including footballers Myers, Rossi, and Rowland. Doug Sale and John Stanich were both basketball stars. This was our first postwar squad and we were a combination of war veterans and young players. The same was true for all the college teams we faced and it made for an interesting season. We certainly had a nucleus of players from which to build in the future.

STORY 65:

1948 Bruins—
Playing More Against the Pros

We had a winning season in 1948 ending up with a 23-15 record. Again, Art Reichle, UCLA '41, was our coach. He continued to direct baseball at UCLA until 1974.

Our team was composed of Bob Andrews, Jack Brooks, Jim Fairman, Del Goodyear, George Gruell, Hal Handley, Bill Hicks, Joe Hicks, Ed McKenzie, Kiko Munoz, Jack "Moose" Myers (Captain), Ken Proctor, Gene Rowland, Doug Sale, Bob Selzer, George Stanich, John Stanich, Phil Steinberg and Marty Weinberger. As is usually the case, I could write a paragraph or more about each of these teammates. But I will simply say that we were a very unified group and enjoyed the game together.

Goodyear, at Culver City High School, and Joe Hicks, at Long Beach City College, became coaches and had some very good teams. Gene "Skip" Rowland coached high school football at Long Beach following graduation. Rowland and Myers starred for the Bruin football varsity.

Brothers John and George Stanich were both outstanding players for the Bruin basketball team.

I will say a word about a fine teammate. Recently I called Doug Sale who is retired and lives in Red Bluff, California. We reminisced over the past. He had recently driven to Southern California and had breakfast with John Wooden. He played basketball and played for coach Wooden in the late 1940s and was an assistant coach in that program in the early 1950s. Also, he assisted Coach Reichle in baseball. Doug was a great teammate and a credit to UCLA in those years. We roomed together on out-of-town games. He went on to become an outstanding educator in California. Please see Story 70 (1953 Team), fourth paragraph, about Doug as a speaker for our Chaffey High School baseball banquet that year.

The military teams were pretty much gone by now and we played our pre-season games against some of the professional teams who did their spring training in the Southern California area. This season we played the Los Angeles Angels, St. Louis Browns, Hollywood Stars and the Cleveland Indians.

When we played Cleveland I recall seeing Larry Doby on their roster. He was the first African-American in the American League. I saw him hit the highest pop fly I had ever seen. It was hit so high and the wind blew it around so much that we misplayed it and Larry had a double out of it. Please see Story 10 (A Major League Pop Up by Larry Doby) for more about this fine player.

I would like to mention two pitchers that impressed me. One was Bill Moisan of the Angels. His ball had plenty on it and his fast one had a tendency to sail. He could throw very hard. The other hurler was with the Hollywood Stars, or Twinks as they were sometimes called. His name was Art Schallock and he had a lefty curve ball that looked like it dropped off a table. Both players went up to the majors shortly thereafter, Moisan with the Cubs and Schallock with the Yankees. Please see Stories Nos. 128 (Bill Moisan) and Nos. 139 (Art Schallock).

This was my third year of varsity baseball. I had one more year of eligibility. It was possible to play four years at that time because of military service when they allowed a player to play varsity in his freshman year.

STORY 66:

1949 Bruins—My Last Year in College Baseball

This was my last year of eligibility to play baseball at UCLA. I decided early on to stay out of basketball and concentrate on baseball. I had been in the basketball program under Coach John Wooden and would like to have continued. But, it seemed my future probably was stronger in baseball and I wanted to give it my best shot.

We had another fine team with good unity. Ten returning lettermen gave us a pretty good base from which to start. The team ended up with a 21-16 won-loss record and an 8-6 mark in the conference. Six of our overall losses were to teams composed of professional players.

The roster was as follows: Bob Andrews, John Corrigan, Jim Fairman, Mike Gazella, Del Goodyear, Hal Handley (Captain), Wayne Harding, Bill Hicks, Bill Jones, Paul Krupnick, Bill Lundquist, Pete Moody, Mario Nitrini, Ray O'Conner, Ken Proctor, George Stanich, Phil Steinberg, Jack Taylor, Paul Treat, and Marty Weinberger.

I am still in touch with Hal Handley and George Stanich. Hal had two cousins playing in the major leagues, Gene Handley with the Cubs, and Lee Handley with the Pirates. George was also a high jumper having placed third on the Olympic team in 1948. Occasionally, they would fly George from a track meet to a baseball game, or vice-versa, when events occurred on the same day. Also, George signed a professional baseball contract and played for the Oakland Acorns (sometimes called the Oaks) of the Pacific Coast League. Also, George continued to star for

Coach Wooden's basketball team. Gazella's father scouted for the Boston Braves. Please see Story 11 (Mike Gazella).

In the off-season of this year our team and the crosstown rival USC Trojans were asked to go to Wrigley Field to participate in a baseball movie titled, "It Happens Every Spring." It starred Ray Milland, Bill Bendix, and Jean Peters. We spent about two weeks at the park with each player earning $22.00/day. Most of our time was spent sitting around waiting for them to actually do the filming. It is an enjoyable movie and I recommend your seeing it if the opportunity arises. In fact, I believe you can rent it at one of the "old film" renting establishments. As you may have noted, the movie and song title were the same. It is listed in the group of "Baseball Titles in Story 46."

This was a memorable year for us because soon after the season ended Marilyn and I were wed. That was on July 24, nearly fifty-seven years ago. It concluded many enjoyable years of baseball at UCLA and a new beginning for a happy marriage.

STORY 67:

UCLA Baseball Hall of Fame— Eighty-One Members to Date

The UCLA Baseball Hall of Fame was established in 1988 under the direction of Coach Gary Adams. The first player named was Jackie Robinson who played several sports at UCLA including baseball. By 2005 a total of 81 players have been inducted. UCLA has been playing baseball for 86 years or an average of less than one per year. Please see Story 107 (Marvin Gudat) about a major league player who played at UCLA in the early 1920s.

A selection committee of eighteen former players decides on qualifying nominees. It is called The Tenth Player committee. Membership is based on rigid criteria of each candidate's exploits both on and off the field of play. The photo plaques of all members hang on the walls at the Jackie Robinson Stadium Clubhouse for all to see.

The first induction ceremony was held on the UCLA campus in the Alumni Center in 1988 and attended by 265. There were twelve charter members including the outstanding Jackie Robinson. Since the first banquet the event has been held at the Faculty Club on the UCLA campus.

When USC baseball coach, Mike Gillespie visited the campus he told Coach Adams that he was going to start a similar program at their university. USC has

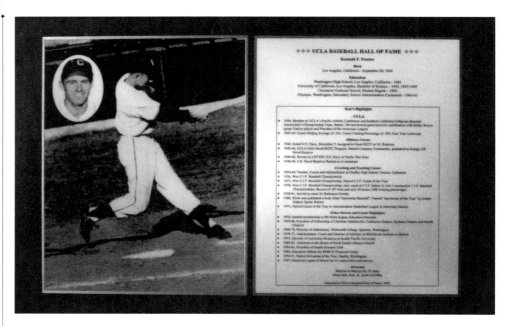

Ken Proctor UCLA Baseball Hall of Fame plaque

an excellent web site for their entire baseball program.

When new members are inducted, an entire day is dedicated to festivities. The following was the schedule of events when I was inducted:

10:15 am	Batting practice
11:35 am	Home run contest
Noon:	Old-Timers (Blue and Gold) Game
1:00 pm	Ceremony for Hall of Fame inductees
1:30 pm	Professional players pre-game infield practice
1:40 pm	UCLA pre-game infield practice
1:50 pm	UCLA Varsity vs Professional players
7:00 pm	Hall of Fame induction banquet

I was inducted with four other players including Ray Arrington (retired Los Angeles County Deputy Sheriff), Guy Hansen (former major league scout and pitching coach), Bill Haselman (Texas Ranger catcher), and Rick Kester (educator and former major league pitcher, retired). I was excited because 32 of my former coaches, players, and friends attended. Ray and Lori Lundeen came from Seattle, Howard Collins from Phoenix, Frank Battino from the Bay Area, old friends Hal Thomas, Don and Allie Miller, Tony and Mary Sully, and many others came from areas around Southern California. Jim Bryant, our sportswriter from The Daily Report (Ontario) came with my former fellow coach, Clyde Francisco. Other former players included Vernon Pritchett, Jim McGuire, Hal Reniff, and Jerry

Johnson. Our son Mike, grandson Jesse, and brother-in-law Howard Knudson, were guests. My wife, Marilyn, my best baseball buddy, and I sat together. Larry Burnett, ESPN anchorman, was the master of ceremonies. There were more than twenty Bruin major league players in the audience.

The 81 current Hall of Fame members are as follows:

Bob Adams, Lee Alarid, Earl Altshuler, Rich Amaral, Bob Andrews, Ray Arrington, Jim Auten, Dave Baker, Steve Bailey, Ted Bashore, Bill Bonham, Bill Brasher, Dr. Bobby Brown, Joe E. Brown, Judge Lynn "Buck" Compton, Chris Chambliss, Floyd Chiffer, Jim Coletto, Jeff Conine, Curt Counts, Mickey Croft, Dennis Delaney, James Devere, Pat Dodson, Tim Doerr, Vern Followell, Tebbie Fowler, Mike Frankovich, Mike Gallego, Rick Ganulin, Mike Gerakos, Jack Gifford, Sid Gilmore, Brian Graham, Dan Guerrero, Guy Hansen, Wayne Harding, Bill Haselman, Joe Hicks, Alan Hoops, Eric Karros, Rick Kester, Steve Klausen, Tim Leary, Andy Lopez, Sam Lovullo, Shane Mack, Mike Magnante, Ryan McGuire, Glenn Mickens, Jack "Moose" Myers, Tim O'Neill, Hoyt Pardee, David Penniall, Rick Pope, Ken Proctor, Art Reichle, Mike Riskas, Jackie Robinson, Gary Robson, Ernie Rodriguez, Ron Roenicke, Gene "Skip" Rowland, Steve Runk, Gary Sanserino, Dave Schmidt, Randy Schwartz, Frank Schwengel, Don Sealy, Don Slaught, George Stanich, Phil Steinberg, Ed Stewart, Jack Theriault, Kenny Washington, David Weiner, Jim York, Matt Young, John Zaby, and Todd Zeile.

Gary deserves much credit for his efforts in promoting the UCLA baseball program. He helped to bring the baseball program into prominence during his thirty years at UCLA. His influence will be felt for years to come.

Top: Ken & his Chaffey players and friend at Hall of Fame banquet. *LtoR:* (standing) Vern Pritchett, Ken Proctor, Coach Clyde Francisco, Jim McGuire, Howard Collins, (sitting) Jerry Johnson, Frank Battino, Hal Reniff (not in picture)

Bottom: Ken & Marilyn Proctor at Hall of Fame banquet.

Ken Proctor UCLA Baseball Hall of Fame plaque, (closeup left)

◇◇◇ UCLA BASEBALL HALL OF FAME ◇◇◇

Kenneth F. Proctor

Born
Los Angeles, California – September 20, 1924

Education
Washington High School, Los Angeles, California - 1942
University of California, Los Angeles, Bachelor of Science – 1944, 1947-1949
Claremont Graduate School, Masters Degree – 1960
Olympia, Washington, Secondary School Administrative Credential – 1964-65

Ken's Highlights

- UCLA-

- 1944, Member of UCLA's Pacific Athletic Conference and Southern California Collegiate Baseball Association's Championship Team, Batted .340 and formed great keystone combination with Bobby Brown (great Yankee player and President of the American League)
- 1947–49, Career Batting Average of .324, Career Fielding Percentage of .985; Four Year Letterman

-Military Career-

- 1942, Joined U.S. Navy, December 7; Assigned to Naval ROTC at UC Berkeley
- 1943-44, UCLA-USA Naval ROTC Program, Named Company Commander, graduated as Ensign, US Naval Reserve
- 1944-46, Served on LST 839, U.S. Navy in Pacific War Zone
- 1946-59, U.S. Naval Reserve; Retired as a Lieutenant

-Coaching and Teaching Career-

- 1950-64, Teacher, Coach and Administrator at Chaffey High School, Ontario, California
- 1956, Won C.I.F. Baseball Championship
- 1957, Won C.I.F. Baseball Championship, Named C.I.F. Coach of the Year
- 1958, Won C.I.F. Baseball Championship; only coach in C.I.F. history to win 3 consecutive C.I.F. Baseball Championships; Record of 187 wins and only 30 losses (.900 winning percentage)
- 1958-61, Served as scout for Baltimore Orioles
- 1960, Wrote and published a book titled "Successful Baseball"; Named "Sportsman of the Year" by Inland Empire Sports Writers
- 1973, Named Coach of the Year in Interscholastic Basketball League in Honolulu, Hawaii

-Other Honors and Career Highlights-

- 1956, Earned membership in Phi Delta Kappa, Education Honorary
- 1959-86, President of Fellowship of Christian Athletes (So. California Chapter, Spokane Chapter and Seattle Chapter)
- 1964-70, Director of Admissions, Whitworth College, Spokane, Washington
- 1970-75, Administrator, Coach and Director of Athletics at Mid-Pacific Institute in Hawaii
- 1975, Director of University Relations at Seattle Pacific University
- 1980-85, Chairman of the Board of North Seattle Alliance Church
- 1984-85, President of Seattle Kiwanis Club
- 1986, Education Officer for PEMCO Financial Center
- 1990-91, Named Kiwanian of the Year, Seattle, Washington
- 1997, Received Legion of Honor for 45 years of Kiwanis service
- 2006, Wrote and Published a book titled *Baseball Memoirs of a Lifetime*

-Personal-
Married to Marilyn for 56 years
Three sons, Ken, Jr., Scott and Mike

Inducted to UCLA Baseball Hall of Fame, 2002

Ken Proctor UCLA Baseball Hall of Fame plaque (closeup right)

CHAPTER 4

Leading the Chaffey High School Baseball Tigers

In Ontario, California in the 1950s

$\blacklozenge$In February 1950 I was offered a teaching contract in the Chaffey Union High School District. Specifically, I replaced a teacher, George (Bill) Culler, who resigned in mid-year. My job description was to teach five periods of Physical Education and coach the junior varsity baseball squad.

Baseball season began immediately. The turnout on opening day numbered approximately fifty students. I found it a most difficult task to have to cut the excess number of players. Every one of those youngsters wanted to "make the team," and it was traumatic for me to deny them a chance to play. Later in 1953 when I took charge of the baseball program at Chaffey I was able to solve this problem. Please see Story 78 (Commentary)(No Cuts in Baseball, Everyone Plays), about the necessary changes.

Crew-cut Ken in 1950 at age 26.

I worked fifteen years at Chaffey. The first ten was spent coaching baseball, basketball, and football with an emphasis on baseball. In the final five years I worked as the Director of Athletics. The following are some particulars about my teams for my ten baseball seasons at Chaffey from 1950 through 1959.

ART CREDIT TO PAT DOOLEY

STORY 68:
1950 JV Team— My Very First Squad

This was a period of trial for me. It was my first opportunity to coach at the high school level. I spent a good deal of time getting acquainted with the community, the school, my colleagues, but most important, my students and players.

Our opponents were many of the area high schools in that part of Southern California. I soon learned that teams there were very competitive and were generally well coached. Some of our adversaries were high schools from Pomona, San Bernardino, Colton, Redlands, and Riverside. It was known as the Citrus Belt League because of the many orange groves in those cities. Baseball was very popular there. Of course, Southern California weather contributed to that fact because teams could play virtually the year around.

Ken's first Chaffey JV team in 1950

There was no youth baseball there at that time and it occurred to me that it would be good for the community if we had such a program. Later our youth program took a back seat to none. Please see Story 13 (Developing a Youth Baseball Program in Ontario, California).

The following were my players: Tony Aguilar, Buel Anderson, Ralph Barcevac, Ed Brown, Clayton Bryant, Dick Carmichael, Lupe Coronado, Franklin Dorsett, Arlen Downs, Bob Emilio, Dave Farmer, Archie Farrar, Tom Floriano, Chuck Gladson, Clark Goodwin, Bill Johnson, Johnny Keefer, Reginald Keith, Larry Lanier, Vernon Martin (Captain), Jesse Miller, Johnny Moore, Richard Odenberg, Jim Sylvia, Norman Thorpe, and Howard Theurer.

There were a number of talented players on that team and early on I could see that these were a fine group of young men with which to work. I thorough enjoyed each and every personality. A young pitcher, Dave Farmer, and an outfielder, Vernon Martin, were great leaders of this group. One player, sophomore Arlen Downs, obviously had not only good coordination and ability but a deep desire to win. He had a great arm and I primed him for pitching. He had a natural "screwball" that curved inside to a righthanded batter. His pitches broke many bats by striking them on the handle.

I was pleasantly surprised at the end of the season when, on behalf of the team, Arlen brought me a beautiful brass bell with hammer to match. It was special because Arlen made it himself in a foundry where he worked. It sits proudly in my den today. It kind of symbolized my first effort at coaching. I will comment further on Arlen in the story about the 1952 JV team.

We played just twelve games that season, home and home, and ended up with eight wins and four losses.

STORY 69:

1951 JV Team—
We Have Some Experience Now

With one baseball season under my belt, I was eager to get started with my second season. For nine months I planned various strategies for 1951. Incidentally, by now I had positively learned that the students in this school district were generally great kids, easy to coach, cooperative, and eager to learn. The Ontario community had character.

It was a thirteen-game season with similar competition as 1950. Coaches at our opponent schools continued to be great, friendly and professional. The umpiring was well organized and certainly capable. As before we played at our home field about half the time. The fields were well kept, especially for this level of play. In many areas the quality of fields sometimes can be less than desirable. That was not true in our location.

This squad was composed of Gary Adams, Don Africh, Buel Anderson, Rito Armenta, Bill Cowan, Sam Crowe, Arlen Downs (Captain), Bill Elwell, Dave Farmer, Milton Frye, Chuck Gladson, Sam Gold, Clark Goodwin, James Graves, Roman Guiterrez, Ben Hunter, Lee Johnson, Mike Killion, Melvin Loros, Manuel Luna, Chuck McKellar, Dick Messler, Jesse Miller, Tony Munoz, Mike Parra, Jon Patterson, Gil Quesada, Richard Saez, Loren Sanchez, Roger Sawyer, Russ Stanley, and Jim Wiesen.

Arlen was elected captain of this squad. He went undefeated on the mound. And Gold was pitching great baseball and was a great star in the future. Though I did not know it at the time, some of my future players were on this team because I was not aware I would eventually be coaching the varsity. I just recently had an email from one of these players, Milton Frye, who now lives in Salem, Oregon. We keep in touch. Other stars were Adams, Crowe, Goodwin, Quesada, Sanchez, and Wiesen.

We posted eleven wins and two losses for the season.

STORY 70:

1952 JV Team—
Another Great Bunch Of Kids

Some of my 1950 and 1951 players were now with the varsity team and it was enjoyable watching them develop. I did not have much chance to see their games since my JV team was often playing at the same time. But, I did see them at other times.

It was evident to me that the 1952 JV club was going to be tough to beat. I had several returning lettermen whom formed a good nucleus. We opened the season defeating Baldwin Park at Chaffey. We traveled to their field a week later and could not get untracked at the plate as they gave us our only defeat of the year. For the rest of the season we dominated our opponents and went undefeated.

Arlen Downs had now moved up to the varsity squad and was their starting pitcher. With his dazzling screwball, he pitched head coach, Harry Yochem's team into the CIF playoffs where they were barely edged, 3-2 in eleven innings, in the first round against powerful San Diego High School. Downs went on to compete very well at our school district's Chaffey College the following year.

The squad this season was Gary Adams (Captain), Ron Alverson, Carl Bare, Larry Blaylock, Tom Branchetti (who later played at Fontana HS), Joe Bruce, Bob Craft, Lionel Crowley, Joe DiCarlo, Eddie Edwards, Bill Finch, Bob Fowlkes, Gary George, Frank Gomez, Robert Gomez, Roger Heinauer, Louie Ledesma, Ken McCullough, Ray Padilla, Mike Parra, Warren Peters, John Pizzuto, Rex Ralston, John Reese, Richard Saez, Loren Sanchez, Stan Scates, Bill Smith, David Stockwell, Gordon Tedder, Richard Vasquez, Gene Waltman, Jim Wiesen, and Hershell Wilson.

Standouts on this squad were Adams, Bare, DiCarlo, Peters, Sanchez, and Stockwell. Our year ended with eleven wins and one loss. This would end my JV coaching as our varsity coach, Harry Yochem, retired and I was named to replace him. During those three JV coaching years we finished with 30 wins and 7 losses, an 81% victory percentage. The quality of our young men in Ontario made the difference.

STORY 71:

1953 Varsity Team— A Good Varsity Start

Ken's 1953 Chaffey varsity

I was embarking on my first varsity coaching experience and, I must say, it was exciting. Many of my JV kids had already succeeded with Mr. Yochem in 1952 as they won the Citrus Belt League title. And more talented JVs were moving to the varsity as I took over.

We had players from a number of towns and communities near Ontario. They were Upland, Fontana, Montclair, Alta Loma, and South Ontario among others. A significant number of Upland players became star performers in athletics in these years. Our high school had an enrollment of near 4,000 students. Many of the area high schools were similarly large in attendance since students came from the various surrounding communities. It wasn't long before new high schools were built in some of these areas because of the exploding population occurring in California at that time.

Team players were: Gary Adams, Don Africh, Joe Agapay, Ron Alverson, Gene Anguiano, Ed Cantrell, Bill Cowan, Bob Craft, Sam Crowe, Roger Heinauer, Lou Hoyos, Ben Hunter, Joe LeBeau, Del Maple, Tony Munoz, Gil Quesada, Don Rabun (Captain), Hal Reniff, Ron Riccardi, Loren Sanchez, Fred Sylvia, Hershell Wilson.

This team proved to be just that—a team. No one player dominated the scene. Our victories came pretty much the result of team effort. One could imagine that the next year's squad was going to be a good one. We were laying a foundation. We won three straight games in the Pomona Tournament before losing in the semi-finals to Colton High School.

Our speaker at the year-end banquet was Doug Sale. At the time he was assistant to both John Wooden, UCLA basketball coach, and Art Reichle, Bruin baseball coach. When I played at UCLA in the late 1940s Doug was my roommate on out-of-town baseball trips. Also, Doug starred at Sacramento Junior College in both baseball and basketball before attending UCLA. I still am in touch with Doug as he has retired and resides in his hometown of Red Bluff. At the Ontario Kiwanis banquet he did a fine job of recognizing our players and giving an inspirational address. Please see Story 65 (1948 Bruins—Playing More Against the

Pros) for more about Doug.

We had a good year with wins over some of the better clubs in the league. Competition was outstanding and it made for excellent baseball. It turned out to be somewhat of a building year for baseball at Chaffey as succeeding seasons would prove. We finished with fourteen wins and eight losses.

STORY 72:

1954 Varsity Team— Breakthrough, a Great Team

This was a breakout year for us. The team became a dominating force for many years starting with 1954. Fundamentals were entrenched deep into the entire program. As players moved up from one level to another they performed as a unit because all players were basically on the same page. And this situation improved each year. To some degree, Chaffey baseball fundamentals were instilled even in players in the youth leagues. Please see Story 13 (Developing a Youth Baseball Program in Ontario, California).

Ken's 1954 Chaffey varsity

We ended our season with 22 wins and 3 losses and won the Citrus Belt League championship. It was certainly among the best seasons we posted over the years. It was interesting the way it happened. We had beaten Fullerton 9-7 earlier in the year and they were our opponents in the first round of the C.I.F. (California Interscholastic Federation) playoffs. We had them down 2-1 in the bottom of the ninth inning with two outs. A homerun tied the game and we eventually lost in 14 innings, 3-2. It was a great ball game between two fine teams.

It was interesting the way it happened. In the bottom of the ninth inning, Chaffey was leading 2-1 and there were two outs. Sam Gold, our pitcher, and I had discussed the ninth inning batters. I told Sam to keep the ball high and tight to Willie Quezada, their third batter of the inning because he was the one batter than could hit it out. And I knew he could be taken on that high inside pitch. The count was one ball, two strikes on Willie and Sam, indeed, pitched the ball high and tight. But, somehow, Willie managed to get his hands out front and he drove the ball just barely fair over the right field fence to tie the game. The

REWARDS OF VICTORY . . . Pitcher Harold Reniff and Coach Ken Proctor receive trophy after Chaffey defeated Lynwood 3-2 in the finals of the Pomona 20-30 baseball tournament. Reniff worked a total of 11⅓ innings to be the outstanding moundsman of the tournament.

Hal Reniff, Chaffey pitcher, MVP of 1954 Pomona Tournament champions, Chaffey HS, 1954

next five innings were great by both teams but Fullerton squeezed one across in the bottom on the fourteenth inning to win it. We had to give Willie credit for his homerun. He did what he had to do.

However, we had given a signal that we intended to become a force in California high school baseball. And that, indeed, did happen in ensuing years.

Our speaker at the Chaffey Baseball Banquet was Ellsworth "Babe" Dahlgren, the man that replaced Lou Gehrig on May 2, 1939 after the great New York Yankee slugger had completed 2,130 consecutive games, the record that Cal Ripken eventually topped. Babe went on to play in 1,135 major league games, had a lifetime average of .261 with 82 home runs and 509 RBIs. Dahlgren did a fine job in recognizing our players who had such an outstanding season.

Team players were Joe Agapay, Gene Anguiano, Carl Bare, Larry Blaylock, Dick Bumstead (Manager), Odell Carter, Bill Cowan, Joe DiCarlo, Larry Fagan, Sam Gold, Lou Hoyos, John Lewis (Manager), Warren Peters, Dick Peterson, Vernon Pritchett, Gil Quesada (Captain), Hal Reniff, Bill Smith, Jerry Snider, Dave Stockwell, Fred Sylvia, Jerry Williams, and Hershell Wilson.

We were victorious in the Pomona Baseball Tournament as be became the first team in our league to win that distinguished competition. Five consecutive games were won as we defeated Lynwood High School, 3-2, in the final game. Hal Reniff, a sophomore, was voted Player of the Tournament.

1955 Varsity Team— Close Pays Off Only in Horseshoes

Our squad came up with another 20-win season in 1955. We started off with flair as junior Dick Peterson tossed a no-hitter while striking out 10 in our opener against Santa Ana High School. In a sense it was an indication of things to come.

Four all-CBL players were gone from the previous year's club. But, the new youngsters stepped right in and did the job. I just sat back and let it happen. Our local newspaper tabbed them "The Comeback Kids."

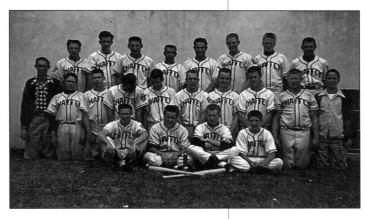

Ken's 1955 Chaffey varsity

We started out by losing our first two league games and came back to win 12 in a row and the Citrus Belt League championship.

The speaker this year was very personable and capable. He was Johnny Lindell, a former New York Yankee outfielder. He was another of the many baseball players out of USC. In 1941 he posted a 23-4 mark as a pitcher. Later he was switched to an outfielder and he spent 10 years with the Yankees and five years moving between the Cardinals, Phillies and Pirates. He played in 854 games batting .273 for a lifetime average and slammed 72 home runs. He played in 12 World Series games batting .324. Late in his career he was sold to the Hollywood Stars of the Pacific Coast League and won 24 games while losing just 9. He was easily the most valuable player that year, 1952.

The squad consisted of the following players: Gene Anguiano, Carl Bare, Chuck Bennett, Odell Carter, Joe DiCarlo, Dick Foreman, David Frye, Lou Hoyos, Jerry Johnson, Joe LeBeau, Jody Marker, Jack Mauch, Carl Ogren, Warren Peters, Dick Peterson, Vernon Pritchett, Frank Reed, Hal Reniff, Bill Smith, Jerry Snider, David Stockwell (Captain), Fred Sylvia, Jerry Williams, and Brian Zenz.

The final statistics had us with a 20-6 record for the year.

1956 Varsity Team— We Catch The Golden Ring

Having won back-to-back Citrus Belt League championships in 1954 and 1955, the team was primed and ready to make it a three-peat. We played a very difficult pre-season schedule against some top teams. We lost three games early. In the tough 32-team Pomona Tournament we were defeated in the semi-finals when we faced future Chicago White Sox star, Camilo Carreon. Although he became the White Sox catcher eventually, he pitched that day. Following that loss the team won 18 consecutive games to win our first California Interscholastic Federation (CIF) championship.

There was a point in the season when excitement was a peak. I recall a game where Chuck Giordano opened with a base hit to centerfield. I waited for the count to be in our favor, two balls and no strikes, and I called for our special first-to-third sacrifice bunt play. Howard Collins dropped a perfect bunt down forcing the third baseman to leave his base to field the ball. In the meantime, Chuck was stealing and upon reaching second base just kept on running to third base. The third baseman tried to get back to the bag to receive a return throw from the first baseman. He, Chuck, and the ball all arrived about the same moment and the ball got by him. Chuck jumped to his feet, dashed home, slid, and in a cloud of dust reached out to touch home plate and score the first run of the game. We had essentially

Ken's Mom, Marie Proctor and Marilyn Proctor watching 1956 Chaffey playoff game in Ontario, California

scored a run on a simple sacrifice play. The opponent was demoralized and we were off and running to another victory. It was one of many moments when our players simply out-thought and out-played our adversaries.

Ken's 1956 Chaffey varsity, Chaffey's first CIF champions.

Our speaker at the Ontario Kiwanis banquet in June was the heralded Frank Kelleher, outstanding outfielder of the Hollywood Stars. Frank was in the middle of one of baseball's greatest brawls in 1953. Please see Story 209 (One of Baseball's Famous Brawls). Kelleher did an outstanding job in his address. He was personable and interesting. Frank had hit 226 home runs in his career and led the Pacific Coast League in batting three times.

The players were: Gary Balding, Frank Battino, Chuck Bennett, Odell Carter, Howard Collins, Dick Foreman, Chuck Giordano, Lloyd "Red" Hunter, Russ Hunter (Manager), Jerry Johnson, Marty Karavanic, Gary Lancaster, Joe LeBeau, Jim Lisec, Larry Maxie, Daryl Moss, Jim McGuire, Dick Peterson, Andy Prevedello, Hal Reniff, John Snell, Jerry Snider (Captain), Reave Warren (Manager), and Brian Zenz.

Many exciting moments occurred in 1956. We played a number of one-run ball games as our season-ending win streak continued. In the final CIF championship game played at Oxnard, California Hal Reniff, who later pitched for the New York Yankees, faced Mike Dalton of Oxnard. Hal bested Mike 3-0 in a well-played game. We cannot point out any one player who made the difference in the game with the exception of Hal. At the risk of expressing a cliché, this was truly a team victory. Every player did his job.

We designed a unique way to flash our signs that day. One of my players, Gary Balding, was given a set of signals that he relayed to the players on the field. I would walk by Gary and quietly comment or give him a physical sign for the play I wanted to occur. He gave signs all day and never made a single mistake. Gary helped to win the championship that day with a job well done.

A most unusual happening occurred in the game. On a high inside pitch to centerfielder Andy Prevedello the ball grazed his hand. The umpire, Eric "Dutch" Bergman, thinking the ball had hit the bat, called it a foul strike. I went out to check on Andy and we could see the stitch marks of the baseball on his hand. I called the umpire over and when he saw the stitch marks he pointed to first base and said, "hit batsman." This was typical of Mr. Bergman. He always tried to correct mistakes and make the right decision, a very competent umpire. Please see Story 19, (Umpires Do a Great Job for more details about this play. Also, please see Story 170 (Andy Prevedello) for another very unique story about Andy.

There are so many stories to tell and so much excitement. Oxnard coach, Burt Killingsworth, and his players did an outstanding job that day. It was a good battle and certainly a game to remember. It was a fitting end to a good season for Chaffey.

STORY 75:

1957 Varsity Team— Two In A Row

Ken's 1957 Chaffey varsity, finished 2rd in league and came back to win 2nd CIF championship.

The pressure was on Chaffey this season following a CIF championship. We lost ten lettermen including our top three pitchers. But we had a nucleus of talented youngsters and a solid group of replacements from the two JV teams of Clyde Francisco and Sol Friedman.

The team was voted by the area sportswriters to win the Citrus Belt League championship once again. The season started well and we won several games in a row. We ran into snags about three times during the season. A sportswriter for the Pomona Progress Bulletin commented that their ball club was one of the few teams to defeat Chaffey during the year. We ended up in a tie for second place with Colton. A playoff victory with them gave us a playoff spot. Please see Story 78 (Commentary—CIF Playoff Record) for a list of our opponents and scores of the five CIF games.

We had batted .259 for the regular season, somewhat low for Chaffey teams. However, in the CIF playoffs we scored 72 runs on 76 hits batting .392 in those five games and won our second consecutive championship.

One story this season could be termed a baseball miracle. In late February at a sliding practice session my first baseman, Brian Zenz, limped over to me and said he had hurt his ankle in the sliding pit. I sent him to see a doctor and he returned an hour later with tears in his eyes. He said the ankle was broken and the doctor estimated that Brian would be in a cast for at least ten weeks. That would take us right up to the end of the season. I can still hear his words. "Coach, there goes my senior year in baseball." I encouraged him to hang in there and hope the injury would heal faster than expected.

Brian stayed with the club and helped wherever he could. He became my assistant coach. The weeks rolled by and, finally, in late April, the doctor said he could get some batting practice. A special cast was placed on his ankle and he was given the green light to play. It was really amazing how well he could move around the diamond with that cumbersome arrangement.

I put Brian in his first league game on April 26 and he drew a base on balls. The Chaffey crowd cheered. By the end of the league season Brian appeared at the plate 12 times and did very well. His movement on the field was hampered, of course, but he performed beautifully. Counting those four games and the five playoff games, Brian had an on-base percentage of .658 and batted .350. In a season of miracles, Brian was one of the key players in bringing another CIF championship to Chaffey.

The Tiger roster was as follows: Tim Bottoms, Howard Collins, Jim Ferris, Chuck Giordano (Co-Captain), Jim Hansen, Daryl Hunter, Russ Hunter (Manager), Jerry Johnson, Gary Lancaster, Jim Lisec, Jody Marker, Larry Maxie, Mickey Mehas, Sherrill McCown, Jim McGuire, Andy Prevedello, Vernon Pritchett, John Snell, Jim Syren, Reave Warren (Manager), and Brian Zenz (Co-Captain).

Pomona Tournament champions, Chaffey HS, 1957, A great comeback team.

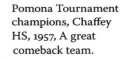

I saw Jim Hansen at spring training in Arizona recently and he is now a physician in Hawaii.

Mr. D. Patrick Ahern, noted baseball enthusiast, did the honors as speaker for the Ontario Kiwanis banquet. He did an excellent job and was roundly applauded by the audience.

STORY 76:

1958 Varsity Team— Back To Back To Back

Chaffey baseball had a very good year in 1958, our first in the Montview League. It was a season of strong defense. We averaged 0.8 errors per game and the pitching was superb. We entered the playoffs with just one loss and defeated five opponents by a composite score of 41 to 6 to win our third consecutive CIF championship. Our record at season's end was 24-1.

This squad consisted of the following players: Gary Balding, Jim Bice, Tim Bottoms, Bob Brown, Ivan Clevenger (Manager), Larry Dyer, Dick Frantzich, Randy Gold, Daryl Hunter, Russ Hunter (Manager), Jim Lisec, Ron Mau, Larry Maxie (Captain), Mick Mehas, Sherrill McCown, Dick Quesada, Jim Roberts, John Snell, and Ray Zak. Larry Maxie was the Player of the Year in the CIF and Jim Lisec earned second team all-CIF honors.

The speaker at the Ontario Kiwanis banquet was Pete Beiden, a longtime baseball coach. The baseball field at Fresno State University in California is named after Pete. He had 601 victories with only 268 losses at Fresno and coached 20 different years without having a losing season. He was one of the top coaches in the nation. He was a graduate of the University of Redlands. He coached several high school and college teams before taking over the Fresno State program. He spent some time in professional baseball as he managed the Visalia Cubs in the California League in 1948. With his vast knowledge of baseball he was very entertaining and did a fine job.

Ken's 1958 varsity, won 3rd CIF championship in a row.

Following the 1958 season we received the following letter from California State Senator Ray Gregory:

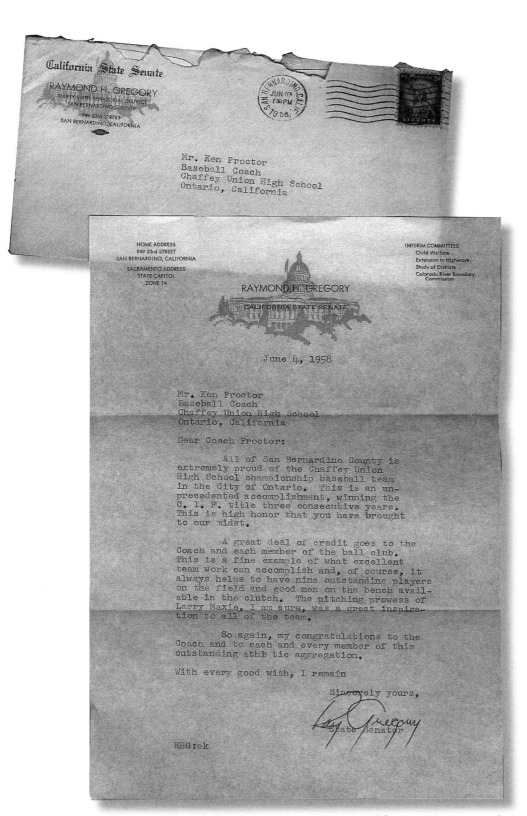

Senator Ray Gregory's letter. Senator Gregory was our California state representative.

1959 Varsity Team— Almost Perfect, 39-1

Once again the pressure was on us to win another CIF championship that would be our fourth in a row. We had a great start and finished our second Montview League season undefeated. We had won the Pomona Tournament for the third time to retire the permanent trophy, and played into the quarterfinals of the CIF as we won our 39th consecutive game. Our final record was 39-1.

Even though we were undefeated right up to the last game of the year we played a number of exciting and close games. The newspaper nicknamed our team as "The Heart Attack Kids." Our final game was a 6-4 loss to Morningside High School.

Team players were: Ed Barrett, Jim Bice, Tim Bottoms, Lowell Bosshardt, Gary Byrnes, John Carlson, Ivan Clevenger (Manager), Curt Cunningham, Larry Dyer, Mike Ensey, Jim Ferris, Greg Goddard, Randy Gold, Bill Gunn, Bill Isaacson, Rick Hunter (Manager), Doyle Lyman, Ron Mau (Co-Captain), Tom McFadden, Dave Myers, Jim Roberts, Jim Stauber, Stan Swerdloff, and Ray Zak (Co-Captain).

It was a very exciting year. The newspapers carried the story throughout the season that Chaffey was undefeated and shooting for a fourth consecutive CIF championship. On April 3 we had a non-league game scheduled with our neighbor, Upland High School. Big brother, Chaffey, was supposed to take our smaller northern neighbor to the cleaners.

Chaffey opened the first inning with four big runs. The rout was on, right? Not on your life. Pitcher Jim Davis of Upland settled down and inning by inning

Ken's 1959 varsity, Pomona Tournament champions and ended season winning 39 games and losing one game, our final contest.

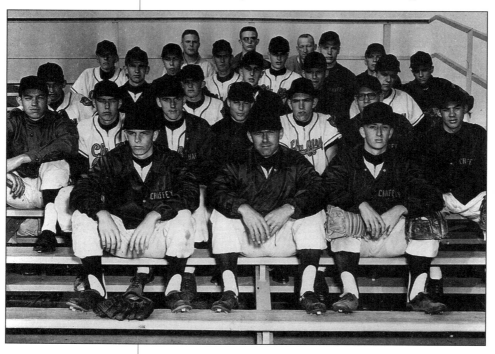

shut Chaffey down as we left eight men on base. In the meantime Upland scored a run in the fourth inning and rallied in the sixth inning to take the lead, 5-4. The impossible was happening. How could they possibly defeat the Chaffey powerhouse who had won the last 90% of their games?

Top: Pomona Tournament champions 1959.

Bottom: Ken in uniform (Ken concluded his high school coaching in 1959 and became Director of Athletics at Chaffey.)

The contest continued on until the eighth inning and I called for a pinch hitter. His name was Jim Ferris who had good power and was used occasionally in pinch-hit roles. Jim stepped up and powered the first pitch over the right field fence to tie the game at 5-5. Darkness was falling on the field and by the time the ninth inning was over, the game was called. It saved our streak and we continued winning until the last pitch of the semi-finals of the CIF giving us a 39-1 season.

I saw Doyle Lyman recently and found that he had been coaching baseball at Bonita and San Dimas High Schools. He was always a good student of the game. Ray Zak headed up the intramural program at UCLA for many years before retiring and Dave Myers became the principal of Chaffey High School. And, Tom McFadden served as the baseball coach at Ontario High School.

It was fitting that this season, my last year coaching varsity baseball at Chaffey, that my college coach, Art Reichle, was the speaker at the Ontario Kiwanis banquet.

I have made a few comments about some of the Chaffey baseball players and what they are doing today. It is difficult to know all of their life stories. I would just like to say that nearly all of these players have made their marks in a positive way. Our students at Chaffey and all other schools in those days produced scores of good citizens and successful people. It was such a privilege to have the opportunity to be with them and be a part of their lives.

STORY 78:

Commentary— Putting It All Together

There are a number of miscellaneous items I want to cover here. Many people are involved in any school or college including school employees, community individuals, and parents. This is an attempt to bring these items into one story.

A. Chaffey School District and Administration Support

I doubt if there ever was a baseball coach who had more support from his administration than I. This was typical of the Chaffey School District in support of it students. We never had an eligibility problem because the district did its job and played by the rules. I could always count on transportation (buses adequate and on time), the best of playing fields, the highest quality food services, clean and sufficient locker rooms, and the best equipment. We had one of the best trainers in the southland in Homer Thompson.

Our student body was always there for us. The janitorial staff did a 100% job. I mentioned good playing fields. The grounds crew always went beyond the call of duty under the direction of Leo Petsuch. The Chaffey faculty and counselors were among the best. Superintendent Dan Milliken. Principal Ernest Payne, Director of Athletics George Thorne followed by Al Smith, the Chaffey coaching staff, and all concerned made our path less difficult. It takes many cooperative people to make a school function properly and we certainly had those people. I owe a great debt of gratitude of everyone involved.

B. No Cuts in Baseball—Everyone Plays

(Please see the two lead paragraphs of Chapter 4). When I had all those youngsters turn out for baseball in 1950 I realized immediately that many of them would not have a place to play baseball because of our limited program. Most programs were that way in the past and hundreds of thousands of young hopefuls were turned away all over the nation. I had recalled trying to make teams myself when I was a young boy. The thought of being cut was devastating. Some people have said that life is that way and people have to learn to live with reality. That may be true but I had another idea.

I did not accept that theory and I made an appointment with the superintendent, Dr. Daniel B. Milliken to discuss the matter with him. I told him I had a plan that would allow every boy in school who desired to play baseball to do so and at very little cost to the school district. My plan was to juggle field use so we could have a varsity and junior varsity plus a group we would designate as "intramural." I had done some groundwork before my appointment and found some men who would serve as coaches. The first two teams would play a home-and-home schedule with other schools while the intramural squad would be broken into teams and play each other only at Chaffey.

The look on Dr. Milliken's face was one I will never forget. He saw the value of such a program and with a twinkle in his eyes he approved the idea and told me to get started. The program was very successful and was a big hit with the community, especially the parents of the young players. And soon we added two more teams, namely, sophomore and freshmen giving us 80 uniformed players and another 50 in the intramural group.

It turned out that we had some freshmen intramural players who, because of the opportunity to play, earned their way to one of the regular teams. I am not sure if other schools tried the same type of program but I do know if I were starting over today, I would initiate it again. I owe much to Dr. Milliken's foresight in recognizing the program's value.

C. Chaffey Baseball Coaches, 1949-1959

1949-1952:
Varsity Harry Yochem
JV Bill Culler
JV Ken Proctor

1953:
Varsity Ken Proctor
JV Bob Schweighardt
Intramural Lyle Fry

1954:
Varsity Ken Proctor
JV, Ray Stark;
Intramural, Lyle Fry

1955:
Varsity Ken Proctor
JV Clyde Francisco
JR-Reserve John Peterson
Intramural Sol Friedman

1956:
Varsity Ken Proctor
JV-Orange Clyde Francisco
JV-Black Sol Friedman
Freshmen Lud Rathbone
Intramural Jim Blake

1957: **Varsity** Ken Proctor
       JV-Orange Clyde Francisco
       JV-Black Sol Friedman
       Freshmen Bob Keeney
       Intramural George Thorne

1958: **Varsity** Ken Proctor
       JV-Orange Clyde Francisco
       JV-Black Sol Friedman
       Freshmen Larry Adler
       Intramural Dick Luciani

1959: **Varsity** Ken Proctor
       JV-Orange Clyde Francisco
       JV-Black Sol Friedman
       Freshmen Larry Adler
       Intramural Angie Antonelli

D. Ontario Kiwanis Club

I was fortunate to be a member of the Ontario Kiwanis Club from 1950 to 1964. We had over 100 members. They came from many parts of our community. We met every Tuesday at noon at the local YMCA where we had lunch, took care of business matters, enjoyed some fun, and had a speaker.

The club supported many community activities. In addition to various youth programs that benefited the youth of Ontario, they provided funding and leadership for the annual baseball banquets. Individual members sponsored awards such as the Most Valuable Player and Most Improved Player for every part of our program (Varsity, JV-Orange, JV-Black, Freshmen and Intramural). In addition they provided varsity trophies for the Outstanding Pitcher Award, Leading Hitter Award, and Most Inspirational Player Award.

A prayer of thanksgiving was provided at each banquet by an area minister. One of the Kiwanis members served as Master of Ceremonies. They invited a high quality special speaker to bring a message to participants. Excellent dinners were served at a very reasonable cost and usually prime rib, incidentally.

My appreciation was always extended to these fine men. They gave some support and recognition to our high school, our program, and the 130 individual players each season.

E. Pomona 20/30 Club Baseball Tournament Participation

The Pomona 20/30 Club Baseball Tournament was one of the great high school baseball competitions in the nation. Thirty-two of Southern California's best high school teams strived each year to win five consecutive games to take the title. Many of the highest ranked teams were involved in this storied action. Dozens of future major league players participated through the years. The Pomona 20/30 Club deserved much credit for providing this excellent tournament. The following are the results of Chaffey teams from 1953 through 1959:

	CHAFFEY	OPPONENT		
1953	8	Rosemead	1	
	11	Covina	3	
	9	Lynwood	6	
	5	Colton	8	(Lost in semi-finals)
1954	4	Montebello	2	
	17	Santa Ana	5	
	10	Santa Monica	8	
		Burroughs	1	
	3	Lynwood	2	(Won the championship, the first CBL team in history to do so)
1955	3	Baldwin Park	6	(Lost in 1st round)
1956	8	Fallbrook	1	
	1	Colton	6	(Lost in second round)
1957	6	Mary Star of the Sea	0	
	4	San Bernardino	0	
	1	Pomona	2	
	2	North Phoenix	2	
	4	Burroughs	3	(Won championship)
1958	8	Arroyo Grande	0	(tournament rained out & called off)

10	San Bernardino	0	
3	Ventura	1	
11	Ganesha	1	
8	Riverside	1	
9	Fontana	4	(Won championship) Overall Pomona Tournament Record Won 20, Lost 3 (87%)

F. Citrus Belt League and Montview League Titles

Chaffey won the Citrus Belt League championship in 1954, 1955, and 1956. We were second in 1957 but went on to win the C.I.F. championship. Chaffey was assigned to the new Montview League and we won titles in both 1958 and 1959.

OVERALL RECORD FROM 1950 THROUGH 1959

The various season won/lost records were as follows:

	WON	LOST
1950 (JV)	8	4
1951 (JV)	11	2
1952 (JV)	11	1
1953 (Varsity)	14	8
1954 (Varsity)	22	2
1955 (Varsity)	20	6
1956 (Varsity)	22	3
1957 (Varsity)	25	5
1958 (Varsity)	24	1
1959 (Varsity)	39	1 (tied one game, Upland)
JV	30	7 (81%)
Varsity	166	26 (87%)
TOTALS	196	33 (86%)

G. C.I.F. Playoff Record

The baseball squads made it to the playoffs every season except 1953. The following is Chaffey's results of the playoff years:

1954:	Lost in first round to Fullerton, 3-2 in 14 innings.
1955:	Lost in first round to Baldwin Park, 6-3.
1956:	Had bye in first round.
	Defeated Mira Costa, 11-1.
	Defeated San Diego Hoover, 4-3.
	Defeated Montebello, 8-6 (walk off home run).
	Defeated Oxnard, 3-0, and won the CHAMPIONSHIP.
1957:	Defeated Chula Vista, 27-12.
	Defeated Anaheim, 13-3.
	Defeated San Diego, 13-4.
	Defeated Muir, 10-0.
	Defeated San Diego Hoover 9-3 & won CHAMPIONSHIP.
1958:	Defeated Helix, 9-1.
	Defeated Montebello, 9-1.
	Defeated Anaheim, 5-3.
	Defeated Oxnard, 4-1.
	Defeated Lynwood, 14-0, and won CHAMPIONSHIP.
1959:	Defeated Burroughs, 8-5.
	Defeated Notre Dame, 4-3.
	Lost in semi-finals to Morningside, 6-4.
	Final CIF record in six years: 16 wins, 3 losses.

Totals   196   33   (86%)

H. Everyone Had a Job

I tried to make each member of the team an assistant coach. Every player on the team had a job to do during a game. For those not actively in the game at the time we assigned them to watch whether or not our opponents touched the bases as they ran. If we saw someone miss a base it was reported to me and I made a decision whether or not we would make an appeal to the umpire at the appropriate time in hopes of getting an out.

Others were assigned to try and pick up signs and signals from the opposing team. Sometimes we could figure out their pitch out, steal, squeeze, etc. signs.

In one of our games I had a player, Tim Bottoms, come to me and tell me he had figured out when the opposing pitcher was going to throw a curve ball. It was simple but effective. The pitcher bit his lip every time he threw a curve ball. For the rest of that game we knew when that particular pitch was coming. Tim went on to become a star pitcher at UCLA. He was a smart young man.

All players were to watch for weaknesses on the opposing team. It could be a weak throwing arm in left field or the inability for an infielder to go right or left. Such knowledge could often provide us an advantage in a given situation.

I. Dimes and Quarters

I hope you find this section interesting. We had to pay $24.00 per dozen for base-balls in those days which was two dollars per ball. They were the quality Pacific Coast League model, A1010. Every time a foul ball went over the roof of the sta-dium, and that was often in most games, our budget was depleted two bucks.

My first year I came up with the idea of paying young kids a dime if they would return the ball to me. I was pretty much working alone at the ballpark and kept a back pocket full of dimes. It worked great the first two or three years.

With hamburgers and malts and other food products going up in price, the kids soon decided a dime was not enough. So, the hard facts of economics took its course and we had to give a quarter for every ball. That seemed to work fine for the rest of our experience there. Today a high quality baseball brings about $5.00 each so I expect the output would be a dollar or two for a returned ball. By the way, just for your information, a good quality wooden bat back then was about $48.00 per dozen (four dollars per bat). Today they cost $720.00 per dozen or SIXTY DOLLARS PER BAT. Perhaps this is part of the reason many high school and college teams are using metal bats.

Regarding baseballs, a quick calculation will show that we saved a lot of money with this process of paying for returned foul balls. And, the kids loved it. Everybody won!

J. Banquet Speakers

In each of my seven varsity seasons (1953 to 1959) we had outstanding speakers at our annual banquets. Each one was excellent in his own right. Please read about these speakers in the sections describing the various baseball seasons.

K. Riverside's Competitive Horsehiders

During our seven-year coaching span in the Citrus Belt and Montview Leagues many fine teams were our opponents. As I have stated previously, the competi-tion was fierce but fair. Everything was done with class and on a high level. Each team involved commanded respect with both character and their abilities to play the game correctly. Although any team could defeat another on any given day, through the years there was one team that stood out a bit above the rest. That would be the Riverside Poly Bears. Our competition with them was always

BUNTS CAN WIN OR LOSE IT - WATCH BALL HIT THE BAT

BE RELAXED CONFIDENT DETERMINED

Dugout sign (these are two of our dugout signs that were reminders for our players.)

played with honor and dignity. Their coach during my tenure was Ben Hammerschmidt. He was a gentleman and a fierce competitor. When we edged them out in the 1957 CIF playoffs even though they had won the CBL league title, we received a congratulatory and encouraging telegram from them as we met San Diego Hoover in the championship game. Hoover had defeated Riverside a few days earlier to edge them out of the playoffs. A Riverside victory in that game would have put two teams from the same league in the finals. To this day I still have friends from that team, one of which is Gary Adams, who coached the UCLA Bruins for over 30 years. His twin brother, Gene, and other teammates are pals. Chris Krug, their catcher, played with the Chicago Cubs and the San Diego Padres in the majors. Others I recall are John Merrill, Greg Shanz, Richie Stalder, Dan Mc-Cune, Anthony Scott, Tony Chavez, and Doug Major. I know there are others who were equally talented. They are all quality men.

L. Attitude of My Players and Managers

The quality of the young men on my teams was obvious. We simply could not have reached our goals without the collective attitude that was present. They were disciplined, responsible, loyal, eager, positive, competitive, resourceful, enthusiastic, spirited, poised, and confident. They were "do'ers."

After each victory we had a tradition of burning one end of the sign showing our opponent's name. It was a small ceremony but an activity the players enjoyed.

As the team spirit built each year, the seniors served as models for the younger players on the squad. They made sure the sophomores and juniors were properly dressed. If a player was not clean-cut they told him to get a haircut. They estab-

Burned signs (A small sign was printed for each opponent. When we won the tip of the sign was burned indicating victory. A different player burned the sign each time.)

lished a precedent whereby the younger players would shine the baseball shoes of the seniors. It became a tradition. The new seniors earned the privilege each year. It was done in good spirit with the end goal serving the best interests of the team as a whole. They were helping the coach to do his job.

They served as leaders at our annual baseball clinics. This assistance extended even into the community as they helped in organizing the youth leagues. It was truly a team effort to make the baseball program top notch both at Chaffey and in the area.

Yes, I have said it before and I will say it again. I was a very fortunate man to have the job of heading up our baseball program. And the type of players and managers I had made it all possible. Thank you, guys! You were and are the best!

M. Sportswriters

Harlow Smith, Chuck Elwell, and Jim Bryant (*The Daily Report*), Bob Speck, Jerry Boyd, Claude Anderson, Sam Feldman, Bruce Brown (*San Bernardino Sun*), Garland Rose (*Riverside Press & Enterprise*), and Jack Sloan and Stan Hochman (*Pomona Progress Bulletin*), Jack Hefley, Gary Smith, and Mel Durslag (*Los Angeles Times*) covered our games. Each of these gentlemen was a fine writer. All were capable and respected in their chosen field.

N. Jim Bryant, Sportswriter Deluxe

The *Ontario Daily Report* (now called the *Inland Valley Daily Bulletin*) was an outstanding newspaper. It received many awards through the years. I recall three sports editors there during my tenure at Chaffey. The first was Harlow Smith, a very bright and intelligent writer. Next was Chuck Elwell who did an excellent job. Both were very thorough.

The next gentleman arrived in Ontario a few years after I came to Chaffey.

His name is Jim Bryant. He was married to his job. His coverage of all Chaffey sports was truly outstanding. He had a way of covering sports in which he dug out the true story, the real facts. Accuracy was his watchword.

Jim was an outstanding photographer. Sometimes I could not understand how he could accomplish so much with his writing and photography work. Carrying his equipment alone was a major chore.

At our scheduled games Jim always showed up with a bag of lemons. It became routine. He never failed. And the players loved those lemons. It was just another thoughtful gesture that was part of Jim.

His stories had flare and were exciting to read. He covered anything associated with the sport including births of children of the coaches. I recall how he tied in the births of our boys, Kenny, Mike, and Scott, with important games we were playing.

Recently, I made a telephone call to Jim. He still lives in the same house in Ontario. We had a good long chat about our baseball days in our community. I discovered something I did not know. I refer you to Story 2 (The Panthers) about Harvard Playground in Los Angeles. That team played in the 1930s and, of all things, Jim was there and knew all about Harvard. We had all those years of fellowship in Ontario in the 1950s and were not aware that we may have crossed paths at Harvard years before.

Chaffey owes a great deal to Jim for his coverage of our sports program. His work was complete and genuine. He covered any and all Chaffey youngsters who went into professional baseball. He kept our community aware of their progress.

Jim Bryant, I salute you. You are a gentleman and writer of the first order. Thanks for your devoted friendship to all of us.

STORY 79:

TBF Torques, Buzzards, and Friends

This interesting acronym, TBF, (Torques, Buzzards, and Friends stands for a group of people who are connected with Chaffey High School in various ways.

The Torques and Buzzards were car clubs at Chaffey in 1950s.

Many of them had their meetings at the Ontario Police Department where they worked on civic activities and safety with the police as advisers. They were more or less social clubs centered around cars.

Mr. & Mrs. Don Warner (Shirley Lambeth), two Chaffey graduates, came up with the idea of getting their old friends together for fellowship and fun. This was in 1995 and the Warners, with the help of Dick Evenhuis, another Chaffeyite, collected enough names to make a list of fifty of the old gang. They booked rooms in Laughlin, Nevada where the rates were inexpensive, the food good, and the weather great. They

Top: Don and Shirley Warner (the leaders of TBF, Torques, Buzzards, and Friends)

Bottom: Five TBF baseball players at Laughlin (Hal Reniff, Jerry Johnson, Lou Hoyos, Joe DiCarlo, Jim McGuire)

held the first meeting at the end of February, 1996, and forty-eight attended. Thus, TBF was born.

In a large sense, Don and Shirley are total baseball fans. They follow the game closely. Don is a devoted Chaffeyite and ties baseball into TBF, especially because so many graduates either played baseball or followed our team closely as fans. They have given special attention to one of our players, Hal Reniff, who played for the New York Yankees. This has been particularly true because we lost Hal to cancer in September, 2004. Please see Stories No. 133 (Hal Reniff) and 33 (Hal Reniff, A Special Guy).

The membership has grown to over 200. Don and Shirley invited their coaches who they felt had helped mold their lives since many TBFers were athletes. This was a real break for Marilyn and me because we became part of the "Friends" group of TBF even though we were not Chaffey graduates. We attend a gathering at every opportunity.

The group gets together every year in Laughlin where they discuss the "old days of our youth." Other gatherings are held from time to time in other locations. In fact, those who live in the Ontario/Upland area get together at local eateries at least once a week to reminisce.

Don and Shirley deserve a world of credit for their endless work in keeping everyone informed. They distribute monthly newsletters and daily emails. It has become an activity of love for the Warners. There is not one member of TBF who does not cherish them dearly for their work in keeping TBF alive and well.

They reside in Lewiston, Idaho. Two sons, Ron and Stewart, live in Lewiston and a daughter, Julie lives in Prosser, Washington. Their children have nine of their own and one of the children has one grandchild.

CHAPTER 5

Stories About Some of My Favorite Major League Players

Through the years I have had contact, known or been friends with many baseball people. Some of these names involved stories about others. I made an effort to find out how many players were professionals through the years. I went to some websites including "BaseballLibrary.com," and the "Society for American Baseball Research" (SABR) and added up the number of ball players listed. It was 12,238 although another source tells me it is closer to 16,000 players. I expect it depends of the definition of a "player." It is evident that there are many stories and interesting facts about all these players. These are comparatively just a few that involved me personally and I hope you enjoy them.

STORY 80:

Rich Amaral— Utility Man Deluxe

We first met Rich and Michelle Amaral at a meeting of the members of the UCLA Baseball Hall of Fame in January, 2002. Rich and I played at UCLA many years apart. We were in Seattle in the 90s and Rich was playing for the Mariners. He was a solid utility man and a very good contact hitter. He had a great on-base percentage and was a very steady fielder. He was fast and had the ability to steal bases. In fact, at one point in his career he stole 46 bases of an attempted 54. He starred at UCLA in the late 70s and early 80s. He played in 727 major leagues games with a .276 average. He had 159 RBIs. A back injury forced him out of baseball in 2000.

Later, Rich was presented with a Mariner plaque and recognition for outstanding play and Marilyn and I had the privilege of sitting with them at that game. They are a great family and we count it a privilege to have them as friends.

STORY 81:

Wally Berger— My Buddy's Uncle

In 1935 I was eleven years old and had a neighbor friend by the name of Neil Johnson. His uncle was Wally Berger of the Boston Braves of the National League. I loved the game and was so impressed that Neil's uncle actually played in the major leagues. Wally Berger was an outstanding player and was involved in many of baseball's exciting years. He

played in 1,360 games in eleven years. He batted an even .300, had 242 home runs, and 898 RBIs. He played in one seven-game World Series. Berger had torn up the Pacific Coast League in 1929 as he starred for the Los Angeles Angels. In 1933 and 1934 he was the starting centerfielder for the National League All Star team. As a rookie in 1930 he hit 119 RBIs for the Braves. To show the immensity of that record, it was not broken for 71 years when Cardinal Albert Pujols, who is active today, had 120 RBIs. Also, in 1993 Mike Piazza had 100 RBIs, 30 home runs and batted .300 and no rookie had accomplished that feat since 1930 when Wally Berger did it.

There is one last interesting connection. I had mentioned having Mace Brown as a colleague on Guam in November 1945 Please see Story 7 (World War II Duty on Guam with Mace Brown). On September 16, 1935, Mace pitched five innings of relief to beat Boston and the only hit he allowed was a double by Berger who hit his third double of the game in the ninth inning. The only thing that kept Berger from being a more well-known baseball star is the fact that he never played on a winning team. With his tremendous ability he could well have been a Hall of Famer.

STORY 82:

Yogi Berra— Funny and Great

When my UCLA teammate, Bobby Brown, played for the New York Yankees, he often roomed with the incomparable Yogi Berra. Bobby said that having Yogi for a roommate was a great experience. We all know about the "Yogi stories." Well, Bobby has some that we do not ordinarily find in books. See the next to the last paragraph in this story. In the late 40s after Bobby had left our UCLA team, he attended medical school at Tulane University in the off-season and played for the Yankees from February to October. Yogi joined the Yankees in 1946 and, except for a few games with the New York Mets in 1965, played his entire 20-year career with the Yankees.

Yogi is known more for his unusual language than his playing. But, he was one of the great catchers and batters in the history of the game. He is one of four catchers to play an entire season without an error (1958). The famous baseballer, Paul Richards, said that Yogi was the most dangerous player in the game in the last three innings. He was, indeed, a clutch hitter. He played on ten World Champions. He was cat-like as a catcher and was said to be one of the great receivers in handling pitchers. His accomplishments are really beyond belief. He seemed to be the linchpin of those great Yankee teams. Though surrounded by many great players, Berra contributed in so many positive ways. Some called him the best "bad ball" hitter to ever play the game.

He played in an unmatched 14 World Series and holds records in the Fall Classic in games played (75), at bats (259), hits (71), and doubles (10). Casey Stengel called him a "great man," and said "he was lucky to have him and so are our pitchers." He was on the All Star team from 1948 through 1962 and was placed in the Baseball Hall of Fame in 1972.

Joe Garagiola told me he and Yogi played American Legion baseball together in St. Louis. They lived right across the street from each other. Both of them are in the St. Louis Walk of Fame, a group of heralded individuals from that great city. Please see Story 47 (Introducing Joe Garagiola),

third paragraph.

Bobby Brown is one of the foremost cardiologists in American medicine. One night in Detroit he and Yogi were rooming together and Bobby was studying his Gray's Anatomy, a huge medical book. Yogi was reading and kept looking over at Bobby. After an hour or so Yogi turned out his bed lamp and said, "Bobby, let me know in the morning how that turns out." Yogi stories are a major part of the fun of baseball fans. They held a "Yogi Berra Night" in St. Louis in 1947 and Yogi spoke into the microphone and said, "I want to thank everyone for making this night necessary." On a comment about inflation, Yogi once said, "A nickel ain't worth a dime anymore." He was asked how he liked school and his pithy reply was "Closed." Commenting about a New York restaurant, Yogi said, "Nobody goes there anymore, it's too crowded." There are entire books written on "Yogi-isms." I asked Bobby if these stories were true. And he replied, "yes, most of them."

Our hats are off to a man who has made this story necessary, Lawrence Peter "Yogi" Berra. He certainly is a great one!

STORY 83:

Hiram Bithorn— First Puerto Rican in the Majors

When I was a youngster in the 1930s I knew of a pitcher with the Oakland Acorns, as they were called at that time. His name was Hiram Bithorn (Spanish pronunciation is Eerom Beethorn). He was a capable pitcher and very popular. He pitched for several Pacific Coast League teams before going to the Chicago Cubs in 1942. Hi stayed with them until 1946 when he was sold to the Pittsburg Pirates. They released him in spring training and he signed with the Chicago White Sox.

Bithorn pitched 509 innings in the majors with a 34-31 record and an ERA of 3.16. In 1943 he posted an 18-12 record with 2.60 ERA and led the National League with seven shutouts.

When Marilyn and I visited Puerto Rico in 1993 we visited Hiram Bithorn Stadium (Estadio Hiram Bithorn). The name jumped out at me since I had remembered Hiram pitching some sixty years previously. The stadium is so-named because Hiram was the first Puerto Rican to make the big leagues in 1942.

Hiram was shot and killed in unusual circumstances in Mexico in 1952. He was there trying to make a comeback in the Mexican League. He was just 35 years old and it was very sad. Bithorn was a successful pitcher and I will always remember him as one of my boyhood heroes.

STORY 84:

Jim Bouton— A Tough Knuckleballer

In 1962 Jim Bouton signed his first professional baseball contract with the New York Yankees. I had followed his interesting career through the 1960s and 1970s but had no idea I would meet and get the opportunity to chat with him someday. In 1970 he wrote a book, "Ball Four," which received a lot of attention. He revealed many stories about the personal lives of his teammates and broke baseball taboos in doing so. He wrote about inside information of contract signings and other facts that the public did not know and he ruffled a few feathers of some players and personnel previously protected by baseball journalism. If you are a baseball fan I would recommend your reading Jim's book sometime.

In May of 2000, one year after I had introduced Joe Garagiola at an ARC of King Country luncheon in Seattle, once again a prominent baseball figure was invited as a guest speaker. That would be Jim Bouton. He did a fine job and gave an entertaining address to the assembled body in a downtown hotel.

Following the meeting I drove Jim to the airport where he caught a flight back to his home on the east coast. We had a good opportunity to exchange conversation. In the early sixties he and my star pitcher from Chaffey High School, Hal Reniff, were friends and teammates on the New York Yankees. Jim shared that Hal saved a number of his games for him when manager Ralph Houk gave Bouton the hook. He said he always felt comfortable when Hal took over his pitching duties.

Jim, a knuckleball specialist, shared an amusing story about Hal. It seems they were playing Cleveland one afternoon and it began to rain in the third inning. Before the game finally ended there were a total of four rain delays and at each delay, more and more fans left the park. As the two players headed for the locker room Hal asked Jim if he had brought his station wagon to the game to which Jim replied, "Yes I did. Why do you ask?" And Hal said, "Well I thought we might give the remaining fans a ride home." That certainly sounded like quick-witted Hal.

Bouton posted quite a record before leaving the game. He pitched 1,239 innings with a 62-63 record. More impressive was his career 3.57 ERA. He participated in 24 World Series innings with a 2-1 record and a phenomenal 1.48 ERA. In 1963 he was 21-7 with a 2.53 ERA and was among the league leaders in most categories. He had six shutouts and allowed the fewest hits per nine innings (6.89). He lost to Don Drysdale of the Los Angeles Dodgers 1-0 in game three of the 1963 World Series. It was one of great pitching duels of the 1960s. Jim said that he set a record in the 1964 World Series. His baseball cap came off his head 37 times. Incidentally, in that series between the Yankees and St. Louis, Jim was 2-0 but the Cardinals defeated New York four games to three.

Jim injured his arm in 1968 and spent the end of that year plus 1969 and 1970 in the bullpen. He tried a comeback in 1978 but he was forced to retire. Since his retirement he wrote about his comeback in a book called "Ball Five." Also, he was involved in several baseball-related businesses and was one of the inventors of "Big League Chew," a bubblegum shredded to resemble tobacco.

I enjoyed meeting and talking with Jim. He is certainly a personable nonconformist and contributed much to the game of baseball. His nickname is "Bulldog," the same as one of my favorite players, Orel Hershiser. It is easy to understand why both of them were given that monicker. Both played the game for keeps!

STORY 85:

Bobby Brown— Destined To Succeed

Various facts and information may be found about Bobby Brown in the following stories:

Story 36: (Yankee Stadium
with Dr. & Mrs. Bobby Brown).

Story 39: (Dick Butler, A Gentleman of Class).

Story 63: (1944 UCLA Team).

Story 82: (Yogi Berra).

Bobby was one of baseball's best hitters in the late 1940s and early 1950s when the Yankees were winning world titles regularly. He signed with the Yankees in 1947 and hit .300 his first year. He equaled that average in 1948. Over his major league career he played in 548 games with a .279 batting average. He hit 22 home runs and had 237 RBIs. He played in four World Series. It would have been six times in the Fall Classic but he was sent to Korea and Japan for assignment there. In World Series play he was in 17 games with a .439 batting average. He still holds the record in one World Series for getting three hits and a walk in four pinch hitting plate appearances. He retired from baseball in mid-1954 to practice medicine. He became a very successful private cardiologist. Thirty years later he left his successful career as a doctor and succeeded Lee MacPhail when he accepted the position of president of the American League (1984-1994).

Bobby has set high standards in both college and professional baseball. He has made a significant contribution to mankind as an outstanding medical doctor. He is a fellow UCLA Baseball Hall of Fame member and has received numerous awards and recognition for his medical contributions. This is an extra comment about Bobby. He is a very patriotic American and has become an expert in the history of the Civil War. It is one of his several hobbies. Also, he is a better-than-average tennis player.

We have enjoyed good comradeship with Bobby and Sara. It was a genuine pleasure to be Bobby's teammate and we cherish his and Sara's friendship.

STORY 86:

Mace Brown— A Great Relief Specialist

Please read Story 7 (World War II Duty on Guam with Mace Brown). My story says it all about Mace. He was a major leaguer in every sense of the word. I was so fortunate to have the opportunity to meet and work with him.

STORY 87:

Dick Butler—A Class Act

Please see Story 39 for specifics about a great baseball man, Dick Butler. I had the pleasure of meeting with Dick each time he visited Seattle to evaluate American League umpires for my friend, Dr. Bobby Brown, President of the American League.

He would call me from Fort Worth, Texas, and we would plan to have breakfast together. We spent the whole time just talking baseball. What a treat!

STORY 88:

Phil Cavaretta— One Of My First Heroes

Please see Story 5 (Phil Cavaretta's Bat). If you would go back and read the story I believe you will feel the emotion of an eleven year-old kid. Now seventy years later I can still feel that thrill of taking that bat home. It brings tears to my eyes. There were many of us out west who never had the chance to see a major league game. That made

the bat acquisition even more exciting. He was one of my heroes. Please look up information on Phil in the aforementioned story. He was a great ball player.

STORY 89:

Roberto Clemente— A Legend Of Puerto Rico

Please see Story 37 (Twenty-eight Ball Parks and Counting) and read down to the (National League—14) to Montreal Expos—Hiram Bithorn Stadium).

Marilyn and I took a trip to Puerto Rico in November 1993. We went to Hiram Bithorn Stadium (Estadio Hiram Bithorn) to see a baseball game. We saw other Puerto Rican ballparks as well on that trip. We had heard that baseball on the island was very popular and that many major leaguers played there in the winter to keep in shape and to improve their chances to secure better contracts.

Immediately next to the Bithorn stadium in San Juan is the Roberto Clemente Sports Complex.

STORY 90:

Ty Cobb—He Did It All

Ty Cobb retired in 1928 and held 90 major league records at that time. He was known for his split-handed grip that gave him more bat control but less power. He actually had a disdain for the long ball and the clamorous Babe Ruth. To prove his point, on May 5, 1925 against the St. Louis Browns, he slid his hands down the bat and hit three home runs that day. He hit two more the next day to drive his theory home. In 1907 he became the youngest player ever to win a batting title.

Batting was not the only talent possessed by this icon of baseball. In 1907 he had 30 outfield assists and led the league in assists in 1908. When he retired he was second all-time in assists and double plays for outfielders.

Cobb set an American League record in 1911 by getting at least one hit in 41 consecutive games. Young Shoeless Joe Jackson of the Cleveland Indians (he was not with the Chicago White Sox yet) was challenging Ty for the batting title that year. But Cobb came on strong in a six-game series between the two teams late in the season and outhit Joe by twelve percentage points, .420 to .408.

Cobb's baserunning was renowned. He stole all bases including home several times to win games. He was the career steal leader for more that fifty years until young Lou Brock broke the record on August 29, 1977 (Maury Wills had broken Ty's single season record with 104 stolen bases in 1962. Marilyn and I were among those in the stands yelling "Go, go, go," when Wills was on first base). He not only won games with his baserunning, but put fear in the hearts of all infielders who tried to tag him out. A young catcher once asked a veteran what to do when Cobb tried to steal second base. The reply was a casual, "throw to third."

Baseball lost one of its most colorful and controversial characters when Cobb passed away July 17, 1961 in Atlanta. He was 74. Please see Story 35 (Happening on Ty Cobb's Home Town) for more on the life of this great player.

Del Crandall— A Winner On and Off the Field

I met Del Crandall in 1951 at an All Star game in Ontario, California. He had signed in 1949 with the Boston Braves and became their regular catcher at age 19. It was a fund-raiser for baseball in our community and players gave their time to support it.

Del was a very impressive young man, a good-looking athlete with lots of energy and drive. Interestingly, as the high school coach and member of our baseball community, I was asked to umpire that game. Since Crandall was catching we had occasion to speak to each other several times. It was evident that Del wanted the umpire to keep on his toes and I worked hard to do a good job.

As the years rolled by Del became the regular catcher of the Milwaukee Braves as they moved from Boston. He was one of the great defensive catchers at that time. He won four Gold Gloves and appeared in eight All Star games. He starred behind the plate as the Braves defeated the New York Yankees, four games to three, in the 1957 World Series. They played again in the 1958 World Series with the New York club turning the tables and winning four games to three. Crandall homered in both series. In three separate seasons he hit more than 20 home runs. His career-high season for batting average was 1962 when he hit .297.

Del was a brainy baseball manager having led the Milwaukee Brewers from 1972 to 1975 and the Seattle Mariners from 1983 to 1984. In both instances he simply did not have the players to compete with other teams in the American League and management put the blame on Del.

On May 31, 1964, Del was involved in the longest baseball doubleheader ever played. The Mets were playing the Giants at home and the whole affair commenced at 1:00 p.m. In the top of the 23rd inning of the second game, Del won it for San Francisco 8-6 with a double to score two runs. After the Mets failed to score in the bottom of the inning, it ended a game that took seven hours and twenty-two minutes, a record. The entire doubleheader was played in 32 innings and took nine hours and fifty minutes—both doubleheader records, as are 47 strikeouts. In addition the Mets struck out twenty-two times in the second game, an overtime contest record. It was quite a day at the ballpark!

It was interesting to me that Del was born in Ontario, California, the same town where I first met him and where I was coaching. His family later moved to Fullerton where he played in his school days.

Del Crandall is a quality man. He was not only an outstanding baseball player but a gentleman of the highest order. It was certainly my privilege to meet and know him.

STORY 92:

Dominic Dallesandro— More Power Per Pound

"Dim Dom" is an unusual nickname but that is, indeed, the actual diminutive of Dominic Dallesandro. It stands for "Diminutive Dominic." Dom was just 5'6" tall and a modest 168 pounds.

Dom played eight years in the major leagues for the Boston Red Sox and Chicago Cubs. He batted .267 with 22 home runs and 303 RBIs. His high year was 1944 when his average reached .304.

I saw Dom play in the Pacific Coast League in the late 1930s. I clearly recall his outstanding timing in hitting a baseball. His size did not prevent him from walloping the long ball. He was a hero for smaller players who realized they could be good hitters with timing rather than sheer strength.

He was certainly one the colorful players of the 1930s and 1940s. Dom passed away in 1988 at the age of 75.

STORY 93:

Dizzy Dean— It Ain't Braggin' When You Can Do It

Please see Story 4 (Dizzy Dean's Promise) about an experience I had with this great player. He referred to himself as "Ole Diz." He was probably one of the most confident men to play the game.

Dean had only six full seasons in the majors. When he signed his first contract in 1930 he was an immediate success. He had a 25-10 minor league record before he pitched a three-hitter for the St. Louis Cardinals on the last day of the season. He returned to the minor league Houston club in 1931 and struck out 303 batters as he had 26 victories. The following year he joined the famous "Gas House Gang," World Champions. He led the league in innings pitched, strikeouts, and shut outs while winning 18 games. In 1933 he absolutely overwhelmed batters and continued so for the next four years. He won 102 games and led the league in complete games and pitched more than 300 innings per season. He even came out of the bullpen between starts to win games.

In the World Series of 1934 between the St. Louis Cardinals and Detroit Tigers, Dizzy and brother, Paul, dominated the pitching. Dizzy won the first game, 8-3. He won the seventh game as he shut out the Tigers, 11-0, to take the series 4-3.

Paul was 2-0 in that series and had an incredible 1.00 ERA.

In 1935 Dean won 24 games and saved 11. He and brother, Paul, won 47 games between them.

Dizzy was a remarkable player. He was a braggart and could back up everything he claimed. Along with his obvious avoidance of the rules of grammar he was a legendary favorite of the fans. They loved him. He was one of the characters who popularized the game of baseball as it was developing into America's best pastime. As we see fans today express their love for baseball we have to give much credit to players such as "Ole Diz," who built some of the foundations of this great spectator sport.

STORY 94:

Joe Dimaggio—Player of the Century, 1869-1969

It is difficult to say that one player is better than all the rest. But, if one were to try and make such a statement, Joe DiMaggio would certainly be among the leaders. I watched Joe play for the San Francisco Seals in the early 1930s and he was sensational. Actually, he was purchased by the Yankees from the Seals in 1934 and allowed to play one more year for San Francisco. He reported to New York in spring training 1936 and proceeded to set rookie records for runs (132) and triples (15), and he hit .323 with 29 home runs and 125 RBIs. He amazed baseball fans everywhere.

Many admired Joe because he did everything with such ease. He was graceful and did not try to be spectacular. It just came natural to him the way he played. He was always in the right place at the right time. He always threw to the correct base and with power and accuracy. In 1947 he made just one error the entire year. Manager Joe McCarthy said he was the best base runner he had ever seen. He did everything stoically with no showmanship. Many of today's athletes could learn a lesson from Joe in that regard.

Please see Story 8 (Playing Against the Yankee Clipper, Joe DiMaggio) for more enlightenment about a player who generally avoided the limelight and was, indeed, named Player of the Century. In this regard, Joe reminds me of our UCLA basketball coach, John Wooden. The last thing Coach wanted to see on the basketball court was a showoff. Many admired Joe for the fact that he refused to rest on his natural skills but instead made an effort to improve his play everyday. One writer commented that he was more than an exceptional athlete, but rather the consummate professional.

STORY 95:

Larry Doby— Check Out His Numbers

Please see Story 10 (A Major League Pop-Up by Larry Doby). This man was truly a Hall of Famer. In his first year, 1948, he hit 16 home runs and batted .301 to help the Cleveland Indians to a World Championship, 4-3, over the New York Giants. His home run won the fourth game, 2-1. He had seven hits in the series and batted .318. He continued to improve and had 32 home runs and a .541 slugging percentage by 1952.

Doby affectionately called Bill Veeck his "godfather." Bill owned the Cleveland Indians and signed Larry four months after Jackie Robinson had broken the color line in Brooklyn. Incidentally, Veeck was instrumental in many changes in baseball over the years.

Larry was born in South Carolina in 1923 and grew up in New Jersey. He passed away in 2003.

STORY 96:

Bobby Doerr—Babe Says He Was "The MVP of the Red Sox"

I met Bobby Doerr at our PEMCO office in Seattle in 1989. Bobby is a friend of George Flood with whom I worked several years. Bobby lives in Oregon and is still playing golf. We see him on occasion.

Doerr was one of my boyhood heroes although he is just six years my senior. When I was 17 years old I recall Bobby playing second base for the Boston Red Sox. In fact, he was one of the players who prompted me to become a second baseman. He was very tough as a hitter and a defensive wizard in the infield. He had great range and was sure-handed having retired with a .980 fielding average.

Robert Doerr's middle name is "Pershing" in honor of General John J. Pershing, World War I hero. He was one of those players who signed with a team, the Boston Red Sox, and stayed with them his entire career. Doerr signed in 1937 with Boston by Hall of Famer Eddie Collins, who was actually part owner of Red Sox at the time. On a recruiting trip to California Collins signed both Doerr

and Ted Williams, quite a catch for the Beantowners. And, in fact, Bobby and Ted became very close friends on the Red Sox team in the following years.

Bobby played fifteen consecutive seasons with Boston and never batted below .270 in his career. He played in 1,865 games with a .288 average, 223 home runs and 1.247 RBIs. He was an All Star from 1941 through 1944, 1946 through 1948, and in 1950 and 1951. His World Series marks are six games and a .409 batting average.

He was forced into early retirement with an injury in 1951 at the tender age of 33. He later coached for both the Red Sox and the Toronto Blue Jays. In 1986 Bobby was voted into baseball's Hall of Fame. In l946 Babe Ruth was asked who was the Most Valuable Player in the American League that year. The Babe replied that Bobby Doerr, and not Ted Williams, was the number one player on the old Red Sox, and deserved the MVP Award.

This man was known by fans, coaches, and players as one of the finest to ever play the game. He has the respect of all as a kind and courteous gentleman. I considered it a rare privilege to have the opportunity to know Bobby Doerr personally.

STORY 97:

Ryne Duren— You Better Duck!

There is some sadness to this story. When I was in the middle of my high school coaching career, I often pointed to Ryne Duren as a reliever who could change the course of a team's success. He had a blazing 95 MPH fastball. He pitched for six different clubs and was at his peak in the late 1950s and early 1960s with the New York Yankees. Ryne had uncorrected vision of 20/70 and 20/200 and wore very thick glasses. As he would squint toward home he would frighten batters. To add to their fear, Ryne would intentionally throw his first warm-up pitch against the backstop. The story goes that in the minors once he hit an on-deck batter.

So, Ryne quickly acquired the nickname of "Blind Ryne." He was an immediate success with New York. In the 1958 World Series against the Milwaukee Braves he made three appearances in relief with a 1.93 ERA. He helped the Yankees to come back from a 3-1 game deficit to defeat Fred Haney's Braves. Also, this was Casey Stengel's seventh world title tying him with former Yankee manager Joe McCarthy for winningest managers in the World Series.

Duren was in the big leagues from 1954 to 1965. He pitched in 589 innings with a 3.83 ERA. He retired with 57 saves. Why is this story sad? Ryne had it made in baseball but he made a quick decline because of his drinking habits. The troubled highway he chose and the difficulties it caused him are described in his autobiography, The Comeback. He was certainly one of the most promising relievers of all time.

STORY 98:

Carl Erskine— In a Rundown Between 1st and Home

Carl Erskine told a very humorous story at a conference of the Fellowship of Christian Athletes in Ashland, Oregon in the late 1950s. Please see Story 30 (The Fellowship of Christian Athletes),

paragraphs number five and six. It involves a story about Carl and the late great Babe Herman, outstanding major leaguer.

Carl was a personable and capable baseball player with the Brooklyn Dodgers who won 61% of his pitching decisions in twelve years with the "Bums." He had a shoulder injury in his rookie year and pitched in pain most of his career. However, Carl had many bright moments on the mound. He was another one of those major leaguers who played for only one franchise, the Dodgers (ten with Brooklyn and two with Los Angeles).

Erskine was a big hit with the young men at the FCA conference in Ashland. He told another story about bunting the ball along the first base line. As the first baseman fielded the ball, Erskine stopped and ran back toward home plate. The first baseman threw the ball home and Erskine reversed his direction again. Carl's next statement brought down the house. He said, "Here I was in a rundown between first and home." He went on to say that he finally headed back towards home and slid in to avoid the tag. He was tagged out and asked umpire Beans Reardon, "Beans, what would I have been if I had been safe?"

Carl gave a good account of himself almost every time he took the mound. His record of 122-78 attests to that fact. He is another of those men who exemplified good character and served as a model for young hopefuls. He resides in the city of his birth, Anderson, Indiana, with his wife, Betty. They have been married for 58 years.

STORY 99:

Bob Feller— They Don't Come Any Better

Please see Story 31 (Will You Pitch Batting Practice to Me, Mr. Feller?) for information about Bob Feller's great pitching career.

To this day Bob is a popular ambassador for baseball. Feller is another of those great Americans who serve as a model for youngsters. When a need arose one could always count on Bob Feller to be there with assistance. This was true when he joined the Armed Services in World War II. And it was true whenever there was a need in helping people.

Our hats are off to you, Bob. Thanks for consistency in everything you have done. You are indeed an inspiration.

STORY 100:

Rollie Fingers— More Saves Than Anyone

When I was coaching at Chaffey High School in Ontario, California, Rollie Fingers was a youngster living in Upland just north of us. Several of my players were from Upland because they had no high school at that time and Upland was in our school district. The Ontario and Upland players through the years were well known to each other. Rollie had played with a number of them in youth baseball in our community.

He was signed by the Oakland A's in 1968 at the age of 22. Rollie was an immediate winner and succeeded as a starter. But his real contribution was

yet to come when he became a relief pitcher. In fact, even though he was a starter in 1969, 1970 and 1971, he finished each year in the bullpen. And from that start many feel he was the best relief pitcher who ever played the game.

Over his 17-year career Fingers pitched 1,701.1 innings with a 2.90 ERA. In the League Championship Series he posted a 3.72 ERA and in 33 World Series games he was credited with a 1.35 ERA. Rollie leads all relief pitchers with 341 saves. Only two others, Bruce Sutter and Rich Gossage sport more than 300 saves.

Fingers made it a point to never pitch more than two innings at a time thereby saving his strength. He led baseball in saves many times and his ERA was often under 2.00. He once joined three other pitchers in tossing a no-hitter for Oakland. They would be Vida Blue, Glenn Abbott, and Paul Lindblad. He was elected into the Hall of Fame on August 2, 1992. Also, he once won the Cy Young Award and the league MVP Award in the same year, 1981. Rollie was known for his handlebar mustache. In fact, he might have pitched one more year by signing with Cincinnati but he refused to shave off the mustache that was the Red's policy.

STORY 101:

Whitey Ford— The Leader Of The Pack

I never met Whitey Ford but I knew much about him through a pitcher I coached in high school who played for the New York Yankees for six years. His name was Hal Reniff. Please see Story 33 (Hal Reniff, A Special Guy). Hal palled around with Whitey and Mickey Mantle. He said Ford was kind of "the leader of the pack." Mickey just went along for the ride. Both Whitey and Mickey played their careers only with the Yankees.

Hal said that Whitey had complete command on the mound when he pitched. His assortment of pitches, change of speeds, and knowledge of hitters was nothing short of phenomenal. In his sixteen years with New York they won eleven pennants. Whitey was usually at the top of the list in every department.

His lifetime marks were 3,170 innings pitched, a record of 236 wins against 106 losses, and an ERA of 2.75. His World Series record was 146 innings with a win-loss record of 10-8, and a 2.71 ERA. He actually broke Babe Ruth's World Series record of 29 2/3 scoreless innings with 33 during the 1961, 1962, and 1963 World Series. Hal was the major right-handed reliever during those years although he said it was rare to come in for Whitey.

Hal said that his friendship with Whitey and Mickey was the most fun he had during those years. Whitey and Mickey were inducted into the Hall of Fame together in 1974.

STORY 102:

Augie Galan— "Joe D." Was His Replacement in the Pacific Coast League

Augie "Frenchy" Galan played infield and outfield for the Chicago Cubs beginning in 1934. This player was a true hero of mine. He could do it all despite having a deformed arm from a baseball accident as a youngster.

How he broke into the major leagues is most interesting. Augie was playing for the San Francisco Seals in the old Pacific Coast League. A group of big leaguers came through town on their way to Hawaii for some exhibition games. They needed a shortstop and invited Augie to come with them. The Seal's owner gave permission for him to leave three days before the season ended if a replacement could be found for Galan. Vince DiMaggio volunteered that his 17-year old brother could fill in for him. The Seals agreed to put young "Joe DiMaggio" at shortstop for the last three games in 1932. The following year Joe batted .340, led the Pacific Coast League with 169 RBIs and hit safely in 61 consecutive games. How about that?

Galan went on to bat .356 in 1933 and collected 265 hits with 51 doubles and 102 RBIs. On top of those marks he scored 164 runs and had 22 triples. Those records earned him a contract with the Cubs, who gave $25,000 and seven veteran players to the Seals in exchange for Augie. Joe signed with the New York Yankees in 1936 and the rest is history. Please see Story 8 (Joe DiMaggio) for more about the Yankee Clipper.

In his career, Augie played in 1,742 games with a .287 batting average, 100 home runs, and 830 RBIs. He was the first everyday player to go an entire season without hitting into a double play although, strangely enough, he did hit into a triple play that year (1935). And he was the first to hit home runs from both sides of the plate in the same game.

This is an interesting part of the story. I recall Augie being the only switch hitter in baseball at that time. Switch hitters did not exist then. I have looked up many records and believe that is true. Please see Story 193 (Lefties and Righties Today) in which my research shows the number of switch hitters today in baseball along with some other facts.

Augie was a speed merchant on the bases. In 1936 he became the first Cub to homer in the All Star Game. He was injured in 1940 and was traded to the Dodgers the following year. But, he continued to produce well batting over .300 each season from 1944 to 1947. After 1945 he batted exclusively left-handed. Incidentally, Augie threw right-handed.

Galan spent fifteen years in the majors with the Cubs, Dodgers, Reds, New York Giants, and Philadelphia Athletics. In his final years Augie managed the Oakland Oaks and the Philadelphia Phillies and also coached under the great Mel Ott. I think of Augie with great admiration. He was Mr. Consistency. Upon retirement, Augie managed a group of meat markets in the Bay Area of San Francisco.

STORY 103:

Mike Gazella— He Faced Walter Johnson

Please see Story 11 (Mike Gazella, A Former Yankee) for some background about this teammate of Babe Ruth and Lou Gehrig.

Mike played on the 1926 World Champion Yankees at third base and shortstop. He had originally spent some time with New York in 1923 and was sent to the minor leagues. He returned in 1926 and was an infield fixture through 1928. He was there when Babe Ruth and Lou Gehrig were in their prime.

Later in 1934 Mike played for the Los Angeles Angels in the Pacific Coast League. From 1937 through 1940, Mike managed the Moline Plowboys of the Three-I League. He led his team to the playoffs two years in succession and won the league championship in 1937.

STORY 104:

Troy Glaus— MVP of the 2002 World Series

I met Troy Glaus on January 24, 2002 at the UCLA Hall of Fame Day at Jackie Robinson Stadium near the campus. There were approximately twenty former Bruin baseball players present who were now in the big leagues. Please see Story 67 (UCLA Baseball Hall of Fame) for more details.

Troy was a member of the Anaheim Angels playing third base. He had led the American League in home runs the previous year with 47. The following season Troy was voted the MVP the World Series against the San Francisco Giants.

The purpose of the UCLA gathering was to induct five former Bruins into the UCLA Baseball Hall of Fame. There was an old timers' game plus an alumni game followed by an evening banquet. I happened to be one of the five to be inducted and brought my wife, son, grandson, and brother-in-law with me. We had an enjoyable day.

Troy has been traded to the Arizona Diamondbacks and currently is their regular third baseman. Barring injury, he should have a great career.

STORY 105:

Ken Griffey Sr.—
A Member of the
Big Red Machine

I am a Seattle resident. I met the two Ken Griffeys when they played on the Mariners team together. When Sparky Anderson was the manager of the Cincinnati Reds I followed Senior on a regular basis.

Senior played eighteen years in the major leagues including 1973-1981 with Cincinnati, 1982-1986 with the Yankees, 1986-1988 for the Braves, back to Cincinnati for 1988-1990, and finally 1990-1991 with the Mariners. Senior and Junior were the only father-son combination to play in the big leagues at the same time.

Senior's records were outstanding. He was a key part of the Big Red Machine, World Champions of 1975 and 1976. He played in 2,000 games with a .297 batting average, 147 home runs and 824 RBIs. He was a heads-up, all around player and a credit to our great game.

STORY 106:

Ken Griffey Jr.—
A Future Hall Of Famer?

Please see Story 43 (Ken Griffey Jr.'s Signature Disappearing Act) about an interesting happening in Seattle when I met the young Griffey. Please see Story 45 (Catching Foul Balls at Baseball Games), paragraphs 3, 4, 5 and 6. It was exciting having both Griffeys in Seattle.

I will not even try to list all of Junior's records here. There are simply too many. Just suffice it to say that he is certainly one of the great players to ever put on a uniform. His batting proficiency and defensive genius are known far and wide. He was a consistent hitter with great power. His current stats show that he was nearing 400 home runs in 2005. He has passed that figure now. Interestingly enough, he has batted a lifetime average (so far) of .299, within two points of his dad. He has well over 1,152 RBIs. Injuries have kept him on the bench much of the time after he went to Cincinnati from Seattle. Marilyn and I were in the Great American Ball Park in Cincinnati recently and we had hoped to see Junior play one more time. But, alas, he was injured and did not play. Hopefully, at age 36 now, he will play a number of years yet.

Here is just one more bit of trivia. We saw the two Griffeys hit back-to-back homeruns on September 14, 1990. That is one for the record books.

We feel that Junior will be in the Hall of Fame someday. Hank Aaron has stated that Junior has the best chance of breaking his all-time home run record of 755. Time will tell. Our best to Ken Jr. for giving baseball fans everywhere a style of play that has excited onlookers for the past seventeen years.

STORY 107:

Marvin Gudat—
Broke Up a No-Hitter

When I watched Marvin Gudat play baseball in the old Pacific Coast League in the 1930s I had no idea that he had played for the UCLA Bruin baseball team in college in the early 1920s. When he played in the Pacific Coast League in mid-1930s, it was only a decade later that I played my first game for the Bruins.

Marv played professional ball in the minor leagues in 1926 through 1928. He signed a contract with the Cincinnati Reds on May 21, 1929. He came up as a pitcher but eventually settled in as an outfielder. He went back to the minors and did so well he was traded to the Chicago Cubs in 1932. When I first saw him he had been sent to Los Angeles and was playing right field for the Los Angeles Angels in 1934. He was a smooth left handed batter who had power and could hit to all fields. That team ended the season with 137 wins and only 50 losses. And Gudat was one of the key contributors. In 1938 Marv had been sent back to the Cubs and actually played in the 1938 World Series between the Cubs and the Yankees.

Back to the Pacific Coast League, he batted over .300 for six seasons and set a PCL record by playing in 393 consecutive games. This was not easy because of Marv's aggressive style of play. He was often injured but played through the problems. He went on to play with the Oakland Acorns, Hollywood, and San Diego through 1945, the year he finally retired. His minor league career average was .306 in 2,103 games. He had 2,211 hits and 214 stolen bases. In 1940 Marv came to the plate with two outs in the ninth inning and pitcher Jess Flores was one out away from a no-hitter. Marv said later he was looking for a screwball he could punch over the infield. That's exactly what he got and he broke up the no-hitter with a base hit.

More recollections of Marv are described in two parts of this book. Those are Story 3 (A Day at the Ball Park), and Story 208 (Four Pitches and You're Out).

More recollections of Marv are described in two parts of this book. Those are Story 3 (A Day at the Ball Park), and Story 208 (Four Pitches and You're Out).

STORY 108:

Fred Haney: First Angel General Manager (American League)

I have fond memories of Fred Haney. Early in his career he played for the Detroit Tigers, Boston Red Sox, Chicago Cubs, and St. Louis Cardinals. He was the Tiger's regular third baseman and played in 622 major league games with a career batting average of .275 and 228 RBIs.

But I knew Fred more as a broadcaster with the Hollywood Stars in 1943 to 1948. He proceeded to manage the Stars winning two pennants in four years. Later he managed the Milwaukee Braves to a World Championship in 1957 and the American League title in 1958.

He also broadcast NBC-TV's "Game of the Week and later was the first General Manager of the expansion Los Angeles Angels owned by movie star Gene Autry.

STORY 109:

Gabby Hartnett— Why "Gabby?"... Because He Was So Quiet

I recall Gabby Hartnett driving baseballs off the left field wall at Wrigley Field in Chicago. But, the memory that sticks in my mind is that they were usually singles. No, Gabby did not have speed on the bases but he was a stalwart with his nineteen years as a Chicago Cub. And he managed the Cubbies to the National League pennant in 1938. This man was one of my favorites in the 1930s.

Gabby was widely known for both his batting and fielding prowess. Many experts considered him to be the greatest catcher in the National League during his years with the Cubs. I always had the impression that his name was given him because he talked a lot. It was just the opposite. He was very reticent, thus, the nickname, Gabby.

I went to Wrigley Field in Chicago to see a game many years later. Outside that old storied stadium are several cement plaques in the ground honoring some of Chicago's famous players. Hartnett's name is there along with some of the greatest to ever play the game. He played in 1,990 games and batted .297 with 236 home runs and 1,179 RBIs. As a manager he went 203/176 in wins and losses.

Gabby was an All Star from 1933 through 1938 and was voted the Most Valuable Player in 1935. He was voted into the Baseball Hall of Fame in 1955.

STORY 110:

Babe Herman— One of Three Men on Third Base

This man was one of the most colorful players of the game. He often had to deny being hit on the head by a fly ball (I guess it really happened). But, Babe often said, "I was a pretty fair country hitter." He was certainly correct about that fact.

Herman played in 1,552 games and had an excellent career batting average of .324. He was more of a line drive hitter as he had 181 home runs but 997 RBIs. In 1930 he batted .393 with an excellent 241 hits.

One of the great stories in major league base-ball is the one in which Babe "tripled" into a double play. Babe had doubled and with head down charged into third base. The runner ahead of Babe had stopped at third and the lead runner, thinking he would be thrown out at the plate, returned to third base. There was even a book written titled "Three Men on Third," highlighting the incident. The newspapers coined one of the greatest quips in baseball when they said, "The Dodgers Have Three Men on Base." To which one reporter replied, "Oh yeah? Which base?"

Please see Story 30 (The Fellowship of Christian Athletes) about Herman's comments when Carl Erskine said he thought he could steal home. Great story!

STORY 111:

Jackie Jensen— Ted Williams Said Jensen was the Best Outfielder He Ever Saw

I include Jackie Jensen in my book because he was one of my adversaries playing for the California Bears in the Pacific Coast Conference collegiate baseball program. He was a hard-nosed competitor and his major league marks proved that fact.

Jackie was heir apparent to Joe DiMaggio's position in center field with the New York Yankees but in college he was often asked to take to the mound. He had a very strong arm and often won games in which he pitched. He beat UCLA on a two-hitter in 1948 on our field. I fortunately had a triple and a drag bunt single that day but could not get around to score. I was very impressed with Jackie.

Emmett Ashford, umpire, was working behind the plate. I recall his calling a high strike on Jackie who did not turn around or give the slightest indication he did not like the call. On the next pitch Jackie hit the ball over 400 feet and out of the park. Later, I told that story to some of my high school players to point up the fact that it is not wise to allow one bad call to affect your batting.

In eleven years in the big leagues Jackie played in 1,438 games, batted .279 with 199 home runs and 929 RBIs. He was an All Star in 1952, 1955, and 1958 winning the MVP Award in the latter year. He also won a Gold Glove in 1959.

In the 1940s in the Pacific Coast Conference, I watched Jackie play halfback for the California Bears. He was a true All American. He was difficult to catch. He might have played many more years in the major leagues except for his fear of flying. His teammate at Boston, Ted Williams, called Jackie the best outfielder he ever saw.

STORY 112:

Walter Johnson—Modest, Decent, Quiet, Awesome!

I was only three years old in Walter Johnson's last year in the major leagues. He had played for Washington Senators his entire twenty-one year career. Walter's numbers take page after page of statistics. He was truly a great baseball pitcher. He was nicknamed "The Big Train" or "Barney," (a reference to his speed since Barney Oldfield was the fastest race driver in America at that time).

A few of his numbers will follow, but as good as he was in baseball, what pleased his fans the most was his exceptional character. He was born in Kansas and grew up on a farm and retained the personality of a warm, modest, friendly individual that exemplified the values that Americans admired and respected. Newspaper reporters called him "The White Knight" and "Sir Walter."

Friend, check out these numbers! They are truly remarkable. Walter amassed 5,914.2 innings on the mound with 417 victories over 279 losses. His career ERA was an incredible 2.17. In 50 World Series innings he was only slightly higher with a 2.34 ERA. He had 200 victories in just eight seasons, an incredible 25 wins per season. He reached 300 wins in only 14 seasons, a mark of more than 21 victories per season. Sixty-five of his losses were by shutouts of which 26 were 1-0 ball games. Obviously, he was playing for a team without a potent offense or his won-loss record would have been even more remarkable.

As was the case with a number of pitchers in the early days, Walter was a starter and a reliever. He was 40-30 in relief with 34 saves. He continued his mild and decent manner throughout his career. He never swore, drank liquor, or argued with umpires. And he never threw at hitters on purpose although in his style of pitching he did pitch inside and ended up hitting 206 batters. They say Ty Cobb would move up in the box and crowd the plate knowing that Johnson would never back him off on purpose.

In one of baseball's favorite stories, the Senators finally made it to the World Series in 1924 (my birth year) and Walter appeared in relief just two days after throwing a complete-game victory, and he won in the final inning. Johnson went 23-7 that year at age 37. Also, please see Story 11 (Mike Gazella, a Former Yankee) of Mike's comment about his greatest thrill in baseball that involved "The Big Train," Johnson's nickname.

His awards, records, and accomplishments are

too numerous to mention. Suffice it to say he was one of baseball's greatest performers. He was one of the five players admitted to the Baseball Hall of Fame when it was established in 1936.

STORY 113:

Marty Keough— A Most Gifted Performer

In Story 205 I write about Billy Kilmer, an incredible athlete and, indeed, he was outstanding. Another man in that same category is Marty Keough. He graduated from Pomona High School in California in the early 1950s. He played football, basketball, and baseball there. In 1952 I was officiating a C.I.F. playoff game between Pomona and Monrovia High Schools. Marty was the quarterback and he had led Pomona to a 35-13 lead. With less than a minute to play Pomona had the ball on Monrovia's three-yard line. Marty went to his knee to run out the clock. He did not want to embarrass his opponent. This was typical of Keough's humility.

Earlier, I was officiating a basketball game at Pomona and saw Marty drive for the basket. He was closely guarded by an opposing player and drove on through flipping the ball from behind the basket, and it went over the top of the backboard without touching anything and went through the hoop. It was one of the most incredible shots I have ever seen.

In 1956 Marty signed a professional baseball contract with the Boston Red Sox. Scout Joe Stephenson signed him up. In the off-season Marty came home and played winter ball with the Ontario-Upland Pirates, my semi-pro team. What a privilege it was to play alongside Marty! He was an excellent player. In a game tied 4-4 in the bottom of the ninth inning, I beat out a drag bunt. Marty hit a 400-foot drive to right centerfield on the first pitch for a triple and the game was over. This was standard for Marty. He could do it all, including hitting, fielding, throwing, and running. Please see Story 14 ((The Ontario-Upland Pirates) for more information.

Marty played eleven years in the big leagues with Boston, Cleveland, Washington (Senators), Cincinnati, Milwaukee, and Chicago (Cubs). He played in 841 games and had a lifetime batting average of .242. He hit 43 home runs and had 176 RBIs. He went on to play baseball in Japan in 1968.

In 1953, my first year of coaching varsity baseball at Chaffey High School, I can recall seeing Marty's brother, Joe, at a Pomona game. He was just seven years old and was practicing his "hook slide" in foul territory down the leftfield line. It was a perfect slide. Everyone marveled at this little kid. I had heard he was another fine athlete like Marty. In 1966, the same year that Marty retired from MLB, Joe signed a professional baseball contract with the Oakland A's. Joey, as he was affectionately known in our area, homered in his first at-bat to defeat the New York Yankees, 4-3. He played in 332 games and batted .246 with 81 RBIs over the next seven years. In addition to Oakland, he played for Kansas City and the Chicago White Sox.

To add icing to the cake, Marty's son, Matt, signed a professional baseball contract with Charlie Finley, Oakland A's owner, in 1976. He first was an infielder and was scheduled to be Sal Bando's successor at third base, but he was converted to a pitcher because his minor league batting did not work out as expected. He could throw very hard. He went on to pitch 1,190 innings with a lifetime ERA of 4.17. He played for Oakland, New York Yankees, St. Louis, Chicago Cubs, and Houston. In one league championship series game Matt pitched eight innings with a 1.08 ERA.

On March 16,1992, Matt was with the Los Angeles Angels and was hit in the head by a batted ball and had emergency surgery for a blood clot. His last game in the major leagues had been in 1986 and that was followed by a short stint in Japan. Matt fully retired after the head injury.

However, we are not finished yet with this amazing athletic family. Marty's brother, Tom, was the kicker (punter) for the California Bear football team in the 1950s. And his father, Zeke, was shooting in the 70s in golf after age 60.

Yes, Marty Keough was an excellent athlete. But, better than that, he is a quality gentleman on and off the field and we are better for having him as a friend.

STORY 114:

Sandy Koufax—A Great and Humble Young Man

There are so many great stories about this young man. He was truly a magician when he pitched a baseball. Willie Stargell, Pittsburg Pirate slugger, once said, "hitting Sandy Koufax's pitches is like eating soup with a fork." Please see Story 22 (Sandy Koufax Strikes Out the Side) when Marilyn and I first saw Sandy pitch for the new Los Angeles Dodgers.

Sandy started out slow in his early years. He signed a professional baseball contract in 1955 with the Brooklyn Dodgers at just 19 years of age while attending the University of Cincinnati. Control was his nemesis. He struggled somewhat with location (control) until 1961 when he suddenly found him-self. During his final six years in the major leagues he was almost unstoppable. He pitched 2,324 innings with a record of 165 wins and 87 losses. His lifetime ERA was 2.76. In World Series play he pitched 57 innings with a 4-3 record and a miraculous 0.95 ERA.

Between 1961 and 1966 he led the National League in wins and shutouts three times, complete games twice, and strikeouts four times. His 382 strikeouts in 1965 set a new major league record. He led in ERA five consecutive years with his best mark of 1.73 in his final year. He pitched a no-hitter in each season from 1962 to 1965 and the last a 1-0 perfect game against the Cubs on September 9, 1965. He won the Cy Young Award in 1963, 1965, and 1966. He and Don Drysdale formed one of baseball's greatest "lefty/righty" combinations.

Koufax retired at the young age of thirty-one and was voted into the Baseball Hall of Fame at the youngest age ever, thirty-six. Because of a little-known circulatory ailment in his pitching arm that caused him arthritic pain, he chose to retire on November 18, 1966 rather than risk crippling his arm permanently.

Sandy is certainly one of the most successful players in baseball history. After Marilyn and I attended the 1959 World Series we later realized what a phenomenal pitcher we had seen participate. His baseball greatness was achieved in the following seven years after that exciting series.

STORY 115:

Chris Krug—I Will Build a Baseball Field for You (Like the Field of Dreams)

In 1957 our Chaffey High School varsity baseball team was battling for the Citrus Belt League championship. Our talented opponent, Riverside Poly High School, was an adversary. They forced us into a playoff game with Colton High School to earn second place and a spot in the CIF playoffs. We won that playoff game and went on to win the CIF Championship. Riverside lost to the team we defeated in the finals. Our two teams came close to doing something that had never been done in CIF baseball history. That would be having two teams from the same league facing each other in the finals of that huge tournament.

The catcher on that team was Chris Krug. He was a husky, burly guy with outstanding talent. Besides being a fine catcher he was one of the best hitters in the league. In recent years I ran across Chris again and we enjoyed talking over old times. He currently owns a company that makes baseball fields. They provide the proper materials to form excellent baseball diamonds. The company is called Athletics Turf, Incorporated.

In 1988 between June 26 and July 10, Chris directed the building of the field in Dyersville, Iowa, thirty miles west of Dubuque, for the movie, "Field of Dreams." He used a mixture of Kentucky blue, fescue, and rye grasses. He said the corn growing in the outfield was about chest high so they put in about eight rows of taller corn on the edge of the outfield to make the cornfield look larger. Chris revealed that now, nearly twenty years later, more than 100,000 people per year visit the site. He said

it is so popular as a tourist attraction that it rivals The Grand Canyon and Mount Rushmore in visitor numbers. In the 1990s, some farmers planted more corn in the field itself but there was so much clamor about leaving the field untouched that they took out the corn. Today, people stand in long lines just to have the opportunity to bat a few baseballs. And there are occasional weddings at home plate. The picture now ranks with some of the great movies of the past such as "Gone With the Wind," "Casablanca," and other notable films.

Chris has worked on such baseball fields as the Los Angeles Angel Anaheim Stadium, UCLA, USC, San Diego State, and numerous colleges and high schools in California. He has been in his baseball field business for twenty years and is still going strong.

Chris played with the Chicago Cubs in 1965 and 1966 and with the Padres in 1969. Chris was part of baseball history when he was one of the last six batters faced by Sandy Koufax in his perfect game in 1965. Following his professional baseball career he was an assistant coach to Gary Adams at UCLA from 1979 to 1984.

I have much respect for Chris. Though he was playing for one of my opponent teams in high school, I always felt as though Chris was like one of my own players. He is an outstanding man.

Rusty Kuntz— One of Sparky Anderson's Guys

In 1989 I had the privilege of throwing out the first pitch at a Seattle Mariner/Toronto Blue Jay game played in the old Kingdome on April 26. My friend, Moose Clauson of the Mariners, was in charge of this special event. My catcher on the "first pitch" was Rusty Kuntz (pronounced Coontz). He was a very friendly gentleman and I enjoyed meeting him.

Rusty Kuntz was the first base coach for the Mariners and was their outfield and base running coach. He played seven years in the big leagues, five with the Chicago White Sox, part of a year with the Minnesota Twins, and two years with the Detroit Tigers. He was on Sparky Anderson's championship Detroit Tiger team in 1984 and drove in the game-winning RBI of the fifth and deciding game of the World Series against San Diego.

Rusty went to Paso Robles High School in California and on to Cuesta College and Cal State Stanislaus. He signed with the Chicago White Sox and made his major league debut in 1979.

After his playing days he coached with Houston in 1987, the Seattle Mariners from 1989 to 1992, the Florida Marlins from 1992 to 2002, and with the Pittsburg Pirates since that time. In 2006 he continues with the Pirates with one of their minor league teams.

Rusty gave me the baseball after I threw the first pitch. I still have it in my den.

Denny Lemaster— A Fireballer From Oxnard

In 1958 the Chaffey High School Tiger baseball team visited Oxnard, California to play what some called one of the greatest pitching duels in high school history. Chaffey's pitcher was young Larry Maxie while Oxnard had Denny Lemaster on the mound. Larry was a big 6'5" hard throwing right hander while Denny was a tall classic southpaw.

It was standing room only at Oxnard's field as 2,500 fans showed up for this unique match up. As expected strikeouts were common as the game proceeded. Each pitcher posted eight K's in the first four innings. At that point in the game Chaffey, not being able to hit Lemaster's offerings, had a player work Lemaster for a base on balls. Following were three two-strike bunts in succession followed by Ray Zak's double giving the Tigers a two-run lead they never relinquished. The final score was 4-1, Chaffey.

Maxie struck out 20 while Lemaster K'd 16, an incredible number between two of the best teams in the California Interscholastic Federation (CIF). Larry went on to be voted the CIF Player of the Year and signed a $60,000 with the Milwaukee Braves. Interestingly, Denny also received $60,000 from the Braves.

Before going to the Braves, Denny once struck out eleven in a row in the minors. Lemaster went on to play eleven years in the big leagues, six with the Braves, four with the Astros, and one with the Expos. He recorded a formidable 3.58 ERA in 1,788 innings and pitched a 90-105 win-loss mark.

Maxie is still in baseball today as a scout for the Chicago White Sox after having some pitching success as the Most Valuable Player in the Texas League in 1961 and a leader in the American Association. An injury forced Maxie to retire from active playing. He then went into scouting with both the Toronto Blue Jays and the White sox.

I understand Denny and Larry have seen each other occasionally and reminisce over the day they fanned 36 batters between them in one game.

STORY NO: 118:

Gene Lillard— An Old and Great Angel

Some of the Pacific Coast League players were my heroes in the 1930s. Gene Lillard was one of them. For a player who was 5'10" and 178 pounds, he had great power. His talent for hitting home runs at Wrigley Field, Los Angeles in the 1930s was renowned. Please see Story 208 (Four Pitches and You're Out) for a good story about Gene and his teammates.

In the 1950s I played on a semi-pro team called the Ontario-Upland Pirates in California. One of our opponents was from Santa Barbara and Gene Lillard was the manager of that club. Please see Story 14 (The Ontario-Upland Pirates) for more about Lillard. After his major league and Pacific Coast League playing days, Gene returned to his hometown. It was great seeing him. We lost Gene in 1991 at age 78. He was a baseball man through and through and a fine gentleman.

STORY 119:

Johnny Lindell— Another Great Yankee

In my young mind in the 1940s, Johnny Lindell was a Yankee and only a Yankee. He was very likeable and an excellent ball player. He had come out of the University of Southern California and many more "Trojans" were to follow. Sam Barry and Rod Dedeaux were the coaching leaders in the collegiate ranks.

Johnny started as a pitcher and was very successful. He was 23-4 at Newark in 1941. However, Joe McCarthy, New York manager, did not believe Lindell had a major league fastball. He switched Johnny to the outfield in 1943. John turned out to be a fine hitter and played on three pennant winners in 1943, 1947, and 1949.

Johnny was returned to Hollywood of the Pacific Coast League and manager Fred Haney put Lindell back on the mound. He proceeded to post a 24-9 pitching record and with his excellent hitting was the MVP in 1952. He returned to the majors but his best days were behind him.

Please see Story 73 (1955 TEAM) when Johnny was the speaker at the annual Chaffey High School baseball banquet. He was a big hit. More of Lindell's records are discussed in that story.

STORY 120:

Walter Mails— "Duster" Was a Character

I first heard of John Walter "The Great" Mails in 1939. Please see Story 6 (An Incredible Event—The Big Baseball Drop) about a unique public relations stunt created by Mails. It typified unusual ideas of Walter. But, let's go back twenty-four years when Mails broke into baseball.

This man was probably in the top ten of baseball characters. He played for the Brooklyn Robins (Dodgers) in 1915 and 1916, injured his arm, and did not return to the majors until 1920 when he was called up from the Pacific Coast League to the Cleveland Indians in August. He won seven straight games to help the Indians get to the World Series against Brooklyn.

During that period he once walked the bases full on twelve pitches and then proceeded to strike out the side. He allowed no hits from that point on and won the game 2-0.

In the World Series he had an incredible ERA of 0.00. Incidentally, it was in that particular series that second baseman, Bill Wambsganss, pulled off the only unassisted triple play in World Series history. Cleveland defeated Brooklyn in that Series. Walter went on to the St. Louis Cardinals in 1925 and 1926 but returned to the Pacific Coast League to finish off his playing career.

Mails was nicknamed "Duster" because he pitched inside often to back hitters off the plate. He self-proclaimed himself as "Walter the Great" and often made his claim hold up. His arm problems kept him from attaining the level to which he was capable. But he was certainly one of the characters who have added color to our great game.

STORY 121:

Eddie Malone— One Tough Cookie

My high school, Washington of Los Angeles, was full of baseball hopefuls. In 1939 the school dropped baseball and in its place started softball. Some of the baseball hopefuls transferred to nearby Fremont High School in order to play baseball. One such player was Eddie Malone. He had baseball experience in the Pacific Coast League at a young age. Finally, in 1949 Eddie signed a contract with the Chicago White Sox and played through 1950.

He played in 86 games batting .257 with one home run and 26 RBIs. Eddie's real strength was defense and handling pitchers. He was an energetic ball player and came to play everyday.

He returned to the Pacific Coast League and was highly successful. In fact, Eddie was in the middle of the famous battle called "The Brawl," between the Los Angeles Angels and Hollywood Stars in 1953. Please see Story 209 (One of Baseball's Famous Brawls).

Eddie represents so many youngsters who had a burning desire to play baseball and, perhaps, never really had a real opportunity. Many of you out there will relate to this story. Regardless of circumstances, however, it was nice to have the dream. Also, World War II affected many of us in those days and several key years were given to our country. We gladly served at that time of need. Eddie Malone was in that category.

Eddie was a tough, down-in-the-dirt, hard-playing catcher who gave 100% every moment he was on the field. Both at high school and in the Pacific Coast League, I had great respect for Eddie. It is highly likely that Eddie's service in World War II kept him from a long, successful career in the major leagues.

STORY 122:

Billy Martin— Wanna Fight? I'm Your Man!

My star pitcher of the 1956 championship Chaffey High School Tigers, Hal Reniff, told me that Billy Martin lived up to every interesting story that was told about him. He could start a brawl at the drop of a hat or start a rally to win a baseball game. He was fiery and ready for action at all times. Hal socialized with Martin, Whitey Ford, and Mickey Mantle when they were on the road.

Billy played eleven years on seven different teams. He was a tough second baseman and scuffled with the best of them. He batted .257 in 1,021 games with 64 home runs and 333 RBIs. In World Series play he hit .333 with 5 home runs and 19 RBIs. Actually, Billy managed in far more games than he played. That would be 2,266 games (1,253 wins and 1,013 losses). He managed with the Twins, Tigers, Rangers, Yankees, and Athletics. His manner of managing the Athletics in 1981 was called "Billy Ball," and it won him an AL West pennant. Billy set a major league record by being hired and fired five times by one club, the Yankees. Despite all the various problems, Billy was named Manager of the Year four times.

The Yankees won the pennant every year Martin was with them except when Billy left for the Army in 1954. In the renowned Yankee-Dodger World Series of 1953 Martin set a record with 12 hits in that six-game set, hit .500, and drove in the winning run in the ninth inning of the Series final game.

Please see Story 18 (Gilmore Field), paragraph 12, for a Billy Martin incident that describes the toughness of this fiery player. Billy made things happen whenever and wherever he played, coached, or managed. He was Casey Stengel's favorite from the time Casey had Billy on his Oakland Oaks Pacific Coast League team in 1948 and 1949. Billy was independent, to say the least. Just to show an example of his competitiveness, in Billy's first major league game on April 18, 1950, he set a major league mark by becoming the first player to get two hits in one inning. When the phrase, "he came to play," was coined, they were probably talking about Billy Martin.

STORY 123:

Cal McLish— Just Call Me "Tuskahoma"

Cal had a checkered career in baseball. He signed with Brooklyn in 1944 at age 18 but he did not spend a full year in the major leagues until 1951. He played with the Dodgers, Pirates, Cubs, Indians, Reds, White Sox, and Phillies. With all these teams, Cal pitched 1,609 innings with a 92-92 won-loss record and a 4.01 ERA.

When I was watching Pacific Coast League baseball in the late 1940s, Cal was pitching for the Los Angeles Angels. He was very popular among the fans and did a creditable job on the mound. I recall a story in the Los Angeles Times that indicated McLish could throw equally well right or left handed. I never saw him pitch lefthanded but they say he was capable of such a feat. In fact, I have a clipping showing Cal throwing both lefty and righty. It is dated 1949 and McLish was pitching for the Los Angeles Angels.

Cal and the renowned Gene Mauch were life-long friends and broke into the majors together in 1944. He pitched for manager Mauch at Philadelphia in the 1960s until arm trouble affected him in 1964. He stayed with Mauch as his pitching coach in 1964 and 1965. Also, he re-joined Mauch as the pitching coach of the Montreal Expos from 1969 to 1975.

Please see Story 203 (Baseball Nicknames are Fun) about Cal's name and nickname. He was one of eight children and may have the most unusual name of any baseball player. It is Calvin Coolidge Julius Caesar Tuskahoma "Cal" McLish.

STORY 124:

Denny McLain— What Might Have Been

Please see Story 26 (Denny McLain Goes for 32nd Win) that tells about my visit to Baltimore Memorial Stadium in 1968. It provides much information about Denny.

I would like to make some comments here about Denny McLain. In his career he pitched with Detroit, Washington, Oakland and Atlanta. Denny was an extrovert. He even did an act in Las Vegas at one time. He was on the Ed Sullivan show and performed in other TV programs. He was the son-in-law of Hall of Fame shortstop Lou Boudreau.

When we talk about characters in baseball, Denny has to be mentioned. Had he kept on a straight line with baseball getting his full attention, he certainly would have ended up amount the great players of the game. But, that did not happen and he ended up broke and in trouble with the law.

STORY 125:

Mickey Mantle—One of the Greats of All Time

This is another occasion where you can read about the great Mickey Mantle and some of his accomplishments. Please see Story 27 (Mickey Mantle's Last Game at Yankee Stadium) when I visited the famous ballpark. Also, more information about Mickey is included in Story 29 (A Great Memory of a 1964 Detroit Conference).

STORY 126:

Willie Mays—An Incredible Performer and Gentleman

Most fans were overwhelmed with Willie May's impact on baseball, particularly in his early years. Please see two stories. First, please see Story 16 (We All Watched Willie in Amazement) and, second, see Story 20 (The Dodgers and Giants Come West). Both cover some of Willie's amazing career. Willie always was a man to be admired. One can read the goodness in him.

STORY 127:

Steve Mesner—
A Pacific Coast League
Phenom

In 1934 young Steve Mesner signed a Chicago Cubs contract. He was just 16 years old. That year and the years following was when I had the opportunity to see him play for the Los Angeles Angels in the Pacific Coast League. He batted .331 and was a team leader. The Cubs had an agreement with Los Angeles and many Angels moved on up to the Cubs. Steve joined Chicago in 1938. After spending an additional year with the Cubs, Steve was traded to the St. Louis Cardinals. After some time in the service, he returned to play for the Cincinnati Reds and stayed with them through the 1945 season.

Steve was a stocky young player with good power. I saw him hit many home runs at Wrigley Field in Los Angeles. It is interesting to note that Steve played American Legion baseball with Bobby Doerr. Bobby's father was the coach of that team.

Mesner's marks in major league play were 451 game, .252 batting average, and 167 RBIs.

STORY 128:

Bill Moisan—He Threw a
Pitch that "Sailed"

You will not find any remarkable statistics on this player. But, in 1948, my junior year at UCLA, he was pitching for the Los Angeles Angels of the Pacific Coast League and I was at the plate. He threw a pitch that I will never forget. It was heading for the strike zone and suddenly darted up and away.

It sailed! The catcher said, "How did you like that one, kid?" He had my attention. It ran through my mind that if the pitch had been at my head, I was history. That was the day I realized I needed to learn how to "turn away" from high inside pitches. Fortunately, I was able to master that ability and it probably saved me a few times.

Bill went up to the Cubs shortly thereafter. He pitched only five innings with a 5.40 ERA. However, I swear that if he could simulate the one he threw at me that day in 1948, he would most certainly be successful. Please see Story 65 (1948 TEAM) about Bill Moisan.

STORY 129:

Wally Moon—
An Excellent Model
to Follow

I mention Wally Moon in two stories in this book. Please see Story 20 (The Dodgers and Giants Come West) and Story 203 (Wally Moon's Baseball Camp). Both are interesting stories about this Los Angeles Dodger star.

Wally Moon was a steady performer who played in the outfield and at first base. He performed five years for the St. Louis Cardinals and seven more for the Los Angeles Dodgers. He played in 1,457 games with a .289 batting average, 142 home runs and 661 RBIs. When he came to the Dodgers in 1959 he fit right in with their race for the World Championship. His inside-out swing allowed him to hit many home runs over the infamous 40-foot screen in left field of the Los Angeles Coliseum. Appropriately, he scored the last run ever scored in that famous stadium where the 1932 Olympic

Games were held.

Wally was a speedy runner and stole many bases. He was an All Star in 1957 and 1959 and won a Gold Glove in 1960. Earlier in his career, Wally hit a home run in his first major league at bat in 1954 for the Cardinals. Also, he batted .304 that year. He was voted Rookie of the Year over Hank Aaron.

I was in the middle of my coaching career when Wally Moon was with the Dodgers and I often referred to him as one of those players they could mimic or copy. He was a performer who fundamentally did everything correctly.

STORY 130:

Stan Musial—Most Say He Was the Most Consistent Ever

When the Dodgers moved to Los Angeles we went to see Stan Musial play at every opportunity. What a model of a man for others to follow. He held this respect not only for those in St. Louis but wherever the game has been played.

As is true with so many talented youngsters, Stan was a pitcher who was wild and inconsistent. But, wiser people sent him to Daytona Beach to develop. Under the wing of the great White Sox pitcher, Dickey Kerr, he compiled an 18-5 record. Also, Dickey played Stan in the outfield and Musial batted .352. An injury later in the year finished Stan's pitching career so he remained in the outfield. The following year he played in the International League and batted .426 in a call-up to the Cardinals.

This is a side note worth mentioning. Dickey Kerr was on the famous Black Sox of the 1919 White Sox. But, Dickey was an honest pitcher and won his first two starts in that infamous year while others were throwing games. He compiled a 21-9 record in 1920 and moved into minor league managing later. He befriended the Musials and years later they repaid Dickey by purchasing a home for him in Houston.

Here is another player who stayed with the same club throughout his 22-year career with the Cardinals. Stan played in 3,026 games with a .331 batting average, 475 home runs, and 1,951 RBIs. He played in 23 World Series games as well. He served as General Manager and senior vice-president of St. Louis for more than 25 years.

His records are outstanding. He was an All Star in 1943 and 1944 and again from 1946 through 1963. He won three MVP Awards in the National League including 1943, 1946, and 1948. He was the NL batting champion in 1943, 1946, 1948, 1950, 1951, 1952, and 1957. He led the league in RBIs in 1948 and 1956. He was voted into the Hall of Fame in 1969. Remarkable!!

Musial seemed to be the most consistent player in the major league ever. He did not have slumps as he had the same number of hits on the road as at home. And his batting average stayed the same throughout his career. And, his consistency held up as a gentleman and a citizen. Truly, Stan the Man was a model for all time.

STORY 131:

Mike Radford— A Cup of Coffee with Kansas City

In 2001 my World War II reunion was held in Branson, Missouri. We went to a daytime show called "Remember When?" It was produced and directed by Mike and Shari Radford and our group enjoyed it very much.

After the show Marilyn and I introduced ourselves and we have found some good friends. I learned that Mike had always wanted to be major league baseball player. He came out of the service in 1969, signed with the Kansas City Royals, and in his only at-bat drove a 95 MPH fastball off the centerfield wall for a double. So, Mike's baseball card shows that he made it to the major leagues and 1.000 is his batting record. As we say in the business, he was up there for "a cup of coffee."

Mike played Little League, Pony League, American Legion, and college baseball. His American Legion coach was the capable Brooklyn Dodger third baseman, Spider Jorgensen. In 1968 he called Mike to arrange a tryout with Kansas City. However, he was 21 years old at the time and they released all rookies over 19. Later Mike's friend, Tommy Heinrich, the old Yankee outfielder, called and said they had wanted to contact him but could not locate him. But Mike and Shari had other things to do in life and are now influencing people with some special programs and presentations. Their ministry is certainly effective and they have great testimonies.

Mike and I keep in touch now. If you want a great motivational speaker contact Mike and Shari at MikeRadford.com. They bring a very positive message and their audiences appreciate them.

STORY 132:

Jimmy Reese— Seventy Eight Years in the Game

In the 1930s Jimmy Reese was one of my Pacific Coast League heroes playing for the Los Angeles Angels. He is known for being one of Babe Ruth's roommates in the big leagues.

Jimmy was in professional baseball for 78 years. He started out as a batboy for the Los Angeles Angels in 1917 and stayed with that job until 1923. He signed with the Oakland Oaks at that time where he played until being sold to the New York Yankees. He roomed with the Babe in 1930 and 1931. His first year with New York he batted .336.

He was playing behind a great second baseman, Tony Lazzeri, and did not have much opportunity to play on a regular basis. He was sold to the St. Louis Cardinals in 1932. Once again, he was playing behind another star, Frankie Frisch, with little chance to advance. However, he did have 742 at-bats and had a .278 average.

He played and managed in the minor leagues at that point and that is when I had the opportunity to see Jimmy play for some very good Los Angeles Angel teams. He entered the Army and upon return he worked as a scout, coach or manager for seven different minor league teams. In 1973 he joined the major league California Angels and was with them until his death in 1994.

A friend of mine, Rob Campbell of Seattle, Washington, wrote to Jimmy in the late 1980s expressing his appreciation for all his years of entertaining fans for so many years. Jimmy, thoughtful man that he always was, responded by sending Rob a California Angels cap, a personal letter that he cherishes, and some other items. Rob was very impressed with Jimmy's courtesy. Please see Story 152 (Rob Campbell).

STORY 133:

Hal Reniff— A Very Competitive Yankee

I refer to Hal Reniff in several locations in this book. However, please see Story 33 (Hal Reniff, A Special Guy) for a complete description of Hal and some interesting facts about his life. He was a very special person to me in many ways.

STORY 134:

Phil Rizzuto—Holy Cow, What a Ballplayer!

Bobby Brown, my teammate at UCLA and subsequent president of the American League of baseball, was on the New York roster with Phil Rizzuto during some of the winning years of the famous Yankee teams. Both were infielders. Phil was seven years older than Bobby and started his Yankee career a few years earlier than Brown.

Many years later Marilyn and I were visiting Yankee Stadium as guests of the Browns. Please see Story 36 (Yankee Stadium with Dr. and Mrs. Bobby Brown) about that visit. When we arrived at the stadium we parked right next to Phil Rizzuto who was the Yankee announcer for many years. His exclamations of "Holy Cow" while broadcasting are legendary.

Phil signed with New York in 1941 and played

two seasons with the club before he went into the service from 1943 to 1945. His numbers were outstanding when he returned from duty and, in fact, placed second in the MVP voting behind Ted Williams in 1949. And by 1950 he earned the MVP Award with a .324 batting average, 125 runs, 91 walks, 36 doubles, and a career-high .439 slugging percentage.

He spent thirteen years with New York, his only major league club. When announcing, Phil made up a mark for the scorecard that was "WW." Someone asked, "What is that mark, Phil?" To which the Scooter replied, "Wasn't watching!"

Rizzuto's number 10 was retired in 1985. He was an All Star in the following years: 1942, 1950, 1951, 1952 and 1953. He was inducted into the Hall of Fame in 1994.

STORY 135:

Jackie Robinson— This Man Played All the Sports

At UCLA the baseball park is known as Jackie Robinson Stadium. As part of the complex there is a Jackie Robinson Museum that displays plaques and other memorabilia of the UCLA Baseball Hall of Fame.

These were made in memory of the great Jackie Robinson, UCLA star in baseball, football, basketball, and track. Jackie went on to star for the Brooklyn Dodgers in the National League. Please see Story 67 (UCLA Baseball Hall of Fame).

Jackie played in 1,382 games with a .311 batting average. He hit 137 home runs with 784 RBIs. In World Series play he played in 38 games with a .234

batting average, 2 home runs, and 12 RBIs. He was an All Star from 1949 through 1954, received the MVP Award in 1949, and was inducted into the Hall of Fame in 1962.

STORY 136 AND 137:

Gary Roenicke—Two Brothers and a Great Dad and Ron Roenicke— (L. A. Angels' Bench Coach)

I choose to put these two players into one story although they are listed separately. When I was coaching at Chaffey High School in Ontario, California in my last year, these two were three and five years old and sons of my good friend, Floyd Roenicke, baseball coach of the Covina High School team. We had many good battles on the diamond through the 1950s.

Gary, the eldest of the two brothers, spent ten years in the majors. He started with Montreal in 1976, played for the Orioles from 1978 through 1985, and finished his career with the Yankees for a year and two years for Atlanta from 1986 to 1988. He played mostly outfield.

Gary played in 1,063 games, batted .247, hit 121 home runs, and had 410 RBIs over his career. He retired in 1988 at age 34.

Ron played with six different clubs from 1981 to 1988. He was with the Los Angeles Dodgers from 1981 to 1983 and spent the last part of the season with the Seattle Mariners. In 1984 he went to San Diego, 1985 to the San Francisco Giants, followed by two years, 1986 and 1987 with the Philadelphia Phillies. His last year in the big leagues was with the Cincinnati Reds.

Since that time Ron has been a coach. He has been the third base coach with the Los Angeles (Anaheim) Angels for several years and provides them an experienced veteran to help younger players. Recently Mike Scioscia named him Bench Coach for the Angels.

Ron is another member of the UCLA Baseball Hall of Fame. He played 527 games in the major leagues with a batting average of .238. He hit 17 home runs and had 113 RBIs.

Last year at the retirement dinner of UCLA baseball coach, Gary Adams, I spoke with Ron about my admiration for his father. He is a quality gentleman and one I estimate will someday manage a major league team.

Though I have not met Gary, I want to extend my best wishes to both of the Roenicke boys. They come from good stock.

Babe Ruth—
The Babe Was and
Is "Baseball"

Meeting Babe Ruth was one of the highlights of my life. What a thrill to shake his hand! Please see Story 9 (Hey Kid, You Got My Number) about this exciting experience.

What can I say about the Babe? The man was beyond belief in his ability to play this game of baseball. We talk about his home runs but they are probably down the list of his accomplishments. He had 29 consecutive scoreless innings in WORLD SERIES PLAY. He posted a 1.75 ERA and nine shutouts in 1916. He rewrote the record books every year. He hit a home run every 11.76 times at bat. No one has matched his slugging average of .847 in 1920. As an outfielder he twice recorded 20 assists in a season. He played his last game on May 30, 1935 when he was with the Boston Braves.

Sportswriter Bill Broeg commented "Trying to capture Babe Ruth with cold statistics would be like trying to keep up with him on a night out." It was an impossible thing to do. He battled on the ball field and on the same day would be seen spending hours of free time with needy children. Yes, he was a free spirit and "the true character of the game." There will never be another like him. Most agree with me on that statement.

Meeting Babe that day in Los Angeles in 1948 was awesome. Here he was dying of cancer and he was out on our bench watching us play. I have one last and frank comment about this man. Babe Ruth was and is baseball!!!

Art Schallock—His Curve
Had Lots of Bite On It

Please see Story 65 (1948 Team) regarding facing some professional pitchers while in college. Art Schallock was one of those pitchers. Art played in 170 games for the Yankees and had a 6-7 win-loss record and 4.02 ERA in five years. His career was short and possibly due to an injury. But, when we faced him during spring training in Southern California, he could throw hard with "lots of stuff."

Arnold "Jigger" Statz—
The Greatest Angel
of Them All

This man was one of the genuine heroes of my youth.

Jigger had two careers, really. He played a total of nine years in the major leagues (New York Giants, Boston Red Sox, Chicago Cubs, and Brooklyn Dodgers) followed by 18 years with the Los Angeles Angels of the Pacific Coast League. When Statz passed away on March 18, 1988, the headline read, "The Greatest Angel of Them All."

His nickname had something to do with his size. The story goes that he was "no bigger than a chigger." Somehow, the name was mixed up and he ended up being called "Jigger." He was only 5' 7 ½" tall and weighed 150 pounds. He did not hit with power but he certainly hit with consistency. In his years with the Angels he had longevity records beyond belief.

These numbers are worth reading. He played in 2,790 games, had 10,657 at bats, 1,996 runs, 3,356 hits, 4,405 total bases, 2,564 singles, 595 doubles, 137 triples, 6,872 put outs, 263 assists, 7,135 accepted chances, and eleven 200-hit seasons. In the big leagues he played in 683 games with a .285 batting average. And the following three records are really beyond belief. He played in 3,473 professional games, had 13,242 at bats and 4,093 hits, the latter being surpassed only by Ty Cobb and Pete Rose.

Jigger scouted for the Cubs from 1947 through 1952. Also, he served as temporary manager of the Cub's farm team at Visalia, California in 1948 and 1949.

It is little wonder that Jigger was so popular. His determination and character were among the highest of anyone who ever played the game. Remember that name, Arnold "Jigger" Statz. It is a great one!

STORY 141:

Lou Stringer— Louie was Quick, Quick, Quick

Lou lived in our neighborhood in Southwest Los Angeles and, like many of our local friends, could often be found playing baseball at Harvard Playground. He was tabbed as the probable replacement for the Cub's regular second baseman, Billy Herman. Lou led National League second basemen in assists in 1941 but did a turnabout and led in errors in 1942.

After a stint in the service he returned to the Cubs and was signed with the Boston Red Sox as a substitute for the injured Bobby Doerr in 1948. He hung on in a utility role for Boston until 1949 when he went to the Pacific Coast League and played several seasons for the Los Angeles Angels and Hollywood Stars.

Lou was not a strong hitter but did manage to bat .242 in 409 games over six seasons. He had 19 home runs and 122 RBIs. He was very quick. He could transfer the ball from glove to hand in a split second.

We knew Lou both as a local player in our neighborhood which was a baseball hotbed, and also because he was the fiancé of our best man's sister. Lou is living today in the Los Angeles area and still is an eager baseball fan.

STORY 142:

Bobby Thomson— In the Giant's All-Time Outfield

This man made one of the memorable plays ever in baseball history. Please see Story 24 (The Shot Heard 'Round the World) about the last second swing of the bat to win the National League pennant. There were so many factors in this story that could have turned the outcome the other way. But, Bobby Thomson put the finishing touch on a remarkable season in 1951.

Thomson played fifteen years in the big leagues, eight with his beloved New York Giants, four with the Milwaukee Braves, a cup of coffee back with his Giants, two years with the Cubs, and another cup or two with the Orioles and the Red Sox to complete his career.

Thomson was a gamer for sure. Many are not aware that in the storied three-game playoff series that determined the National League winner,

Thomas had homered in the first game to erase a Dodger 1-0 lead. That clout was hit off Ralph Branca, the same pitcher hurling for the Dodgers when Thomson hit the "shot heard 'round the world." There is some trivia for you.

Another curious happening occurred in spring training when Thomson broke his ankle. That injury kept Hank Aaron from being sent to the minor leagues and later in the season Aaron ran for Thomson and broke his ankle. More trivia.

In 1969 Thomson was named to the Giant's all-time outfield along with Mel Ott and Willie Mays. I would say, "pretty good company." Bobby played in 1,779 games, batted .270, and hit 264 home runs with 1,026 RBIs for his career. He was an All Star in 1948, 1949, and 1952.

STORY 143:

Nick Tremark— "I Played Some Baseball in New York"

This was a remarkable experience for me. I met Nick Tremark on Guam where we were stationed together in a U. S. Marine Corps unit. I was there working with former major leaguer, Mace Brown, helping to keep the armed forces occupied with various athletic activities until they could go back to the States. Please see Story 7 (World War II Duty on Guam with Mace Brown). Among other things, Nick and I patrolled the island traveling from one side to the other watching for Japanese soldiers who had been sniping at U. S. troops even though the war had ended. Apparently, they did not know the war was over. Part of our job was to transport various items to other units stationed there. We were based near the main town of Agana near Apra Harbor. When food and other goods came in on ships we picked up cargo and delivered it to designated locations.

Of course, we chatted with each other and discovered where each of us lived in the States. We queried one another about our lives at home. One day Mike told me he had played some baseball when he was in New York. I asked him where he played and his answer overwhelmed me. Nick said, "I was on the Brooklyn Dodgers." I could hardly believe it. He was lefty all the way and played outfield. He played from 1934 to 1937 in 35 games with a .247 batting average. He had just 10 RBIs. Nick was just 5' 5" tall and 150 pounds, sort of a Dominic Dallesandro type. He said he was used mostly as a pinch hitter.

After playing for the Dodgers, Nick extended his baseball career by playing for the Los Angeles Angels of the Pacific Coast League. We figured I had seen him play when I was only fourteen years old (Nick was twenty-six at the time).

After our Guam duty ended I returned to Los Angeles and Nick went back to his home in Yonkers, New York. Nick was a great guy and I would like to have seen him again here in the States. He passed away in 2000. We will have to see each other in heaven and talk some more baseball.

STORY 144:

Omar Visquel— This Guy is a Tiger Out There

Please see Story 42 (Throwing Out First Pitch at Major League Baseball Games), paragraph 4. Omar was my catcher at a game between Seattle and Oakland in 1992. Read story for details.

Omar was the star shortstop in Seattle from 1989 through 1993. He was an All Star in both the 1988 and 1989 seasons. His defense was magnificent and he won Gold Glove Awards eight consecutive years from 1993 to 2000. He had 1,620 games with a .276 batting average, 41 home runs, and 515 RBIs. Omar had the ability to get wood on the ball. He put it in play. He had the ability to get rid of the ball quickly if necessary. I will never forget the last out of Chris Bosio's no-hitter in Seattle on April 27, 1993 against the Boston Red Sox. Omar charged and bare handed it and threw the runner out by a step. Incidentally, Bosio walked the first two hitters in that game and finished by retiring 26 batters in a row plus a force play on the first "base on balls" runner.

After playing five seasons with the Mariners and eight with the Indians, Omar was traded to the San Francisco Giants. That adds five more major league seasons to his record. He has certainly been a consistent performer.

At the aforementioned game when Omar was my catcher, Marilyn and I both had the opportunity to meet this fine young ball player.

STORY 145:

Bump Wills— A Quality Young Ballplayer

After coaching at Chaffey High School in Ontario, California for fifteen years I accepted a position at Whitworth College in Spokane, Washington and moved the family there in 1964. Our boys, Kenny, Mike, and Scott were becoming of age to play competitive sports in school. Please see Stories No. 175, 178, and 180 (Ken, Mike, and Scott Proctor) about their playing days.

One of our opponents was Central Valley High School. Our school, Mead High School, had some very competitive contests with Central in all sports. Kenny and Bump Wills were the same age and met each other on the football and baseball fields. I recall one game when Bump returned an opening kickoff 87 yards for a touchdown. On the following kickoff, Kenny ran it back 100 yards tying the score at 7-7 after less than a minute of play. The two played infield for their respective teams in baseball and each performed very well.

Following high school graduation, Bump played in Japan for a few years and went on to play for the Texas Rangers from 1977 to 1981. He was traded to the Chicago Cubs where he played one season in 1982. Bump never attained the notoriety of his famous father, Maury Wills, but he was competitive, had good speed, and earned a living in baseball for a few years.

Bump, who was called Bumpy in school days, played 831 games in the majors with a .266 batting average, 36 home runs, and 302 RBIs. Bump, originally a right handed batter, later became a switch hitter.

STORY 146:

Don Zimmer—A Genuine Credit to the Game

This man is one of my all-time favorite players. He is a baseball man through and through. He claims to have never earned any money except in baseball.

Zim, or Popeye, as he is called, was on an American Legion national championship baseball team in 1947 when Babe Ruth came and congratulated them. One year later I met the Babe at UCLA in June. And the Babe passed away three months later.

In 1953 Zim received the first of many serious injuries that was to be his fate. He was hit in the head while playing in the American Association. He was unconscious for nearly two weeks, lost his speech for six days, and dropped 44 pounds. But, in 1954 he was playing again, and in 1955 played second base along with Junior Gilliam for the Brooklyn Dodgers in the World Series. He continued playing in 1956 when he was hit again and received a fractured cheekbone ending his season. Please see Story 23 for more fascinating information about Zim.

There are some other interesting facts. Zim played for Casey Stengel as an original New York Met in 1962. His name, Popeye, was given him because of his unusual strength. He is built like a fireplug. His high school buddy, Jim Frey, named him the Chicago Cub's manager in 1988. He was creative in his strategic moves. He did not always "follow the book." For example, he often pulled off the squeeze play with the bases loaded. His reasoning was, why not? If the play is performed right there will not be a force at home anyway.

Popeye continues in the game today working for the Tampa Bay Devil Rays. We wish you well, Zim. You are a credit to our great game.

CHAPTER 6

Special Stories About Friends, Fans and Former Players

I very much enjoy writing about people who love the game of baseball. The following friends and fans are some of them. These people have one thing in common. They appreciate the value of competition and have, for the most part, made it a part of their lives. This is especially true for those who love "the grand old game of baseball." All of my former Chaffey High School players are listed in Chapter IV on the various teams. Some of them are listed in this current chapter for special stories and highlights.

STORY 147:

Harry Amend—He Wanted to Be at the Plate

I always thought that Harry Amend might have played in the big leagues if he had so chosen to do so. Harry is a lanky lefthander with a natural motion. We first met in Spokane when I was on staff at Whitworth College and Harry was a student. Soon thereafter we played "slow pitch" softball on an organized team. Harry could do it all both offensively and defensively.

As I had done, Harry chose to be an educator. After teaching a number of years he became an administrator and has been a superintendent of several school districts. Currently, he is the superintendent of the Couer d'Alene School District in Idaho.

Our wives, Sandy and Marilyn, have been good friends, particularly through their commonality in Christian activities. The four of us had been together at the summer conferences in the Fellowship of Christian Athletes in Ashland, Oregon. Both families have grown children.

Harry worked for a time as a scout for the Philadelphia Phillies, another common interest for the two of us. He is a great baseball man and it is a privilege to call him a friend. I recall that when the game was on the line, Harry wanted to be at the plate.

STORY 148:

Gary Adams—A Standing Ovation at Bovard Field

In the late 1950s the Riverside Poly High School Bears had twins playing in their infield. They were Gary and Gene Adams, second base and shortstop,

respectively. They were sparkplugs of that team and were always "in the hunt" for the league title.

Gary went on to play at UCLA and became the captain of the Bruins. He was a formidable hitter and nearly flawless in the infield. He performed well enough that he was asked to become the assistant baseball coach of the University of California at Riverside. Four years later he accepted the head baseball- coaching job at the University of California at Irvine baseball squad. He remained there five years. His teams went to the NCAA playoffs every year and were national champions in his final two years.

UCLA head coach Art Reichle retired at that time and Gary was asked to replace him. Coach Reichle was my coach at UCLA, too. Gary retired in 2004 from UCLA after thirty years of coaching baseball. When his upcoming retirement was announced in his last game against USC at the Trojan's Bovard Field, he received a standing ovation.

Gary has sent many players to the major leagues and had more than 1,000 victories at UCLA. Rod Dedeaux, former USC baseball coach, and Gary, each have more players in the major leagues than any other college baseball coach. He was very popular with his players and was duly honored recently at a retirement celebration with a turnout of 300 at the Strawberry Farms Golf Club in Irvine, California. Marilyn and I flew down from Seattle for the occasion.

Gary and his wife, Sandy, and their two daughters, Jessica and Audrey, live in the mountains north of Los Angeles. They are a fine family and ones we are proud to call friends.

STORY 149:

Gene Adams—Dr. Adams, An Accomplished Professor

The Adams twins were always a force to be reckoned with at Riverside Poly High School when I was coaching baseball in the Citrus Belt League. Gene also played at UCLA with much success. Currently, he is a professor at Fullerton College south of Los Angeles where he has worked for 27 years. His title is Professor of Kinesiology and Health Promotion.

Gene has made significant contributions in his field of study and is well known among his peers and has authored several books. Gene has his Bachelors and Masters degrees from the University of California at Los Angeles (UCLA) and his PhD from the University of Southern California (USC).

He and his wife, Jan, live in Southern California. His son, Manny, 34, played baseball for brother, Gary, at UCLA. His daughter, Shaun, lives in the area and is a UCLA graduate.

I had a letter recently from Gene and he is doing well and continues to be a good friend and colleague of Marilyn and me. He is a true gentleman of class in his daily life and his profession. He is highly regarded by his associates.

STORY 150:

Chuck Bennett—Should I Go For It, Coach?

One of my most memorable coaching experiences occurred on June 1, 1956 in a CIF semi-final baseball game played on our home field, John Galvin Park in Ontario, California between Chaffey and Montebello High Schools. It was the ninth inning and the score was tied 6-6. There were two outs and centerfielder Andy Prevedello, who had singled, was on first base. The winner of this game would move into the finals for the California Interscholastic Federation championship.

Chuck Bennett, our leftfielder, with bat in hand, came by the dugout where I was standing. He sensed the opportunity of the moment and with a low and serious tone he said, "Shall I go for it, Coach?" This was an eighteen-year old high school player asking me if he should hit one out of the park. I was thinking, "Hey, this is Babe Ruth stuff," like pointing at a spot beyond the fence in the deep outfield. Today, they even have an ad on television depicting such a happening. I can remember it like it was yesterday and, actually, it was nearly fifty years ago. My mind was going a mile a minute but I gathered my thoughts long enough to reply, "Chuck, pick a good pitch."

The first pitch was a ball at the shoulders. Chuck swung on the second pitch and drove it far and high against the outfield screen some 400 feet away. The crowd went crazy. All our players streaked to home plate to greet the two runners. We have newspaper pictures showing this scene. It was bedlam! I had never experienced anything like it. The moment is frozen in my mind like it just happened—right now! We were in the finals!!! It excites me just to think about it. Please see Story 214, Item No. 16 (Quotes in Baseball).

Ben (Terry) Cain— A Quality Pair of Friends

At Chaffey High School I had a student athlete who was always positive and carried a big smile on his face. In those days he was known as Terry Cain. Now most friends call him Ben. He and his lovely wife, Barbara, live just a few miles from us in Mill Creek, Washington.

Terry is a CLU and has his own business. Basically, he helps people direct their business affairs. That is a good business for him because he was always a "helper." He cares about people. He and Barbara are two of a kind. They have gentle spirits, are both very capable, and give their love away freely. I have seen many times when they were there for people when the need arose.

As a matter of fact, I probably would not be writing this book had it not been for Terry. He took me to a business friend, Kurt Gorham, who has been instrumental in the book's formation. You will find the Cains in the Acknowledgments of the book. In addition, Terry told me that baseball was and is his favorite sport.

They adore their grandson, Colton. He is fortunate to have two wonderful grandparents like Terry and Barbara. We, too, treasure their friendship and count it a blessing that we have reunited after all these years.

Rob Campbell—A Veritable Baseball Encyclopedia

When I was on staff at Seattle Pacific University in Seattle, Washington, I met many fine individuals at that outstanding institution. One of them was an energetic student named Rob Campbell. He loved baseball with the utmost passion. We spent hours talking about the great game.

Rob had played in high school but, unfortunately, SPU did not have a baseball team. He played intramural ball and satisfied his baseball needs by keeping up with action in the major leagues and attending Mariner games at the Kingdome in the city. He and his family moved to the Bay Area for a time and we kept in touch by mail. We traded baseball information back and forth.

He is now the Vice President of Finance for the popular Nordstrom Company whose headquarters is in Seattle. Rob and wife, Cam, have three sons, Todd, Jay, and Steve. Jay is playing baseball at the University of Montana, Steve is a freshman basketball player at Washington State University, and Todd is a basketball and football player in junior high school.

One of his best stories is about contacting Jimmy Reese of the Los Angeles Anaheim Angels. Please see Story 132 (Jimmy Reese) about this interesting incident.

Rob is one of the most interesting baseball fans I know. He has consistently sent me good articles about baseball. He is very knowledgeable about baseball players, past and present. I was always impressed that Rob, even in his younger years, had a thorough comprehension of baseball history. He is a great friend and one I admire and enjoy.

STORY 153:

Moose Clauson— He Brightens Up a Room

When Moose and Dorothy Clauson were made they broke the mold. What a fine and generous couple! Marilyn and I have known them for many years. Moose is an administrator with the Seattle Mariners. He is one the most likeable people one would ever meet. When we go to Safeco Field, home of the Mariners, just mentioning Moose's name brings big smiles on the faces of those with whom he works.

He grew up as Al Clauson and has been an outstanding individual wherever he has worked. He was nicknamed Moose because of his diminutive size. Moose is a guy who walks in and brightens up a room. He was in the insurance business in Seattle for years and a friend of all. He was extremely successful in his work. The Mariner organization recognized that fact and he has been with them since the early days of the club.

Marilyn and I consider Moose and Dorothy as extremely close friends. They just don't come any better!

STORY 154:

Howard Collins—A Good Man to Have on Your Side

Howard is one of my former baseball players from the championship teams of Chaffey High School in the 1950s. He lives and works in Phoenix, Arizona. He is a former FBI man now retired from that responsibility.

After an excellent batting average and playing a solid third base at Chaffey, Howard went on to star at Chaffey College and UCLA in baseball. In fact, though an infielder in high school, he had such a good arm that he was used to pitch in college. He has the distinction of shutting out USC, the Bruin's cross town rivals, 3-0, in a game in the 1960s, the first to accomplish that feat in fifteen years. He had a number of other shut outs and had a 1.96 ERA in his junior year and was listed in the College Baseball Handbook as one of the lowest in the nation.

Many scouts sought after Howard. His fastball was estimated at about 94 MPG. Unfortunately, a campus bicycle accident injured Howard seriously and it brought to an end his lifetime dream of pitching in the major leagues.

We see Howard every year when we go to spring training. He is still a total baseball fan and follows the grand old game regularly.

STORY 155:

Ross Cutter—Baseball is His Middle Name

In 1964 we left Ontario, California to join the staff at Whitworth College in Spokane, Washington. This small Christian college in north Spokane has been a shining light in that city. Part of the reason it has been so popular is because of people like Dr. and Mrs. Cutter (Ross and Shirley). Both of them have been models for thousands of students there for nearly fifty years. They are the kind of people who have given themselves to the education of American youth and have done an outstanding job.

Ross attended the University of California at Berkeley as a physical education major. He graduated in 1942. He played sports as a youth including tennis and baseball. Prior to going to what is known as "Cal-Berkeley," he graduated from University High School in Oakland. From 1948 through 1954 Ross coached baseball at Liberty High School in Brentwood, and Stockton and Franklin High Schools in Stockton. He briefly coached Whitworth College as acting coach on a three-game road trip in 1961 for a team that went on to win the NAIA National Championship. That team featured Ray Washburn, an eventual St. Louis Cardinal star pitcher.

Ross's accomplishments in tennis coaching are legendary. He spent thirty-three years coaching Whitworth College teams and was voted into the NAIA Hall of Fame in 1986. He served on the NAIA National Committee for eighteen years. The tennis courts at Whitworth have been named after Ross since 1990.

We are the best of friends with the Cutters. The four of us go each year to Arizona to attend spring training baseball games. They started this activity many years ago and we have joined them since the late 1990s. Ross is a very knowledgeable baseball aficionado as he follows the game throughout the year.

It was a great day when we met the Cutters more than forty years ago. We are making plans right now for another spring training experience in March. Please see Story 41 (Spring Training Fun).

Marcia Dashiell—An All American in Sports and Life

As you may note I am writing about people alphabetically by last name. It is certainly appropriate that this lady follows the Cutters regardless of alphabet. Marcia was a student of Dr. Cutter at Whitworth College. Marcia was probably the best female basketball player to attend Whitworth in the 1950s, 1960s, and 1970s. She led the Pirates to victories over the University of Washington, Washington State University, and Gonzaga. She had a career-high 32 points against Gonzaga as a sophomore. She was named on several All American teams. And she knows baseball inside and out.

Following graduation in 1968 she continued to play on touring AAU teams and other squads. In 1975 she was invited to try out for the first-ever United States Olympic team. In the 1970s and early 1980s she traveled to Central America and Europe playing with various teams.

She participated as a player/coach from 1993 to 1996. She recently retired from coaching and teaching for 30 years in Oregon including eight years at Cascade High School in Turner and eighteen years in the North Clackamas School District.

More recently, Marilyn and I have met Marcia and she has become a close personal friend. In fact, because of Marcia and her friends, Ruth Cassanova and Darlene Walker, I became excited about writing this book. They inspired me.

Marcia has a great family, including her parents, Mel and Lillie, who live in central Washington. We have been with them and Marcia in the springtime recently to watch some spring training baseball games. Marcia is a died-in-the-wool Atlanta Braves fan and she knows the game like the back of her hand. We thoroughly appreciate our valued camaraderie with this fine lady. Marilyn and I cherish her Christian friendship.

STORY 157:

Joe De Maggio—A Colleague Who Has Earned Respect

Because of his name, Joe always raised eyebrows when he introduced himself. Of course, this Joe's last name has one letter different from the Yankee Clipper, the "e" instead of "i" after the "D." Joe and I graduated from Washington High School in 1942. We played baseball and football together. Also, we previously had attended Horace Mann Junior High School in Los Angeles.

Joe was a marvelous athlete. He could play any sport very well. I recall he held the record at Horace Mann for "dropkicks in succession" for seniors. He put 69 kicks through the uprights. I was the junior record holder at 61 kicks and was always trying to catch him. The status, senior or junior, was based on height, weight, and age. Also, Joe was outstanding on his various teams on through high school.

While I was earning my degree at UCLA, Joe was across town securing his sheepskin from USC. Many of our large graduating class of over 800 went to one or the other of those two great universities. Both did a great job of preparing their students for the future.

Later in the 1950s and 1960s, Joe coached at Redlands High School when I was at Chaffey High School. Both schools were in the old Citrus Belt League. We had some great contests versus each other in baseball and football.

I always admired Joe, not just for his accomplishments on the athletic fields that, in fact, were very good, but for his attitude and manner. He is a great model for his students.

STORY 158:

Pat Dooley—Pat and Dixie, Two Talented and Valued Friends

At the outset, let me say that Pat Dooley, professional artist, has one of his artworks in the Baseball Hall of Fame in Cooperstown, New York. Pat did sketches for this book. They are truly outstanding and add a rich quality to the book. He is an extremely talented gentleman. Please allow me to start Pat's story in the 1950s and bring you up to date.

He is another Chaffey High School graduate who has gone on to succeed famously in his chosen profession. He told me when he was young he entered in every art class available and every art competition.

Following graduation from high school, Pat worked in the newspaper industry in all facets. He was a pressman, photographer, editor, advertising salesman, advertising director, circulation manager, controller, and publisher. His last ten years in that business was with Script's League Newspapers.

When Pat turned 50 he retired from the newspaper business and took up art on a full time basis. He and his wife Dixie have spent 40 to 60 hours a week at this craft. They have owned two galleries and a framing business. Pat does the painting and Dixie does the promoting.

Pat's paintings have been purchased and collected by individuals and corporate businesses throughout the United States. He and Dixie have won dozens of awards and honors in the past seventeen years. Pat is a most talented artist.

Pat states, "I create my best work when I'm emotionally involved with the subject. It's almost always the light. I am a painter of light. The subject is not nearly as important or emotionally stimulating as the light hitting it. The light and the atmosphere it creates is the inspiration for all my paintings."

In 1995, Pat was commissioned by the University of Oregon to do a painting honoring the retiring Womens' Athletic Director there. He worked with Oregon Athletic Director, Norve Ritchey. This lady was the main subject in the movie, "A League of Their Own." The beautiful 24"X30" painting was placed in the Baseball Hall of Fame in Cooperstown, New York.

Please see Pat and Dixie's picture in the Photo and Art Credits in the beginning pages of this book.

STORY 159:

Elvin C. "Ducky" Drake— My Coach, Trainer, and Brother

I knew this man in three different locations in my life. First, he was my junior high coach at Horace Mann Junior High School in Los Angeles. He was very popular with the students and was known to all of us as "Mr. Drake." Secondly, when I arrived at UCLA and went out for athletic teams, there was Mr. Drake serving as head trainer for the athletic department. He was known to all Bruin athletes as, "Ducky." And, finally, after teaching for a number of years, I became involved with the Fellowship of Christian Athletes. When I arrived to join the staff

at Southern Oregon College in Ashland, once again, there was "Ducky" serving on the same staff.

"Ducky" Drake was a role model for all of us in all three areas. He "walked the talk," as our young men like to say. He did not allow any profanity in his training room and he demanded discipline. He was teaching all of us to be responsible for our own actions and to be mentally tough. When he came to Spokane with the John Wooden UCLA basketball team in the 1960s I asked him if he would speak to my Fellowship of Christian Athlete group of 60 young men. He gladly accommodated us and did an outstanding job of bringing a meaningful message.

If you have the opportunity to see pictures of any of the great UCLA basketball or football teams, look for "Ducky." He will be in the background somewhere. Every athlete that ever attended UCLA looked up to "Ducky," a great man.

STORY 160:

John Fabian— Mr. Baseball Fan

From 1975 to 1985 I worked for the PEMCO Financial Center and the Washington School Employees Credit Union in Seattle. I met many great friends and colleagues during those years. One young gentleman in the credit union was John Fabian. I single out John because he is a totally devoted baseball fan. He loves the game. He keeps abreast of all the various teams and their activities and knows about all trades and business developments in the game. And the best part is that John has opinions about these baseball facts and expresses them exceedingly well.

After I retired I missed seeing John. Occasionally, I will go back and "talk baseball." I really enjoy seeing this wonderful friend.

STORY 161:

Chuck Giordano— Best Second Baseman in the CIF—1957

One of the key players of the 1956 and 1957 Chaffey Tiger CIF championship baseball teams was Chuck Giordano. He was a second baseman with a big heart. Chuck learned well. I recall his fundamentals. Like most of the Chaffey players, you had to tell Chuck something just once.

He made one error in his senior season to allow a runner to reach first base. On the same play he picked a runner off third base. He always had his head in the ball game. He batted .369 in his junior year and .560 in CIF play in his senior year. Chuck was selected to the All-CIF first team as a second baseman.

Chuck has developed a group of restaurants in Southern California. He has built a successful business and makes it happen just like he did on the baseball diamond.

STORY 162:

Hal Handley—This Great Catcher Could Nail Them

This gentleman is one of my good buddies from UCLA baseball days. He was one of the most intelligent catchers I knew. His ability to keep runners close to the bases they occupied was exceptional. I was the second baseman and Hal and I worked out a set of signals between us to try and keep base runners close to the bag. They had to be worried about being picked off because of Hal's quick reaction time and fine throwing arm.

Hal's cousins, Lee and Gene Handley, both played in the major leagues, Lee spending most of his years with Pittsburg and Gene with the Philadelphia Athletics.

A retiree now in Southern California, Hal and Donna Handley enjoy themselves in their home city. Hal and I keep in touch via telephone and email often.

STORY 163:

Jerry Hendon—A Loyal Baseball Fan Saw the Finals

I learned about this story just recently. Jerry was a football player from Chaffey High School and when the baseball team was scheduled to play Oxnard in the CIF Finals in 1956 Jerry was bound and determined to see that game.

He said he made his plans, somehow left school early on Friday, borrowed his mother's car and headed for Oxnard. The distance from Ontario to Oxnard is almost 100 miles and in those days we did not have the high-speed highways as today. Jerry said he must have broken all speed limits to get there. He made it shortly after the first pitch.

That is the kind of loyalty our students had for their teams. Jerry watched the game and celebrated with us for a while afterward. Thanks for your great effort, Jerry. We are glad you made it safely.

STORY 164:

Ben Hines—If You Want to Learn About Batting, See Ben

In 1962 I had the assignment to hire coaches for one of our athletic departments in our district at Montclair High School. The baseball coach I chose was an outstanding player and baseball man. He had played his baseball at LaVerne College (now the University of LaVerne) in La Verne, California. His name was Ben Hines.

He was a fine prospect and a coach the students liked very much. Later Ben accepted the post of baseball coach for LaVerne College, his alma mater.

When Marilyn and I moved to Seattle we became acquainted with various players and coaches of the Mariners. And who should be on the roster as team batting coach but Ben Hines? I understand that he was very good at his trade. Soon thereafter, Ben accepted the same position with the Los Angeles Dodgers. Also, Ben worked with the California Angels in their hitting instruction program.

I am not sure where Ben is today but I did see an ad for a baseball clinic where Ben is teaching more about hitting. I am sure he will always be around baseball. He is a coach who always had my respect.

STORY 165:

The Knudsons— A Baseball-Loving Family

(Dolly, Luther, Lyle, Howard, Marilyn, & David)

This was a baseball family since they lived up in Roger Maris country in Fargo, North Dakota. The boys, Howard and Lyle, went to Castleton High School and played different sports there. David was a young fellow at that time and his later talents led him to music and he became very good at it. In fact, he has been and still is a professional musician.

When the family moved to Los Angeles in the early 1940s Luther took the kids to baseball games at Gilmore Field. They watched the Hollywood Stars. Please see Story 18 (Gilmore Field), paragraph 8 about the Knudsons and Gilmore Field.

My wife, Marilyn, has become a baseball aficionado. She knows the game inside and out. She loves to go to the ballpark. Lyle and Howard still love sports and watch games whenever the opportunity arises.

STORY 166:

Jim Lisec—Steady Jim Always Did the Job

I had a telephone call from Jim Lisec just recently. We talked a bit about Chaffey High School baseball days and recalled that his dad, Joe Lisec, was always there to mend our gloves, chest protectors, and anything associated with the baseball team. Joe did it out of the kindness of his heart. Jim said, "Would you like to talk to Joe?" "Would I?" I said. "Put that great guy on the phone." Joe, now over 90, and I had a great talk. He sounded terrific.

Jim was an outstanding first baseman and starred on the 1958 team. Please see Story 76 (1958 Chaffey Team). He was a steady hitter and uncanny with his ability to cover first base. He fielded everything that came his way. Jim was honored by selection to the All-CIF Second Team.

As I have said before, we were a "team" kind of squad, all for one and one for all. When we won we all won, and when we lost we all lost. This kind of story could be applied to every one of those great players I was privileged to coach. Jim was a great team man.

Jody Marker—A Fine Player With A Big Heart

Just south of Ontario, California is a school by the name of Boys' Republic. It is a placement center for troubled youth 14 to 18 years of age. The average stay there is six months to a year. They have an incredibly high success rate with their boys.

Jody Marker went to work there in 1970 and retired in 1994. He began as the Supervisor of Grounds. Some of the students were assigned to help Jody with this work. Soon, Jody was offered the job of Wreath Production Supervisor. Many may be aware of the beautiful Della Robbia Christmas Wreath Program at Boys' Republic. The revenue generated by this program provides 25% of the support to operate the school.

The help that Jody gave these young men cannot be measured. Steve McQueen, the famous movie star, was one of Jody's boys. Also, John Babcock of ABC Sports graduated as one of Jody's students. And there were hundreds of others. It did not surprise me at all when I learned of Jody's experience all these years.

Jody was an outstanding baseball player. He was quicker than greased lightning and very coordinated. Because of some confusion of school district boundaries Jody played in a neighboring community and I did not have the opportunity to have him on my team. That was my loss. He did finally play at Chaffey and was always a good contributor in any activity he tried. We are so proud of Jody for the many youth he assisted through the years. It is a pleasure to call him "friend."

Larry Maxie—CIF Player of the Year—Twice

In 1958 Larry reached the pinnacle of high school success by being named CIF Player of the Year for the second time. He signed a baseball contract with the Milwaukee Braves under the direction of a scout named Johnny Moore, a scout with the club. Moore was a major league star in his own right.

Larry won 18 consecutive games that year and was a key figure in earning Chaffey the CIF Championship. He was a great young man to coach. He was very humble and considerate but a fierce competitor.

This man was the supposed successor to Milwaukee's great left-handed pitcher, Warren Spahn. Larry started at Eau Claire, Wisconsin in the Braves chain and eventually was the Most Valuable Player of the Texas League. An injury forced him out of baseball and he signed on with the Toronto Blue Jays as a scout. Today he is scouting with the Chicago White Sox.

I had the privilege of coaching Larry for three years as our team won the CIF title each of those years. He was a fine player and took instruction very well.

Daryl Moss— 130 Pounds of Dynamite

Ever so often a young man comes into a coach's life who will not be beaten or take a back seat to anyone. There you have Daryl Moss. Daryl spent much of his early life without the benefit of a father to give him direction. But, with his mother's help and his dogged spirit, today he is a retired Marine Corps hero and a fine father and husband.

Daryl was a catcher for me, all 130 pounds of him. In the finals of the CIF in 1956 he had bruised ribs about which he told no one. It was not until after we accepted the trophy that we learned of the injury. He was the catcher for the New York Yankee pitcher to be, Hal Reniff.

I went back through the records and noticed that Daryl was always in the thick of things. Despite his small size he always did his part. I am very proud of him. The nicest thing Daryl ever said to me was that I was his surrogate father for a part of his high school life. Daryl, I am humbled for you to say such a thing. I am honored. Thank you!

STORY 170:

Andy Prevedello— Kept Centerfield Under Control

This guy was everywhere. He patrolled centerfield for our Chaffey ball club like a caged tiger. There was no fly he could not run down. He had the speed and arm to go with it. And he was a tough hitter.

Andy signed with the Pittsburg Pirates upon graduation out of high school. There is a great story to be told about one of Andy's minor league teams. On August 19, 1958 he was playing for the Douglas (Arizona) Copper Kings against the Chihuahua Dorados in Ciudad Delicias, a small town southeast of Chihuahua, Mexico. A small crowd of 614 persons witnessed a most unusual event. In fact, this event has never happened at any level in professional baseball.

In that game, every player on the Copper Kings hit a home run. They won the ball game 22-8 and the game was called at the end of eight innings due to darkness. Bob Clear, the manager and pitcher that day for Douglas currently works for the Los Angeles Angels as a roving special assignment instructor.

This is a related oddity. On September 4, 1999, eight different Cincinnati Reds homered during a 22-3 drubbing of the Phillies at Vet's Stadium. But the Douglas team still holds the record when every player homered.

Andy was a great young man to coach. He was enthusiastic and positive. He was instrumental in Chaffey's winning ways. Andy is retired now and living in Surprise, Arizona.

STORY 171:

Hannah Proctor— A High Quality Young Lady With a Good Eye

This young lady, Mike and Penny's daughter (and our granddaughter), is a music major in her third year of college at Northwest University. She has accomplished much in many areas in her young years. She was an exceptional basketball player in high school and college. She also played softball. She was a member of the Tacoma (Washington) Junior Symphony Orchestra. She is truly a professional in her music work.

Hannah has already graduated from a Bible College in California. Her talents and abilities are evident. It will be interesting to us to see her grow and make a significant contribution to others. Her love for people is her energy.

As with all our grandchildren, Hannah is a gem.

STORY 172:

Jesse Proctor—A Fine Athlete and Gentleman

Jesse Proctor in Little League (an all-around athlete).

Jesse proved to be a clutch athlete in his playing days. In Little League we saw him hit a grand slam one time. In another game he struck out the final batter with a one run lead, the bases loaded, and two outs. After the game I said, "Jesse, what were you saying in your mind about that last hitter." And Jesse replied, "You're going down!" And one other time we saw Jesse score five consecutive three-point shots in a high school basketball game.

Jesse, Mike and Penny's son (and our grandson) is a good athlete. His future appears to be in music, computers, or some kind of ministry. He is one of the most capable drummers I have ever seen. Now he is playing guitar and bass as well. He and a friend started their own web site building business at age 17. He will graduate from college in the next year or so. He, too, is currently attending Northwest University in Kirkland, Washington.

He is a great young man and will certainly make his mark in this world.

STORY 173:

John Proctor—My Dad Was Everybody's Friend

My father, John Proctor, was a fine man. Please see Story 1 (Dad Gave Me a Baseball When I was Four). He had a tough start as a young child when his father was killed early in life. He liked sports but because of home responsibilities had to work to support his mother and sister. I think his athletics were done in bits and pieces. He told me he won a handball championship tournament one time that gave him lots of pleasure.

All through the years my dad was there for me. He tried to never miss a game when I was coaching my teams at Chaffey. He and my mother both were very loyal.

John Wooden told us last year that his father was his model and taught him much about life. I feel the same way about my father. Though not educated, he seemed to know more about the real issues of life than most men. He certainly was my hero.

STORY 174:

Ken Proctor Jr.— A Smooth-Hitting Lefty

Our sons were all baseball players. Ken Jr. was a left-handed batter and right-handed thrower. He was fast and had a great arm. Kenny started all three years in high school. He played third base and pitched. Also, he was a very good football player. We saw him return a kickoff 100 yards for a touchdown and a punt 80 yards for another TD.

He and his brothers certainly enjoyed their baseball and other sports as they grew up. I had one last opportunity to coach Kenny and Mike when the boys were high school age in the 1960s. I managed a sponsored American Legion team in Spokane and we had a successful year. It was kind of a bonus. I had figured my coaching days were over by that time.

Kenny has his own boys in Hawaii now. He is 53 years old this year and doing fine. He still finds time to surf over there. He was in the business of making surfboards and wind surfboards at one time. He is a computer expert and has been selling automobiles for several years. His home is on Maui.

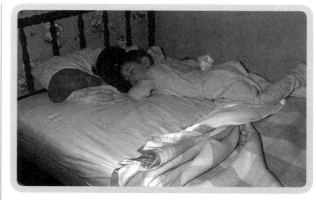

Kenny sleeping with catcher's glove. (He always slept with his athletic equipment).

Top: Kenny sliding into home (He started early in baseball.

Middle: Kenny & Mike, ages 5 & 3, with bats. (Both ended up very fine hitters)

Bottom: Kenny swinging bat in high school game. (He was a sharp batting left hander as a young man).

STORY 175:

Marie Proctor—She Could Lick a Polar Bear

My mother, Mary Lou "Marie" Proctor, was an ardent sports fan. She loved our local professional teams in Los Angeles and particularly the teams on which I played and coached through the years.

One thing I learned from my mother was to be competitive. Her famous line that the family recalls is, "I could lick a polar bear." And I wouldn't doubt that statement. She was a tiger. Also, I never knew a word she could not spell.

To my baseball-loving mother, Mary Lou, we will always love and admire you.

STORY 176:

Marilyn Proctor— This Lady Makes Things Happen

This is an incredible woman. Her talents know no end. The day she accepted my proposal of marriage was the day my life became a true blessing. We have had a marvelous life together and it is still going strong.

Please see Story 12 (Marilyn Proctor, My Best Baseball Buddy). Our love for the Lord Jesus Christ is our linchpin and holds us together. And, among many other interests, baseball ranks high in our camaraderie.

Marilyn is quite an athlete in her own right. She loves the outdoors and is one of the strongest hikers I have ever seen. We have hiked as much of 25 miles in one day. Also, we have biked together for many years. We are approaching some 3,000 biking miles together. She has a servant's heart and has a talent to "make things happen." She loves to garden, is a great cook, and keeps the cleanest and nicest home one could desire. She is at the top of the list as a wife, mother, grandmother, a friend, and baseball buddy.

Thank you for everything, Sweetheart! I love you!

STORY 177:

Mike Proctor— His Talents Know No End

When he was very young we knew that Mike would make a deep impression on others in his life. Today he and wife, Penny, are parents of three great children. Mike is a firefighter and an ordained minister. He does an excellent job at each career.

Mike swinging bat in high school game. (Mike was another excellent hitter. He was the leading hitter of his team as a senior and tops in the league).

Mike and Kenny in American Legion Simchuk uniforms.

I had the privilege of working with Mike as his high school coach. He played three sports including baseball, basketball, and football. In high school he concentrated on baseball and basketball and was all-league in both. He played first base in baseball and power forward in basketball. He was an excellent batter.

Graduating from the University of Hawaii, Mike majored in art and is an excellent graphic artist today. In fact, he is doing much of the work in the development of this book.

Mike has become a professional musician. He writes, directs, organizes, and plans all types of Christian music for their ministry, Elisha's Request. Thus far, with his family, he has produced four CDs

and is in the process of doing a fifth one. He, Penny, and children, Hannah, Rebekah, and Jesse have ministered in Australia, Africa, Mongolia, Alaska, Hawaii, and in many areas of the United States.

STORY 178:

Penny Proctor—What a Gal—She Does It All!

Marilyn and I could not ask for a better daughter-in-law. Penny is a charming and beautiful lady who is everybody's friend. She has done a marvelous job in making a comfortable home for her family and, with husband Mike, has raised three talented children.

The Penny/Mike Proctor household is in constant use. It seems as though houseguests are there every month. Their guests include those from Mongolia, Australia, Germany, and the United Kingdom. And Penny is the premier hostess. Her delectable cooking is something to behold and she has passed her talents along to all three children.

I first met Penny in Hawaii and found her to be an excellent athlete. She was winning tennis tournaments at the time. We jogged together from time to time. When Marilyn and I joined the family for a day at the park, Penny could field long fly balls with the best of them. And she could bat them out as well.

As Marilyn and I agreed one day after being with Penny for a family gathering, "What a gal! She does it all!"

Rebekah Proctor— Music, Basketball, Graceful Character

This is another of Mike and Penny's children (another granddaughter). She, too, will graduate from Northwest University in the near future. "Bekah," as we call her, is an exceptional athlete. She is currently a senior and captain of the Womens' Basketball Team at Northwest U. Along with Hannah, she has played basketball since elementary school days. She also played softball and volleyball.

We do recall one incident worth repeating. Her high school, South Kitsap, was playing in the state playoffs about six years ago against Spokane's Shadle Park. They were down one point with just twelve seconds on the clock. The ball was brought downcourt and a shot was taken. Hannah batted the ball to Bekah with four seconds remaining and she made a ten-foot jumper to win by one point with no seconds of the clock. We later saw it on a television replay.

Rebekah also loves music and plays keyboard. Music will always be part of her life. We are very proud of her.

Scott Proctor— A Great Son and Athlete

Our third son, Scott Proctor, was born April 20, 1957. He was a husky little guy at birth weighing 9 pounds, 14 ounces. He was a good athlete from his earliest days. When old enough for baseball it became evident that he could play the game if he so chose.

When fourteen years old he joined a baseball league in Hawaii where he proved to be an excellent pitcher. He had a good fast-ball, a sharp-breaking curveball, and fine control. Also, he took to basketball and started at guard every year in high school. He was an excellent shooter and his passing was even better. He earned All-League honors and averaged over 16 points a game. Also, he ran some track and was very strong in the 440-yard dash.

He loved music and possibly owned more CDs and records than anyone we knew. His music obviously came from within. Scott loved the mountains that probably came from the many happy days he spent in back country and wilderness areas with our family.

Eventually, he moved and worked up in the Cas-

Scott Proctor pitching (Scott was a very fine athlete).

cade Mountains in Washington State. Regretfully, Scott took a snowmobile deep into the mountains one day and lost his life. He was alone at the time. We miss him dearly but cherish the forty-four years we had the privilege to see and be with him. He certainly was a talented young man.

STORY 181:

Dave Reinhart— Super Dad, Therapist, and Sports Fan

In the 1990s I had some injuries that required a physical therapist. This resulted in my making a very good friend who loves baseball and is total sports fan. His name is Dave Reinhart and he works at a medical facility in Seattle.

Dave can speak with you on any baseball subject. He played the game in his younger days and now coaches his own kids. He deep understanding of the game has given me many pleasant moments of discussion.

STORY 182:

Harry Reinhart— Fine Dad & Musician Who Loves the "Sox"

Marilyn and I were in Chicago on June 7, 1998 riding the Red Line (Chicago elevated) to Wrigley Field to see a Cub's baseball game. We met Harry Reinhart on the train and had a great time talking baseball with him. We have contacted Harry, Patti, and his two children and kept in touch with them.

We congratulated Harry with the White Sox World Series victory in 2005. His prayers have been answered. Also, Harry is a professional musician.

STORY 183:

Jerry Snider— A Clutch Performer

I was directing a baseball clinic in Ontario, California one evening and I saw a young third baseman charge and go through the motions of fielding a ground ball and faking a throw to first base. He fooled everyone in the park including the base runner coming from second to third. The fielder wheeled and ran back to third base to tag out the runner who had rounded the bag. I looked at that play and said to myself, "I would like to have that kid on my ball club."

His name is Jerry Snider and a few years later led the CIF in batting average edging out a Long Beach player named Ron Fairly of Dodger fame. Please see Story 55 (Ron Fairly).

Snider helped lead our 1956 team to the CIF title. Jerry was voted the all-CIF first team shortstop.

Jerry signed with Boston by Red Sox scout, Joe Stephenson.

STORY 184:

Phil Sultz—
A Genuine Friend,
Artist, & Baseball Fan

Do you remember the articles titled "The Most Unforgettable Character I Have Ever Met?" It is certainly possible, and perhaps even probable, that my friend, Phil Sultz, fits into that category. Phil and his wife, Jan, live in a small community in upstate Maine. Both are excellent artists. Phil paints and draws and Jan is a potter. She can make anything out of clay, wood, or otherwise, a real talented lady. I saw a wooden plate she made one time and it was truly outstanding. She has the touch. Phil's paintings and drawings have won many contests in various art shows. He is an authority in western art and, in particular, photography in the Jackson Hole, Wyoming area.

Phil and I were rangers together in the late 1950s and early 1960s in Grand Teton National Park. He loves "the game." He told me he had been on his high school baseball squad for three years. He had a batting average of .500. Phil followed that information by telling me he bunted successfully in his first at bat and struck out the next time. He said, "that is .500, isn't it?" You sense what is coming with this guy. His school was Buffalo Technical High School that consisted of about 1,000 boys. He took me back when he mentioned wearing a kind of burlapy uniform. The materials were not that great in those days.

Phil played lots of basketball and, in fact made 49 out of 50 free throws in a contest. He one time made 48 points in one game, an achievement in itself.

He recalls playing in a softball game and one-

handing a long ball against the fence. His comment was, "softball is a great game but it ain't hardball."

The Buffalo Barons, a farm team of the Detroit Tigers, played in the International League. He said it cost 35 cents to get into the grandstand. He remembers seeing Hank Greenberg hit a double in an exhibition game and recalls that Jackie Robinson played for Montreal.

I enjoyed this recent letter from Phil describing the visit he and Jan made to Chicago to see their daughter. They took in a White Sox game and these were his reflections: "Been a few years since our last big league game. A bit overwhelming. Not the game, but everything else. Let's call the experience a big fat deli sandwich almost too large to manage, even with two hands, and the game itself the mustard in between. The electronic pseudo organ noise and strips with ads and corporate logos and instructions to the attending crowd when to yell and the beer sellers blocking our sideways view toward home plate every five minutes and the unbroken stream of folks going and coming with hot dogs and everything else.

Beginning with color guards and the national anthem, well that's to be expected, but the big booming voice asking every veteran to stand. The intro of the players was way over the top. Loud, slow motion baloney like talking to a brain-damaged mule. Now the manager is going out to talk to his pitcher, time for a corporate plug and six short blasts of six tunes and boom box man telling the crowd what they can do two weeks from today.

Meanwhile six different boards are lighting up all the time and the fan activity is still basically beer and buns. No let up, and long lines at the men's room. A little strip around the field for a vehicle to show up between innings and tee shirts fired into the crowd at the fans waving frantically as if they had been marooned on an island without drinking water. Anyway, we had a good time. It was worth it just to see Shawn Green stroke one into the right field seats. His uniform, his motion, his looks. He's a knockout. Reminds me of Ted Williams."

Phil and Jan are two of our best friends. It was good we ran into each other in the Tetons in the 1950s and we are very much reconnected now.

STORY 185:

Hal Thomas— Los Angeles Angels Forever and Good Buddy

In June of 1949 Hal Thomas and I graduated together from UCLA. We were both Naval Reserve Officer Training Corps cadets and participated in various athletic programs. Hal was a javelin thrower. He is one of the most ardent baseball fans I know, especially when it comes to the Los Angeles (Anaheim) Angels. When they lose he goes and hides for a few days. I keep telling him to cherish the World Series they won in 2002. Some teams never get there.

Hal and his wife, Jo, were friends of our's for many years. We had many good times together. Hal lost Jo a few years ago and everyone misses her. Hal still comes and visits us every July in our Seattle home. Seattle was Jo's hometown and I think Hal knows the city better than we do.

I wanted to get this devoted Angel baseball fan in my book. He is a quality gentleman who gave much of his life to young people as a schoolteacher and administrator in the Los Angeles School District. Our hats are off to you, buddy!

STORY 186:

Darlene and Terry Walker— Great Grandma and Grandpa Baseball Fans

When I added my Story 194 (Grandmas Like Baseball, Too), I gathered my information from Darlene Walker. She and husband, Terry, love this game through their son, daughter-in-law, and grandchildren. They follow the game religiously.

Darlene and Terry typify devoted baseball fans throughout America. They are loving, caring people who understand the importance of this game to our nation. They truly tie in their love for baseball with their children and grandchildren.

What a joy it is to call them and Marcia Dashiell "baseball pals."

Please see Story 156 (Marcia Dashiell).

STORY 187:

The Tim Walkers— Total Baseball Family

(Tim, Mary, Joshua, Jesse, and Shay)

This book would not be complete without telling about the Tim Walkers. Tim, Mary, Joshua, Jesse, and Shay live in a small Oregon community southeast of Portland. They are total baseball fans and love Oregon State University.

Marilyn and I had the pleasure of visiting their home and observing the love they have for one another. Darlene and Terry (see Story 186) are grandma and grandpa. I saw a book that Shay had given his grandmother. It was a beautiful baseball book that Darlene cherishes. It has formed a bond between the two that will last forever.

We do appreciate their friendship and look forward to good fellowship with them again soon.

STORY 188:

Don And Shirley Warner— TBF Leaders and Baseball Fans

These are two of the most generous and loving individuals Marilyn and I have ever met. They have organized a group called "TBF." Please see Story 79 (TBF). They make their home in Lewiston, Idaho and have a great family. I mention "baseball" in their story in a special way. It ties in with this love we baseball fans have for this game. Don and Shirley, you are the best!

STORY 189:

Gary Wright— Top of the Line PR Man

Gary Wright is the lead public relations director for the Seattle Seahawks National Football League team. He is a very capable individual having been with the Seattle team for the last twenty-five years. I attended a Kiwanis meeting recently and Gary, the speaker for the day, introduced himself and told me he was aware of my baseball experiences in Southern California. I found he had attended Long Beach State College and later became the Sports Information Director there. He knew about my Chaffey baseball teams of the 1950s.

When Gary talked about certain players and some of the specifics about my teams, it made me realize how knowledgeable he was in his public relations work. When former Seahawks coach, Chuck Knox, was honored recently in Seattle, it was Gary who was given credit for the work he did on behalf of this outstanding coach.

Gary knows baseball through and through and I certainly have enjoyed getting to know him better.

CHAPTER 7

Extra Innings

STORY 190:

Baseball Is a Perfect Game (Almost)

As I watch a baseball game I am stunned at how perfect are the dimensions of the infield. Play after play is so close that it takes repeated camera shots to determine if a runner is safe or out. Even then it is not always clear. Ninety feet between bases absolutely could not be better. If it were more or less either the defense or the offense would have a distinct advantage. We always hear the phrase, "it was a bang-bang play," meaning that the foot hit the bag or the ball hit the glove nearly simultaneously.

Generally speaking, on tag plays, umpires have developed a rule that if the ball reaches the base before the runner, the runner is usually out. Occasionally, a clever runner will decoy the baseman and reach his hand or foot to the bag before being tagged.

Likewise, the pitching distance of sixty feet, six inches also seems to be perfect. What a battle it is between pitcher and batter. It is a constant war as to whether that batter is strong enough to put the bat on a ball coming in between 90 and 100 miles per hour. The pitcher changes speeds and the conflict continues. If the distance between the pitching rubber and home plate were any different what might we expect? In fact, many fans do not know that prior to 1893 the pitching distance was 50 feet rather than the 60', 6" that we all know. Can you imagine facing a ball coming 100 MPH at 50 feet?

On the other hand just about every ballpark has varying distances to the outfield fences. All kinds of differences occur in the different parks. So, the game is not perfect in that part of the field. Outfielders learn how to play to advantage on their particular home fields. I can recall in the old days how some teams would change their fences to fit strategies. Pittsburg once developed an area in left field that became known as "Greenberg Gardens," whereby they moved the fences in somewhat to give an advantage to long-ball-hitting Hank Greenberg. There have been other occasions where certain changes were made to the benefit of a hitter, a group of hitters, or a team.

On May 5, 1949 at old Comiskey Park, the Chicago White Sox took down a five-foot chicken wire fence. It had been erected to cut the distance for a home run by twenty feet. It resulted in eleven homers being hit in eight games. However, their opponents hit seven of them. After this incident, the American League ruled that fences are not to be moved more than once a season. It would seem more logical to have standard distances in all parks but that is not likely to happen.

Nevertheless, those "bang-bang" plays in the infield continue to occur to the delight of the fans. The poor umpire sometimes is between a rock and a hard place trying to make the correct call. All in all it seems to work out and I, for one, am thankful that the founders of the game made the current dimensions. It really seems like a miracle that these distances have never changed and, consequently, the plays are still very competitive even today.

Tips On Watching Baseball Games

Some of these tips may help a fan better enjoy a game. The following are some thoughts on (1) DEFENSE, (2) PITCHING, (3) OFFENSE, and (4) MISCELLANEOUS. Please let me say that I would expect various opinions on some of these philosophies. Baseball people debate these issues constantly and there are many varying viewpoints. These are for your consideration:

DEFENSE

All bases covered at all times: This is an old baseball adage. All bases and home plate must be covered on every play.

Bare hand play on bunts at third base: This is a very tough play and must be practiced over and over again. Timing has to be perfect to get a fast runner. The third baseman must keep his eye on the ball as he charges, grab it and throw it as he bends forward. He will not have time to stand up and throw.

Covering bases on sacrifice, first to second: When the sacrifice is in order to move a runner from first to second, the second baseman covers first base and the shortstop covers second base. The first and third basemen try to field the bunt but they must retreat to their respective bases if necessary, particularly the third baseman. It is best if the pitcher can handle the bunt in any sacrifice situation. That gives the defense an extra fielder. The third baseman attempts to stay at third base for a play if necessary. If he has to field the bunt his best choice is to throw out the bunter at first base unless he is sure he can force the runner at second base. The offense will try to make the first baseman field the ball if they are smart because he has to hold the runner at first base and cannot get to the ball quickly.

Covering bases on sacrifice, second to third: The batter will try and make the third baseman field the ball so as to leave third base uncovered for the runner on second base to go there. Many times this bunt is made to move two runners (on first and second) to second and third. The shortstop must cover second base. Also, this puts a possible force play in order at third base. A quick fielder can make that force play if the bunt is not good or is bunted too hard. Occasionally, the pitcher can handle the bunt and the third baseman must retreat quickly to accept a possible throw.

Deciding when to cut-off throw to plate: This usually occurs when a ball is thrown from the outfield to a cut-off man in the infield. The catcher has to determine if they have a chance to tag the runner out at the plate. If that is the case he yells, "leave" or "leave it." If he determines that he cannot tag out the runner he yells, "cut," "cut-second," or "cut-third," as the case may be. I always liked to have my first baseman be the cut-off man. Some strategists like to use the third baseman for that job. I liked to have my third baseman be available to cover third base for a possible play there. If the throw is cut-off you will want to have second and third covered for sure to tag the advancing runner.

Decoys: Anytime a fielder can make a runner slow down, stop, or return to a base unnecessarily, he should do so. He does this by making the runner think he is fielding a ball or, in some cases, not fielding a ball. For example, if a runner is coming into third base, the baseman can relax and look casual even though the throw is coming his way. At the last minute, he catches the ball and fools the runner into standing up (not sliding) and places the tag on him. Outfielders can try and make runners slow down, stop, or return to a base by making it appear they are catching a fly ball. Decoys are clever means of fooling base runners.

Dropped third strike, throwing to first or tagging batter: I always made it a point to have my catcher tag a batter on a missed third strike just to be safe. In a recent league championship series game between the Angels and White Sox, there was a question as to whether a ball hit the dirt on a third strike. The umpire called "strike" because the batter swung and missed. This being the third out of the inning, the catcher rolled the ball out to the pitcher's mound. The batter ran to first base. The umpires discussed the matter and determined the ball had hit the dirt and the catcher should have tagged the batter. As it turned out, that play cost the Angels the game when the runner on first stole second and scored the winning run on a base hit. If the catcher had tagged the batter out or even thrown to first base, the inning would have been over. The umpire was correct in calling the pitch a strike but he had not called the batter out until the tag or throw had been completed.

Fielding a slowly hit ground ball: I have found that the best rule here is to charge the ball. If one tries to play the big hop he will miss throwing out the runner most of the time. Learning how to field the ball that is "between hops" is the best method. Also, by charging, an infielder generally will find

that he plays the ball rather than allowing the ball to play him. Then, of course, a quick release becomes very important.

Getting body in position for throw after catching fly ball: When a fly ball is hit to the outfield the fielder wastes valuable time if he (a) catches the ball and then has to get in throwing position. I always taught my outfielders to position themselves for the throw prior to catching the ball. In fact, clever outfielders can actually get themselves "in motion" to make the throw. This positioning can get the ball to a base or home plate one to three seconds sooner than in (a). The advantage is obvious.

Giving "who covers" sign to each other (SS & 2B): With a runner on first base the shortstop and second baseman must signal to each other who will cover in case of an attempted steal. It is general knowledge in professional baseball that the fielder to cover the base will hold his glove sideways in front of his face and close his lips as though to say "me." The other fielder will do the same with his glove and open his mouth as though to say "you." The next time you watch a game look for this sign from those two fielders.

Knocking down ball to prevent run from scoring: When an infielder can get to a batted ball that is heading for the outfield, he can help his team immensely by "knocking the ball down." In most cases it will keep a runner heading to third base from scoring.

Outfield positioning with winning run on third base and one or no outs: When a fly ball will score the winning run on a tag up play, the outfielders must come in close enough to throw the runner out at home if he chooses to try and score. Another advantage for the defense is that a blooper is not likely to fall in for a hit. The disadvantage, of course, is that an average fly ball will go over the head of the drawn-in outfielder. Note: When a foul ball is hit deep enough to allow a runner to tag up and score the winning run from third base, the outfielder would want to let the ball drop. They would then have a chance to get him out on the next play.

Neighborhood play: When a runner is forced at a base the umpire will call him out if the baseman is "in the neighborhood" of the base. This allows the baseman to get out of the way of the oncoming runner and protects him from being injured unnecessarily.

Playing close to base lines late in game to prevent runner from getting to second base to be in scoring position: The first and third basemen generally play within a few feet of the baselines in the late innings when the score is close and the defense is trying to keep the runners out of scoring position.

Routine outs at first base: The first baseman is generally allowed to leave the base a split second early to keep from being stepped on by the oncoming runner. This is an accepted practice. However, this allowance would not apply if the throw pulls the first baseman off the bag.

Shifting for pull hitters: When a batter generally pulls the ball (righthanders hit the ball to left field almost all the time, or lefthanders hit the ball to right field predominantly) the defense can over shift. This over shifting usually takes place with a lefthanded hitter at the plate. The first such shift, in my recollection, was known as the famous (Ted) Williams Shift. The rightfielder plays close to the first base line, the centerfielder moves to right centerfield, the second baseman moves deep in the hole between first and second bases, and the shortstop moves to the first base side of second base.

Throwing quickly after fielding ground ball: Some of the great fielders in baseball increased their ability to throw out a runner at first base by getting rid of the ball quickly.

Throwing quickly and on one hop after fielding a ground ball: Some players have improved their ability by fielding a ground ball and throwing the ball low so as to skip off the grass to the first baseman. However it is done, the idea is to get the ball to first base as quickly as possible.

Throwing runners out at bases: In general, if the throw beats the runner the umpire will call him out. However, it the runner obviously can get around the tag and touch the base, he can be called safe even if the throw beats him.

When to bring infielders in to cut off runner at the plate: Normally, the infielders are brought in only in the late innings of a close or tie game. With none or one out the team wants to keep that go-ahead run from scoring. Sometimes in a close pitchers' battle the infield will come in even in the early innings.

When to place infielders halfway: With a runner on third, occasionally, a team will keep the third and first baseman in close and put the shortstop and second baseman halfway back. The theory is that on a hard hit ball the runner can still be thrown out at the plate but the infielder can decide if he wants to throw the runner out at first or go for a 6-4-3 or 4-6-3 (shortstop, second, to first, or second, shortstop to first). Much of the decision here is based on the importance of the run to be scored.

When to place outfielders in the infield: This is a very unusual play but there could be times when one outfielder can come in give the defense five infielders instead of the usual four. If that happens the defense will place the outfielders in left centerfield and right centerfield to balance them out somewhat. It would be extremely rare to see this play in major league baseball but it is possible and could be a winning strategy.

PITCHING

Brush back pitch: Most pitchers feel they must throw inside to be effective with their pitching. The inside pitch is sometimes called the "brush back pitch."

Dreaded base on balls, The: Much has been written about the base on balls. To be honest, I could devote an entire chapter about this subject. Some experts have said when the first batter in an inning gets a walk he will score 70% of the time. I am not sure of that figure but it would not surprise me. I had a sign in my dugout that said, "No Three Ball Counts." I realized that the pitcher has to work on the batter to get him out but I figured if we did not give a batter three balls he could not draw a base on balls. In this section I am writing about a former player named Jack Salveson. His theory was to throw strikes and issue NO walks. I think the base on balls is the coach's or manager's worst enemy. It becomes an uncontested advantage for the batting team.

General philosophy on pitching to the average batter: I like to get ahead of the hitter by throwing a strike on the first pitch. Many hitters do not like to swing at the first pitch and he can get ahead early that way. I like to stay ahead of the hitter. I do not like my pitchers to fall behind even at two balls, one strike. I would prefer not to go to a three-ball count. If you do not go to three balls you cannot walk a batter. Except for errors, a .300 hitter theoretically gets on base just three times out of ten. So, obviously, it is wiser to let him hit the ball rather than walk him. When working a batter inside it is well to hit your target. Otherwise, it is too easy to hit the batter.

Giving signs, catcher to pitcher, or reverse: The standard method is to have signals given from catcher to pitcher. Some teams change their signs every three innings to eliminate the possibility of a runner at second base stealing signs. Sometimes the catcher can go through his signs but the actual sign is not the fingers as is normally seen, but position of the arms or how the catcher sets himself. There are all kinds of possible variations. Some pitchers like to give signs to the catcher. Then, of course, often the signs come from the dugout to the catcher and then to the pitcher. The important thing is to be on the same page. We want to be sure the pitcher does not cross up the catcher by throwing a pitch he is not expecting. That can easily lead to a passed ball.

Holding runners on the various bases (pitcher's mindset): I like my pitchers to separate their concentration into two parts when runners are on bases. Their first consideration should be to satisfy themselves that the runner does not have too large of a lead. This is true of any base but particularly first and second bases. He should throw over to drive the runner back when he feels that lead is too big. Once he is satisfied that the runner is where he wants him, he can then concentrate on the batter. Too many times pitchers are so concerned about the runner that they forget what they are trying to do with the batter. And some pitchers forget almost completely about the runner and concentrate only on the batter. They must be thinking about both runner and batter but separately. Also, I like my pitcher to go into the stretch position with a runner on third base. It holds him there at least momentarily in case of a squeeze play.

How to determine whether a strike or ball when you are not directly behind the plate: This is a difficult thing to do under the best of circumstances. But when you want to know where the pitch is located the best thing to do is watch the catcher's glove and see where it is when the ball is caught. Even then it is difficult to tell. One has to depend on the umpire to call it correctly. It is much easier to check on a high pitch rather than one that is inside or outside.

Jack Salveson: Jack pitched six seasons in the major leagues. He was the last rookie signed by the great John McGraw and was a control specialist. This man was a childhood hero of mine in the 1930s. The reason we liked him so well was that he threw strikes and systematically ended baseball games early. He did not waste his time walking batters. Jack won 204 games in the Pacific Coast League in just 16 years. He was the biggest influence on me regarding my philosophy of throwing strikes. Most of the time his nine innings game (he usually finished them himself) lasted about an hour and a quarter to two hours. Jack generally threw no more than 90 pitches in a nine-inning game.

Masterpiece: A well-pitched game with few hits allowed and little or no walks. It would probably be a shutout.

No three ball counts: This is my own philosophy. Professional players might say it is impossible. I do not think so. If one stays away from three ball counts by throwing strikes he cannot walk any player. Walks are the downfall of pitchers. I am not saying that there could be times to try and nip the corner. But, in general, I prefer to try and get the batter out without going to the three-ball count.

Number of pitches: Generally speaking, I like my pitchers to throw no more than an average of twelve pitches per inning. If a pitcher throws nine innings it would total 108. I would prefer the count to be even less. In this way it is possible to pitch a complete game without being relieved. However, in this day of the "closer" this may not be practical and I would certainly want my good finisher in there.

Pitchers hitting "the black": Pitchers can throw so fine these days that they can well hit "the black edge of home plate" with some regularity. That is what a pitcher should try to do. Pitches on the black should be called strikes.

Pitchers taking advantage of hitters' weaknesses: Most major league teams and pitchers keep a book on batters. They generally know weaknesses of the various hitters. When a batter has a known weakness the pitcher should take advantage of it. Some of the weaknesses are (a) can't hit a curve ball, (b) can't hit a low pitch, (c) can't hit a high pitch, (d) has difficulty with a change up, etc.

Pitchers with good stuff, fastball, good location: A good live fastball is a tremendous advantage. If a pitcher can throw the pitch where he desires he is even more effective. Change of speeds to go with the fast stuff is a definite advantage. And, of course, an effective curve ball or slider helps very much.

Pitchers with slow stuff who are tough to hit: Through the years there have been pitchers with great change of speeds to go along with their different types of pitches. A good example is a sinker. Just offhand I recall Stu Miller, Bruce Sutter, Willie Hernandez, and Jamie Moyer who have kept batters off balance with their array of pitches. When I was a youngster I recall watching a Pacific Coast League pitcher by the name of "Jittery" Joe Berry (see Baseball Humor, Chapter 8). He led the 1944 Philadelphia A's in relief wins (10) and saves (12) as a 39-year old major league rookie. His unusual motion gave him his name and his slow stuff was very effective.

Pitching rhythm: Using a good selection of pitches, getting ahead on the count, and mixing up his pitches, a hurler should get in a smooth pitching rhythm early in the game. He should try to keep things under control and put the offense off balance. This is especially important from a mental perspective. Such a plan tends to spread confidence to the all players.

Setting up a batter: As a pitcher, I want to get ahead of the hitter as soon as possible. That means getting the first strike over the plate. With that advantage the pitcher can "set up the batter" by getting him to swing at bad balls (out of the strike zone) or at a pitch that is the batter's weakness.

Shaking off signs: By shaking off signs a pitcher can get the batter to guess what is coming. Sometimes a pitcher will shake off signs and come back to the original sign just to get the batter to start guessing. Theoretically, however, a good pitcher/catcher combination would not "shake off signs" often because the catcher knows pretty much what his pitcher wants to throw. But, occasionally, it can pay off.

Starter/Middle reliever/Set-up man/Closer: In my perfect world of pitching, there would be no relief pitchers because I would like my starter to go all the way. But, knowing this will not happen all the time, we go on the theory that a middle reliever will come in after the starter has reached his predetermined number of pitches. The set-up man would follow which means he will take over for the middle reliever and turn the ball over to the closer in the last inning. Also, I am not adverse to bringing in my closer in the eighth inning, if necessary.

Steady target by catcher: To be frank, I do not like to see the catcher's glove moving around during a pitch. I prefer that he provide a steady target for the pitcher. He may wish to wait until the pitcher is almost ready to throw so as to not give the location away. But, at that point, I like to see a steady target.

Three and two count philosophy: Because the runners may run on this count (and always will run with two outs), I like to see the pitcher hold the runner close to first. With less the two outs this protects the pivot men at second base on an attempted double play or a force play at second. A throw or two to first base can certainly be in order here. I always told my pitchers to let them know you have not forgotten them. As described earlier in this section (holding runners on the various bases), I encouraged my pitchers to give full attention to base runners. Then, and only then, the pitcher should turn his thoughts to the batter and not lose concentration.

Throw strikes: One time I recall Coach Wooden telling us to concentrate on a spot when we make a lay-in with the basketball. The same theory applies to pitchers hitting spots. He should concentrate on hitting his target. This is especially true for throwing strikes. Concentration is the key.

OFFENSE

Get your pitch: Swinging at bad pitches has kept some players out of baseball. I like to see a batter reduce his strike zone until he has two strikes. In other words, he should hit "his pitch." I recall in the late 1950s a quote by Mickey Mantle. He said he was "taking the American League pitchers off the gravy train." He said he meant he was not going to swing at bad pitches anymore. It was revealed in an article in the newspaper and I cut it out and put it on the bulletin board. I said if one of the greatest hitters in the game needs to hit only good pitches, so does everybody else.

Green lighting the batter: When the batter has a three-ball, no strike count on him, he normally "takes" the next pitch. But, occasionally the manager or coach will "green light" him. This means he can swing at the 3-0 pitch if he so desires. Sometimes it is a "fat fast ball" and the batter can drive it.

Guarding the plate: Above I spoke of "getting your pitch." But, if a batter has two strikes on him, I believe he must "guard the plate." That means he must swing at any pitch that might be called a strike. Taking a third strike is unacceptable in my book. Many major league players do not change their swinging plan even with two strikes. In my opinion the "swing hard with two strikes method" can win or lose a ball game. The percentages of hitting a long ball are against a batter with two strikes and one or two balls. Why? It is because the pitcher is likely to throw a waste pitch. Guarding the plate and making contact puts the percentages in your favor.

On deck and in-the-hole batters: The on-deck hitter should be readying himself to go to bat. Also, he should be ready to serve as a base coach giving the "slide or stand up" sign to an oncoming runner. I rarely see this happen in the big leagues. Also, I like to see the on-deck hitter get a bat out of the way of an oncoming runner. That usually does not happen, either. The in-the-hole batter should be selecting his bat and protective hat.

Setting a line-up: A lead-off batter should have a high on-base percentage, be quick, intelligent on the bases and very selective at the plate. The second batter should be able to bunt well, be able to hit to the right side and have high on-base percentage. The 3, 4 and 5 hitters must be able to drive in runs. They will get this opportunity often. The 6 & 7 batters will get many opportunities to drive in runs so should be contact hitters. Some baseball people feel the two lowest batting average hitters should be in the 8 & 9 spots.

Everyone does not agree on that theory. Recently I saw a major league manager alternate his batters like "left, right, left, right, etc." There are all kinds of thoughts in this matter. Some managers like to have a speedy runner hitter in the nine-spot. Some like their best hitter in the three-position while others like that hitter in the four-position (clean up hitter).

Slumps: If someone could solve this baseball problem he could bottle it and become a millionaire. A slump is when a batter cannot make proper contact with the ball. All kinds of solutions have been tried with no apparent success with any of them. Sometimes managers allow the slumping batter to take a few days off. Some give him extra batting practice. I will tell you the solution I often tried. Starting the batting practice I would coach the player to shorten up on the bat (choke it) and hit the ball back at the pitcher's feet. I found that hitting low line drives back through the middle often cured the slump.

Tough with two strikes: I have discussed this in different ways previously. But, to summarize it, I think it is largely a matter of attitude of the batter. He must decide that nothing gets by him. He can shorten up (choke the bat), foul off pitches, and be very tough mentally.

MISCELLANEOUS

Figuring averages: The" batting average" is determined by dividing the number of official at bats into the number of hits made. For example, if a batter has 21 at bats and 7 hits, he has a .333 batting average. A "fielding average" can be found by dividing the number of chances (attempts to field a ball) by the number of successfully completed plays. A fielder having 25 chances and completing 20 of them would have a .800 fielding average. The "earned run average" (ERA) can be computed by dividing the number of earned runs by the number of innings pitched times (x) 9. So, a pitcher having thrown 180 innings and allowing 40 earned runs would have a 1.998 or 2.00 ERA.

Gloves on the field: Players formerly were allowed to leave their gloves on the field when they went to bat. However in 1954 a rule was made that offensive players must carry their gloves and all other equipment off the field. Before that time, after three outs almost all defensive players would throw their gloves on the field near their defensive positions. It was difficult to get out of the habit.

Keeping score: There are many systems of keeping score. I like the old Peterson Scoremaster books. We kept a record of every pitch and the order in which it was thrown. I could go back in the book and check on the pitch count at any point in the game. Almost all books use the following numbers to refer to the various positions: pitcher, 1; catcher, 2; first base, 3; second base, 4; third base, 5; shortstop, 6; leftfield, 7; centerfield, 8; rightfield, 9. The letter, K, is a strikeout and a "c" is added if it is called strike. There are more designations. I would recommend getting a scorebook at a sporting goods store if you are so interested. Also information is available on the Internet. Many individuals have fun keeping score at the ballpark.

Slugging average: This average can be determined by dividing the total bases by the number of "at bats." For example, if a player has 650 "at bats" and 370 total bases for a given period of time, his slugging average would be .567 or 370 divided by 650. To be in the official baseball records list, a player is required to have at least 1,000 career games. Babe Ruth is the all-time leader with a slugging average of .690. The current leading active player has .616 (Todd Helton).

Strike zone: This subject has been a matter of controversy over the years. As a youth I was always taught that a strike was a ball that is over the plate including the corners and from the armpits to the top of the knees. I recall at one point they stopped calling high strikes and the ball had to be just above the waist. More recently, they raised it and the high strike is more or less as it was formerly. The day may come when they use electronics to determine strikes. But, polls indicate that fans do not want that to happen. There may be some instant replay on other actions, however.

Total bases: A homerun counts as four bases, a triple as three bases, a double as two bases, and a single as one base. The number of total bases is a summation of the number of bases hit by an individual player. For example, a player getting a homerun, double, and single in a game would have seven total bases.

STORY 192:

Baseball's Language of Its Own (Baseball Lingo)

There are so many colloquialisms, adages, sayings, truisms, and special meanings in baseball that one could not assemble them all in a story. But, I shall try and provide a few which have had some meaning to me through the years. They allow an individual to communicate with a fellow fan in a language that is dear to the hearts of each person. I hope you enjoy these observations.

(1) In Baseball Itself

A buck ninety-six: Sometimes an announcer, referring to a players' batting average, will say it in terms of money. As a kind of idiom, he will say "He is batting a buck ninety-six" for some batting .196.

A shot: In the larger sense of the word, a shot is usually a hard hit live drive deep in the outfield and, perhaps, over the fence.

Around the horn: After an out the infielders usually throw the ball "around the horn," or throw to each other with the ball ending up with the third baseman who gives it to the pitcher. It refers to the shape of certain horns.

BP: Batting practice (Let's take some BP).

Bags are loaded: This is one way of saying that all three bases are occupied by players of the team at bat.

Balk: A balk is an action made by the pitcher that, by rule, allows baserunners to advance one base. To my knowledge there are eleven ways to balk. Look it up in a rule book.

Baltimore chop: A high bouncing ball that hits off the plate. Sometimes it goes so high that the runner can reach first base even before it is fielded.

Band box: Refers to a small ballpark in field size.

Base knock: Another name for a base hit.

Base on balls: A runner reaches first base after receiving four ball calls (non-strikes).

Belted: A term used to indicate that a ball is hit long and hard. Usually it is out of the park.

Big dance, The: Some use this term to refer to the World Series.

Bigs, The: Refers to the "big leagues," major league baseball.

Blooper: A short pop up or fly that falls in for a hit.

Blue dart or blue darter: A line shot or line drive hit by a batter.

Bobble: An error or a misplay by a fielder.

Booted it: When a player misplays a ball or makes an error.

Brush back pitch: A pitch that is thrown inside to a batter. It may back him off the plate. Sometimes called chin music.

Bush league or bush leaguer: This term comes from the olds days of baseball indicating that an action is unacceptable (bush league) or a player who does not play according the rules or is unwise with his play (bush leaguer).

Butterflies: A wheezy feeling in the body when one is nervous.

Can of corn: A term indicating a weak fly ball to the outfield.

Change up: A change of speeds or let up pitch. Sometimes called "pulling the string."

Chucker: Refers to the pitcher or hurler.

Chin music: Similar to a brush back pitch or one that backs the batter off the plate.

Circuit clout: A home run, a dinger, a fourmaster, or round tripper.

Comebacker: A term used to describe a ball hit directly at the pitcher. It comes back from the bat to the mound.

Count on the batter: It is fairly common practice to refer to the count as a two-digit number. When the count is three balls, two strikes on the batter one will often say the count is "thirty-two."

Cup of coffee: A term meaning a player is with a team for a very short period of time. For example, "I had a 'cup of coffee' with them."

Daylight play: When a pitcher can see "daylight" between a runner at second base and the shortstop (that is, the runner is more toward third base than is the fielder) a signal can be given for an attempted pick off. Usually, it is done by a pre-arranged "count," so that the ball and fielder arrive at the base at the same time.

Dinger: A home run, circuit clout, fourmaster, or round tripper.

Dish: A reference to home plate.

Doctoring the baseball: Refers to a pitcher doing something to a baseball to make it move so the batter cannot hit it.

Don't get your dauber down: Generally speaking, it means don't lose your spirit or morale. Stay positive.

Double play: When the defense gets two outs on the same play.

Ducks on the pond: Means runners on base or bases occupied.

Duster: A pitch close to a batter's body, inside pitch.

Foul pole (fair pole): The poles down the left or right field lines. It has been known as the foul pole but a ball hitting it is fair. But, the term for the lines is "foul line" and the pole is best known as the foul pole.

Foul tip: A pitched ball that is "tipped or touched" by the bat. The word is "tip" and not "tick," as youngsters sometimes use as a misnomer.

Fourbagger: A home run, a dinger, a circuit clout, a round tripper.

Free pass: A walk or base on balls (four called balls to the batter).

Frozen rope: A line drive or blue dart.

Fungo: A lightweight bat to hit balls to the infield or outfield. The infield fungo is usually 34" long while the outfield fungo is 35" long and slightly larger in size. Sometimes used as a verb. That is, a coach decides to "fungo" some balls to the fielders.

Game of inches: You will hear this term in various sports. In baseball just a few inches each way can change the outcome of a game.

Gapper: A ball hit in the left or right centerfield alleys. It is usually a double, sometimes a triple with a faster runner.

Giddy-up: A term used to indicate that a pitcher can throw hard. His ball has some "giddy-up" on it.

Giving pitcher a cushion: Scoring an early run or several runs will give the pitcher the lead in the game and he, in a sense, gets a cushion.

Go the other way: Phrase meaning the batter is hitting the ball to the opposite field, righties to right field, and lefties to left field.

Good wood on it—Good metal? Traditionalists will say, "he got good wood on it." Metal bats are used in college and high school baseball today for budgetary reasons. They do not break. However, I have never heard the expression, "He got good metal on it."

Gopher ball: A pitch that a batter can hit out of the park, a home run.

Grand old game, The: It is often referred to as "The Grand Old Game of Baseball."

Great American pastime: Another term of endearment to the game. It is the "Great American Pastime."

Guarding the plate: This refers to a batter making sure he hits the ball when he has two strikes on him. With two strikes on him he makes sure he "guards the plate" and does not get called out on strikes.

Hard stuff: Fastballs or pitches with some speed.

Has a gun on him: Suggesting that a player has a good arm (can throw well).

Has his hitting shoes on: This implies that a batter is hitting well on a given day.

He couldn't hit his hat size: Implying that a batter is weak and incapable.

He couldn't hit his way out of wet paper bag: A put down on a batter's ability to hit.

He runs like a truck: An implication a runner is slow afoot.

Heater: A fastball, a blazer.

Hidden ball trick: A situation when a fielder hides the ball from the runner and tags him out. Hidden ball tricks are rare in the game today.

Hit it where it's pitched: Indicates the batter is hitting the ball to the right or left side depending on where the pitcher throws it.

Hitting the cover off the ball: A term often heard when a team or a player is having a good day batting.

Home plate: The rubber at home where the angle of the plate extends down each foul line. It has black edges on it.

Horsehide: Another name for a baseball.

Hot corner: Third base.

Hot stove league: When people sit around the fire and talk baseball.

Hurler: The pitcher or chucker.

Ice cream cone: A term referring to the white baseball almost falling out of a glove on a defensive play, particularly a fly ball.

In a pickle: This refers to a baserunner who is caught between bases or home. He is said to be "in a pickle."

In the hole: The batter who is scheduled to be batting after the on-deck batter.

In the well: A ball that is going to be or has been caught. The announcer will say, "It is in the well."

Indifference: A term used to indicate that the pitcher and catcher allow a runner to steal a base without trying to throw him out. He gets the base due to "indifference."

Infield fly rule: The rule designed to prevent the defense from getting a double or triple play by intentionally dropping a pop fly ball. The rule states that a batter is automatically called out when, with less than two outs, he hits a fair pop fly that can easily be handled by an infielder when there are runners on first and second or bases are loaded. Runners advance at their own risk.

Intentional pass: This describes a base on balls given to a batter on purpose. All four pitches must be made.

Jacked it out: A term usually heard on the bench indicating the batter has hit the ball out of the park, a home run.

Jammed him: Indicates the pitcher throws the ball "inside," to the batter.

Jug: Another name for a curve ball or Uncle Charlie.

Keep trademark up: A term often heard when we were kids. You keep the trademark up to help prevent breaking the bat. Holding the trademark up keeps the grain of bat in a position so as not to break the grain. One goes against the grain, so to speak.

Key to the pitcher's box: A joke in the early days usually pulled on a rookie. He would be asked to go get the "key to the pitchers' box."

Kicks foul: This is a term I first heard by Dodger announcer, Vin Scully. It is simply a ball that is fouled off and bounces foul.

Knock: A term for a base hit.

Leather man: A good fielder.

Let up pitch: A change up or change of speeds. The pitcher "lets up" on a pitch to slow it down. Sometimes it is referred to as "pulling the string."

Level playing field: A term to indicate that both sides have an equal opportunity to accomplish a goal.

Listed as day-to-day: When a player is injured but has a chance of playing soon, he may be listed as day-to-day.

Lucky seventh, The: An old saying in baseball that the seventh inning can be the lucky one.

Lumber: The assortment of baseball bats on a team.

Make it go through: Please see Story 32. This refers to a situation whereby the runner on second base should stay there on a routine ground ball to the left side. If that does not happen there is a good chance that the runner can be thrown out at third base by the shortstop or tagged out between bases.

Moving runner over: There are various situations where the runner should be moved up a base (first to second, second to third). The term means to make that happen.

On deck batter: The batter scheduled to bat next.

On the black: A pitched ball that crosses over the black rubber edge of the home plate.

Passed ball: A ball that gets by the catcher so that a runner or runners may advance (not a wild pitch).

Pepper league: A game with a long history. Four or five players get together with one batting and three or four fielding. The ball is thrown to the batter who hits the ball back toward the fielders who are about 30 feet away. They continue this "game" until a different batter takes over. Sometimes at certain ballparks a sign can be seen stating, "No Pepper League Here." It chews up the ground in and around home plate and is better played on grass.

Pitch around him: A term indicating the pitcher will not give the batter anything good to hit. He would rather walk him than let him hit.

Pitchout: A ball intentionally pitched wide to give the catcher a better chance of throwing out a stealing runner.

Poetry in motion: A term used about a graceful player whose natural motion is a thing of beauty.

Pop up: A ball hit in the air somewhere in the vicinity of the infield. There is some confusion on this name. Some announcers now call a ball a pop up even if reaches the deep outfield. My view is that a pop up is on or near the infield. Deeper hits are fly balls, not pop ups.

Popped him up: A term used by announcers to indicate a pitcher has caused a batter to pop up

Power alleys: This refers to the alleys in left and right centerfield.

Protective cup: A plastic or rubber device that fits in a supporter to protect the groin area of a player.

Pulled the string: A term indicating the pitcher has thrown a change up or slower speed pitch. Sometimes called a let up pitch.

Puts the ball in play: When the batter makes contact and hits a ball in the field of play.

Rally caps: Turning one's cap inside out or fixing it in some way to show he is in a rally mode.

Rhubarb: An old baseball term to indicate there is a disagreement on the field resulting in argument or physical contact.

Rang him up: A term meaning the pitcher puts **down the batter**

Ribbys, ribbies, or RBIs: A term meaning "runs batted in." If it were accurate it would be RsBI (runs batted in) but it would be confusing so we simply call it RBIs.

Ripped: A ball that is hit hard or belted. A shot or blue dart.

Rookie: A new player never having been in the big leagues before.

Round tripper: A home run, dinger, circuit clout, or four bagger.

Rube: A term used for a "character" or unusual personality. Perhaps started from a player named Rube Waddell near the turn of the century.

Rundown: A play where one or more runners are caught between bases and the defense plays a "rundown" to get one or more outs.

Scalded it: Meaning the batter hit the ball hard. I first heard this term by Dusty Baker when he played for the Dodgers. On an interview when asked about a particular home run Dusty hit, he replied, "I scalded it!"

Scoring position: Refers to a runner who is on second or third base.

Seventh inning stretch: An old term indicating the fans will stand and stretch before the last half of the seventh inning. Tradition has brought about singing during that time, "Take Me Out to the Ball Game," and more recently, God Bless America."

Shag flies: A term meaning players will practice catching fly balls during practice. Shag means, "go after it."

Show, The: This refers to the major leagues, themselves. A player will say, "I finally made it to The Show."

Soft stuff: Change ups, or pitches with little speed on them.

Southpaw: A left-handed pitcher, or port sider.

Stay up: When I was playing baseball it was courteous to tell the stealing runner, especially from first to second on a steal, to "stay up," and not slide. The point was to not have the runner slide and open

himself to injury. I am not sure if that is still happening today.

Staying alive: It means a team is "hanging in there," and "staying alive" so as to have a chance to win the game.

Stepping In the bucket: A term meaning that a batter is stepping away from the plate.

Sticker: A term meaning batter.

Tablesetter: This expression is often heard when players get on base to set up the situation where some runs can be scored.

Tag up: Means to return to a base when a fly ball is hit in order to "tag up" and run to the next base.

Tailor-made double play: A perfect, easy to make double play, not difficult, where the ball has a big hop.

Take a strike: This is a term meaning that the batter will receive pitches until a strike is called.

Take something off: When a pitcher takes some speed off the pitch to fool the batter. It can be a change up but speed can be taken off in various amounts.

Taking some cuts: Taking some swings in batting practice.

Texas leaguer: A batted ball that falls in for a hit, a blooper.

Throwing aspirin tablets: When a pitcher throws so hard it is difficult to follow the ball, he is said to be "throwing aspirin tablets" (ball looks small).

Throwing smoke: When a pitcher throws exceptionally hard.

Tomahawk: Refers to a slashing motion by the batter in which he drives the ball hard.

Tools of ignorance: Catchers' gear.

Touches 'em all: When a batter hits a long ball one may hear a coach say, "touch 'em all," meaning touch all the bases.

Triple play: The rare instance when a team gets three outs on one play. Please see Story 215, item 4, about unassisted triple plays.

Turn 'em loose: A term used when the manager wants to allow the runners to run hard. This will occur on a three ball, two strike count with two outs.

Turnstiles: This is an old rotating device that allowed fans to enter the park through the "turnstiles." Today's "turnstiles" are more modern.

Twin killing: Refers to a double play.

Uncle Charlie: A curve ball.

Waste pitch: A pitch that is thrown out of the strike zone with the hope the batter will go for it. This occurs when the pitcher is ahead in the count.

Watch out for the wheelbarrow: A joking term implying to the fielder that a wheelbarrow is in his path.

Went deep: Meaning the batter hit the ball deep into the outfield, a long ball.

Wheel house: This refers to the batter's arc of his swing. A ball in "his wheel house" is one that he likes to hit. It would be his power spot.

Wild as a March hare: An idiom suggesting that a pitcher is wild and cannot find his target. It, too, is a very old term.

Wild pitch: A pitch that gets by the catcher due to the fact that the pitcher threw the ball too wild for the catcher to stop it.

Wood man: A good hitter.

Yard, The: Referring to the ball field. Occasionally, one will hear an announcer say "the yard will hold it," meaning it will stay in the field of play.

(2) In Our Daily Lives

A ball park figure: Meaning one would like an amount close to the actual cost.

A whole new ball game: Inferring that a situation is brand new and not as before.

All our bases are covered: Implying that in a given situation we have done everything necessary.

Bush league: It was a bush league operation meaning the mode of procedure was less than desirable.

Couldn't get to first base: Meaning an individual or group could not even get started.

He had two strikes on him to begin: Implying that a person was nearly failing before he began a project.

He threw me a curve: Indicating a person was surprised by how he was treated, something he did not expect.

He's out of my league: Meaning this guy is much better than I.

Hit a home run: He hit a home run with that accomplishment meaning he did a great job.

Hit it out of the park: Referring to an accomplishment, speech, or otherwise, that a person or group did the best possible.

I call 'em as I see 'em: Indicating that someone evaluates a situation the way he observes it (as a baseball umpires would say).

In a league of his (her) own: A player who is individualistic.

Major league: They did a major league job on that project.

Out in left field: Inferring that a person is not getting something right or correct.

Pinch hit for him: He can't do it now so I will have someone "pinch hit" for him.

Play the field: They prefer to "play the field" rather than zero in on one person.

Rain check: I can't do it now but I will take a "rain check" on it.

Right off the bat: Meaning let's get it done immediately, "right off the bat."

Smash hit: Her results were a "smash hit" meaning she did a great job with her effort.

Steps up to the plate: Suggesting that a person gets the job done; he steps up and does it.

Struck out: Implying that an individual did not get the job done.

They play hardball: Meaning they are really serious the way they operate. They play "hardball."

Touch base: I will "touch base" with you soon meaning we should keep in touch.

Two strikes: He was born with "two strikes" on him meaning he had a disadvantage in the beginning.

STORY 193:

Lefties, Righties, and Age Today

I did a study of switch-hitters, left and right-handed pitchers, and average ages of players on various teams. It seems remarkable that in the 1930s I can recall only one player who hit from both sides of the plate. His name was Augie "Frenchy" Galan who played all through the 1930s for the Chicago Cubs. He played for the Dodgers, Giants, and Reds in the majors plus San Francisco and Oakland in the Pacific Coast League. Please see Story 101 (Augie Galan) for details about this outstanding player.

The following numbers change, of course as players come and go. But, the American League has 117 right-handed and 61 left-handed batters. They have 31 switch hitters. The National League has 126 right-handed and 65 left-handed batters. And their switch hitter count is 45. That makes a total of 76 switchers combined in both leagues. These batters are position-players and there are about 15 to 18 per team. There are 14 American League teams and 16 National League clubs.

The American League has 142 right-handed

pitchers and 55 portsiders. The National League has 171 right-handers and 62 left-handers. Pitching staffs are usually about 14 in number.

The ages are similar in both leagues. The average age of players is near 29 years. In the American League the highest average is the New York Yankees at 34 years while the lowest is the Minnesota Twins at 27.8 years. In the National League the highest average is the San Francisco Giants at 32.3 years. The lowest average is the Colorado Rockies at 26.9 years.

STORY 194:

Grandmas Like Baseball, Too

Story after story is told about dads or moms or both taking their kids to baseball games. It is an American tradition and it is great. However, a new breed is developing out there. Please let me explain.

We know lots of grandmas that love baseball. Marilyn and I see them all the time when we go to a ballpark. Sometimes they bring a grandson and granddaughter with them. Ever so often we find one that keeps score and follows the game like a sportswriter. The best part is when they wear attire

"Rainy" Revling and Lue Gibbs, grandma baseball fans. We met these Chicago Cub fans at Spring Training,

with the logo of their favorite team, or, better yet, to watch them whoop and holler over the success their team is experiencing.

You can find these people in any baseball park in America. They are American treasures. People are already writing about them in books.

Oh, by the way, sometimes they are called "grandpas" and they do the same things. And, sometimes, they even go to the games together as Marilyn and I do. If you happen to be in any of these categories and have not yet been out to the ballpark, give it a try. We think you will like it.

Marilyn and I were at a spring training game in Mesa, Arizona when we met Rainy Revling and Lue Gibbs. They came all the way from the midwest to see their favorite team, the Chicago Cubs. We became friends and now write to each other on occasion. They love this game.

One grandma and grandpa we met live in a town in Oregon called, get this, Harmony. Isn't that a great name? Their names are Darlene and Terry Walker. They showed us a book given to them by their grandsons, Josh, Jesse and Shay. What a great book! They cherish the book mightily. They would not part with it for the world. The whole family, including the kids' parents, Tim and Mary, loves baseball. And Grandma and Grandpa Walker are right there with them. Baseball is their common bond. Please see Stories No. 186 and 187 about these fine families.

STORY 195:

Baseball As Told to a Foreigner

We have friends in other countries, many who have never experienced a baseball game. American teams and players going to Japan for exhibition games have been happening for many years. In fact, it happened so much that Japan has had it's own leagues for years. The sport is extremely popular there. Please see Story 40 (Baseball At the Tokyo Dome with Yashitoka).

Richard Weston is our British friend who lives in Wimbledon, England, the famous tennis city. He has expressed an interest to us of wanting to know more about American baseball. Richard is an expert and performer in what the Brits call "Athletics," but known in America as "Track and Field." Someday we would like to take Richard to a baseball game in America.

So, how does one describe baseball to a foreigner? The following is one version:

BASEBALL
(AS EXPLAINED TO A FOREIGN VISITOR)

You have two sides, one out in the field and one in.

Each man that's on the side that's in goes out and when he's out he comes in and the next man goes in until he's out.

When three men are out, the side that's out comes in and the side that's been in goes out and tries to get those coming in out.

Sometimes you get men still in and not out.

When both sides have been in and out nine times including the not outs, that's the end of the game.

STORY 196:

Batting Practice Around America

As soon as our children were old enough to wield a baseball bat it became routine for the family to go out and have "batting practice." It didn't matter where we were. Sometimes it happened on vacation in Utah, Colorado, Oregon, or the park down the street near our home.

We would go to a local ball diamond if possible. That type of location lacking, we would simply find a big field. Each person was allowed a certain number of hits and, of course, those not batting would chase down the balls. Many times, Marilyn would serve as the catcher and dad would pitch. As the boys were older we would trade around at all positions.

A bag of balls and several bats were always kept in the car. It was generally not known exactly when we might decide to have practice.

Occasionally, other kids would see us playing and join the fun.

But most of the time it was just the five of us.

Those were grand memories. As I write, it makes me want to go right this minute and "take some more cuts with the kids."

When we went to the Louisville Slugger Museum recently, I thought about BP, as we called it in our youth. Please see Story 34, paragraph 17, (Visiting Hillerich and Bradsby, Louisville Slugger Bats). They have a wonderful cage there. A batter can select a bat, don a helmet, and take some swings. The cost is just one dollar. I had a great time taking some batting practice.

STORY 197:

Baseball Fun Games As Kids

Various types of fun baseball games have served as an activity for groups and families to enjoy. Of course, these often occurred at a family picnic or outing. Sometimes a group of kids could just make up their own games at a park or even out in the street. I can think of the many times we had to stop playing because a car was coming. Playing in the street today is obviously not a good idea. Cars move too fast and driving is a lot different than in the earlier days.

I think the most popular game I can recall is "Hit The Bat." A person would toss the ball in the air and hit it to a group in the field. If someone caught the ball on the fly, that person would come in and take his or her turn at bat and the batter would move to the field. If the ball was dropped or it was a grounder, the batter would put the bat down horizontally and allow the thrower to roll the ball toward the bat. If the ball hit the bat, the batter had to catch it to remain at bat. Sometimes we would limit the batter to five hits in order to give someone else a chance to bat.

Do you remember "Three Flies and You're Up?" The batter would toss the ball up and hit fly balls until a fielder caught three of them in the air. That person would take over with the batting. Sometimes we would give the batter three chances to hit a fly ball or he would have to give us his batting spot. Again, we often limited the number of balls hit, fly balls or otherwise, to give others a chance with the bat.

When we were a little older (ten years and up) we had a great game called "Over The Line," or "Hit Through Infield." We had special rules for the game and usually four of us would play nine innings. We often played in the summer when watermelons were ripe. Sometimes they were just one penny per pound. Other times entire melons could be purchased for 10 cents each. The losers of the game would treat the winners. A big watermelon filled us up when we quartered it.

Newspaper ad, watermelons 10 cents each.

Another game I enjoyed was called "Work Up." Nine positions were filled on the field with four batters at the plate. As outs by a batter, he would go to right field and fielders would move up one position in a certain order until they reached home and had a chance to be a batter. Sometimes we would play that game for hours.

I recall that we played a softball game with regular rules except for one thing. The batter had to hit a fair ball before fouling it off three times. What did we call that game? It was called "Three Fouls and You're Out."

There are many more fun baseball games available. These are just a few. Kids often made up their own baseball games. When you think about it, baseball was invented in America and children have been playing various kinds of baseball-related games since the late 1800s. There are few of us who have not had some experience with this great American game.

Softball vs Baseball

There is a distinct difference between baseball and softball. The size of the diamond, rules, and type of equipment make each unique. And there are variations, too. For example, softball has developed "Mountain Ball," or "Slow Pitch," as it sometimes called. It is extremely popular today, particularly among young adults. They have all kinds of leagues and competition even to the extent of playing for national championships. Slow Pitch is more of an offensive game and games will often end up with big scores.

After I graduated from college I played "Fast Pitch Softball." We were sponsored by various businesses that funded the entire operation. It is a very fast game and is still being played today. The emphasis is more on defense and there are many low-scoring games. Girls' fast pitch softball has developed over the years and is a very exciting game to watch.

I played on various semi-professional baseball teams as well. We often called it "hardball" in those days. Once again, the teams were sponsored by businesses and were often played on Sunday afternoons. In Ontario where I coached I played on a team a semi-professional team. Please see Story 14 (The Ontario/Upland Pirates). We played Sunday afternoons and also on weeknights since we had a very nicely lighted field.

Semi-professional teams gave many players the opportunity to have some baseball experience. It gave them a recreational activity away from their day jobs and an opportunity to get some vigorous physical activity in an enjoyable way. It was fun, too, for the fans and relatives.

It is regretful that the International Olympic Committee voted to eliminate baseball and softball from competition at the 2012 Summer Olympic Games. They will be held in the 2008 Summer Olympic Games and another vote will take place at that time. Since these sports are being played around the world now it seems logical that they be included in the regular format.

STORY 199:

Family Fly Ball Fun and Batting at a Local Park

Hitting baseballs and having batting practice has been a great activity for our family as adults. We enjoyed having batting practice when the children were young. Please see Story 196 (Batting Practice Around America).

This fun is usually organized around a meal or picnic. We hit fly balls to each other and have a couple of good rounds of batting practice.

STORY 200:

Scott Proctor's Kitty League

Our family, dad Ken, mom Marilyn, children, Kenny, Mike, and Scott had some great family fun for our entire time together.

As far back as I can remember, Scott, our youngest son, loved baseball. When he was only seven years old he invented a game he called "Kitty League." He loved cats and developed his entire plan around kitties. He had a "cat" name for each player. Some of the names were actual cats we had owned through the years.

When we went camping the first thing Scott would do is set up a baseball diamond in the dirt somewhere near the campfire. He marked fouls lines, set up home plate and bases, and even put up markers and a line indicating the fences. He used tiny balls of foil for the baseballs and pencils for bats. He would line up his teams on a score sheet and have a game right there in the campground. He would toss up the foil ball and hit it with the pencil. He would determine whether it was a hit or an out and mark it on the score sheet.

Later in Spokane, Scott built an entire ballpark out of cardboard. We had a green carpet and that was his field. He even made elaborate colored advertisements on the outfield fences. He had a sign on one of them that said, "Hit this sign and win $50." There were American flags everywhere. He improved the field constantly and gave it a genuine look.

Scott lost his life in the mountains in 2002. We miss him dearly. But, ever so often we get out his Kitty League field and recall the enjoyment he had with it. The field reminds us of Scott and all the great times we had together as a family. We lost him at age 44 but there was much joy wrapped up in those years.

Scott Proctor's Kitty League field in campground

American League Roster

Pitchers	No.	Throws	Bats	Club	
Jeff	34	Right	Right	NO	
Milt	36	Right	Right	NY	
Jason	37	Left	Left	SL	
Miles	38	Left	Right	SL	
Mickey	40	Right	Right	SL	
Willard	41	Right	Right	GB	

Catchers	No.	Throws	Bats	Club	
Floyd	27	Right	Right	GB	*
Willie	28	Right	Both	SL	

Infielders	No.	Throws	Bats	Club	
Erik	1	Right	Right	GB	
Clint	7	Right	Both	GB	
Jerry	20	Right	Right	NO	
Leon	25	Right	Left	SL	*
Keith	30	Right	Right	NY	*
Ross	31	Right	Right	SL	*
George	32	Left	Left	GB	
Louis	42	Right	Right	NO	*

Outfielders	No.	Throws	Bats	Club	
Norman	11	Right	Right	NO	*
Rick	17	Right	Both	SL	
Ralph	18	Left	Left	NY	
Aaron	22	Left	Both	NO	*
Jack	23	Right	Right	GB	*
Kawika	24	Right	Right	NO	

*Indicates Starter

Scott Proctor's Kitty League stats #1 and 2.
(Scott was very creative, he made this
program live.)

...ter

			Throws	Bats	Club	
			Right	Right	SF	
			Right	Right	KC	
			Right	Right	SD	
			Right	Right	SD	
			Left	Left	SF	
			Right	Both	LA	

			Throws	Bats	Club	
			Right	Right	SD	*
			Right	Right	KC	

			Throws	Bats	Club	
			Right	Both	KC	
			Right	Right	SD	*
			Right	Both	SF	*
			Right	Both	SF	
			Left	Right	KC	*
Israel	32		Right	Right	LA	
Trojan	44		Right	Right	KC	*
Barney	45		Left	Left	LA	

Outfielders	No.		Throws	Bats	Club	
Felix P.	10		Right	Both	SD	*
Rod	11		Right	Both	LA	
Tico	12		Right	Both	KC	*
Pepper	15		Left	Both	KC	*
Tigger	18		Right	Right	SD	
Henry	24		Left	Both	SF	

* Indicates Starter

STORY 201:

A Telephone Call From Out of Past (57 Years Ago)

Recently I received a telephone call from a gentleman who lives in two locations in California. In the warmer months he resides at Newport Beach and in the winter his home is at Indian Wells in the desert.

He identified himself as Marshall Cox. At first I did not recognize the name but when he said "Sonny Cox," I knew him immediately. He had been one of the young boys in a YMCA group I led in the late 1940s, over 57 years ago. I was back from the Navy and attending UCLA at the time. I led the group at Western Knoll Congregational Church in Los Angeles.

We had a great time talking about our early days together. It was inspiring for me just to hear from him. He overwhelmed me when he said how much I had influenced his life. I had no idea of this fact. He recalled some of the lessons we were learning in those days. I was learning as well. And those kids were joyful to be around.

Sonny was a very good athlete and played baseball, football, and basketball on the teams I coached. He said he was starting to go down the wrong road at the time and our group helped to straighten him out. He saw my UCLA baseball jacket I wore and it inspired him to attend the University in Westwood, California.

He did, in fact, go to UCLA and successfully graduated. He went on to form a company in nuclear medicine. I will not get specific but he developed three companies in total and has made an incredible contribution to mankind with his work.

Marshall & Donna Cox, Ken & Marilyn Proctor. Marshall was one of my former YMCA boys in the 1940s.

He has been unbelievably successful in every way.

He and his wife, Donna, invited us to their home in California. We were in Phoenix at the time attending spring training baseball games and we drove over to their home in just a few hours. We had a delightful visit and Donna is a wonderful lady and now a good friend. She and Marilyn hit it off very well.

It was so good to see Marshall after all these years and to realize how the Lord works in our lives when we have no idea of our relationships. "Sonny" is a quality leader in his business field and still directs his various boards. He said the sports we played back in the 1940s were some of his most enjoyable moments in his life. I feel blessed that we have revived our friendship. We plan to keep in touch with them and would very much like to host them in Seattle.

Watching World Series— A Tradition

The Fall Classic, the World Series, has been a great time of baseball enjoyment for fans all over the world. Attending a World Series "live" is a special event for most people and comparatively very few have that privilege. But, for thousands upon thousands of others, it is an opportunity to gather together and watch this timeless and treasured rivalry.

Marilyn and I went to one "live" World Series game. Please see Story 21 {Our First (and Only) Live World Series Game.} That occurred in 1959 in a contest between the Los Angeles Dodgers and the Chicago White Sox. Incidentally, those tickets cost us FOUR DOLLARS EACH. Can you believe it?

Now, many years later, we have started another tradition. Every year at Fall Classic time we select a day with our local Seattle friends, Pete and Jennifer Prekeges, and have a delicious dinner and an enjoyable evening watching a World Series game. We trade homes each year for this annual custom. It really does not matter which teams are playing. It is just the camaraderie and enjoyment of watching part of this great event that occurs in October every year.

There we sit, four of baseball's self-appointed experts, enjoying the culmination of a long season. Our gathering is really not a party. Rather, it is a great tradition that baseball gives us. It is a time to watch and celebrate this wonderful game in the spirit of good friendship. Play ball!!!

Baseball Nicknames Are Fun

There are, perhaps, thousands of nicknames in professional baseball. They have become part of the game. I guess nicknames are prominent in life. We recall when we lived in Hawaii, most kids, and even adults, had nicknames.

Imagine someone named "PeeWee," "Schoolboy," "Babe," "Twinkletoes," or "The Wild Thing." Some are endearing, some very accurate, some funny, and some quite descriptive. If you were called "The Splinter," you would understand what was meant, wouldn't you?

The following are generally players, with some managers, broadcasters, umpires and others thrown in for interest. Here are a few to ponder:

Walter "Smokey" Alston

George Lee "Sparky" or "Captain Hook" Anderson

Luke "Old Aches and Pains" Appling

Frank "Home Run" Baker

Johnnie B. "Dusty" Baker

Ernie "Mr. Cub" Banks

Walter "Red" Barber

David Gus "Buddy" Bell

David Russ "Gus" Bell

Lawrence Peter "Yogi" Berra

"Jittery Joe" Berry

Harry "The Cat" Brecheen

Mordecai Peter Centennial "Three Finger" Brown

William "Billy Bucks" Buckner

Merritt "Sugar" Cain

Gary "The Kid" Carter

Bill "The Inspector" Caudill

Orlando "The Baby Bull" Cepeda

William Jones "Boileryard"
   or "Noisy Bill" Clarke

Roger "The Rocket" Clemens

Tyrus Raymond "Ty" Cobb
   (The Georgia Peach)

Gordon Stanley "Mickey" Cochrane

Rocco Domenico "Rocky" Colavito

James Anthony "Ripper" Collins

Charlie "The Old Roman" or "Commy" Comiskey

Frank "The Crow" Crosetti

Tony "Chick" Cuccinello

Hazen Shirley "Kiki" Cuyler

Alvin "Blackie" Dark

Charles Theodore "Chili" Davis

Ray Thomas "Peaches" Davis

Andre "The Hawk" Dawson

Charles Frederick "Boots" Day

Russell Earl "Bucky" Dent

Jay Hanna "Dizzy" Dean

Paul "Daffy" Dean

Dominic "The Little Professor" DiMaggio

"Joltin' Joe" DiMaggio

James Alberts "Cozy" Dolan

Patrick Henry "Patsy" Dougherty

Ryne "Blind Ryne" Duren

Leo "The Lip" Durocher

Dennis "The Eck" Eckersley

Johnny "The Crab" Evers

Bob "Rapid Robert" Feller

Mark "The Bird" Fydrich

Vernon "Lefty" or "Goofy" Gomez

Leon "Goose" Goslin

Richard Michael "Goose" Gossage

Robert Moses "Lefty" Grove

Ron "Louisiana Lightning" or
   "The Ragin' Cajun" Guidry

Charles Leo "Gabby" Hartnett

Floyd Caves "Babe" Herman

William Jennings Bryan "Billy"
   Herman

Michael Franklin "Pinky" Higgins

Elon Chester "Chief" Hogsett

Miller "Hug" or "The Mighty Mite" Huggins

Joe "Shoeless Joe" Jackson

William Chester "Baby Doll" Jacobson

Randy "The Big Unit" Johnson

Walter "The Big Train" Johnson

Willie "Hit 'Em Where They Ain't" Keeler

Carroll Walter "Whitey" Lockman

Ernie "The Schnoz" Lombardi

John Walter "The Great" or
   "Duster" Mails

Frank Edwin "Tug" McGraw

John "Little Napoleon" McGraw

Calvin Coolidge Julius Caesar Tuskahoma "Cal"
   McLish

Mickey "The Mick" or
   "The Commerce Comet" Mantle

Alfred Manuel "Billy" or
   "The Kid" Martin

John "Pepper" Martin

Willie "Say Hey" Mays

Joe "Ducky" Medwick

Saturino Orestes Arrieta Armas
   "Minnie" Minoso

Stan "The Man" or "The Donora
   Greyhound" Musial

Frank "Lefty" O'Doul

Herb "The Squire of Kennett
   Square" Pennock

Charles Gardner "Old Hoss Radbourn"

Phil "The Vulture" Regan

Harold Henry "Pee Wee" or
    "The Little Colonel" Reese

Harold "Hal" or "Porky" Reniff

Phil "Scooter" Rizzuto

Pete "Charlie Hustle" Rose

Lynwood "Schoolboy" Rowe

George Herman "Babe" Ruth (The Sultan of Swat)
    and (The Bambino)

Nolan "The Ryan Express" Ryan

Chris "Spuds" Sabo

Ryne "Ryno" Sandberg

Tom "Terrific" Seaver

George "Twinkletoes" Selkirk

Truett Banks "Rip" Sewell

Edwin Donald "Duke" Snider

George Tucker "Tuck" Stainback

George Robert "Birdie" Tebbetts

Paul "Dizzy" Trout

Virgil "Fire" Trucks

George Edward "Rube" Waddell

Bill "Wamby" Wambsganss

Lloyd "Little Poison" Waner

Paul "Big Poison" Waner

Mitch "The Wild Thing" Williams

Ted "The Splendid Splinter" Williams

STORY 204:

Jinxes And Superstitions

Nickel in red hankerchief: I guess I am just as superstitious as any of them. I carried a large red hankerchief in my rear pocket with a knot in the end. The players wondered what I had tied up in that piece of cloth. The main item was an Indian Head nickel. I carried it for good luck. I had some other things, too. When we won the CIF championship in 1956 the players were jumping around celebrating and a bunch of them came over and said, "What is in the hankerchief, Coach?" I took it out and untied the knot to show them the nickel. It could have been anything in there but it was fun opening it up together to see it.

Stepping on lines: I never stepped on the baselines when I cross them. Why? I don't know. It was just the way we did it. Watch the players today in the major league games. Very seldom do they step on the baselines. Bad luck? Who knows? It is just something baseball people do. I think I saw one player step on a baseline this year, just one!

Wearing same clothes: This is pretty common among baseball players. Some wear the same socks until they get a hit. Some won't change underwear until they get a double or better. They have all kinds of these things going on in their routine. I heard of one major leaguer that did everything in threes. He would tap his bat three times on the plate before hitting. He would say three special words each inning in the field. "Eyes on ball, eyes on ball, eyes on ball." It could be anything.

Carrying lucky charms: I mentioned the Indian Head nickel. You never know what a player might carry with him. Sometimes is is an item the player has had for years, or something his wife or girlfriend gave him, or something special he had found.

Following same routines: Baseball players can be a strange bunch. I have known players who will never break a game day routine for fear of losing. They may drive to the game the same route every time, park in the same or similar location, put on the uniform in a certain order, eat the same foods, and on and on. They have all kinds of routines that they carry out to the smallest detail. Of course, using certain bats mean a lot to many players. Some will not allow a teammate to borrow a bat for fear of breaking it. Some sit in a certain location in the dugout or will shave or not shave on certain days. I had one teammate who would not play until he had touched every bat in the bat rack.

A special story: In the 1958 season one of my pitchers, Larry Maxie, tore a big hole in the right knee of his uniform. Some eighteen games later a sports reporter, Tom Youlden, asked Larry if he couldn't get a different uniform for the playoff games. Larry replied, "Couldn't do it. Wouldn't want to change our luck!"

STORY 205:

Billy Kilmer—An Incredible Athlete

When I was coaching in high school I officiated football games in the fall and basketball games in the winter. I was too busy in baseball season to call games although I have done that in my earlier years.

One evening I went to Citrus High School to officiate a basketball game. They were playing Chino High School and the game came down to the wire. I was about to observe one of the most amazing performances I had ever seen.

Chino was leading Citrus by seven points with fourteen seconds to play. This was before the three point shot was in force. A Citrus player had the ball, shot and made the basket and was fouled. He made the point. Chino now led by four points with nine seconds to play. As the Chino player threw the ball in, this same player leaped in the air, intercepted the ball, scored a basket and was fouled. He made the free throw. Chino now led by one point with four seconds to play. Once again this same player jumped, intercepted the ball, scored a basket with no seconds on the clock and Citrus won by one point.

The player was Billy Kilmer who went on to star for the UCLA Bruin football team, the San Francisco 49ers, and the Washington Redskins. His high school baseball coach told me he batted .675 in his senior year. Billy could do it all.

Billy and Marty Keough were two of the most capable athletes I had every witnessed. Each simply got the job done in any sport. It was a pleasure just to watch them perform.

STORY 206:

Wally Moon's Baseball Camp

Following my annual spring baseball season I would pack up the car and head for my summer ranger job in one of the national parks. For six years I worked in Glacier National Park while we were in Grand Teton National Park for four. Both parks were outstanding and the family always looked forward to those three-month "vacations." Of course it wasn't a vacation for dad who had to put in forty hours a week on the job. But, nevertheless, we all had many great family experiences together.

In 1959 I received a telephone call in the spring from the Los Angeles Dodgers. They were starting a Wally Moon Baseball Camp on a college campus near our home. They wanted to know if I would be interested in directing it. I must say it was tempting to accept such a challenge. I had just completed ten years of high school coaching at Chaffey and it seemed like a natural to step in such a position. But, we had been in the National Park Service (summers) for seven years and the family dearly loved to return each June. So, with a family decision, we turned down the opportunity.

I often wondered if I might have been still working for the Dodgers had I accepted. This probably would not have happened. Baseball is a business and ownerships change, CEOs and executives change, personnel changes, and there was no certainty one would have a permanent job. But, in any event, we left it behind us and once again chose family over career. I have always felt comfortable with decisions based on what is best for the family.

Wally Moon's career with the Dodgers ended six years later in 1965. But, it would have been enjoyable working with a man of Wally's caliber. He was just 29 years old at the time and six years my junior.

STORY 207:

The Old Pacific Coast League

There are so many stories of the old Pacific Coast League. In the early days I really had no idea that there were thoughts of making the "PCL" the third major league. Some of the players in that league were making more money than those in the majors.

But, when Walter O'Malley and Horace Stoneham brought their Dodgers and Giants west, any thoughts of major league status in the PCL went up in smoke.

Many of the old timers had their starts out west. It was the home of hordes of players including Ted Williams, the DiMaggio brothers, Joe, Vince, and Dom, Wally Berger, Bobby Brown, Jackie Robinson, Bobby Doerr, Rollie Fingers, Babe Herman, Billy Herman, Ernie Lombardi, Walter "The Great" Mails, Jo Jo White, Marty Keough, Denny Lemaster, Johnny Lindell, Billy Martin, Frank "Lefty" O'Doul, Augie Galan, Lefty Gomez, and dozens of others.

While baseball was emerging in the east and Midwest in the late 1800s, it was also developing in the west. Prior to 1900 there developed the California League first starting in San Francisco. In 1903 the Pacific Coast League was born.

Teams I recall as a youth were the San Francisco Seals, the Los Angeles Angels, the Portland Beavers, and the Seattle Rainers. Others were added such as the Hollywood Stars, Oakland Oaks or Acorns, Sacramento Solons, and San Diego Padres. The Los Angeles club had ties to the Chicago Cubs and many of the Angels went on to play there.

It was a great league and a wonderful recreational outlet for west coast baseball fans.

STORY 208:

Four Pitches and You're Out

I did not realize it at the time but in 1934 the Los Angeles Angles Triple A team was one of the best minor league teams to play the game. They went

137-50 for the season. That is better than 73% victories, an incredible percentage for a professional baseball team. I went to watch the Angels meet the Oakland Acorns. It was one of those moments in one's life where you remember every detail.

Arnold "Jigger" Statz (see Story 140) hit the first pitch of the game deep to left field. Jigger was not known for his power. He had more triples by far than home runs. The left field wall at Wrigley Field, Los Angeles, was thick. The ball hit right on top of the wall, bounced up in the air, came down and hit it the second time, and disappeared on the other side. Score: Angels 1, Acorns 0.

The second batter, Marvin Gudat (see Story 107), took a pitch for a ball. On the second pitch he hit a live drive against the right field bleacher screen for a double.

The third batter, Gene Lillard (see Story 118), hit the first pitch over the center field wall at the 400-foot mark. Score: Angels 3, Acorns 0.

The Oakland manager came out and took the pitcher out of the game after those four pitches. It was the only time in my memory that I saw a pitcher knocked out of the box that quickly. The Angels went on to win the game 11-2.

STORY 209:

One of Baseball's Famous Brawls

This event was so much off the wall that it has become known as "The Brawl." It occurred when I was in my first coaching job at Chaffey High School during the 1953 baseball season. It was during a game between the Los Angeles Angels and the Hollywood Stars at Gilmore Field on August 2. It was so wild and violent that it took 50 uniformed police officers to break it up.

There were thirty full minutes of fighting before order was restored. But controlling it was not easy. Police were placed at each clubhouse and nine players were allowed outside at a time. On top of this fact, yet another game had to be played since it was a doubleheader.

It was described as a gouging, spiking, and slugging battle of uniformed baseball players. It was the third melee in three days but this one was the most ferocious. The fighting started in the sixth inning and was quieted by the umpires. But, it resumed a few moments later. The melee was observed by a television audience that included Police Chief William H. Parker. He immediately dispatched 50 police officers to assist the umpires.

Hollywood Star Frankie Kelleher was at the center of the problem though not at all his fault. He was a thorn in the Angels side the whole series. He had won the first two games for the Stars with pinch hits and in the third game he got the Angels' dander up by singling in a run in the first inning. In the fourth inning Angel pitcher Joe Hatten gave Frankie some "chin music," and Kelleher promptly tripled to center and then scored on a squeeze play to put the Stars up 2-0.

Then came the sixth inning when after two more bean balls by Hatten, Kelleher was hit in the middle of the back. Frankie strode to the mound and began pummeling the pitcher. Joe retaliated and the battle was on. Kelleher was tossed out and his replacement, Teddy Beard, later went into third baseman, Moe Franklin, with spikes flying and another confrontation started. Fights broke out all over the field with almost every player on both teams participating. Eddie Malone (see Story 121) was spiked in the leg and others had bruises, gashes, and black eyes.

All of this action increased the attendance to a record number of 63,017 for a three-game series. Fortunately, no fans were involved or there might have been a serious riot.

An interesting observation in this story is that Frankie Kelleher was our banquet speaker at Chaffey High School in 1956, just three years after the brawl. When asked how he survived the incident he just laughed and said the encounter was forgotten by all. Another interesting fact is that in 17 years of professional baseball Kelleher had never been in a fight or ejected from a baseball game.

STORY 210:

Brothers in Baseball

As a youngster I recall several brother combinations such as Dizzy and Daffy Dean, Walker and Mort Cooper, Rick and Wes Ferrell, and Paul and Lloyd Waner. It seemed rather unusual that two men from the same family would be in the big leagues.

I did a study on this subject recently and came up with some surprising results. There has been over 350 brother combinations in major league baseball through the years. And there are more than two brothers in one family who have played the game at the same time. The all-time record is held by the five Delahanty brothers who played baseball at the turn of the century. They were fifteen years apart in age. From eldest to youngest, they were Ed, Tom, Joe, Jim, and Frank.

There are two sets of four brothers. One group played at the turn of the century. They are the O'Neill brothers, from eldest to youngest, Jack, Mike, Steve, and Jim. Jack and Mike were born in Ireland. The second set is current players. They are

the Molina brothers. From eldest to youngest there are Bengie, Gabe, Jose, and Yadier.

There are 15 sets of three brothers. The Alou brothers, one of those groups, all played for one team at the same time and set the record for the most number of games played by brothers at 5,129.

There have been some famous names in these groups including DiMaggio, Boyer, and Sewell, all sets of three. Some are not aware that ESPN's Harold Reynolds has a brother, Don, who spent two years with the San Diego Padres. The slugger, Vladimir Guerrero has a brother, Wilton, who is in his ninth year in the major leagues. The list goes on and on and is an interesting subject.

The Boone family is a story in itself. Ray played for years in the majors with Cleveland and Detroit as has his son, Bob, followed by his grandchildren, Bret and Aaron. The Gus Bell family is another incredible story of baseball players. Besides Gus are his son, Buddy and his grandson, David.

This baseball brother story is very interesting. Over 350 brother combinations is a surprising number.

STORY 211:

Rip Sewell's Eephus Pitch

In 1932, Truett Banks "Rip" Sewell had a five-game tryout with the Detroit Tigers but was returned to the minors. However, in 1938 he was signed by Pittsburg and went on to pitch nine consecutive years with the Pirates. Part of his foot had been shot off in a hunting accident keeping him out of World War II.

He pitched 2,119 innings with Pittsburg and had a very respectable record of 143 victories and

97 losses and a 3.48 ERA .He was named National League Pitcher of the Year in 1943. Rip was an exceptional fielder having handled 12 chances in a single game. In 1941 he had eleven assists in a game and set a major league record with three assists in one inning.

Sewell was a celebrated figure because of an extraordinary pitch he developed. It was coined the "eephus pitch" by one of his teammates, Maurice Van Robays. He would toss the pitch in the air from 18 to 25 feet above the playing surface and had the ability to put it in the strike zone. They did not play slow pitch softball in those days but Rip's pitch was similar to one used in that game. Some called it a "dew drop pitch." He was quite effective with it. However, on July 9, 1946 in the All Star game Ted Williams hit one of Rip's blooper pitches into the right field bleachers for a home run. Incidentally, it was Ted's second dinger of the ball game.

Rip was an individualist and had a mind of his own. He fought against any organized union for the players that started to appear after World War II. His comments were, "First they will want the hamburger, then the filet mignon, eventually the cow, and, finally, the entire pasture."

STORY 212:

Mordecai "Three Finger" Brown

I had read about this player when I was just a little kid and always wanted to know more about him. I decided to put his name in my book even though I had no personal contact with him. He played until 1916 and was elected into the Baseball Hall of Fame on May 9, 1949 when I was 24 years old.

Just his unusual name alone made this player one of the most unique in baseball. Mordecai made the most of a handicap. As a seven-year old boy he caught his right hand in a corn grinder on his uncle's farm. Almost all the forefinger had to be amputated, his middle finger was saved but pretty badly mangled and remained crooked, and his little finger was stubbed. He learned to add spin to the ball with his deformed hand by releasing it off the stub. He pitched for thirteen years with the Cardinals, Cubs, Reds, and the St. Louis Terriers.

Considering his handicap he had an incredible 2.06 ERA as he pitched 3,172 innings. He won 239 games while losing just 129 for a 65% victory percentage. For you statistic buffs, that is an incredible winning record. He was the pitching mainstay of the Chicago Cubs when they had the famous Tinker to Evers to Chance double play combination.

Many of his pitching battles were against the great Hall of Famer, Christy Mathewson. Pitching for the Cubbies against their fierce rivals, the New York Giants, he was credited for the victory in the renowned "Merkle Boner" game in 1908 that decided the National League pennant. Please see Story 216 (Baseball Trivia), item 3.

STORY 213:

Casey Stengel— God Love His Soul

I never met Casey Stengel. That was my loss. But three friends of mine either played for him or saw him from time to time at Yankee Stadium.

First, my pitcher at Chaffey High School, Yankee Hal Reniff, told me about Casey's dropping by Yankee Stadium now and then in 1961 and 1962. Casey had just won ten American League pennants and seven World Championships as the New York manager. Unbelievably, he was fired a few days after the famous walk-off home run by Pirate Bill Maseroski to beat the Yanks four games to three in the 1960 World Series. The reason given for the firing was, "he is too old." To which Casey quipped, "I'll never make the mistake of being seventy again."

Jim Bouton commented to me about Casey being one of the most interesting baseball men he ever met. He, too, was on the 1961 Yankees with Hal Reniff.

My old keystone (double play combination) partner from UCLA, Bobby Brown, played for Casey as his regular third baseman in 1949, 1950, and 1951. Bobby said that Casey had his own ideas about the game and often outfoxed his opponents. He had played since 1912 for the Brooklyn Robins (they did not become known as the Dodgers until the 1930s), Pittsburg Pirates, Philadelphia Phillies, New York Giants, and Boston Braves (then called the Bees). He was excited to play for the Giants who were managed by the great John McGraw. Casey played on three pennant winners for McGraw in 1921, 1922 and 1923 and learned much about managing during those years.

Casey managed a total of 23 years, his most successful with the Yankees when he won five consecutive World Championships. He was with New York from 1949 to 1960 winning ten league pennants and seven world titles. He used a platoon strategy that he had learned from Brooklyn manager, Wilbert Robinson and the Giant manager, McGraw. Soon other teams were using the system and it continues today.

Stengel personally trained Mickey Mantle how to play balls off the walls at Yankee Stadium. They say Mickey was astonished that Casey was so knowledgeable. But, he played on outstanding teams in the early years. In fact, He hit two game-winning home runs in the 1923 World Series. His inside-the-park homer with two out in the ninth inning of Game One left the fans shocked. He was thirty-three years old at the time. This is just a side note for your interest. I recall in the early 1950s as I listened to a Stengel interview when Casey called Mickey, "that fella in center field."

After his huge success with the Yankees in the 1950s Casey was named manager of the newly formed New York Mets. Stengel's famous comment was, 'It is nice to be back in the Polar (Polo) Grounds again with the New York Knickerbockers." He managed until 1965 when he retired.

I was in Southern California then and I recall that he lived in Glendale, California at that time and worked for a bank there. He had a sign on his desk that read, "Stengelese Spoken Here." Casey was known for his own personal language that was called "Stengelese." Some of his quotes are classic. He once said that, "Brooklyn is a borough of churches and bad ball clubs, many of which I had." When he was named the Yankee manager in 1949 he commented, "This is a big job, fellows, and I barely have had time to study it. In fact, I scarcely know where I am at." He once stated, "The secret of managing is to keep the five guys who hate you away from the five who are undecided." And, then, with the Mets in 1962 he had some vintage quotes with, perhaps, the most memorable being, "Can't anybody here play this game?"

A story about Casey from 1948 tells how some baseball history might have been changed forever. The celebrated construction magnet and co-owner of the Yankees, Del Webb, attended a night game at the Oakland Park in Emeryville, California. Casey was managing the Pacific Coast League team there. After the game Del and Casey sat around and talked baseball.

At eight o'clock the following morning Del drove by the park on his way to a construction job on his schedule. He heard a baseball being hit inside the park. He was curious to see who was working out so early. To his astonishment, there was Casey hitting infield to a bunch of kids and giving pointers to them. Del said he made up his mind then that anyone with that kind of enthusiasm for baseball at fifty-seven years of age belonged in the major leagues. He said later, "I knew then that I had the next Yankee manager."

Incidentally, Del Webb went on to build Sun City near Phoenix, Arizona, where thousands of retirees now live. Currently, they are still building and developing other Sun City communities. Mr. Webb and his family have made great contributions in other ways including education, medicine, etc., all for Americans in many locations.

Stengel played 1,277 innings with a .284 batting average. He had only 60 home runs since he was basically a line drive hitter. And he had 535 RBIs. In World Series contests he played in twelve games and batted .393. Despite his ups and downs with different types of teams, he was certainly a prime prospect for the greatest manager in baseball history. His impact on the game is classic.

Casey's first name came about because he was originally from Kansas City (K.C.). He contributions and accomplishments in baseball are monumental. When he finally retired he had a quote that might describe Casey more than any other. He said, "There comes a time in every man's life and I've had plenty of them."

I have a tape at home of the great Vin Scully wrapping up a World Series. In the background we hear Casey commenting in Stengelese about baseball. And Vin says, "Casey Stengel, God love his soul."

CHAPTER 8

Baseball Quotes, History, Trivia and Humor

STORY 214:

Memorable Quotes In Baseball

(1) "Baseball is the very symbol, the outward and visible expression of the drive and push and rush and struggle of the raging, tearing, booming, nineteenth century." (Mark Twain)

(2) "To the pioneers who were the moving spirit of the game in its infancy and to the players who have been elected to the Hall of Fame, we pay just tribute—but I should like to dedicate this museum to all America." (Kenesaw Mountain Landis, Commissioner of Baseball, July 12, 1939 in the dedication of the Baseball Hall of Fame).

(3) "The City of Angels offered him (Walter O'Malley) more than the keys to the city. It gave him the keys to the kingdom. New York City balked at "twelve acres" and Los Angeles enthusiastically proffered "three hundred acres." This is the biggest haul since the Brinks robbery." (Sportswriter Tim Cohane on the Dodgers move to Los Angeles from New York).

(4) "Show me a guy that can't pitch inside and I'll show you a loser." (Sandy Koufax, Brooklyn and Los Angeles Dodger pitcher).

(5) "Ya gotta believe." (Tug McGraw, Philadelphia Phillies pitcher).

(6) "Hitting against Sandy Koufax is like eating soup with a fork." (Willie Stargell, Pittsburg Pirate outfielder).

(7) "Slump, I ain't in no slump. I just ain't hitting."(Yogi Berra, New York Yankee catcher).

(8) "As one of nine men, Joe DiMaggio is the best player that ever lived." (Connie Mack, owner and manager, Philadelphia Athletics).

(9) "Pete Rose is baseball." (Sparky Anderson, Cincinnati manager).

(10) "Chuck him (Honus Wagner) the ball as hard as you can and pray." (John McGraw, Manager, New York Giants)

(11) "Get in front of those balls, you won't get hurt. That's what you've got a chest for young man." (John McGraw)

(12) "No matter what I talk about, I always get back to baseball." (Connie Mack).

(13) "You are born with two strikes against you, so don't take a third one on your own." (Connie Mack).

(14) "There is but one game and that game is baseball." (John McGraw).

(15) "I demand respect on the field from managers and players. To me, that's 75% of umpiring." (John "Jocko" Conlon, former major league player and umpire).

(15) "CLEAN BALL is the MAIN PLANK in the American League platform, and the clubs must stand by it religiously. There must be no profanity on the ball field." (American League President Ban Johnson in a directive to team owners in a letter dated May 8, 1901.

(16) "Coach, should I go for it?" (Chuck Bennett, Chaffey High School leftfielder, June 1, 1956). Chuck went by the dugout, paused, and asked me that question. I thought to myself, " here is an 18 year-old high school player asking if he should go for a home run to win a game tied 6-6 in the bottom of the ninth inning that would put us in the championship finals of the CIF." Are we talking "Babe Ruth pointing here?" Chuck did, indeed, hit a 400-foot dinger and we won the championship the next game. Please see Story 150 (Chuck Bennett) for details.

(17) "There was almost no power in my right arm. Even when batting, the chips remaining caused the arm to swell twice its size." (Augie Galan, Chicago Cubs, 1939 describing his feeling after surgery.)

(18) "If one of our guys went down (from an inside pitch) I just doubled it. No confusion there. It didn't require a Rhodes scholar." (Don Drysdale, Los Angeles Dodgers, 1960.)

(19) Rogers Hornsby, asked what he does in the winter when there's no baseball, he replied: "I'll tell you what I do. I just stare out the window and wait for spring."

(20) Willie Mays played his first major league game on May 25, 1951 and went 0 for 5 at the plate. He started his career going 1 for 25 and told his manager, Leo Durocher: "I can't do it, Mr. Leo. You better bench me."

(21) Casey Stengel played his first major league game on July 27, 1912 and went 4 for 4 at the plate. He commented later in his life as follows: "I broke in with four hits and the writers promptly decided they had seen the new Ty Cobb. It took me only a few days to correct that impression."

(22) "The kid who was lucky enough to come up with a real league ball or a store-bought bat automatically became team captain." (Ford Frick, National League President, 1973).

(23) "I see great things in baseball." (Walt Whitman, Poet.)

(24) "I couldn't have done it without my players." (Casey Stengel in 1953 after winning his fifth consecutive World Series championship).

(25) When speaking of Yogi Berra, Casey Stengel said: "He would fall in a sewer and come up with a gold watch."

(26) "You can't tell the players without a scorecard." (Scorecard vendors at ballparks).

(27) "When you're playing, awards don't seem like much. Then you get older all of it becomes more precious. It is nice to be remembered." (Hank Greenberg, at the induction ceremony at the Baseball Hall of Fame, 1956).

(28) "Baseball was, is, and always will be to me, the best game in the world." (Babe Ruth near the end of his career).

(29) "I always heard it couldn't be done, but sometimes it don't always work." (Casey Stengel)

(30) "You could look it up." (Casey Stengel)

(31) "There are three types of ball players, those who make things happen, those who watch it happen, and those who wonder what's happening." (Tommy LaSorda, former Dodger manager).

(32) "I think there are some players who are born to play ball." (Joe DiMaggio).

(33) "The good Lord was good to me. He gave me a strong body, a good right arm, and a weak mind." (Dizzy Dean in 1936 on why he was so successful).

(34) "I tell you what, I think baseball has spread. But, if we are talking about anything spreading, we would be talking about soccer. You can go over in Italy and I thought they would never know DiMaggio every place. And, my goodness, you mention soccer, you can draw fifty or a hundred thousand people. Over here you have a hard time to get soccer on the field, which is a great sport, no doubt." (Casey Stengel on soccer vs baseball).

(35) "He wanted to see poverty, so he came to see my team play." (Casey Stengel, manager of the New York Mets, about President Lyndon Johnson).

(36) "I don't like them fellas who drive in two runs and let in three." (Casey Stengel).

(37) "I was such a dangerous hitter that I got intentional walks during batting practice." (Casey

Stengel—by the way, this is Casey's old number, 37).

(38) "Most ball games are lost, not won." (Casey Stengel).

(39) "I never saw a man who juggled his lineup so much and who played so many hunches successfully." (Connie Mack about Casey Stengel).

(40) "Pitchers have to possess more than mere speed. A pitcher has to have other pitches to go with it so that he can mix 'em up and shake your timing." (Joe DiMaggio, 1961).

(41) "I want to make sure the kids graduate. I want to teach them everything I know about baseball and I want to teach them everything I know about life." (Tony Gwynn, San Diego State baseball coach, 2001).

STORY 215:

History of the Grand Old Game

Probably developed from the games of cricket, rounders, and town ball, baseball has been played in America for over 150 years. Some records claim that the first game was played in 1846 under the direction of Alexander Cartwright who had invented the game. Old records show he even umpired that first game. There are others who say that Abner Doubleday was the creator of baseball. However it occurred, there is no doubt that the game has captured the interest of Americans.

When Marilyn and I visited the Great American Ball Park in Cincinnati recently, we took advantage of that time to go to the Cincinnati Hall of Fame. It is a marvelous hall and full of baseball history. Please see Story 37, National League, Great Ameri-can Ball Park, paragraph 2. It describes details of the first professional baseball team in Cincinnati in 1869.

Near the turn of the century professional leagues developed and the first World Series was held in 1903. The game grew in popularity and larger and larger stadiums became necessary to handle the crowds. Baseball heroes delighted the fans with great hitting, fielding, base running, and strategy. The Ty Cobb and Babe Ruth eras were significant. The breaking of the "color line" with Jackie Robinson and Larry Doby made great changes.

It is interesting to note the relationships American presidents have had with baseball. Ulysses S. Grant was president when the first professional game was played and when the National League was formed. On June 6, 1892, Benjamin Harrison was the first president to attend a major league game. Cincinnati defeated Washington that day, 7-4. William Howard Taft was the first president to throw out the first pitch on April 4, 1910. Every president except one since has performed that function. The exception: President Jimmy Carter.

More recently than President Taft, Ronald Reagan was a radio announcer for the Chicago Cubs and he re-created games as well. In his movie acting he played a baseball player several times. George W. Bush dreamed of following the footsteps of the great Willie Mays. Prior to becoming President of the United States and Governor of Texas, he was a managing partner for the Texas Rangers. He opened the White House lawn to T-ball players in 2001 and this has become a tradition.

Today there are 112 countries in the International Baseball Federation and numerous professional teams are playing in many countries.

With that many countries in the federation and with baseball being played in so many areas of the world it would seem logical to have both baseball and softball in the Olympic games. However, both events are scheduled for elimination after the 2008 Summer Olympic Games. Please see Story 198 (Softball vs Hardball) for more information on this subject.

Baseball has a great past. An entire book could be written on the history of the fascinating sport that has captured a nation.

STORY 216:

Trivia For Horsehide Fans

(1) On September 20, 1960, Carroll Hardy pinch-hit for Ted Williams, the only time a player hit for him. He hit into a double play. Hardy also hit for Roger Maris on May 18, 1958 in Cleveland and hit his first major league home run.

(2) Robert McCullough of the Cooper Bessemer baseball team threw a fast breaking curve ball to one of the "Lambs" batters in Mt. Vernon, Ohio in September 1938 and broke his arm in four places on this one pitch.

(3) No baseball book is complete without mention of the famous "Merkle boner" game played in the 1908 National League pennant race between the New York Giants and Chicago Cubs. Nineteen-year old Giant first baseman, Fred Merkle, was the runner on first base with outfielder Harry "Moose" McCormick on third. The score was tied 1-1 and there were two outs. Jack Pfiester lined a single into right centerfield and McCormick crossed the plate for the apparent winning run. Merkle went halfway to second and, seeing McCormick touch the plate, headed for the clubhouse in centerfield. But quick-thinking Cub second baseman Johnny Evers called for the ball—any ball—and stepped on second

claiming a force out that made McCormick's apparent run moot. The force out ruling was held up and the two teams had to play another game to determine the National League pennant winner for 1908. The Cubs won and defeated the Detroit Tigers for the World Series title as well. Some say the ball that Evers used was not the actual game ball. Joe "Iron Man" McGinnity may have thrown the ball into the stands. Famed manager, John McGraw, until his death in 1934, claimed Merkle had been unjustly blamed for the loss.

(4) There have been eleven unassisted triple plays in major league baseball. One of note was on July 8, 1994 by John Valentin of the Boston Red Sox on the Seattle Mariners. In addition, Valentin hit a homerun in Boston's 4-3 victory. This game was the major league debut of Alex Rodriguez.

5) The first movie about baseball was made in 1898 by Thomas Alva Edison. It was titled simply, "The Ball Game." Since that time more than 250 more have been produced. If you are interested in knowing more about baseball movies I would recommend surfing the Internet on the subject.

(6) Harry Hartman, Cincinnati announcer in 1929, is the first to utter the following homerun phrase: "Going, going, gone!"

(7) On August 31, 1959, in the Los Angeles Coliseum Sandy Koufax tied Bob Feller's major league record of 18 strikeouts in one game watched by 82,974 fans. Wally Moon's three-run homer beat San Francisco, 5-2, in the bottom of the ninth inning.

(8) There are 58 professional baseball players listed whose last names are Williams.

(9) In 1968 Frank Howard of the Washington Senators hit ten home runs in just six days in the month of May. He hit 44 dingers for the year.

(10) On June 23, 1971 Rick Wise of the Philadelphia

Phillies pitched a no-hitter and hit two home runs, one a two-run shot.

(11) On May 13, 1942 Jim Tobin, pitcher for the Boston Braves, hit home runs in three consecutive at bats. Two years later he tossed a no-hitter and hit a home run.

(12) In 1934 Cincinnati became the first team to use an airplane for transportation, Cincinnati to Chicago.

(13) On May 24, 1935 Cincinnati hosted Philadelphia for the first night game ever played.

(14) In 1929 Roy Carlyle of the Oakland Oaks of the old Pacific Coast League, hit what is thought to be the longest home run in baseball history. It was measured at 618 feet.

(15) The first professional baseball game was played in 1869 in Cincinnati. The teams were the Cincinnati Reds versus The Great Western of Cincinnati. The Reds won almost all of their seventy games that season.

(16) The last out at old Comiskey Park in Chicago was made by ESPN sportscaster, Harold Reynolds. The game was played on September 30, 1990.

(17) In 1953 the Cincinnati Reds changed their name to the Cincinnati Redlegs because of the communist connotation of the name, "Reds." But, fans and sportwriters continued to call the team "The Reds." The name was officially changed back to the Cincinnati Reds in 1959.

(18) In 1959 through 1962 there were two All Star games played each year. The All Star game originally started as an idea by Chicago Sportswriter, Arch Ward, to coincide with Chicago's Century of Progress Exposition. The first All Star game was played on July 6, 1933.

(19) Connie Mack was an amazing man. He spent

60 years in baseball, 50 of which he had an ownership interest in the team he managed. He still holds the record for most wins by a manager, 3776. He also holds the record for the most losses by a manager, 4025. He passed away in 1956 at the age of 93.

(20) Sparky Anderson is the only manager to win a World Championship in each league (Cincinnati 1975 & 1976; Detroit 1984).

(21) On July 6, 1933 in Comiskey Park, Connie Mack and John McGraw, two of the most colorful men in baseball, fittingly managed the American League and National League teams, respectively, in the first All Star game ever played. The American League won, 4-2.

(22) Speaking of Charlie Comiskey, many are not aware that he did more than own the White Sox. He played thirteen years for the St. Louis Browns and the Chicago White Stockings in the late 1800s. He played in 1, 385 games with a .266 batting average, 29 home runs, and 883 RBIs. After the turn of the century he became very successful as an owner and was involved in baseball his entire life. He was voted in the Baseball Hall of Fame in 1939.

(23) On January 22, 1929, the New York Yankees announced they are putting numbers on the back of all uniforms. The numbers are placed according to the player's position in the batting order. Thus, the leadoff hitter is number one, second hitter number two, etc. That is why Babe Ruth had number three and Lou Gehrig had number four. The Yankees were the first team to start continuous use of numbers. Soon thereafter, the Cleveland Indians announced they, too, are using numbers. By 1931 all American League teams had planned to use numbers. It was 1933 before all National League players were numbered.

(24) On April 17, 1929, Babe Ruth and actress Claire Hodgson were married at 5:00 a.m. at Yankee Stadium. The early hour was chosen to avoid crowds. However, the Yankee/Red Sox game that day was

rained out and the wedding party continued uninterrupted.

(25) On June 23, 1917, starting pitcher Babe Ruth walked the first batter. Ruth disputed the call on each pitch leading to the base on balls. He came in and punched umpire Brick Owens in the jaw. Ruth was immediately ejected. Reliever Ernie Shore was brought in and runner Ray Morgan was thrown out on the next pitch. Ernie proceeded to put down the next 26 batters in a row for a perfect game winning 4-0. Ruth was suspended for nine days and fined $100.

(26) Ted Williams batted .406 in 1941. If his six "sacrifice fly outs" were not counted as "at bats," his average would have been .412. The sacrifice fly rule as not counting as an at bat was reinstated in 1954. This is the history of this rule: 1908: sacrifice fly counts, no time at bat; 1926: sacrifice fly counts if runner advances (any base); 1931: no sacrifice fly rule; 1939: sacrifice fly counts if runner scores; 1940: a sacrifice fly awards batter an RBI if runner scores but counts as a time at bat; 1954: the sacrifice fly rule was reinstated and an "at bat" does not count.

(27) May a player switch batting positions (right to left or left to right) in one plate appearance? Yes, but he cannot hold up the game. He must be ready.

(28) The following are retired numbers of the New York Yankees: 1, Billy Martin; 3, Babe Ruth; 4, Lou Gehrig; 5, Joe DiMaggio; 7, Mickey Mantle; 8, Yogi Berra and Bill Dickey: 9, Roger Maris; 10, Phil Rizzuto; 15, Thurmon Munson; 16, Whitey Ford; 23, Don Mattingly; 32, Elston Howard; 37, Casey Stengel; 44, Reggie Jackson; 49, Ron Guidry.

(29) Honus Wagner was the first 20th century player to steal home two times in one game. Another player, Joe Tinker, stole home twice in 1910 and again in 1911. Ty Cobb holds the record for the most steals of home in a season, six. It occurred in 1912. Cobb stole home 54 times during his career.

(30) On June 18, 1915, Ty Cobb, Bobby Veach, and George Burns pulled off a triple steal. Ty scored a run on the play. Catcher John "Bull" Henry was knocked unconscious on the play and left the game. It was during this year that Cobb ran the bases with daring outwitting his opponents many times.

(31) Thirty-eight players went on to become major league umpires. The first, in 1891, was Bob Emslie and the most recent, in 1976, was Tom Gorman.

(32) On September 12, 1930, Al Lopez, eventual Chicago White Sox manager, bounced a ball into the leftfield bleachers at Ebbetts Field for a home run. It was the last "bounced home run" in the major leagues because the National League follows the American League by calling such a play a "ground rule double." That rule still exists today. Lopez passed away in 2005.

(33) Casey Stengel, of New York Yankee fame, managed the Brooklyn Dodgers from February 24, 1934 to October 4, 1936.

(34) On January 24, 1934, New York Giant manager, Bill Terry, when asked what he thought the Dodger chances were to win the National League pennant, replied, "Brooklyn? Is Brooklyn still in the league?" He may have later regretted that comment. On September 29 of that same year, Dodger pitcher, Van Lingle Mungo, knocks the Giants out of the league lead, 5-1. And a Dodger victory over the Giants a day later completed the job and St. Louis won the pennant.

(35) John "Beans" Reardon, the colorful umpire for many years, was a friend of Mae West, renowned movie star of the 1930s. He appeared in several of her films. Beans was behind the plate when Babe Ruth hit his 714th and final home run.

(36) Roger Clemens, Mr. K for strikeout, and his wife have four sons. Appropriately, their names are Koby, Kory, Kacy, and Kody.

(37) On August 21, 1979, an unusual situation occurred. In a protested game, the Mets were defeating the Astros 5-0 with two outs in the top of the ninth inning. Jeff Leonard was at bat with Doug Harvey umpiring behind the plate. Jeff flied to center field apparently to end the game. Harvey ruled that time had been called. Leonard then singled to right field but the Met's had no first baseman in position. Harvey rules "no play" and orders Leonard to bat a third time. Jeff then flied to left field and the game was over.

(38) Jim Palmer of the Baltimore Orioles gave up 303 home runs in his career but never a grand slam. Harvey Haddix of Pittsburg allowed over 200 homers but no grand slams.

(39) Speaking of home runs, the park that allowed the most home runs is Wrigley Field in Chicago. The famous old park has had 11,173 round trippers hit there since 1914. This number has grown slightly larger since mid-September, 2005.

(40) Only twice did a person manage two different National League teams the same season and it was the same man. (Leo Durocher, Dodgers/Giants, 1948; and Leo Durocher, Cubs/Astros, 1972).

(41) Any player refusing obedience to his captain, an exercise of lawful authority, shall pay a fine of fifty cents. (Rules of the old New York team, the Knickerbockers.)

(42) Penalty enforced by Commissioner Kenesaw Mountain Landis for attacking an umpire: In 1927 it was a 90-day suspension. In 1948 it was changed to a one-year suspension.

(43) Many have heard of the famous run scored from first base by Enos Slaughter of the St. Louis Cardinals in the seventh game of the 1946 World Series. Here are some other facts. The double that drove Slaughter home was hit by Harry Walker. Also, Harry "The Cat" Brecheen was awarded the victory that gave him three wins in the Series. He won the sixth and seventh games, the only pitcher to accomplish that feat. My friend, Joe Garagiola was the Cardinal catcher and had a great series. Joe had four hits and three RBIs in game four. The Cards defeated a powerful Red Sox team.

(44) Harry "The Hat" Walker, the same man who drove in the winning run in the World Series described in Trivia Item 43, went through 20 caps a season by tugging at his cap on every pitch. Also, Walker led the National League in batting in 1947 with a .363 average.

(45) Talk about history, please read this one. Marilyn and I made friends with a very pleasant gentleman and a great baseball fan, Steve Kim, at a Mariner/Angel game at Safeco Field on August 14, 2005. We received an email from him shortly afterwards with the following great trivia story: On Saturday, June 24, 1876, the Cincinnati Reds lost 8-7 to the Boston Red Caps. One day later, Sunday, June 25, was the battle of the Little Big Horn (General George Custer's last stand). Thanks, Steve!

(46) The name, Bill Wambsganss, always intrigued me. I recall seeing it when I was reading about baseball as a kid. "Wamby," as he was known in the early days, pulled off an unassisted triple play for Cleveland against Brooklyn on September 10, 1920 in game five of the World Series. Two other "firsts" happened in that game. Indian outfielder Elmer Smith hit the first grand slam in a World Series off Brooklyn Robin pitcher, Burleigh Grimes. And Jim Bagby, Cleveland pitcher, hit a three-run homer off Grimes, the first dinger by a pitcher in a World Series.

(47) The first known scorecard was found in 1845 and involved the old Knickerbocker Baseball Team of New York.

(48) Babe Ruth is the only player caught stealing to end a World Series. It happened in Game Seven of the 1926 fall classic.

(49) Billy Sunday, the famous evangelist, played eight years in the major leagues for the Cubs, Pirates, and Phillies from 1883 to 1890. He had 12 home runs, 170 RBIs, 84 stolen bases, and batted .248.

STORY 217:

Humor on the Diamond

(1) I learned that you shouldn't go through life with a catcher's mitt on both hands. You need to be able to throw something back. (Author unknown)

(2) Lou "The Mad Russian" Novikoff, played for the Los Angeles Angels in 1940. He won the Triple Crown with a batting average of .343, 171 RBIs and 41 home runs. Lou was on second base with the bases loaded one time and tried to steal third base. When asked his reasoning, Lou said, "I couldn't resist. I had such a great jump on the pitcher."

(3) On July 11, 1961 Stu Miller, San Francisco reliever, was literally blown off the mound by strong winds during the All Star game at Candlestick Park. He was charged with a balk that tied the game, 3-3. But, Stu and the National League came back to win 5-4 in ten innings. I always liked Stu because of his craftiness in serving up a series of slow pitches to get batters out. Opponents said he had three pitches, slow, slower, and slowest. One player said, "he threw a pitch that stopped." He was a nemesis to Dodger batters in those days.

(4) "Jittery" Joe Berry played with the Chicago Cubs, Philadelphia Athletics, and the Cleveland Indians in the early 1940s. Joe was a favorite of mine when I watched him pitch for the Los Angeles Angels in the 1930s. Joe weighed just 135 pounds when he pitched for the A's. In one game a gust a wind came along and he was blown off the mound and charged with a balk, just as with Stu Miller in the 1961 first All Star game.

(5) Fred Haney, manager of the Milwaukee Braves, said that outstanding pitcher, Lew Burdette, "would make coffee nervous." The interesting thing about this story is that, while Burdette was constantly talking and fidgeting on the mound, his teammate, Gene Conley, said he had ice water in his veins. Nothing bothered him. He won 203 games while losing only 144 in the big leagues. His lifetime ERA was 3.66.

(6) "I talked to the ball a lot of times in my career. I yelled, "Go foul, go foul." (Former New York Yankee pitcher, Lefty "Goofy" Gomez).

(7) "I've got my faults, but living in the past isn't one of them. There's no future in it. (Sparky Anderson, former Detroit and Cincinnati manager).

(8) "In Yankee Stadium it gets late early." (Yogi Berra, New York Yankee catcher).(For more Yogi Berra humor please see Story 82, paragraph 5).

(9) "A nickel ain't worth a dime anymore." (Yogi Berra)

(10) An interviewer asked Yogi Berra about two hits he had the previous evening. Yogi replied, "I had three hits." The interviewer apologized and said he had checked the newspaper and the box score indicated two hits for Yogi. He said, "The third hit must have been a typographical error." To which Yogi responded, "No way, it was a clean single to left."

(11) "Son, what kind of pitch would you like to miss? (Dizzy Dean, St. Louis Cardinal pitcher, to a young batter in 1934)

(12) "He (Branch Rickey) must think I went to the Massachusetts Constitution of Technology." (Dizzy Dean, in the Sporting News, 1936).

(13) "I never threw an illegal pitch. The trouble is, once in a while I toss one that ain't never been seen by this generation." (Satchel Paige).

(14) "I ain't ever had a job. I just always played baseball." (Satchel Paige).

CHAPTER 9

Major League Clubs' Names & Location Changes

STORY 218:

Club Names
and Location Changes

The history of professional baseball clubs, their names and location changes through the years is absolutely intriguing. Most historians recognize the year, 1869, as the year of the first professional teams. The Cincinnati Red Stockings are generally credited with being America's first professional baseball team.

Since then teams have changed names and locations, and some teams have become defunct. The following is a summary of the various major league clubs and franchises:

AMERICAN LEAGUE FRANCHISES

AL-1
Baltimore Orioles
1954—present

St. Louis Browns
1902—1953

Milwaukee Brewers
1901

AL-2
Boston Red Sox
1908—present

Boston Americans
1901—1907

AL-3
Chicago White Sox
1904—present

Chicago White Stockings
1901—1903

AL-4
Cleveland Indians
1915—present

Cleveland Naps
1905—1914

Cleveland Blues
1901—1904

AL-5
Detroit Tigers
1901—present

AL-6
Kansas City Royals
1969—present

AL-7
Los Angeles Angels
2005—present

Anaheim Angels
1997—2004

California Angels
1965—1996

Los Angeles Angels
1961—1964

AL-8
Minnesota Twins
1961—present

Washington Senators
1901—1960

AL-9
New York Yankees
1913—present

New York Highlanders
1903—1912

AL-9 (continued)
Baltimore Orioles
1901—1902

AL-10
Oakland Athletes
1968—present

Kansas City Athletics
1955—1967

Philadelphia Athletics
1901—1954

AL-11
Seattle Mariners
1977—present

AL-12
Tampa Bay Devil Rays
1998—present

AL-13
Texas Rangers
1972—present

Washington Senators
1961—1971

AL-14
Toronto Blue Jays
1977—present

NL-1
Arizona Diamondbacks
1998—present

NL-2
Atlanta Braves
1966—present

Milwaukee Braves
1953—1965

Boston Braves
1941—1952

Boston Bees
1936—1940

Boston Braves
1912—1935

Boston Rustlers
1911—1911

Boston Doves
1907—1910

Boston Beaneaters
1883—1906

Boston Red Caps
1876—1882

NL-3
Chicago Cubs
1902—present

Chicago Orphans
1898—1901

Chicago Colts
1890—1897

Chicago White Stockings
1876—1889

NL-4
Cincinnati Reds
1959—present

Cincinnati Redlegs
1953—1958

Cincinnati Reds
1890—1952

Cincinnati Red Stockings (AA)
1882—1889

NL-5
Colorado Rockies
1993—present

NL-6
Florida Marlins
1993—present

NL-7
Houston Astros
1965—present

Houston Colt .45s
1962—1964

NL-8
Los Angeles Dodgers
1958—present

Brooklyn Dodgers
1932—1957

Brooklyn Robins
1914—1931

Brooklyn Dodgers
1911—1913

Brooklyn Superbas
1899—1910

Brooklyn Bridegrooms
1890—1898

Brooklyn Bridegrooms (AA)
1889—1889

Brooklyn Trolley Dodgers
1884—1888

NL-9
Milwaukee Brewers
1998—present

Milwaukee Brewers (AL)
1970—1997

Seattle Pilots (AL)
1969

NL-10
Philadelphia Phillies
1883—present

NL-11
Pittsburg Pirates
1891—present

Pittsburgh Alleghenys
1887—1890

Pittsburgh Alleghenys (AA)
1882—1886

NL-12
St. Louis Cardinals
1900—present

St. Louis Perfectos
1899—1899

St. Louis Browns
1892—1898

St. Louis Browns (AA)
1883—1891

St. Louis Brown Stockings (AA)
1882—1882

NL-13
San Diego Padres
1969—present

NL-14
San Francisco Giants
1958—present

New York Giants
1885—1967

New York Gothams
1883—1884

NL-15
Washington Nationals
2005—present

Montreal Expos
1969—2004

All American League franchises are still active. However there are ten National League franchises that are defunct. They are as follows:

D-1
Baltimore Orioles
(pre-1900 Orioles)
1892—1899

Baltimore Orioles (AA)
1882—1891

D-2
Buffalo Bisons
1879—1885

D-3
Cincinnati Red Stockings
(pre-1882 Reds)
1876—1877

Cincinnati Reds
1878—1880

D-4
Cleveland Blues
1879—1884

D-5
Cleveland Spiders
1889—1899

Cleveland Blues (AA)
1887—1888

D-6
Detroit Wolverines
1881—1888

D-7
Kansas City Cowboys
1886—1886

D-8
Providence Grays
1878—1885

D-9
Troy Trojans
1879—1882

D-10
Worcester Ruby Legs
1880—1882

CHAPTER 10

Coach John Wooden's Favorite Sport

The First Time I Saw John Wooden

One sunny day in the spring of 1947, the UCLA baseball team was having a practice session at Joe E. Brown Field on campus. I noticed a gentleman standing and observing practice behind the third base dugout. He was wearing some athletic gear and appeared to be a coach. It wasn't long before we figured out that this was our next basketball coach, John Wooden, who recently came from Indiana.

Sketch of John Wooden, Marilyn Proctor, and Ken Proctor.

ART CREDIT TO PAT DOOLEY

It crossed our minds that it was nice to see the basketball coach looking us over. We soon learned that he was interested in baseball, a sport in which he had great interest for many years.

I decided that I would try and play basketball as well as baseball and add to my coaching abilities in another good competitive sport. I had played high school basketball and turned out to try for Coach Wooden's team. I played in the program during 1948 on the JV team and learned much from Coach. In fact, in future years in my baseball coaching I applied many of the lessons learned from Coach, many about attitude and cooperation.

Immediately, we learned that Coach Wooden wanted us on the practice floor at 3:30 p.m. He did not want us there at 3:31 p.m. or 3:32 p.m. but precisely at 3:30 p.m. That was our first lesson. "Always be on time," Coach would say. I am sure you have heard that Coach taught us how to put on our sox and shoes properly. Yes, he did that and I never saw any of us get a blister. He was the master of detail. It was evident from the beginning that his organization was superb. Is it any wonder that a coach of any type of sport (or business) could learn from this gentleman?

I am so happy that I had those times under Coach Wooden. I was a player who did not have the basketball success that many of our men experienced. But, just to be there and learn from Coach was invaluable.

Please see Story 66 (1949 UCLA Baseball Team) about some of my basketball efforts and decisions.

STORY 220:

My Annual Notes to Coach Wooden

When Coach Wooden won his first NCAA basketball title in 1964 I sent him a note of congratulations. As he continued to win NCAA titles I sent him annual notes. All of us were so proud of him. We were pleased with his victories, of course, but even more, we were excited about his manner of teaching and the kind of example and model he was setting for athletes everywhere, far beyond UCLA. I tried to apply his theories and character building to all my baseball players. Coach is simply the best.

STORY 221:

Coach's Early Days of Baseball

Coach was born in Martinsville, Indiana on October 14, 1910.

He led his high school to the basketball Indiana State Championship in 1927. He made all-state honors for three years in 1926, 1927, and 1928. He also played summer baseball and set his sights on being a professional baseball player. He had a very strong arm and could throw with the best of them. He was a shortstop.

He went to Purdue University and led them to the National Collegiate Basketball Championship in 1932 and was named the College Basketball Player of the Year. Also, he earned All America honors in basketball in 1930, 1931, and 1932 and captained the 1931 and 1932 teams. In 1929 he played summer baseball and had been hit by a pitch that left him with a shoulder injury. His great throwing arm was gone. My friend, Doug Sale, my UCLA baseball teammate, told me his baseball playing was finished at that point. Doug served as one of Coach's assistants in his early years at UCLA.

With the injuries, his hopes for baseball were diminished. But, interestingly, his love for the game continued and to this day "it is still his favorite sport". He told me that one of the great thrills of his life was throwing out the first pitch at a 2002 World Series game in Anaheim, California.

STORY 222:

Marriage and Coaching

1932 was a banner year for John Wooden. He and his high school sweetheart, Nell Riley, were married. They had been baptized together when juniors in high school in 1927. She was the only girl Coach ever dated. I knew Nell Wooden and she was a gem, a wonderful wife, and a lovely lady. She and John were married for 53 years before she passed away in 1985. The basketball floor at UCLA is now called "The John and Nell Wooden Court."

In 1932 Coach went to Dayton High School in Kentucky where he began his coaching career and coached in all sports. Two year later he went to South Bend Central High School in Indiana to coach basketball, baseball, and tennis. Also, he taught English for nine years which he claims as one of his favorite activities. When Marilyn and I visited John in his home in November 2004 we asked him to recite several poems for us and he did not miss a beat. Also, his eleven-year prep coaching record was 218 victories and only 42 losses, an 84% win record.

STORY 223:

Enjoying the Game Through the Years

Coach said he has enjoyed baseball since his youth and follows the various teams and players. It gives him much pleasure especially since he knows the game so well. Coach would be successful in any effort he attempts. He probably would be managing in the major leagues today had his injury not occurred. On the other hand his love for teaching and character building might have found him as the premier coach of college baseball.

Some Final Words

I hope you have enjoyed reading *Baseball Memoirs of a Lifetime.* It was meant to be enlightening, pleasurable, and informative. Baseball is a common thread woven through the fabric of my life and the lives of many Americans. This great game marks history, provides lighthearted fun and enjoyment, and gives ways to discover and express our deepest passions and values. Thank you for allowing me to share part of my life with you through some of my fondest baseball memories.

The revised edition of my book, *Successful Baseball,* will soon be available. The book deals with the fundamentals of baseball, organizing a program, developing player skills, details of special plays, how to win games, and the mental aspects of becoming a better player.

Baseball forever,
KEN PROCTOR

BIBLIOGRAPHY

Alderson, Richard "Sandy".
MajorLeagueBaseball.com

Associated Students of Chaffey High School.
Fasti Yearbooks. 1950 through 1959

Associated Students of UCLA. *Southern
Campus Yearbooks. 1944, 1947, 1948, 1949*

Bouton, Jim. *.Ball Four.* Cleveland: The World
Publishing Co., 1970

Holmes, Dan. **The Baseball Page.com** 1995

Holtz, Sean. **BaseballAlmanac.com.** 2000

Lollis, Dean. **HistoricBaseball.com.** 2000

O'Donnell, Michael. *Salon Brilliant Careers—*
Vin Scully. 1999

Proctor, Ken. *Successful Baseball.* The Mar-Ken
Publishing Co., 1960

Rickey, Branch. *Branch Rickey's Little Blue Book.*
New York: Macmillan, 1995

Schaap, Dick and Gerberg, Mort. *Baseball Humor.*
Doubleday, New York, 1992

Shatzkin, Mike. *The Ballplayers:***BaseballLibrary.
com.** The Idea Logical Press, 1999

Thorn, John. *Treasures of the Baseball Hall of Fame.*
New York: Villard Books, 1998

Wales, Jimmy. *The Wikipedia Foundation—*
Mel Allen: St. Petersberg 2003

Warner, Gary. *The Home Team Wears White.*
Grand Rapids, Michigan: Zondervan Publishing

Whittingham, Richard. *World Series Almanac.*
Contemporary Books, Inc., 1984

INDEX

A

Adams, Gary 9, 18, 151, 160, 161, 162, 181, 207, 217

Adams, Gene 224 *See* Dr. Adams

Adler, Larry 176

Ahern, D. Patrick 169

Allen, Mel 15, 24, 127, 128, 137, 299

Amaral, Rich 16, 156

Amend, Harry 18, 224

Anderson, Claude 182

Anderson, Sparky 17, 24, 87, 91, 97, 143, 201, 208, 280, 284, 287

Antonelli, Angie 176

Ashford, Emmett 50, 51, 204

B

Barber, Red 129, 143, 146

Baseball Hall of Fame, The 15, 62, 84, 106, 108, 125, 128, 130, 133, 137, 138, 139, 144, 151, 188, 189, 191, 200, 203, 205, 206, 216, 217, 229, 230, 275, 280, 281, 284, 299

Beiden, Pete 170

Bennett, Chuck 18, 165, 167, 225, 280

Berger, Hal 15, 28, 129, 138

Berger, Wally 16

Berra, Yogi 16, 188

Bithorn, Hiram 42, 189

Blake, Jim 175

Boisseau, Vickie 82

Bottoms, Tim 169, 170, 172, 179

Bouton, Jim 70, 77, 190, 276

Bratton, Adrienne 7, 51

Brown, Bruce 182

Brown, Dr. and Mrs. Bobby 15, 78, 86, 91, 93, 106, 107, 108, 109, 146, 154, 190, 191, 192, 216

Brown, Mace 14, 16, 32, 188, 192, 220

Buck, Jack 15, 130, 131

Butler, Dick 15, 17, 108

C

Cain, Barbara 226

Cain, Ben (Terry) 226

Cain, Terry 226 *See* also Ben Cain

Campbell, Kathy 7

Campbell, Rob 18, 215, 216, 226

Caray, Harry 131

Cavaretta, Phil 30

Chaffey High School 40, 43, 49, 51, 63, 67, 72, 76, 78, 79, 112, 134, 149, 173, 184, 190, 198, 205, 207, 208, 209, 211, 217, 221, 223, 226, 227, 229, 231, 232, 273, 274, 275, 280, 299

Chavez, Tony 181

Clauson, Moose 18, 113, 208

Clemente, Roberto 17, 42, 58, 100, 192

Cobb, Ty 15, 17, 83, 84, 85, 91, 108, 192, 193, 204, 219, 281, 282, 285

Coleman, Ken 132

Collins, Howard 18, 112, 152, 166, 167, 169

Cox, Donna 267

Cox, Marshall 267

Crandall, Del 193,194

Cross, Harley 22, 23, 24, 25

Culler, Bill 175

Cutter, Ross 94, 126

D

Dahlgren, Ellsworth "Babe" 164

Dallesandro, Dominic 17, 194, 220

Dashiell, Marcia 6, 112, 113, 242

Dean, Dizzy 14, 15, 17, 28, 29, 64, 125, 133, 194, 281, 287

DeMaggio, Joe 18

DiCarlo, Joe 161, 164, 165, 184

DiMaggio, Joe 14, 17, 35, 44, 58, 66, 76, 79, 87, 119, 120, 121, 146, 195, 199, 203, 280, 281, 282, 285

Doby, Larry 37, 38, 149, 150, 195, 196, 282

Doby, Larry 37, 38, 195, 196

Doerr, Bobby 17, 80, 196, 213, 219, 272

Dooley, Dixie 4, 6

Dooley, Pat 18, 78, 229

Doubleday, Abner 48, 107, 282

Drake, Elvin C. 18

Duren, Ryne 196

Durslag, Mel 182

E

Elwell, Chuck 182

Erskine, Carl 197, 203

F

Fabian, John 230

Fairly, Ron 15, 134, 240

Feldman, Sam 182

Feller, Bob 17, 58, 72, 73, 114, 198, 283

Fellowship of Christian Athletes, The 14, 72, 197, 203, 224, 230

Fingers, Rollie 17, 198, 272

Ford, Whitey 17, 58, 77, 78, 198, 211, 285

Francisco, Clyde 67, 152, 153, 168, 175, 176

Friedman, Sol 168, 175, 176

Fry, Lyle 175

G

Galan, Augie 17, 69, 261, 272, 281

Garagiola, Joe 125, 139, 143, 189, 190, 286

Gazella, Mike 14, 17, 38, 150, 151, 200, 204

Gear, John T. 24

Gilmore Field 14, 39, 45, 47, 49, 99, 211, 232, 273

Giordano, Chuck 166, 167, 169, 231

Glaus, Troy 17, 200

Gorham, Kurt 7, 226

Gorham, Norma 7

Gorham Printing 7

Gregory, Ray 170, 171

Griffey Jr., Ken 15, 17, 88, 113, 201

Griffey Sr., Ken 17

Gudat, Marvin 17, 26, 151, 201, 273

H

Hammerschmidt, Ben 9, 181

Handley, Hal 35, 148, 149, 150

Haney, Fred 17, 197, 202, 209, 287

Hartnett, Gabby 17, 202

Harwell, Ernie 135

Hefley, Jack 182

Heinrich, Tommy 215

Hendon, Jerry 231

Herman, Babe 17, 47, 197, 272

Hillerich and Bradsby 30, 80, 81, 82, 263

Hines, Ben 19, 232

Hochman, Stan 182

Hodges, Russ 15, 62, 137, 139

Horn, Bill 22, 23, 24, 25

J

Jack "Moose" Myers 37, 147, 149, 153

Jensen, Jackie 203

Jewell, Anne 4, 7, 82

Johnson, Jerry 165

Johnson, Walter 17, 38, 73, 84, 108, 204

Jorgensen, Spider 215

K

Keeney, Bob 176

Kelleher, Frank 49, 273, 274

Keough, Marty 17, 41, 205, 206, 271, 272

Kim, Steve 286

Knudson, Marilyn 25, 39

Knudsons, The 19, 232

Koufax, Sandy 59, 64, 99, 206, 207, 280, 283

Krug, Chris 17, 181, 207

Kuntz, Rusty 17, 113, 208

L

Landis, Kenesaw Mountain 108

Lemaster, Denny 50, 208, 272

Lillard, Gene 27, 41, 209, 273

Lindell, Johnny 165, 209, 272

Lisec, Jim 167, 169, 170, 232

Louisville Slugger 7, 14

Louisville Slugger Bats 81

Luciani, Dick 176

M

Mails, Walter 17, 31, 32, 210

Major, Doug 181

Malone, Eddie 17, 49, 210, 273

Mantle, Mickey 14, 18, 58, 65, 66, 69, 70, 76, 77, 78, 79, 92, 121, 198, 211, 212, 253, 276, 285

Marker, Jody 19, 165, 169, 233

Martin, Billy 17, 78, 211, 272, 285

Mathewson, Christy 84, 108, 275

Maxie, Larry 19, 167, 169, 170, 208, 271

Mays, Willie 43, 56, 58, 62, 67, 105, 121, 136, 137, 220, 281, 282

McClendon, Gordon 15, 138, 139

McCune, Dan 181

McGuire, Jim 152, 153, 167, 169, 184

McLain, Denny 14, 17, 64, 65, 89, 212

McLish, 211

Merrill, John 181

Mesner, Steve 213

Miller, Don 22, 23, 24, 25, 147

Miller, Jon 15, 139, 140

Milliken, Dan 174

Milliken, Dr. Daniel B. 175

Moisan, Bill 18, 150, 213

Moon, Wally 18, 20, 55, 100, 101, 213, 214, 272, 283

Moss, Daryl 19, 77, 167, 233

Musial, Stan 18, 34, 79, 125, 214

N

Nelson, Lindsey 141

O

O'Malley, Walter 53, 54, 272, 280

Ontario-Upland Pirates, The 14, 41, 205, 209

P

Panthers, The 14, 23, 25, 183

Payne, Principal Ernest 174

Peterson, John 175

Petsuch, Leo 174

Prekeges, Pete and Jennifer 268

Prevedello, Andy 19, 50, 167, 168, 169, 225

Proctor, Hannah 19, 234

Proctor, Jesse 19, 235

Proctor, John 19, 235

Proctor, Ken Jr. 19, 74, 236

Proctor, Marie 19, 166, 237

Proctor, Marilyn 6, 39, 166, 237

Proctor, Mike 6, 19, 74, 237, 238

Proctor, Penny 19, 238

Proctor, Rebekah 19, 239

Proctor, Scott 19, 239, 265

R

Radford, Mike 215

Radford, Sherri 215

Rathbone, Lud 175

Reagan, Reagan 129, 138, 141, 282

Redman, Rick 7, 80

Reese, Jimmy 18, 215, 226

Reichle, Art 35, 148, 149, 153, 162, 173, 224

Reniff, Hal 14, 18, 76, 78, 152, 162, 164, 165, 167, 185, 190, 198, 211, 216, 234, 275, 276

Riverside Poly High School 207, 224, 225

Rizzuto, Phil 34, 86, 216, 285

Robinson, Jackie 37, 38, 51, 58, 80, 151, 153, 196, 200, 216, 241, 272, 282

Roenicke, Gary 217

Roenicke, Ron 153, 217

Rose, Garland 182

Ruth, Babe 22, 33, 35, 37, 38, 67, 77, 79, 81, 84, 87, 107, 108, 121, 125, 192, 196, 199, 200, 215, 218, 222, 225, 254, 280, 281, 282, 284, 285, 286

S

Sale, Doug 37, 148, 149, 162, 295

Schallock, Art 150, 218

Schweighardt, Bob 175

Scott, Anthony 181

Scully, Vin 15, 53, 57, 59, 127, 129, 142, 258, 277, 299

Shanz, Greg 181

Shaputis, Kathleen 7

Shatzkin, Mike 299

Sloan, Jack 182

Smith, Al 174

Smith, Gary 182

Smith, Harlow 182

Spring Training 15, 126, 228

Sprinz, Joe 32

Stalder, Richie 181

Stan Hochman 182

Stark, Ray 175

Statz, Arnold 18, 24, 219, 273

Stringer, Lou 18

Successful Baseball 12, 297

T

Thomson, Bobby 18, 61, 80, 123, 137, 138, 219

Thorne, George 174, 176

Tokyo Dome 109, 262

Tremark, Nick 220

U

UCLA 13, 15, 35, 36, 37, 38, 45, 50, 51, 85, 86, 92, 106, 108, 112, 130, 134, 136, 145, 146, 147, 148, 149, 150, 151, 152, 153, 162, 173, 179, 181, 188, 191, 195, 200, 201, 203, 207, 213, 216, 217, 222, 224, 225, 227, 229, 230, 231, 242, 267, 271, 276, 294, 295, 299

V

Visquel, Omar 113

W

Wagner, Honus 81, 84, 108, 280, 285

Walker, Darlene 228, 242

Walker, Darlene and Terry 6, 228, 242, 262

Warner, Don and Shirley 80, 184, 185, 243

Wertz, Vic 43

Williams, Ron and Susan 7

Wills, Bump 18, 69, 221

Woodall, Larry 32

Wooden, Coach 10, 13, 20, 151, 252, 294

Wooden, John 13, 20, 35, 92, 149, 150, 162, 195, 230, 235, 294, 295

World Series 13, 14, 17, 20, 28, 30, 33, 34, 35, 38, 43, 51, 57, 58, 59, 61, 63, 64, 65, 67, 68, 69, 77, 80, 85, 87, 92, 95, 100, 101, 102, 105, 107, 126, 128, 129, 130, 132, 134, 140, 165, 188, 189, 190, 191, 193, 195, 196, 197, 198, 199, 200, 202, 204, 206, 208, 210, 211, 214, 216, 222, 240, 242, 255, 268, 276, 277, 281, 282, 283, 286, 295, 299

Wrigley Field, Los Angeles 14, 24, 26, 28, 30, 34, 39, 43, 44, 45, 47, 91, 93, 95, 96, 97, 99, 131, 151, 202, 203, 209, 213, 240, 273, 286

Y

Yamashita, Yashitoka 109

Yochem, Harry 161, 175

Youlden, Tom 271

Z

Zenz, Brian 165, 167, 168, 169

Zimmer, Don 60